THE NEW CAMBRIDGE SHAKESPEARE

ASSOCIATE GENERAL EDITOR

A. R. Braunmuller, *University of California, Los Angeles*

From the publication of the first volumes in 1984 the General Editor of the New Cambridge Shakespeare was Philip Brockbank and the Associate General Editors were Brian Gibbons and Robin Hood. From 1990 to 1994 the General Editor was Brian Gibbons and the Associate General Editors were A. R. Braunmuller and Robin Hood.

KING RICHARD III

King Richard III is one of Shakespeare's most popular and frequently performed plays. Janis Lull's introduction to this new edition, based on the First Folio, emphasises the play's tragic themes – individual identity, determinism and choice – and stresses the importance of women's roles in the play. It also underscores the special relationship between *Richard III* and *Macbeth*, demonstrating that the later tragedy re-examines issues raised in the earlier one. A thorough performance history of stage and film versions of *Richard III* shows how the text has been cut, rewritten and reshaped by directors and actors to enhance the role of Richard at the expense of other parts, especially those of the women. This updated edition contains a new introductory section covering recent criticism and performances – including the RSC cycles of the history plays – of this perennially popular play. The notes define the play's language in terms easily accessible to contemporary readers.

THE NEW CAMBRIDGE SHAKESPEARE

KING RICHARD III

Updated edition

Edited by
JANIS LULL
University of Alaska Fairbanks

CAMBRIDGE
UNIVERSITY PRESS

CAMBRIDGE UNIVERSITY PRESS

Cambridge, New York, Melbourne, Madrid, Cape Town, Singapore, São Paulo, Delhi

Cambridge University Press
The Edinburgh Building, Cambridge CB2 8RU, UK

Published in the United States of America by Cambridge University Press, New York

www.cambridge.org
Information on this title: www.cambridge.org/9780521735568

First published 1999
Updated edition 2009

Printed in the United Kingdom at the University Press, Cambridge

A catalogue record for this publication is available from the British Library

Library of Congress Cataloguing in Publication data
Shakespeare, William, 1564–1616.
King Richard III / edited by Janis Lull. – Updated ed.
   p.   cm. – (The new Cambridge Shakespeare)
Includes bibliographical references.
ISBN 978-0-521-51474-3
1. Shakespeare, William, 1564–1616. King Richard III.   2. Richard III, King of England,
1452–1485 – Drama.   3. Great Britain – History – Richard III, 1483–1485 – Drama.
I. Lull, Janis.   II. Title.   III. Series.
PR2821.A2L85   2009
822.3′3 – dc22   2009004914

ISBN 978-0-521-51474-3 hardback
ISBN 978-0-521-73556-8 paperback

To David

CONTENTS

ILLUSTRATIONS

ACKNOWLEDGEMENTS

I am grateful to colleagues who have discussed *King Richard III* with me over the years, and to Georgianna Ziegler and the excellent staff of the Folger Shakespeare Library. The emphasis of this edition differs from earlier ones, but it also builds on the scholarship of the editors who came before me, especially Antony Hammond. My general editor, A. R. Braunmuller, has supported and gently corrected me every step of the way, and I could never have done it without him. I am also indebted to Paul Chipchase and Sarah Stanton for their careful attention to my work and tactful suggestions for making it better.

Linda Shenk not only inspired me during our many conversations about *King Richard III*, but also contributed indispensably to this edition with her heroic work on the collations. I thank the University of Alaska Fairbanks for the chance to be Linda's teacher, as well as for sabbatical leave support. The University of Oregon graciously allowed me faculty access to their libraries.

Thomas Clayton first taught me about scholarly editing and generously took time to comment on the early stages of this work. Linda Anderson, as always, acted as a friend and colleague throughout the project, catching me up on errors and stupidities large and small. Those that remain are nobody's fault but my own.

I am grateful to Peggy Shumaker, Allison Hawthorne Deming, and Stephanie Pearmain, as well as to the University of Arizona English Department and the University of Arizona Library for help in preparing the updated edition. Thanks again to Linda Anderson for reading everything twice.

ABBREVIATIONS AND CONVENTIONS

1. Shakespeare's plays

Shakespeare's plays, when cited in this edition, are abbreviated in a style modified slightly from that used in the *Harvard Concordance to Shakespeare*. Other editions of Shakespeare are abbreviated under the editor's surname (Rowe, Eccles) unless they are the work of more than one editor. In such cases, an abbreviated series title is used (Cam.). When more than one edition by the same editor is cited, later editions are discriminated with a raised figure (Collier²). All quotations from Shakespeare, except those from *Richard III*, use the lineation of *The Riverside Shakespeare*, under the general editorship of G. Blakemore Evans.

Ado	*Much Ado About Nothing*
Ant.	*Antony and Cleopatra*
AWW	*All's Well That Ends Well*
AYLI	*As You Like It*
Cor.	*Coriolanus*
Cym.	*Cymbeline*
Err.	*The Comedy of Errors*
Ham.	*Hamlet*
1H4	*The First Part of King Henry the Fourth*
2H4	*The Second Part of King Henry the Fourth*
H5	*King Henry the Fifth*
1H6	*The First Part of King Henry the Sixth*
2H6	*The Second Part of King Henry the Sixth*
3H6	*The Third Part of King Henry the Sixth*
H8	*King Henry the Eighth*
JC	*Julius Caesar*
John	*King John*
LLL	*Love's Labour's Lost*
Lear	*King Lear*
Mac.	*Macbeth*
MM	*Measure for Measure*
MND	*A Midsummer Night's Dream*
MV	*The Merchant of Venice*
Oth.	*Othello*
Per.	*Pericles*
R2	*King Richard the Second*
R3	*King Richard the Third*
Rom.	*Romeo and Juliet*
Shr.	*The Taming of the Shrew*
STM	*Sir Thomas More*
Temp.	*The Tempest*

TGV	*The Two Gentlemen of Verona*
Tim.	*Timon of Athens*
Tit.	*Titus Andronicus*
TN	*Twelfth Night*
TNK	*The Two Noble Kinsmen*
Tro.	*Troilus and Cressida*
Wiv.	*The Merry Wives of Windsor*
WT	*The Winter's Tale*

2. Other works cited and general references

Abbott	E. A. Abbott, *A Shakespearian Grammar*, 3rd edn, 1870 (references are to numbered paragraphs)
Adelman	Janet Adelman, *Suffocating Mothers: Fantasies of Maternal Origin in Shakespeare's Plays, 'Hamlet' to 'The Tempest'*, 1992
Alexander	Peter Alexander, *Shakespeare's 'Henry VI' and 'Richard III'*, 1929
Arber	E. Arber, *A Transcript of the Registers of the Company of Stationers of London 1554–1640*, 5 vols., 1875–94
Barton and Hall	John Barton and Peter Hall, *The Wars of the Roses*, 1970
Bentley	G. E. Bentley, *The Jacobean and Caroline Stage*, 7 vols., 1941–68
Boswell-Stone	W. G. Boswell-Stone, *Shakespeare's Holinshed: The Chronicle and the Historical Plays Compared*, 1896
Braunmuller	A. R. Braunmuller (ed.), *Macbeth*, 1997 (New Cambridge Shakespeare)
Brewer	E. C. Brewer, *The Dictionary of Phrase and Fable*, 1981
Bullough	Geoffrey Bullough, *Narrative and Dramatic Sources of Shakespeare*, 8 vols., 1957–75
Cam.	*Works*, ed. William Aldis Wright, 9 vols., 1891–3 (Cambridge Shakespeare)
Campbell	Lily B. Campbell, *Shakespeare's 'Histories': Mirrors of Elizabethan Policy*, 1947
Capell	*Mr William Shakespeare his Comedies, Histories, and Tragedies*, ed. Edward Capell, 10 vols., 1767–8
Chambers	E. K. Chambers, *The Elizabethan Stage*, 4 vols., 1923
Churchill	George Bosworth Churchill, *Richard the Third up to Shakespeare*, 1900
Cibber	Colley Cibber, *The Tragical History of King Richard III, c.* 1700; reprinted 1969
Clemen	Wolfgang Clemen, *A Commentary on Shakespeare's 'Richard III'*, first published in German, 1957; trans. Jean Bonheim, 1968
Colley	Scott Colley, *Richard's Himself Again: A Stage History of 'Richard III'*, 1992
Collier	*Works*, ed. John P. Collier, 8 vols., 1842–4
Collier²	*Works*, ed. John P. Collier, 1853
Crowland	*The Crowland Chronicle Continuations, 1459–1486*, ed. Nicholas Pronay and John Cox, 1986
Davison	*The First Quarto of King Richard III*, ed. Peter Davison, 1996 (New Cambridge Shakespeare)

Dent	R. W. Dent, *Shakespeare's Proverbial Language: An Index*, 1981 (references are to numbered proverbs)
Dyce	*The Works of William Shakespeare*, ed. Alexander Dyce, 6 vols., 1857
Dyce²	*The Works of William Shakespeare*, ed. Alexander Dyce, 9 vols., 1864–7
Eccles	*The Tragedy of Richard the Third*, ed. Mark Eccles, 1964 (Signet Shakespeare)
ELR	*English Literary Renaissance*
F	*Mr William Shakespeares Comedies, Histories and Tragedies*, 1623 (First Folio)
F2	*Mr William Shakespeares Comedies, Histories and Tragedies*, 1632 (Second Folio)
F3	*Mr William Shakespear's Comedies, Histories and Tragedies*, 1663–4 (Third Folio)
F4	*Mr William Shakespear's Comedies, Histories and Tragedies*, 1685 (Fourth Folio)
Greg	W. W. Greg, *The Editorial Problem in Shakespeare*, 3rd edn, 1954
Griggs facsimile	William Griggs's facsimile of Q *Richard III*, 1885
Gurr	Andrew Gurr, *The Shakespearean Stage 1574–1642*, 3rd edn, 1992
Hall	Edward Hall, *The Union of the Two Noble and Illustre Famelies of Lancastre and York*, 1548, reprinted 1809, reprinted 1965 (cited here)
Hammond	Antony Hammond (ed.), *King Richard III*, 1981 (Arden Shakespeare)
Hankey	Julie Hankey (ed), *Richard III*, 1981 (Plays in Performance)
Hanmer	*The Works of Shakespear*, ed. Thomas Hanmer, 6 vols., 1743–4
Hassel	R. Chris Hassel, Jr, *Songs of Death: Performance, Interpretation, and the Text of 'Richard III'*, 1987
Holinshed	Raphael Holinshed, *Chronicles of England, Scotland, and Ireland*, second edn, 1587, reprinted in 6 vols., 1808, reprinted 1965 (cited here)
Honigmann	E. A. J. Honigmann (ed), *King Richard the Third*, 1968 (New Penguin Shakespeare)
Honigmann, *Stability*	E. A. J. Honigmann, *The Stability of Shakespeare's Text*, 1965
Honigmann, 'Text'	E. A. J. Honigmann, 'The text of *Richard III*', *Theatre Research* 7 (1965), 48–55
Ioppolo	Grace Ioppolo, *Revising Shakespeare*, 1991
Irace	Kathleen O. Irace, 'Origins and agents of Q1 *Hamlet*', in Thomas Clayton (ed.), *The 'Hamlet' First Published (Q1, 1603)*, 1992, pp. 90–122
Johnson	*The Plays of William Shakespeare*, ed. Samuel Johnson, 8 vols., 1765
Jones	Emrys Jones, *The Origins of Shakespeare*, 1977
Kelly	Henry Ansgar Kelly, *Divine Providence in the England of Shakespeare's Histories*, 1971

The London Stage	Emmett L. Avery, Charles Beecher Hogan, *et al.* (eds), *The London Stage: A Calendar of Plays, Entertainments and Afterpieces, 1660–1800*, 11 vols., 1960–5
McKellen	Ian McKellen and Richard Loncraine, *William Shakespeare's 'Richard III'*, 1996 (screenplay)
Maguire	Laurie E. Maguire, *Shakespearean Suspect Texts: The 'Bad' Quartos and Their Contexts*, 1996
Malone	*The Plays and Poems of William Shakespeare*, ed. Edmond Malone, 10 vols., 1790
Mancini	Dominic Mancini, *The Usurpation of Richard III*, ed. C. A. J. Armstrong, 2nd edn, 1969
Marlowe	*The Complete Works of Christopher Marlowe*, ed. Fredson Bowers, 2nd edn, 2 vols., 1981
More	Sir Thomas More, *The History of King Richard the Third*, ed. Richard S. Sylvester (*The Complete Works of St Thomas More*, vol. 2), 1963
NQ	*Notes and Queries*
OED	*Oxford English Dictionary*
Ornstein	Robert Ornstein, *A Kingdom for a Stage: The Achievement of Shakespeare's History Plays*, 1972
Oxford	*William Shakespeare: The Complete Works*, ed. Stanley Wells and Gary Taylor, 1986
Patrick	David Lyall Patrick, *The Textual History of 'Richard III'*, 1936
Pope	*The Works of Shakespeare*, ed. Alexander Pope, 6 vols., 1723–5 (vol. 4)
Q	[William Shakespeare], *The Tragedy of King Richard the third*, 1597 (first quarto)
Q2	[William Shakespeare], *The Tragedy of King Richard the third*, 1598 (second quarto)
Q3	[William Shakespeare], *The Tragedy of King Richard the third*, 1602 (third quarto)
Q4	[William Shakespeare], *The Tragedy of King Richard the third*, 1605 (fourth quarto)
Q5	[William Shakespeare], *The Tragedy of King Richard the third*, 1612 (fifth quarto)
Q6	[William Shakespeare], *The Tragedy of King Richard the third*, 1622 (sixth quarto)
Q7	[William Shakespeare], *The Tragedy of King Richard the third*, 1629 (seventh quarto)
Q8	[William Shakespeare], *The Tragedy of King Richard the third*, 1634 (eighth quarto)
RES	*Review of English Studies*
Ribner	Irving Ribner, *The English History Play in the Age of Shakespeare*, 1957
Richmond	Hugh M. Richmond, *King Richard III*, 1989 (Shakespeare in Performance)
Riverside	*The Riverside Shakespeare*, ed. G. Blakemore Evans, 1974

Robinson, P. M. W.	*Collate: Interactive Collation of Large Textual Traditions, Version* 2, 1995. Computer Program distributed by Oxford University Computing Service, Oxford
Rossiter	A. P. Rossiter, *English Drama from Early Times to the Elizabethans*, 1950
Rous	John Rous, *Joannis Rossi Antiquarii Warwicensis Historia Regum Angliae*, ed. T. Hearne, 1745
Rowe	*The Works of Mr William Shakespear*, ed. Nicholas Rowe, 6 vols., 1709
Rowe²	*The Works of Mr William Shakespear*, ed. Nicholas Rowe, 2nd edn, 6 vols., *c.* 1709
Rowe³	*The Works of Mr William Shakespear*, ed. Nicholas Rowe, 3rd edn, 8 vols., 1714
SB	*Shakespeare Bulletin*
SD	stage direction
Seneca	Lucius Annaeus Seneca, *Senecca's Tragedies with an English Translation*, trans. F. J. Miller, 2 vols., 1917
SH	speech heading
Sher	Antony Sher, *The Year of the King*, 1987
Smidt	Kristian Smidt, *Iniurious Impostors and 'Richard III'*, 1963
Smidt, *Memorial*	Kristian Smidt, *Memorial Transmission and Quarto Copy in 'Richard III': A Reassessment*, 1970
Spivack	Bernard Spivack, *Shakespeare and the Allegory of Evil*, 1958
SQ	*Shakespeare Quarterly*
Steevens	*The Plays of William Shakespeare*, ed. George Steevens and Isaac Reed, 4th edn, 15 vols., 1793
subst.	substantively
Taylor and Warren	Gary Taylor and Michael Warren (eds), *The Division of the Kingdoms: Shakespeare's Two Versions of King Lear*, 1983; reprinted 1986
Thayer	C. G. Thayer, *Shakespearean Politics: Government and Misgovernment in the Great Histories*, 1983
Theobald	*The Works of Shakespeare*, ed. Lewis Theobald, 7 vols., 1733
Thompson	A. Hamilton Thompson (ed.), *The Tragedy of King Richard the Third*, 1907 (Arden Shakespeare)
Thomson	W. H. Thomson, *Shakespeare's Characters: A Historical Dictionary*, 1951
Tilley	M. P. Tilley, *A Dictionary of the Proverbs in England in the Sixteenth and Seventeenth Centuries*, 1950 (references are to numbered proverbs)
Tillyard	E. M. W. Tillyard, *Shakespeare's History Plays*, 1944; reprinted 1962
TLN	Through line numbering (from Charlton Hinman, *The Norton Fascimile of Shakespeare*, 1968)
TLS	*Times Literary Supplement*

True Tragedie | *The True Tragedie of Richard the Third*, 1594; reprinted as *The True Tragedy of Richard the Third*, ed. W. W. Greg, 1929 (Malone Society)

Urkowitz | Steven Urkowitz, 'Reconsidering the relationship of quarto and Folio texts of *Richard III*', *ELR* 16 (1986), 442–66

Variorum | Horace Howard Furness (ed.), *The Tragedy of Richard the Third*, 1908 (New Variorum Shakespeare, vol. 17)

Walker | Alice Walker, *Textual Problems of the First Folio*, 1953

Walton | J. K. Walton, *The Copy of the Folio Text of 'Richard III'*, 1955

Weimann | Robert Weimann, *Shakespeare and the Popular Tradition in the Theater*, 1978

Wells and Taylor | Stanley Wells and Gary Taylor, *William Shakespeare: A Textual Companion*, 1987

Wilson | J. Dover Wilson (ed.), *Richard III*, 1952 (New Shakespeare)

Unless otherwise specified, biblical quotations are given in the Geneva version (1560).

INTRODUCTION

In the histories section of the First Folio, only *Richard III* is called a 'tragedy'.[1] It unites the chronicle play, a form Shakespeare had developed in the three parts of *Henry VI*, with a tragic structure showing the rise and fall of a single protagonist. Like Christopher Marlowe's *Dr Faustus*, written at about the same time, Shakespeare's play concerns the damnation of an unrepentant soul, but Shakespeare also grapples with the problem of determinism. In his opening soliloquy, Richard says he is 'determinèd to prove a villain' (1.1.30), and the play develops this ambiguous statement into an exploration of determinism and choice appropriate to both history and tragedy.[2]

History and meaning in *Richard III*

Richard III is the last in a series of four plays – following three about the reign of Henry VI – that dramatise the English Wars of the Roses. As he had in the *Henry VI* plays, Shakespeare used the chronicles of Edward Hall and Raphael Holinshed as sources of historical material for *Richard III*.[3] Hall's *Union of the Two Noble and Illustre Famelies of Lancastre and York* (1548) incorporated a version of Sir Thomas More's *History of Richard III* (written about 1513). Holinshed's *Chronicles of England* (second edition, 1587) adapted More's *History* from Hall, so that More should be regarded as the primary historiographic source for Shakespeare's *Richard III*. More's unfinished work, however, deals only with Richard's rise to the throne. Shakespeare relied on Hall and Holinshed for Richard's decline and final defeat at Bosworth, and those chroniclers had relied on the early Tudor historian Polydore Vergil. Nevertheless, it is More's ironic attitude toward Richard that pervades both the chronicle sources and Shakespeare's play.

Much has been made of the tendency of early Tudor historians to vilify Richard III in order to glorify Henry VII (Richmond) and his descendants.[4] It is true that the concept of history writing in the fifteenth and sixteenth centuries included the selective use of historical events to teach political and moral lessons, a practice most modern historians would reject. However, many of the stories of Richard's villainy

---

[1] The play is called *The Tragedy of Richard III* on its first page in the Folio, but subsequent pages carry the running title 'The Life and Death of Richard the Third'. The word 'tragedy' may have been taken from the printed quartos, all of which use it.

[2] On Richard's pun as a play on providential determinism, see David S. Berkeley, '"Determined" in *Richard III*, I.i.30', *SQ* 14 (1963), 483–4.

[3] Shakespeare may also have used the *Chronicle At Large* of Richard Grafton (1569), but this repeats Hall almost word for word, making it impossible to tell which one Shakespeare employed.

[4] See Tillyard, Campbell and Ribner.

originate in accounts written in Richard's own time or soon after.[1] It is impossible to tell whether these early narratives consciously promote propaganda or merely reflect the traditional literary and didactic aims of medieval historiography. The earliest known portrait of Richard as a usurper (first discovered in 1934) was recorded by the Italian priest Dominic Mancini. It cannot have been intended to advance an established Tudor dynasty, since Mancini wrote in 1483, when the victory of Henry Tudor over Richard III was still two years in the future. Neither can this early date guarantee Mancini's objectivity. Yet no matter how the reign of Richard III was perceived by those who lived through it, by Shakespeare's time, and probably much earlier, stories of Richard as a tyrant and a child-murderer were accepted as fact.

In addition to the chronicle sources, Shakespeare's *Richard III* draws upon a wide range of literary influences, especially the cycle plays and moralities of the native English drama. The influence of classical drama can be seen, not only in the women of *Richard III*, who have been compared to Seneca's Trojan women, but also in the play's formal rhetoric, its ghosts, its villain-hero, perhaps even in Richard's stoic end. Closer to home, Shakespeare drew inspiration from other sixteenth-century English dramatists writing in the Senecan tradition, especially Thomas Kyd and Christopher Marlowe. *A Mirror for Magistrates*, a sixteenth-century collection of verse 'tragedies' about the fall of historical figures, was available to Shakespeare. He may have read it for passages spoken by Richard, Clarence, Hastings, Edward IV, the Duke of Buckingham, and even Jane Shore, although he does not dramatise her story. An unpublished Latin play, Thomas Legge's *Ricardus Tertius*, which was composed around 1579, does not seem to have been used by Shakespeare, though he may well have known it.[2]

The True Tragedie of Richard the Third, an anonymous English play, was published in 1594 but probably composed several years earlier.[3] There seem to be passages in which *The True Tragedie* anticipates Shakespeare, notably in Richard's call for a new horse (scene 18):

> *King.* A horse, a horse, a fresh horse.
> *Page.* A flie my Lord, and saue your life.
> *King.* Flie villaine, looke I as tho I would flie

It is possible that the anonymous playwright borrowed from Shakespeare rather than the other way around. Even if *The True Tragedie* was written first, the printed version could have picked up this famous exchange from Shakespeare's later but more popular play, perhaps via a copyist. Yet the text of *The True Tragedie*, often disparaged as

---

[1] See Dominic Mancini, *The Usurpation of Richard III* (*c.* 1483), ed. C. A. J. Armstrong, 2nd edn 1969; *The Crowland Chronicle Continuations, 1459–1486* (*c.* 1486), ed. Nicholas Pronay and John Cox, 1986; and John Rous, *Joannis Rossi Antiquarii Warwicensis Historia Regum Angliae* (*c.* 1487–91), ed. T. Hearne, 1745.

[2] Shakespeare's contemporary, Francis Meres, names Legge along with Shakespeare as among 'our best for Tragedie' (*Palladis Tamia*, 1598). See Jones, pp. 139–40.

[3] *The True Tragedie of Richard the Third*, 1594; reprinted by the Malone Society as *The True Tragedy of Richard the Third*, ed. W. W. Greg, 1929.

a 'bad quarto'[1] or merely 'contaminated',[2] emerges in Laurie E. Maguire's recent analysis as a coherent play with few of the traditional signs attributed to pirated scripts or 'memorial reconstructions'.[3] It appears more likely, then, that Shakespeare echoed *The True Tragedie* rather than the other way around.

Another parallel, in George Peele's *The Battle of Alcazar* (1594), offers a triangle of possible influences for the 'horse' passage:

> *Moore.*   A horse, a horse, villain a horse
>   That I may take the river straight and flie.
> *Boy.*   Here is a horse my Lord.   (1413–15)[4]

As Antony Hammond has pointed out, this dialogue seems more remote from Shakespeare's than that of *The True Tragedie*,[5] not so much because of the differences in the famous line itself, but because Peele's Moor wishes to fly, while in *The True Tragedie*, as in *Richard III*, the protagonist has no intention of escaping. A possible line of descent for this passage, then, runs from Peele to Anonymous to Shakespeare. In addition to the verbal echo of 'a horse, a horse', George Bosworth Churchill, Geoffrey Bullough and John Dover Wilson all trace structural parallels between *The True Tragedie* and the last four acts of Shakespeare's play. Emrys Jones and Hammond, on the other hand, stress how much *The True Tragedie* and *Richard III* differ in their emphases. As Jones puts it, 'one is surprised to find out how undominating, by comparison, another playwright's Richard could be'.[6] A reasonable supposition might be that Shakespeare used 'a horse, a horse' from *The True Tragedie* and borrowed whatever structural elements he thought would work, just as he did from many other literary sources.

Shakespeare's own earlier plays also provided him with source material, especially *Henry VI, Part 3*, where Richard first emerges as an arch-villain. In *Henry VI, Part 2*, Richard appears as a warrior trying to take the crown away from Henry VI and give it to his own father, the Duke of York. Richard's enemies mention his deformity, but his chief characteristics in this play are devotion to his father and warlike anger: 'Sword, hold thy temper; heart, be wrathful still: / Priests pray for enemies, but princes kill' (5.2.70–1). In *Henry VI, Part 3*, Richard adds to his loyalty and wrath a certain cunning. He persuades York to break a promise of peace because the oath was not sworn before a 'true and lawful magistrate' (1.2.23), then plunges eagerly into the next round of civil war. After York is killed by Queen Margaret, Richard begins to assume the character of a universal antagonist. Although he continues to fight fiercely to avenge his father and to put his brother Edward on the throne, he also mocks Edward's love of women, Elizabeth Grey in particular (3.2), and begins the process of fashioning himself into the monster he will be: 'Ay, Edward will use women honourably. / Would he were wasted, marrow, bones, and all, / That from his loins no hopeful branch may spring, / To cross me from the golden time I look

---

[1] See Wilson, p. xxix.   [2] Hammond, p. 83.   [3] Maguire, pp. 317–18.
[4] See W. W. Greg, *Two Elizabethan Stage Abridgements: 'The Battle of Alcazar' and 'Orlando Furioso'*, 1922.
[5] Hammond, p. 83.   [6] Jones, p. 196.

for!' (3.2.124–7). As Philip Brockbank points out, when Richard 'takes the stage for his first exercise of the soliloquy-prerogative he inherits from York', he immediately begins to speak of his ambitions in terms of birth, or rather of rebirth, since his first has proved unsatisfactory:[1]

> Why, love forswore me in my mother's womb:
> And for I should not deal in her soft laws,
> She did corrupt frail nature with some bribe,
> To shrink mine arm up like a wither'd shrub,
> To make an envious mountain on my back,
> Where sits deformity to mock my body.   (3.2.153–8)

Just as he does in *Richard III*, Richard blames his inability to love on his abnormal birth – and, by extension, on his mother – and invents a new self-birthing process that will make him king:

> And I – like one lost in a thorny wood,
> That rents the thorns, and is rent with the thorns,
> Seeking a way, and straying from the way,
> Not knowing how to find the open air,
> But toiling desperately to find it out –
> Torment myself to catch the English crown.   (3.2.174–9)

The personality Richard reveals or creates in this passage is much like the one he displays in the opening soliloquy of the present play, and actors from Colley Cibber in the eighteenth century to Laurence Olivier in the twentieth have freely borrowed lines from *Henry VI, Part 3* for productions of *Richard III*. From the middle of *Henry VI, Part 3* on, Richard appears as a full-blown villain, confiding his treacherous self-absorption to the audience even as he pretends to support the new Yorkist king, Edward IV. At the end of the play, Richard murders King Henry in the Tower, and the audience understands that he has killed not for his brother, but for himself: 'I have no brother, I am like no brother; / And this word "love", which greybeards call divine / Be resident in men like one another / And not in me: I am myself alone' (5.6.80–3).

Richard III is a sequel to *Henry VI, Part 3*, and was probably written soon after it. *Henry VI, Part 3* must have existed before September 1592, when the dying playwright Robert Greene parodied a line from the play in his pamphlet, *Greenes Groatsworth of Witte*, in which he criticised Shakespeare. Greene transformed York's bitter words to Margaret, 'O tiger's heart wrapped in a woman's hide!' (*3 Henry VI* 1.4.137), into an attack on the playwright, whom he called 'an vpstart Crow, beautified with our feathers, that with his *Tygers hart wrapt in a Players hyde*, supposes he is as well able to bombast out a blanke verse as the best of you' (sig. F1). Greene probably saw *Henry VI, Part 3* performed in London some time before June 1592, when the London theatres were closed because of plague. For Greene to suppose that his

---

[1] See Philip Brockbank, 'The frame of disorder – "Henry VI"', in *Early Shakespeare*, ed. J. R. Brown and B. A. Harris, 1961, reprinted in Brockbank, *On Shakespeare*, 1989, p. 102.

parody of Shakespeare would be effective, he must have believed that many in his audience had seen *Henry VI, Part 3* and that the line he chose to burlesque was a memorable one. Although a London acting company may have taken the play on tour in the provinces during the summer of 1592, Greene's confidence in a theatrical experience shared with his readers suggests a milieu of city theatre-goers and repeated performances rather than of plays glimpsed out of town. Whether *Henry VI, Part 3* was a finished play in the spring of 1592 or was written that summer, however, the continuity between the two plays implies that *Richard III* was developed immediately after *Henry VI, Part 3*, even if Shakespeare was also working on other projects at the same time.[1] *Richard III* was probably completed by 1593, although it may not have been performed in London until the next theatrical season in 1594.

There is very little evidence to help establish the earliest date at which *Richard III* could have been written. Shakespeare's career as a playwright was already well under way, and he had written *Henry VI, Part 3*, but whether these things happened in the early 1590s or before is a matter of conjecture.[2] Since both *Henry VI, Part 3* and *Richard III* use material from the 1587 edition of Holinshed's *Chronicles*, they cannot have been written earlier than that date. Sidney Shanker conjectured that Shakespeare used the character Sir James Blunt to flatter the Blunts of Stratford, even though a Blunt of that family was not actually knighted until 1588.[3] If this guess is right, 1588 would be the earliest date for *Richard III*. Harold F. Brooks argues that Christopher Marlowe's *Edward II*, probably Marlowe's penultimate play, echoes *Richard III*.[4] *Richard III*, by this argument, must have existed long enough for Marlowe to borrow from it and write both *Edward II* and *Dr Faustus* before his death in the spring of 1593. Hammond agrees with Brooks's speculation and suggests a date of 1591 for Shakespeare's play,[5] but as Stanley Wells and Gary Taylor point out, the verbal parallels Brooks finds between *Edward II* and *Richard III* are mostly commonplace and may derive from other sources.[6] Marlowe's *Dr Faustus* also seems to echo Shakespeare's ghosts ('despair and die'), and this borrowing, if it is one, can be reconciled with a composition date of 1592–3 for *Richard III*.

DETERMINISM AND HISTORY

The civil conflicts portrayed in Shakespeare's first tetralogy extended from the death of the Lancastrian Henry V in 1422 through the chaotic reign of his son, Henry VI, Henry's overthrow by the house of York, the rule of the Yorkist kings Edward IV and Richard III, and finally to Richard's defeat in 1485 by the Earl of Richmond, who then became Henry VII, the first Tudor king. Scholars once believed that Shakespeare and most of his contemporaries saw the calamitous wars between the house of Lancaster

---

[1] Stanley Wells and Gary Taylor argue, using rare word analysis, that *1H6* was written after *3H6* (*William Shakespeare: A Textual Companion*, p. 217). They also agree with Marco Mincoff, who says in *Shakespeare: The First Steps*, 1976, that Shakespeare wrote *Titus* between *3H6* and *Richard III* (p. 115).
[2] See Honigmann, *Shakespeare, the 'Lost Years'*, 1985.
[3] Sidney Shanker, 'Shakespeare pays some compliments', *Modern Language Notes* 63 (1948), 540–1.
[4] Harold F. Brooks, 'Marlowe and early Shakespeare', in *Christopher Marlowe*, ed. Brian Morris, 1968, pp. 65–94.
[5] Hammond, p. 61.   [6] See Wells and Taylor, p. 116.

(whose supporters wore a red rose) and the house of York (white rose) as divine punishment for the unlawful deposition of Richard II in 1399. According to this view, Shakespeare's *Richard III* reflects the 'Tudor Myth', which held that the Wars of the Roses resulted from a divine curse that was finally purged by Henry Tudor. Later critics, however, have generally rejected the idea that Shakespeare wrote his plays simply as Tudor propaganda, and most have also rejected the notion that there was any widespread Tudor consensus about God's will and the Wars of the Roses.[1] Disagreement continues over whether Shakespeare's plays generally tended to support or undermine the Tudor–Stuart political order.[2]

As a descendant of the man who overthrew Richard III, Queen Elizabeth I certainly benefited from the impression that Richard had been a wicked king. Yet this villainous portrait of Richard was not a Tudor invention. It had been developing since Richard's own time, gradually taking on the characteristics that critics would later associate with the Tudor Myth.[3] For Shakespeare, the most influential disseminator of Richard's bad reputation was Sir Thomas More – not an Elizabethan but a contemporary of Elizabeth's father, Henry VIII. More's account, which he took from fifteenth-century chroniclers and probably from the personal reminiscences of people still living who remembered Richard, was borrowed by the sixteenth-century chroniclers Hall and Holinshed, and thus became an important source for Shakespeare's play. It was More who first made Richard a character suitable for drama by concentrating on vivid events in his reign and further enhancing his reputation as a criminal tyrant.

Whether More saw Richard's rule as divine punishment is open to question, but there is no question that this interpretation is available in Shakespeare's play.[4] It is articulated by Queen Margaret, who proclaims the justice of Richard's turning on his own family: 'O upright, just, and true-disposing God, / How do I thank thee, that this carnal cur / Preys on the issue of his mother's body' (4.4.55–7). According to Margaret, however, the crimes avenged by Richard's murders are specific actions taken against her family by the house of York, not ancestral political crimes. Margaret gives voice to the belief, encouraged by the growing Calvinism of the Elizabethan era, that individual historical events are determined by God, who often punishes evil with (apparent) evil. Yet her vision of Richard as providential agent or 'scourge of

---

[1] For a strong argument against reducing Shakespeare's histories to the 'Tudor Myth', see Ornstein.

[2] Linda Charnes, for example, has recently argued that Shakespeare used the received portrait of Richard III as one of the themes of his play: '[N]o matter how engaged the play may be with the ideological uses to which Richard's legend can be put, it is even more engaged with what it would feel like to be subjected by and to that legend, with what it would be like to have to *be* Richard III, surrounded by the language and signification of a hundred years of writings about oneself.' According to Charnes, Shakespeare's Richard is a character trying to escape the determinism not of natural causation but of historiography – the works of 'Rous, Morton, More, Holinshed, and other "historians" whose authority cannot and must not, in the reign of Elizabeth, be denied because the playwright himself is subject to the immediate political constraints of his material'. See Charnes, *Notorious Identity: Materializing the Subject in Shakespeare*, 1993, pp. 68–9. For a portrait of Shakespeare as an underminer of political orthodoxies, see Thayer.

[3] See Kelly for an account of the gradual development of Richard's reputation.

[4] If More intended his *History of King Richard III* to promote the interests of the Tudor dynasty, he made no use of it, for he left it unfinished and never published it. See Richard S. Sylvester's introduction to More.

God' is both limited and biased, representing only part of what it means for Richard to be 'determinèd to prove a villain'.

While Margaret regards Richard as the instrument of God's vengeance for crimes against the Lancasters, Richard attributes Margaret's suffering to her own crimes against the Yorks, and others agree with him:

> RICHARD   The curse my noble father laid on thee
>   When thou didst crown his warlike brows with paper
>   And with thy scorns drew'st rivers from his eyes,
>   And then to dry them gav'st the duke a clout
>   Steeped in the faultless blood of pretty Rutland –
>   His curses then, from bitterness of soul
>   Denounced against thee, are all fall'n upon thee,
>   And God, not we, hath plagued thy bloody deed.
> ELIZABETH   So just is God, to right the innocent.
> HASTINGS   Oh, 'twas the foulest deed to slay that babe,
>   And the most merciless, that e'er was heard of.
> RIVERS   Tyrants themselves wept when it was reported.
> DORSET   No man but prophesied revenge for it.   (1.3.172–84)

Shakespeare uses such curses and prophecies as dramatic devices to represent both the long conflict between Lancaster and York and the particular conflict – Richard against everybody – embodied in *Richard III*. Repeated invocations of providence also raise the general question of historical causation, reminding the audience that human events may be viewed as the thoughts of God made visible, manifestations in time of the timeless divine will. The play presents the issue of historical determinism – inseparable in Shakespeare's time from issues of religion – not as an assertion, but as one side of an argument.

On the other side stands Richard himself, representing a secular theory of history that finds the causes of human events in individual actions rather than in providential will. Richard is both a stage 'Machiavel' and a personification of the Machiavellian view of history as power politics.[1] Richard delights in confiding his intentions to the audience and then demonstrating how he can accomplish even the most outrageous of them:

> For then I'll marry Warwick's youngest daughter.
> What though I killed her husband and her father?
> The readiest way to make the wench amends
> Is to become her husband and her father.   (1.1.154–7)

At the end of the 'wooing of Anne' scene (1.2), Richard again turns to the audience to crow over his victory: 'Was ever woman in this humour wooed? / Was ever woman in this humour won?' (1.2.231–2).

---

[1] Niccolò Machiavelli appeared in the Elizabethan popular imagination as an advocate of tyranny and on the stage as a type of the villain. Christopher Marlowe's *The Jew of Malta*, for example, written in 1589, uses Machiavelli as a character. He speaks the prologue to the play and introduces his disciple, the villain Barabas.

From the first word of the play, Richard woos the audience as he woos Anne, with the strength of his personality: his wit, his confidence, his 'bustle'. His evil-yet-appealing character has ancestors in both classical and native English drama. In addition to the Machiavel, he is related to the Senecan criminal-hero, the Herod-tyrant from the medieval 'mystery' or religious cycle plays, and the Vice from the morality plays. Scholars have disagreed about the direct influence of Seneca on Elizabethan drama, but as Jones says, 'Whenever tyrants are in question in Shakespeare, there is likely to be a Senecan feel somewhere in the diction', as there certainly is in the patterned rhetoric of *Richard III*.[1] Certainly Elizabethan revenge tragedy shares many conventions with the plays of Seneca, including, as James E. Ruoff lists them, 'the revenge theme, the ghost, the play-within-the-play, the dumb show, the soliloquy, the declamation and bombast, the emphasis on macabre brutalities, insanity and suicide'.[2] Shakespeare's Richard, however, displays what A. P. Rossiter calls 'a most un-Senecan sense of humour'.[3] The idea of the tyrant who is both evil and funny probably came to Shakespeare through the native English drama. Herod, familiar from the Bible as an angry tyrant (see Matt. 2), had achieved popularity in medieval religious plays as a figure almost comic in his ranting violence.[4] But it was the secular moral drama of the same period, and especially its leading character, the Vice, that brought to the English stage a full-blown conception of comic evil. According to Robert Weimann, the Vice, an allegorical figure with a name such as Iniquity or Mischief, combined 'magician, doctor, and fool all in one'. Like Richard, this character manipulated others in the play while interacting, as though on another plane, with the audience. To the delight of spectators, the Vice would introduce himself and his schemes directly, sometimes moving among the audience asking for money.[5] Vice characters were noted for puns, audience rapport and a subversive energy that the morality plays quashed in the end, often by banishing the Vice to Hell.[6]

The hybrid tradition of the morality-play Vice prefigures the audacious combination of tragic and comic that marks Shakespeare's *Richard III*. When Richard tells the audience that he is 'determinèd to prove a villain', he summarises the tragic conception of the play in a joke. His primary meaning is that he controls his own destiny. His pun also has a second, contradictory meaning – that his villainy is predestined – and the strong providentialism of the play ultimately endorses this meaning. Yet in spite of characters like Margaret who insist that God is on their side, the divine determinism at work in *Richard III* does not seem to be the 'special providence' that minutely arranges each event in human history; God does not necessarily contrive or even notice the fall of every sparrow. Queen Elizabeth, for example, rails against divine indifference to the deaths of her sons: 'Wilt thou,

[1] Jones, p. 270.

[2] See James E. Ruoff, *Crowell's Handbook of Elizabethan and Stuart Literature*, 1975, p. 404.

[3] A. P. Rossiter, 'Angel with horns: the unity of *Richard III*', from *Angel with Horns* (1961), reprinted in *Shakespeare: The Histories: A Collection of Critical Essays*, ed. Eugene M. Waith, 1965, p. 83.

[4] Weimann, p. 67.   [5] *Ibid.*, p. 114.

[6] For the Vice in relation to Shakespeare see Spivack and Weimann. On the mystery plays, see Rossiter.

O God, fly from such gentle lambs / And throw them in the entrails of the wolf? /
When didst thou sleep when such a deed was done?' (4.4.22–4). Margaret immediately answers that injustices have happened before: 'When holy Harry died, and my
sweet son' (25). The providence of *Richard III* is rather the grand design of human
salvation and damnation. God's will is shown not by the victory of one faction or
another, but by the fate of the human soul – in this case, Richard's.[1] He is in this
sense a tragic hero, opposing the will of the universe with his own, 'all the world to
nothing'.[2]

WOMEN AND DETERMINISM

In the first three acts of *Richard III*, Shakespeare almost seems to be on Richard's
side, showing us the world of the play from Richard's point of view. Eventually, however, the play and presumably the audience withdraw their sympathy from Richard,
turning instead to his victims, especially the relatively 'flat' female characters. Like
Richard himself, the prophesying women in the play have links to characters in
both classical and English drama. The scene of the 'wailing queens' (4.4), for example, has been compared to the lamentations of Helena, Andromache and Hecuba in
Seneca's *Troades*.[3] In addition, patterns of audience identification grounded in the
English religious plays probably helped shift the attention of Shakespeare's spectators away from Richard and toward the women. In their scenes together, the female
characters in *Richard III* suggest responses conditioned by the Resurrection plays,
specifically by the motif of the three Marys – Mary Magdalene, Mary Salome and
Mary the mother of James – at the tomb of Jesus. Like the raging tyrant Herod
and the crowd-pleasing Vice, the three Marys formed part of the native theatrical
heritage for playwrights and playgoers of Shakespeare's generation.[4] In contrast to
these male figures, however, the three Marys were associated with solemnity and the
central mystery of Christianity, the Resurrection of Jesus. Shakespeare makes use

---

[1] Camille Wells Slights points out that Margaret, too, is an unrepentant soul, and that she seems already
to be suffering a kind of purgatory in this play. See 'Cases of conscience in Shakespeare's tragedies', in
The Casuistical Tradition in Shakespeare, Donne, Herbert, and Milton, 1981, pp. 67–132.

[2] As Robert G. Hunter explains it, 'Chance does not exist in the providentially controlled world which
is suggested as a possibility in *Richard III*. Richard begins his last speech with the lines: "Slave, I have
set my life upon a cast, / And I will stand the hazard of the dye" (5.4.9–10). The play answers Richard
with Einstein's reply to Bohr: "Der Herr Gott würfelt nicht." The Lord God does not throw dice.' See
Hunter, *Shakespeare and the Mystery of God's Judgements*, 1976, p. 100.

[3] See E. Koeppel, 'Shakespeares *Richard III*. und Senecas *Troades*', *Shakespeare Jahrbuch* 47 (1911), 188–
90. For other perspectives on Seneca and the women's scenes, see Harold F. Brooks, '*Richard III*:
unhistorical amplifications: the women's scenes and Seneca', *Modern Language Review* 75 (1980),
721–37.

[4] The cycle plays, which were associated with Roman Catholicism, were discouraged by the Protestant
authorities under Elizabeth, but they were still being performed in Shakespeare's youth. Alan C.
Dessen compares Shakespeare's borrowings from the morality plays to contemporary filmmakers' use
of conventions from the classic cinematic Western. See *Shakespeare and the Late Moral Plays*, 1986,
p. 8. As Dessen says, the conventions of earlier English drama – the religious cycle plays as well as the
secular 'moralls' – continued to form part of the heritage of the Elizabethan theatre long after these
plays had subsided as popular forms.

of these conventions to direct the audience's sympathy away from Richard in the second part of the play.[1]

Each of the surviving Resurrection plays portrays three fundamental actions: the lamentation of the three Marys, the women's approach to the tomb – where they learn of the Resurrection from an angel or angels – and finally their testimony about what they have learned. The three female-group scenes in *Richard III* – all composed of triads or quasi-triads of women – echo these three traditional elements of the Resurrection plays. In 2.2, three women (and a boy) lament for Richard's victims, in 4.1, three women approach the tomb – here the ominous Tower of London – and in 4.4, after another great lamentation, three women bear witness to Richard's evil.[2] The most important of these scenes is 4.4, but the female characters' contributions in that scene depend on associations developed in the earlier female-group scenes that link them to the Marys and to the revelation of divine will. As the tradition of the Vice helped influence the Elizabethan audience's reaction to Richard, so the tradition of the three Marys helped turn them away from Richard's individualism toward acceptance of the final act's stately determinism.

The first of the play's two parts – 1.1 through 4.1 – focuses on Richard and his evil energy. In 4.2, however, the protagonist begins to decline. As Wolfgang Clemen puts it, 'There is a restless urgency about IV, ii, a quickening of tempo; one is conscious of the approaching catastrophe. The rise must now be followed by the fall.'[3] The interest of the audience is directed away from Richard's perversely appealing personality toward the enormity of his crimes and ultimately to the opposing virtues embodied in Richmond. Several earlier scenes prepare the audience for this turning. In 1.4, both Clarence and the Second Murderer speak movingly of repentance, a double contrast to Richard's incorrigible joy-in-wickedness. In 2.2, the Duchess, Clarence's children and Queen Elizabeth lament their losses – which the audience knows to be Richard's work. In 3.3, Rivers, Vaughan and Grey endorse Margaret's prophecies just before they are put to death.

The strongest preparation for the play's major turn occurs in 4.1. The entire scene presents an inverse analogue of the approach to Jesus's tomb in the Resurrection plays. The Duchess, Elizabeth and Anne salute each other as 'daughter' and 'sister', approach the Tower, and bewail rather than celebrate what they learn there – that Richard holds the princes captive and will soon be king. This scene, with its formal rhetoric and its links to the motif of the Marys, probably evoked religious contexts

---

[1] Dessen discusses the two-phased structure of *Richard III* against the background of a similar two-part action in the late morality plays. He argues that the second phase of *Richard III*, as it draws away from Richard and toward Richmond, would have been familiar and acceptable to Shakespeare's audience because of the still-remembered conventions of the moral drama (*Shakespeare and the Late Moral Plays*).

[2] J. F. Royster, while also recognising Senecan parallels, pointed out similarities between *Richard III* 4.4 and the *Planctus* of the three Marys in Resurrection plays from several of the mystery cycles. See 'Richard III, IV.4 and the Three Marys of mediaeval drama', *Modern Language Notes* 25 (1910), 173–4. E. Koeppel ('Shakespeares *Richard III*. und Senecas *Troades*') disagreed, arguing that the discord between Elizabeth, Margaret and the Duchess made them too unlike the three Marys for the medieval motif to have been a source.

[3] Clemen, p. 164.

for Shakespeare's audience much more readily than it does today. In Elizabethan England, with its Calvinist emphasis on predestination, these associations must have suggested that the women in the play are not only on the side of right, but also on the side of destiny.

In the cycle plays, the three Marys – often almost indistinguishable as individual characters – act as stand-ins for the audience in their personal discovery of the Resurrection. So the Duchess, Elizabeth and Anne, by interrogating Richard's crimes and their own involvement with him, represent Shakespeare's spectators and help detach them from their earlier sympathy for the devil. Anne repents that she 'Grossly grew captive' to Richard's persuasions, and Elizabeth emphasises the innocence of Richard's victims, while the Duchess acknowledges her own 'accursèd womb'. Recent critics have stressed the psychological effects on Richard of his mother's rejection, sometimes blaming her for his deformed character.[1] In the play, however, the emphasis falls not on Richard's suffering in his relationship with his mother, but on the Duchess's grief and shame at her own intimacy with evil. The Duchess's clear-eyed acknowledgement of her role in nurturing Richard and her rejection of what he has become match the audience's initial identification with and ultimate repudiation of the protagonist.

The most significant female triad in the play occurs in 4.4. In the preceding scenes, Richard has begun to lose his Vice-like confidence, sinking into himself rather than reaching out to the audience in his monologues: 'I must be married to my brother's daughter, / Or else my kingdom stands on brittle glass' (4.2.61–2). And Tyrrel, himself a villain, has denounced the 'tyrannous and bloody' murder of the princes. In 4.4, three grieving women – Margaret, the Duchess and Elizabeth – again lament their losses at Richard's hands. Like Rivers, Grey and Hastings, Elizabeth comments on the accuracy of Margaret's earlier predictions:

> Oh, thou didst prophesy the time would come
> That I should wish for thee to help me curse
> That bottled spider, that foul bunch-backed toad.   (4.4.79–81)

As Margaret has predicted, her final function in the play is to teach the other women how to curse.[2] In her curses, Margaret speaks as the voice of destiny, but she stands outside the action of the play. Richard cannot hurt her, nor can she hurt him, at least not directly. When she transfers her cursing power to the other two women, however, that power comes as a kind of revelation. The Duchess and Elizabeth, who have feared and avoided Richard, now denounce him to his face for the first time in the play:

---

[1] See, for example, C. L. Barber and Richard P. Wheeler, *The Whole Journey: Shakespeare's Power of Development*, 1986, pp. 86–124; Bernard J. Paris, *Character as a Subversive Force in Shakespeare*, 1991, pp. 31–52; and Adelman, pp. 1–10.

[2] As Madonne M. Miner points out, these women, united in cursing, display a concord achieved by no other major group of characters in the play. See '"Neither mother, wife, nor England's Queen": the roles of women in *Richard III*', in *The Woman's Part: Feminist Criticism of Shakespeare*, ed. Carolyn Ruth Swift Lenz, Gayle Greene and Carol Thomas Neely, 1980, pp. 35–55.

> DUCHESS   Thou toad, thou toad, where is thy brother Clarence,
>   And little Ned Plantagenet, his son?
> ELIZABETH   Where is the gentle Rivers, Vaughan, Grey?
> DUCHESS   Where is kind Hastings?   (145–8)

By confronting Richard (and the audience) with what he is and what he has done, the women relieve the tension and dread described by the Scrivener (3.6):

> Who is so gross that cannot see this palpable device?
> Yet who so bold but says he sees it not?
> Bad is the world, and all will come to naught
> When such ill dealing must be seen in thought.   (3.6.11–14)

The Duchess and Elizabeth carry the bad news of Richard's crimes, but the fact that they speak out is good news. They bear witness to an evil heretofore only 'seen in thought' by most of those at court (always excepting Margaret). The Duchess vows to pray for Richard's adversaries, and Elizabeth holds her own against him as he seeks her daughter's hand. Although the Duchess and Elizabeth cannot overthrow Richard, the tide has turned. To reinforce the sense of relief that the women's testimony brings, Shakespeare has constructed a pattern of association between the play's major female characters and an ancient and solemn dramatic structure of lamentation, discovery and affirmation. If such associations are lost today, actors and directors must find ways to suggest their dramatic tone as part of an artistic context for the women in *Richard III*. When the women's parts are shortened or eliminated, both the female characters and the providential resolution of the plot can seem inadequate as foils to Richard's vitality.

IDENTITY AND CHOICE

Richard must lose everything unless he repents, and like Marlowe's Dr Faustus he refuses to repent. All the ghosts of Richard's victims order him in his sleep to 'despair and die', the same words Faustus says to himself when he abandons hope (scene 12). In spite of the ghosts' repeated commands, however, Richard does not despair. Starting out of his dream, he momentarily shakes off the theological dilemma of repentance versus despair and veers instead into a state Harold Bloom calls 'self-overhearing'. Bloom suggests that some characters in Shakespeare overhear their own speeches 'and pondering those expressions, they change and go on to contemplate an otherness in the self, or the possibility of such otherness'.[1] In *Richard III*, Shakespeare portrays this self-contemplation for the first time:

> Give me another horse! Bind up my wounds!
> Have mercy, Jesu! Soft, I did but dream.
> O coward conscience, how dost thou afflict me?
> The lights burn blue. It is not dead midnight.
> Cold, fearful drops stand on my trembling flesh.
> What? Do I fear myself? There's none else by.

[1] Harold Bloom, *The Western Canon*, 1994, p. 70.

1   David Garrick, who made his London debut as Richard III in 1741, in an engraving by William
Hogarth. Richard is surrounded by objects he has dishonoured, including 'my George, my Garter, and
my crown' (4.4.370)

Richard loves Richard, that is, I am I.
Is there a murderer here? No. Yes, I am.
Then fly. What, from myself? Great reason why:
Lest I revenge. What, myself upon myself?
Alack, I love myself. Wherefore? For any good
That I myself have done unto myself?
Oh, no. Alas, I rather hate myself
For hateful deeds committed by myself.
I am a villain. Yet I lie, I am not.
Fool, of thyself speak well. Fool, do not flatter.
My conscience hath a thousand several tongues,
And every tongue brings in a several tale,
And every tale condemns me for a villain.
Perjury in the highest degree,
Murder, stern murder, in the direst degree,
All several sins, all used in each degree,
Throng all to th'bar, crying all 'Guilty, guilty!'
I shall despair. There is no creature loves me,
And if I die no soul shall pity me.
Nay, wherefore should they, since that I myself
Find in myself no pity to myself?   (5.3.180–206)

Many critics have seen in this passage the beginnings of modern tragedy. As Robert Weimann says, in *Richard III* 'It is not *Schicksalsdrama*, not the inscrutable workings of the gods, that finally tips the scales of life and death but the *Charakterdrama* of an individual passion and a self-willed personality.'[1] '[D]eterminèd to prove a villain' from the first, Richard unexpectedly confronts the possibility of repentance ('Have mercy, Jesu!'), then reaffirms his earlier course. He makes this choice not from despair, but as an assertion of will. Finding no pity in himself, he will ask for none, not even from God.

Richard does not really love Richard, in the sense that he harbours no tender feelings for himself, but neither will he hate himself. His remarkable self-overhearing on the day of battle results in the same outcome as if he had despaired, fallen into self-hatred, and so taken revenge on himself, as Anne once predicted (1.2.86–7). He will die and be damned. Yet psychologically, there is a difference. By electing to remain himself, Richard insists on free will in the face of determinism. As Coriolanus banishes Rome rather than passively suffer banishment, so Richard assumes his predestined identity as his own choice. This interior moment is the play's final gloss on the paradoxical pun of the opening soliloquy. Richard is – he always has been – 'determinèd to prove a villain', and he refuses to surrender his own part of the pun, his human determination, to cosmic determinism. He has no choice, but he chooses anyway, and in this gesture against fate he partakes of tragic heroism.

Following Richard's monologue on Bosworth morning, he regains his ruthless courage and dies bravely. Meanwhile, the female characters, whose ritualised formality and association with providence helped distance the audience from Richard, have disappeared from the play. The result is a curiously flat triumph by Richmond, who says all the right things – pardons Richard's soldiers, promises peace and does not forget to ask after young George Stanley – but somehow evokes no joy. It is not Richard we mourn for, exactly, but his tragic defiance, and *Richard III* makes space for such mourning at the end. As Jones points out, the play supports determinism from the outset, not only by dealing with historical events of known outcome, but also by repeatedly reminding us of what we know (*Origins*, pp. 222–3). Throughout the wooing of Elizabeth, for example (4.4), 'the terms in which the dialogue is couched are such as to induce us to contemplate the future – the real future – of the Queen's daughter, "young Elizabeth", who we know will marry Richmond'.[2] Yet Richard's heroic end, like the sketchiness of Richmond's part and the withdrawal of the women from the end of the play, allows playgoers to leave the theatre a little defiant themselves, still a little on the side of choice, although mainly reconciled to determinism. Perhaps, as Jones says, a play in which the appearance of free will yields to a sense of higher determinism 'can achieve its fullest effect only in a society officially committed to a belief in God'.[3] Some such opinion about the changing

---

[1] Weimann, p. 160. See also Norman Rabkin, *Shakespeare and the Common Understanding*, 1967, p. 251: 'At this moment, crucial both in the play and in Shakespeare's career, the play turns to tragedy.' Not all critical readers agree. Adelman, for example, says that in this passage 'the effect is less of a psyche than of diverse roles confronting themselves across the void where a self should be' (p. 9).

[2] Jones, p. 223.   [3] *Ibid.*, p. 199.

H. Fuseli R.A. del.   J. Neagle Sc.

The Ghosts vanish. King Richard starts out of his Dream.

K. R. *Give me another horse —*
— the lights burn blue. —

Publish'd by C & E. Rivington, London, Feb. 13th 1804.

2   *The Ghosts vanish. King Richard starts out of his Dream*: an eighteenth-century engraving of the dream scene (5.3) by Henry Fuseli, showing triads of ghosts

faith of the audience may inform the many productions of *Richard III* that reduce the play's emphasis on providential destiny and overplay Richard's delicious wickedness. But perhaps in an era committed to a belief in science and natural law, the conflict between determinism and human will can be as relevant to audiences as it must have been in a climate of official Protestantism. Questions that arise in *Richard III* trouble philosophers still: do people create themselves, or are they created by chains of causation reaching back to a first cause? If determinism is true, is anyone really free?[1] Like Richard, we want to believe that we are ourselves alone, but like the play Richard inhabits, the universe we live in seems to hint that we are no such things.

Richard III and *Macbeth*

Shakespeareans have long recognised the similarities between *Macbeth* and *Richard III*. In 1817, for example, the actor-manager John Philip Kemble published *Macbeth and King Richard III*, in which he defended Macbeth's personal courage against a charge by Thomas Whately that, by contrast with the intrepid Richard, Macbeth was constitutionally timid. Although Whately and Kemble differed in their opinions of the leading characters, the fact that they compared the protagonists at all implies that they saw fundamental likenesses in the two plays. The many parallels suggest that Shakespeare saw such likenesses, too.[2]

   Macbeth revisits the issue of the villain-hero that Shakespeare first addressed in *Richard III*. As Rossiter says, 'Richard Plantagenet is alone with Macbeth as the Shakespearian version of the thoroughly bad man in the role of monarch and hero.'[3] Both protagonists are warriors, at their best when they 'bustle', and both maintain their warrior defiance to the end. Yet their own energies transform these soldiers into schemers who end up wallowing in rivers of blood. Richard, after ordering the young princes killed, muses that 'I am in / So far in blood that sin will pluck on sin' (4.2.64–5). Macbeth, contemplating the murders of Banquo and Fleance, repeats and expands Richard's figure: 'I am in blood / Stepped in so far, that should I wade no more, / Returning were as tedious as go o'er' (3.4.135–7). The relationship of Macbeth's line to Richard's may serve as an emblem for the relationship of the two plays. *Macbeth* echoes, revises and deepens *Richard III*, exploring again the tragic contradiction between a universe ordered by causation and a heroic conception of human free choice.

   Richard ambiguously asserts that he is 'determinèd to prove a villain', but the cosmic joke is on him. The play he inhabits suggests that his half of the pun, his

---

[1] For a non-technical treatment of such issues by a contemporary philosopher, see Ted Honderich, *How Free Are You? The Determinism Problem*, 1993.

[2] There are, of course, many differences between Richard III and Macbeth. Most critics would probably agree to some extent with James L. Calderwood's summary: 'Richard embraces the bestial difference that sets him apart from and beneath humankind. Macbeth unwillingly falls into bestiality in an effort to attain the regal difference that will raise him above beasts and other men.' See Calderwood, *If It Were Done: Macbeth and Tragic Action*, 1986. One might add that Macbeth is not a misogynist, at least not to the degree that Richard is.

[3] Rossiter, 'Angel with horns', p. 76.

determination, is illusory. Since Richard cannot be other than he is, cannot do other than he does, how can he be either a hero or a villain? Yet dramatically, he is both. The play makes him so, not by examining his inner life, but structurally, by provoking first identification and then distance in its audience. *Macbeth* treats the same paradoxes, but in another style. As A. R. Braunmuller puts the questions for *Macbeth*, 'If the prophecies are true before the play begins, or before Macbeth and Banquo hear them, or before Macbeth and Banquo have acted, where is the willed action that allows the audience to discover responsibility and hence to experience guilt? If Macbeth could never act otherwise, could never *not* choose to murder Duncan, and if, putatively, Banquo could never resist thoughts of usurpation, "the cursèd thoughts that nature / Gives way to in repose" (2.1.8–9), where is the tragedy, the dire consequence of an ignorant or misunderstood act, of these events? If, alternatively, the prophecies only become true when they are enacted by responsible and hence arguably tragic and guilty human agents, how may they be called "prophecies" at all?'[1]

Where *Richard III* uses dramatic technique and cultural memory to involve the audience in the clash between Richard's individualism and his fate, *Macbeth* uses psychology. Only following the dream scene in *Richard III*, and then only once, does Richard talk *to* himself rather than *about* himself. Macbeth does it from the first:

> This supernatural soliciting
> Cannot be ill, cannot be good. If ill,
> Why hath it given me earnest of success,
> Commencing in a truth? I am Thane of Cawdor.
> If good, why do I yield to that suggestion,
> Whose horrid image doth unfix my hair
> And make my seated heart knock at my ribs
> Against the use of nature?   (1.3.130–7)

Between the two plays, Shakespeare has shifted from a medieval to a modern conception of character. Yet structural and verbal memories of *Richard III* pervade *Macbeth*. The recurring female-triad scenes of *Richard III* are echoed in *Macbeth* by the highly dramatic appearances of the three witches. In both plays, groups of three women are associated with fate. When the female characters in *Richard III* appear together in triads, they align themselves not just with destiny but with a distinctly Christian providence. *Macbeth* makes the symbolic association between female triads and fate even clearer by linking the women overtly to prophecy and the supernatural. At the same time, by transforming the three women into witches, *Macbeth* renders their connection to the liturgical–theatrical tradition of the Three Marys almost untraceable, allowing the audience to regard them as suspicious and alien. Like many of the other common elements shared by *Richard III* and *Macbeth*, the motif of the three women becomes more equivocal in the latter.

The association between female triads and witchcraft may have been suggested in part by Margaret's first scene in *Richard III* (1.3). She assumes the same kind of prophetic role as the witches in *Macbeth*, and Richard calls her a 'Foul wrinkled

---

[1] See Braunmuller, p. 42.

witch' (162). Margaret also seems to be magically immune from retaliation, either for cursing the queen and courtiers or for violating her banishment. Although she only later (4.4) becomes part of a threesome of women, perhaps the idea of the three fates as witches arose from these two different aspects of Margaret in *Richard III*. Certainly some modern students of Shakespeare have made the connection between the witches of *Macbeth* and the women of *Richard III*. In a recent regional production of *Richard III*, Margaret had the power to freeze the other actors in their tracks while she spoke her asides to the audience, and in 4.4 she executed a trancelike circle dance with Elizabeth and the Duchess of York, the three of them chanting Margaret's lines: 'Earth gapes, hell burns, fiends roar, saints pray, / To have him suddenly conveyed from hence' (4.4.75–6).[1]

Another device that works similarly in both plays is child murder. Both protagonists recognise that they have crossed a moral line when they first decide to move against the young: Richard against the princes, Macbeth against Fleance. Both killers defend the step by recalling that they are deep in blood already, but this self-justification can only alienate further an audience previously conditioned to regard the murder of innocents with horror. When he fails to kill Fleance, Macbeth turns savagely on the family of Macduff. Reflecting the greater psychological immediacy of *Macbeth*, Shakespeare stages the later child killings, which he clearly avoided doing in *Richard III*. *Macbeth*'s mother-and-child murder scene, 4.1, focuses on little Macduff, a direct descendant of sharp-witted little York. After the children are killed, both plays raise doubts about divine concern for innocents. Macduff's anguished question at the deaths of his family, 'did heaven look on, / And would not take their part?' (4.3.223–4), recalls Elizabeth's protests to God over her own slaughtered children, 'When didst thou sleep when such a deed was done?' (4.4.24). A reply of a sort seems to come in the mental experiences of the protagonists. God's wakefulness shows in the wakefulness of Richard and Macbeth; they have murdered their own sleep. The first hint of Richard's disturbed rest comes from Anne, who complains that 'never yet one hour in his bed / Did I enjoy the golden dew of sleep, / But with his timorous dreams was still awaked' (4.1.83–5). Macbeth speaks of 'these terrible dreams / That shake us nightly' (3.3.18–19). After their climactic child killings, both tyrants are also haunted by the ghosts of their victims. In the double dream of Richard and Richmond, the ghosts of the slain princes predict that Richmond will survive the battle 'and beget a happy race of kings', the Tudor dynasty (5.3.160). In a mirror moment in *Macbeth*, the witches show Macbeth a line of future kings (including James I) who will spring from Banquo (4.1.111–23).

In the end, both tyrant-heroes are alone. Just as Blunt observes that Richard 'hath no friends but what are friends for fear, / Which in his dearest need will fly from him' (5.2.20–1), Macbeth tells the doctor that 'the thanes fly from me' (5.3.49), and Malcolm describes Macbeth as deserted: 'none serve with him but constrainèd things / Whose hearts are absent too' (5.4.13–14). Richard has his moment of conscience on Bosworth morning, but reverts quickly to his usual ruthless behaviour. (Colley Cibber's adaptation of 1700 underscores the reversion by having Richard announce,

---

[1] Lord Leebrick Theatre Co., Eugene, Oregon, directed by Chris Pinto, 1998.

'*Richard's* himself again' (p. 52). Cibber's line, making explicit what Shakespeare only implies, endured in the performance tradition for more than two centuries.) Macbeth also has a last moment of doubt near the end: 'I pull in resolution, and begin / To doubt th'equivocation of the fiend / That lies like truth' (5.5.41–3). Then he, too, becomes 'himself again', warlike and doomed: 'Blow wind, come wrack; / At least we'll die with harness on our back' (*Macbeth* 5.5.50–1). Both villains go out fighting, speaking memorably brave exit lines; Richard's 'A horse, a horse, my kingdom for a horse!' (5.4.7, 13) parallels Macbeth's 'Lay on, Macduff, / And damned be him that first cries, "Hold, enough!"' (5.8.33–4).

The list of correspondences large and small between the two plays might be lengthened, but these are enough to show that Shakespeare, like Whately and Kemble, regarded the two dramas as closely related. *Macbeth* reworks themes and issues from *Richard III* in light of all the ways the author's writing had changed in the decade or more that separated the plays. Returning to the problem of the villain as tragic protagonist, *Macbeth* again raises issues of fate and personal responsibility. It poses similar questions about audience identification with a strong, smart 'hero' who is also evil. To modern spectators, *Macbeth* probably leaves the answers even less clear than *Richard III* does. With its steady stream of introspective soliloquies, *Macbeth* places the audience *inside* the central character, which is a harder place for contemporary playgoers to retreat from than the moral theatre of *Richard III*.

Plot and language in *Richard III*

Richard III focuses on the rise and fall of Richard. For all its huge cast, the play has no subplots. Opposing groups of characters – Margaret, Richard's brothers, Elizabeth's family, the York women, the York children, courtiers such as Hastings, Stanley, Buckingham, Ratcliffe and Catesby, and the Earl of Richmond – all are juxtaposed in various combinations to advance Richard's story. This single focus gives the play a classic pyramid structure: 'rising' action to the peak of the pyramid, climax and crisis, then 'falling' action to the end.[1] Beginning with the exposition in Richard's opening soliloquy, the rising action – Richard's ascent to the throne – continues until 4.2, often called the 'coronation' scene, although in Shakespeare's script the crowning takes place offstage.[2] Richard has achieved the kingship, and this is the peak of his fortunes. Immediately, the crisis or turn occurs. The new king begins to falter, expressing an uncharacteristic lack of confidence to the evidently puzzled Buckingham:

> Thus high, by thy advice and thy assistance,
> Is King Richard seated.
> But shall we wear these glories for a day?
> Or shall they last, and we rejoice in them?

---

[1] This triangular structure is sometimes called Freytag's Pyramid, after Gustav Freytag, who described it in his *Technique of the Drama*, 1863.

[2] Many productions add a silent coronation ceremony here, often quite elaborate.

BUCKINGHAM   Still live they, and forever let them last.
RICHARD   Ah, Buckingham, now do I play the touch
    To try if thou be current gold indeed.
    Young Edward lives; think now what I would speak.
BUCKINGHAM   Say on, my loving lord.
RICHARD   Why, Buckingham, I say I would be king.
BUCKINGHAM   Why, so you are, my thrice-renownèd lord.   (4.2.4–14)

The falling action begins immediately, as Richard begins to lose his earlier skill at controlling his environment. He continues his murders, killing the princes and possibly Anne, but Richmond gathers strength at a distance, and Margaret scents catastrophe:

> So now prosperity begins to mellow
> And drop into the rotten mouth of death.
> Here in these confines slyly have I lurked
> To watch the waning of mine enemies.
> A dire induction am I witness to,
> And will to France, hoping the consequence
> Will prove as bitter, black, and tragical.   (4.4.1–7)

Historically, Margaret left England in 1476 and died in 1482, three years before Richard's defeat at Bosworth. Her anachronistic appearance in Shakespeare's play serves several dramatic purposes. In her first scene, 1.3, Margaret foreshadows the main action with her curses and prophecies. She returns at the beginning of 4.4 to underscore the prophecies' fulfilment, which the audience has already seen in the deaths of King Edward, Rivers, Hastings and the Prince of Wales, and in the declines of Buckingham and Elizabeth. The evident association of Margaret with destiny marks her as Richard's antagonist, as does her relationship to the audience. Alone among the characters, Margaret and Richard say things that only the spectators can hear, even while other characters occupy the stage. This makes them both more and less 'real' than the other figures in the play: more real because they are closer to the audience, less real because they break the dramatic illusion with their soliloquies and asides. Their equivocal status, both in and out of the action, sets these two apart. Richard and Margaret oppose each other as if across a crowded room, speaking over the heads of characters who inhabit only the stage-play world.

The theatrical vocabulary of Margaret's opening soliloquy in 4.4 – words such as 'induction' and 'tragical' – calls attention to the rhetorical neatness of the play's shape. This neatness lies not only in the pyramidal structure of the action and in Margaret's prophetic antagonism, but also in paired or 'mirror' scenes that enhance the atmosphere of prophecy and confirmation. The wooing of Anne is matched and to some degree inverted by the wooing of Elizabeth (1.2 and 4.4). Clarence's dream and the murderers' debate about conscience (1.4) are matched by Richard's dream and his debate about conscience with himself (5.3). Similarly, Margaret's speech at the start of 4.4 matches and transforms Richard's famous self-introduction at the beginning of the play and carries on the imagery of seasonal change. In Richard's

3 *The Two Murderers of the Duke of Clarence*: Henry Fuseli portrays the two assassins as distinct characters
(*c.* 1780–2)

soliloquy, the winter of discontent, his home season, gives way to a 'glorious summer' that he does not want. Now it is autumn, the season most congenial to Margaret, and she watches greedily while Richard's overripe prosperity starts to 'drop into the rotten mouth of death'. As she tells the Duchess, 'I am hungry for revenge, / And now I cloy me with beholding it' (4.4.61–2). The wheel has turned, and once again a lurking, isolated speaker observes the change both with triumph and with bitterness. The drama begins again, only this time it is Margaret's play instead of Richard's.

In addition to the structure of its scenes, the play's design also includes its highly patterned language. Critics have often noted, for example, the contrast between the formality of the women's dialogue and the casualness of Richard's speech.[1] This difference in styles reinforces the thematic division between the women's identification with the social group and Richard's individualism. But while Richard uses a more informal idiom than other characters – homely expressions such as 'I run before my horse to market' (1.1.161), and sudden, 'plain' remarks such as 'I wish the bastards dead' (4.2.19) – he, too, employs the repeating figures of formal rhetoric. They are an important thread in the verbal fabric of the entire play.

Rhetoric formed the basis of Shakespeare's humanist education, and he often deployed it more overtly in the early plays than he did later in his career.[2] *Richard III*, however, depends heavily on rhetoric not because it is an early play, but because its subject, the end of a long and necessarily repetitive civil war, fits the repetition-with-variation that lies at the heart of formal rhetoric. Recurrent verbal patterns suit Richard's ironic description of a peace he hopes to turn into another war: 'Our bruisèd arms hung up for monuments, / Our stern alarums changed to merry meetings, / Our dreadful marches to delightful measures' (1.1.6–8). Figures of repetition also suit the play's lamentation scenes, with their similar sorrows and denunciations, as when the Duchess of York grieves with Queen Elizabeth and Clarence's children:

> She for an Edward weeps, and so do I;
> I for a Clarence weep, so doth not she.
> These babes for Clarence weep, and so do I;
> I for an Edward weep, so do not they.

The mourning women in *Richard III* are closely associated with such prominent figures of repetition as *anaphora* – beginning each clause in a sequence with the same word – and *epistrophe* – repeating the same word at the end of each clause.[3] Margaret often uses such language:

> Though not by war, by surfeit die your king,
> As ours by murder to make him a king.
> Edward thy son, that now is Prince of Wales,

[1] See Hammond, p. 114.
[2] On Shakespeare's education, see T. W. Baldwin, *William Shakspere's Small Latine & Lesse Greeke*, 2 vols., 1944.
[3] For a more complete analysis of rhetoric in *Richard III*, see Brian Vickers, 'Shakespeare's use of rhetoric', in *A New Companion to Shakespeare Studies*, ed. Kenneth Muir and Samuel Schoenbaum, 1971, pp. 83–98.

> For Edward our son, that was Prince of Wales,
> Die in his youth by like untimely violence.   (1.3.195–9)

Similarly, male characters rise to formal rhetoric when they look back over the war and its consequences. Earl Rivers, on his way to death at Pomfret, admits the efficacy of Margaret's curses:

> Then cursed she Richard,
> Then cursed she Buckingham,
> Then cursed she Hastings. O remember God,
> To hear her prayer for them, as now for us.   (3.3.17–20)

The patterns of formal rhetoric occur abundantly in *Richard III*, suggesting the patterns of death, sorrow and revenge engendered in civil war. Rhyme, on the other hand, is relatively infrequent. Fewer than ten per cent of the verse lines in *Richard III* are rhymed – a proportion similar to those in *Henry VI, Part 2*, and *Henry VI, Part 3*, but smaller than in the early comedies or *Titus Andronicus*, the earliest tragedy.[1] Rhyme is used for emphasis, as when Richard suggests that his birth was a comfort to his mother, and she replies: 'No, by the holy rood, thou know'st it well, / Thou cam'st on earth to make the earth my hell' (4.4.166–7). A couplet often provides a sense of closure at the end of a speech or scene: 'Let's lack no discipline, make no delay, / For lords, tomorrow is a busy day' (5.3.17–18). Rhyme in the ghost scene, more frequent as the parade of victims draws to an end, implies closure in the form of victory for Richmond:

> [GHOST OF BUCKINGHAM]
> (*To Richmond*) I died for hope ere I could lend thee aid.
> But cheer thy heart and be thou not dismayed.
> God and good angels fight on Richmond's side,
> And Richard fall in height of all his pride.   (5.3.176–9)

Within the limits of its often end-stopped blank verse line, *Richard III* reveals metrical effects corresponding to the dynamics of character and scene. Sometimes, as G. T. Wright has pointed out, the play's verse is quietly regular, the natural rhythms of speech matching the metrical pattern with no sense of strain: 'I fear our happiness is at the height' (1.3.41); 'I thank my God for my humility' (2.1.73). Elsewhere, the demands of special emphasis may be so strong that a line with a single inverted foot will sound as if it has broken the pattern altogether: '*If*? Thou protector of this damnèd strumpet' (3.4.73; emphasis added).[2]

The variety and restraint with which Shakespeare controls such devices as rhyme and metre in *Richard III* support the idea that his flamboyant use of rhetorical figures serves thematic purposes. Formal rhetoric marks the distinctive style of *Richard III* not because a young Shakespeare was showing off his education, but because figures of repetition underscore the cycles of aggression and suffering in the play. As productions like Ian McKellen's film have shown, brutal cutting of these patterns can

---

[1] See Wells and Taylor, p. 98.
[2] See George T. Wright, *Shakespeare's Metrical Art*, 1988, pp. 48, 242.

make the dialogue of *Richard III* sound almost like that of a contemporary movie. To do this, however, is also to eliminate the verbal oxygen of Shakespeare's play.

Richard III in performance

The lead in *Richard III* has always been regarded as one of Shakespeare's choicest parts. The first famous actor associated with the role was Richard Burbage, one of Shakespeare's partners in the Lord Chamberlain's Men (the King's Men after 1603). We know of Burbage's performances only through anecdotes and allusions, but these are enough to suggest that the play and its star enjoyed great popularity.[1] The fact that *Richard III* appeared in six quarto editions before the Folio of 1623 and in two more after it also attests to the play's continuing appeal in the period leading up to the English Civil Wars. On 16 November 1633, the play was acted at the court of Charles I, the only early performance of which a record has survived.[2]

The theatres were closed in 1642, at the onset of civil war, and they remained dark during the Commonwealth and Protectorate periods, when England was governed by a Parliament generally opposed to the drama. With the Restoration of Charles II in 1660 came the re-opening of London theatres and a return to aristocratic patronage of acting companies. Once again there was a King's Company performing Shakespeare's *Richard III*, although the play probably did not please the new audiences as much as it had the old.[3] In 1700, the playwright-actor and poet laureate Colley Cibber revised *Richard III* to appeal to contemporary taste, and the influence of his adaptation continued well into the twentieth century.

THE CIBBER TRADITION

Cibber greatly simplified *Richard III*, focusing tightly on the title character by eliminating King Edward, Clarence, the two murderers, Hastings and Margaret, among others. From Shakespeare's very long script, some 3,800 lines in the Folio, Cibber retained about 800 lines, which he combined with fragments from several other Shakespearean history plays and over 1,000 lines of his own. The resulting dialogue makes many matters clear that Shakespeare chose to leave ambiguous or implicit. For example, when Shakespeare's Richard courts Lady Anne, he says only that he wants her 'not all so much for love / As for another secret close intent / By

---

[1] See John James Monro (ed.), *The Shakespeare Allusion Book*, rev. edn, 1932. Probably the most famous story about Burbage also concerns *Richard III*. On 13 March 1602, John Manningham wrote in his *Diary*: 'Upon a tyme when Burbidge played Rich. 3 there was a citizen greue soe farr in liking with him, that before shee went from the play shee appointed him to come that night unto hir by the name of Ri: the 3. Shakespeare overhearing their conclusion went before, was intertained, and at his game ere Burbidge came. Then message being brought that Rich the 3.^{d} was at the dore, Shakespeare caused returne to be made that William the Conqueror was before Rich. the 3.' Quoted from E. K. Chambers, *The Elizabethan Stage*, 4 vols., 1923, III, 212.

[2] See Nigel Bawcutt, *The Control and Censorship of Caroline Drama*, 1996, p. 184.

[3] Shakespeare's *Richard III* seems to have been infrequently performed in the Restoration period. *The London Stage* lists a prologue written for the play in 1672 (I, 188), and J. G. McManaway discovered a cast list for a performance *c*. 1690 written in a copy of Q8 (*TLS*, 17 June 1935).

marrying her which I must reach unto' (1.1.158–60). Cibber's Richard, by contrast, is in love: 'But see, my Love appears: Look where she shines, / Darting pale Lustre, like the Silver Moon / Through her dark Veil of Rainy sorrow' (p. 11).[1] Later, when he falls out of love and wishes Anne dead, he is equally explicit: 'Why don't she die? / She must: My Interest will not let her live. / The fair *Elizabeth* has caught my Eye, / My Heart's vacant; and she shall fill her place' (p. 26). Nor are Richard's the only motives that Cibber clarifies. Elizabeth tells the audience in an aside that she has no intention of giving Richard her daughter: 'Yet I may seemingly comply, and thus / By sending *Richmond* Word of his Intent, / Shall gain some time to let my Child escape him' (p. 43).

   The Restoration and early eighteenth century saw many adaptations of Shakespeare's plays, but Cibber's *Richard III* survived on stage far longer than any of the others. In part, this is because Cibber shrewdly exaggerated the play's potential as a star vehicle, initially for himself. Shakespeare's Richard speaks nearly a third of the lines in the play, but Cibber's Richard has more than forty per cent.[2] Cibber's deletion of Clarence also omits the early appeal to mercy and repentance that temporarily drives Richard from the stage (1.4). The ritual pattern of female triads is broken, and Margaret, the strongest of the women, is removed completely. There is nothing left to balance Richard's overwhelming dominance of the stage and the story. Cibber's Richard is a bad man, but a comprehensible one, which makes it easier for audiences both to appreciate his energy and avoid implicating themselves in his evil. Shakespeare's Richard weakens once he achieves the throne – as when he issues incomplete orders to Catesby and Ratcliffe, then loses his temper and strikes a messenger (4.4). Cibber's remains in control. He still suffers a crisis of conscience after the ghost scene, but it is brief and simple:

> Have mercy, Heaven. Ha! – soft! – 'Twas but a dream:
> But then so terrible, it shakes my Soul.
> Cold drops of sweat hang on my trembling Flesh,
> My blood grows chilly, and I freze with horror.
> O Tyrant Conscience! how dost thou aflict me!
> When I look back, 'tis terrible Retreating:
> I cannot bear the thought, nor dare repent:
> I am but Man, and Fate, do thou dispose me.   (p. 52)

Catesby enters, and Richard recovers, uttering Cibber's most famous line, 'Conscience avant; *Richard's* himself again.' Thereafter he fights – and speaks – heroically: 'Hark! the shrill Trumpet sounds, to Horse: Away! / My Soul's in Arms, and eager for the Fray' (p. 52).

   To the male actor-managers of the eighteenth-century theatre, this boldly dominant character proved irresistible. The most important of these was David Garrick, who made his London debut as Richard in 1741. Using Cibber's script, but evidently transcending Cibber's declamatory acting style, Garrick took the London theatrical

---

[1] See Colley Cibber, *The Tragical History of King Richard III*, c. 1700; reprinted Cornmarket Press, 1969.
[2] Richmond, p. 51.

world by storm. Thereafter, a rise in the popularity of *Richard III* paralleled Garrick's own rise. While Cibber's adaptation had played 84 times in the 40 years after it was written, it was performed 213 times in the 29 years between 1747 and 1776, when Garrick managed the Drury Lane Theatre.[1] Cibber had extracted an essential feature from Shakespeare's complex work: its focus on a single extraordinary character. As Shakespeare wrote it, and as Cibber perceived, the role of Richard offers an unparalleled opportunity for virtuoso display. 'Richard is a performer', as Julie Hankey says, 'and whether he is the transparent exhibitionist of Colley Cibber's eighteenth-century adaptation or the masked Proteus of Shakespeare, he is a gift to the actor.'[2]

Following Garrick's triumph, *Richard III* became a kind of 'test piece', which 'would have been as strange for the chief tragedian of the day to neglect as *Hamlet*'.[3] One after another, the great male players took up the role. John Philip Kemble, George Cooke and Edmund Kean all left their marks on the part in the late eighteenth and early nineteenth centuries. Kemble and Cooke restored the first four lines of Shakespeare's play, the famous beginning of Richard's first soliloquy, but otherwise played Cibber's text.[4] Kean, 'the quintessential romantic actor – virtually a Byronic force on the stage', played Richard as a warrior, reasserting his grandeur with a wave of his sword on Cibber's 'Richard's himself again.'[5]

In 1821, the actor-manager William Charles Macready attempted to restore part of Shakespeare's text in his performances of *Richard III*, but the experiment was not a critical success. He returned to Cibber's script, keeping only the betrayal of Hastings (3.4) in place of a scene Cibber had invented, in which Richard urges Anne to kill herself.[6] Finally, in 1845, Samuel Phelps produced a version of Shakespeare's text, cut and restructured, at the Sadler's Wells Theatre. Mary Amelia Warner played Margaret to Phelps's Richard, and both won critical approval. In 1849, Phelps repeated his staging of the Shakespearean version with Isabella Glynn as Margaret. At the same time, however, Edmund Kean's son Charles enjoyed a popular success at the Princess's Theatre with Cibber's familiar version of the play (1854). Whether influenced by this competition or by the lack of a strong actress to play Margaret, Phelps reverted to Cibber's text for his final *Richard III* in 1861.

Meanwhile, in 1821, one of Edmund Kean's competitors, Junius Brutus Booth, had left the London stage for America, taking with him the tradition of the English actor-manager and the popular role of *Richard III*. Booth found acclaim in his new country with Cibber's text, restoring a few Shakespearean touches such as Richard's response to the news of Richmond's approach: 'Is the chair empty? Is the sword unswayed? / Is the king dead? The empire unpossessed?' (4.4.476–7). When Booth's son Edwin came to maturity on the New York stage, he, like Macready and Phelps, attempted to produce Shakespeare's version of *Richard III* (1878), but met with mixed reviews.[7] In London, however, Henry Irving had already (1877) enjoyed a hit with Shakespeare's text, and his victory at last overturned a two-hundred-year

[1] Colley, pp. 18, 39.   [2] Hankey, p. 9.   [3] *Ibid.*, p. 41.   [4] See Hankey, p. 41; Colley, p. 55.
[5] Colley, pp. 62 and 75.   [6] *Ibid.*, p. 86.   [7] *Ibid.*, pp. 110–11.

4 *The Rival Richards or Sheakspear in Danger*. William Heath's cartoon (1818) shows Junius Brutus Booth (left) and Edmund Kean (right) in nearly identical costumes for their competing productions of *Richard III*

tradition of using Cibber's words in place of Shakespeare's. But this triumph did not end the practice of focusing narrowly on the title role. Of Shakespeare's 3,800 lines, Irving retained about two-thirds. He cut historical references and the parts of other characters, leaving 'the rest of the cast neutralized so as to give Irving as clear a field as possible to present his own special character study'.[1] Even when Irving revived the production in 1896, only Margaret (Geneviève Ward) among the secondary characters gained much attention,[2] perhaps because Irving for the first time restored Margaret to the climactic female triad in 4.4.[3]

The early twentieth century saw both traditional and novel presentations of *Richard III*. The American actor John Barrymore continued the tradition of 'theatrical giants who staked their reputations upon success in the role of Richard III'.[4] Like Irving's, Barrymore's *Richard III* was a one-man show, subordinating all other parts and business to those of the lead. Barrymore also followed the custom of editing and rearranging the text to make it resemble Cibber's, although the lines were Shakespeare's. By adding five scenes from *Henry VI, Part 3* to the beginning of the play, Barrymore managed to postpone Shakespeare's opening, 'Now is the winter of our discontent / Made glorious summer by this son of York', until half way through the

---

[1] Hankey, p. 65.   [2] *Ibid.*, p. 65.   [3] Colley, p. 135.   [4] *Ibid.*, p. 151.

show. The opening night performance (6 March 1920) ran four-and-a-half hours, finishing after one a.m.[1] In the same year, Leopold Jessner offered audiences in Berlin an expressionist *Richard III*. Notable in part for its later influence on the Polish critic Jan Kott, Jessner's play 'ignored the psychological states of the characters who made up the cast to concentrate upon their symbolic function in the political allegory'.[2] Symbolism permeated Jessner's set, which was dominated in the second half by a blood-red staircase leading up to Richard's throne room. The effects of Jessner's approach continue to be felt in English-language productions of *Richard III*, although their full impact had to wait for the post-Nazi period and for Kott's *Shakespeare Our Contemporary* (1966) to open the way. In 1937, Tyrone Guthrie 'attempted to produce Emlyn Williams as a casebook Richard suffering from maternal deprivation and sibling rivalry',[3] an interpretation that foundered at the time, but would return to influence productions mounted later in the century.

The first significant *Richard III* of the Second World War starred the English actor Donald Wolfit, who in 1942 incorporated his impressions of Hitler into the part. In spite of this new inspiration, Wolfit's *Richard* was a 'roaring melodrama'[4] in the mode of Cibber. It is worth noting that Wolfit gladly retained the female triad mounted against Richard in 4.4, calling it 'the core of the play'. 'Here Shakespeare used the fate motif as he used the witches in *Macbeth*.'[5] Old-fashioned though it was in many ways, Wolfit's interpretation met with a popular success that similar productions had failed to achieve in the 1920s and 1930s. As Colley says, 'The havoc wreaked by this Richard made sense in the context of a country consumed by war.'[6]

After Wolfit's revival came Laurence Olivier's version at the Old Vic in 1944, directed by John Burrell. Destined to be the most important *Richard III* of the century and perhaps of any century, in part because it was preserved on film, Olivier's interpretation combined the influences of the entire Cibber tradition with the actor's own resources of intellect, voice and physical power. The production toured Europe in 1945 and Australia and New Zealand in 1948, and was revived in London in 1949. Although Olivier's first Margaret, Sybil Thorndike, matched him in power, she was confined to the first act.[7] When this version was filmed in 1955, with Olivier himself directing, Margaret was cut entirely and the parts of the Duchess and Queen Elizabeth were reduced almost to walk-ons. Olivier kept Anne, of course, since winning her is Richard's greatest triumph. As in Cibber, however, Anne appears only with Richard. Emphasis shifts from groups of women as ritual opponents to single women as sexual objects, especially since Olivier also adds a silent part for the courtesan Jane Shore, who lurks suggestively around King Edward and Hastings in several scenes. In Shakespeare's play, Shore receives mention, but never appears. Like Cibber, Olivier also rejected the decline in Richard's power that Shakespeare built in to the second half of his script. In an abbreviated ghost scene, some of

---

[1] *Ibid.*, p. 155. [2] *Ibid.*, p. 159. [3] Hankey, p. 66. [4] Colley, p. 168.
[5] Donald Wolfit, *First Interval*, 1954, p. 206, quoted by Colley, p. 169. [6] Colley, p. 169.
[7] See Samuel L. Leiter, *Shakespeare Around the Globe: A Guide to Notable Postwar Revivals*, 1986, p. 600.

5   Edwin Booth as Richard III, Boston, 1872, by Henry Linton after a work by John Hennessy

Margaret of Anjou (Geneviève Ward)

6 Geneviève Ward as Margaret of Anjou, *c.* 1896

7   Laurence Olivier as Richard III and Claire Bloom as Lady Anne in the film directed by Olivier (1955)

the spirits appear to Richard (not to Richmond), but they speak only a few words each. Olivier then shakes off his dream and returns to warrior form with Cibber's 'Richard's himself again', spoken as an aside to the camera as he leans down from his horse. Richmond is reduced to a handsome face speaking a dozen or so lines. It is not surprising that this golden-haired nonentity cannot kill Richard by himself. It takes Richmond's whole army hacking away at the tyrant to finish him off, and even then Olivier prolongs Richard's death with convulsive struggles executed on his back, suggesting the character's almost superhuman energy.

Partly because of its distortions of Shakespeare's script, Olivier's film, as Hugh Richmond remarks, offers 'a distillation of the whole theatrical history of the play' – a kind of dynamic museum of past interpretations.[1] This synthesis was made easier by the fact that past interpretations had been so similar. Nearly all productions since 1700, whether they used Cibber's script or a modified Shakespearean version, had cut characters, scenes and lines with the aim of focusing all attention on Richard. The most successful Richards had been active, sometimes heroic, figures who knew how to gain the sympathy of the audience. There was also a standard Crookback costume – doublet and hose, fur-lined coat, boots and black pageboy hair. A recently rediscovered silent film of *Richard III* (1912) shows the veteran stage actor Frederick Warde, who had worked with Edwin Booth, wearing the traditional look. Even Garrick had dressed this way for *Richard III*, although he had worn eighteenth-century clothes for *Macbeth* and *King Lear*.[2] Olivier, too, adopted the customary costume, adding a touch of his own in the form of a huge nose.

AFTER OLIVIER

In addition to bringing the whole Cibber-based performance tradition of *Richard III* into the twentieth century, Olivier's success perpetuated the custom of using the part to advance one's acting career by overshadowing the previous Richard. As generations of actors had perceived, Cibber's arrangement of the play, if not always his script, fits such a purpose even better than Shakespeare's. Yet Olivier's global success seemed to exhaust the Cibber inheritance. It proved impossible to erase the memory of Olivier's clipped tenor voice, his physical force, his black wig. Critics compared Alec Guinness's sneering (Stratford, Ontario, 1953) to Olivier's sneering and pronounced Guinness less powerful.[3] They compared Christopher Plummer's masterly diction (Royal Shakespeare Theatre, 1961) to Olivier's masterly diction and found Plummer less imposing.[4] Perhaps reflecting the distant influence of Tyrone Guthrie's psychological reading in 1937, Glen Byam Shaw directed Marius Goring at Stratford-upon-Avon in 1953 as 'the first of the long line of post-war lunatic Richards'.[5] But the critics, remembering Olivier's melodramatic Crookback, said Goring's villain was underplayed, and one, Kenneth Tynan, thought Goring was upstaged by his own Buckingham.[6]

More successful in overcoming Olivier's ghost was the Peter Hall/John Barton *Richard III* of 1963. This production closed a three-play sequence called *The Wars of the Roses*, which included the three *Henry VI* plays conflated into two. *Richard III* now appeared as the culmination of Shakespeare's depiction of a long civil war. Hall remembers finding 'great support' for his production in Kott's *Shakespeare Our Contemporary*, which he read in proof while travelling to the first rehearsal of *The Wars of the Roses*.[7] The symbolic bloody stairs from Jessner's 1920 *Richard III* became in

[1] Richmond, pp. 58, 59.   [2] *Ibid.*, p. 135.   [3] Colley, p. 184.   [4] *Ibid.*, p. 190.
[5] *Ibid.*, p. 197.   [6] *Ibid.*, p. 199.   [7] Barton and Hall, p. xi.

8 Frederick Warde as Richard III in the oldest surviving American feature film (1912)

Kott's book a metaphor for the 'Grand Mechanism' of Shakespeare's histories. Each claimant to the throne climbs the staircase of power only to be thrown down by the next ambitious climber. In keeping with Kott's concept of Shakespeare as a lens for viewing one's own time, Hall and Barton set *Richard III* in a police-state atmosphere that seemed to be poised somewhere between the 1400s and the 1930s. 'The costumes and choreography of the battle scenes evoked those of Brueghel, stressing the smoke, grime, and harshness of war with a powerful soundtrack of gunfire and clashing metal.'[1] Ian Holm played an understated Richard who was 'at once a gifted and powerful political leader and yet, obviously, quite mad'.[2] Holm rejected larger-than-life melodrama for what one critic called 'insect insanity',[3] presenting a character shaped both by his own chaotic era and by the mechanism of power-seeking in any age. Some reviewers thought that Holm's diminutive Richard (the actor is five feet six inches tall) was dwarfed by the larger design of the production. Peggy Ashcroft's Margaret, on the other hand, drew strength from her continuing role in the sequence. As the only character to appear in all of the *Henry VI* plays and in *Richard III*, Margaret became a more central figure, and Ashcroft was allowed

---

[1] Richmond, p. 79.   [2] Colley, p. 227.   [3] *Ibid.*, p. 226.

to develop her from a young princess to a 'tough old Amazon'.[1] Nevertheless, as Richmond points out, Barton and Hall followed the Cibber legacy in severely cutting the women's parts in *Richard III*, thereby emphasising 'untempered male aggression and nihilism, very much against the ritual grain and accumulated affirmations of the original script'.[2]

The Wars of the Roses, seen at the time as a watershed production, appears even more so in retrospect. This *Richard III* brought together two strands of interpretation that had been developing in opposition to the Cibber tradition of individualist melodrama – explorations of Richard's motives and political readings of the play. In addition, Ian Holm's drab Richard seems to have banished for good the conventional stage prince familiar from Garrick's time to Oliver's. In 1967 John Hirsch and his leading actor, Alan Bates, offered an alienated, Brechtian *Richard III* at Stratford, Ontario. In the final battle, Richard effectively committed suicide by tossing his dagger to the disarmed Richmond. Terry Hands directed a black-leather-and-steel *Richard III* at Stratford-upon-Avon in 1980, with Alan Howard portraying the title character as a man driven to paranoia by his humiliating deformities. In an acclaimed production in London in 1980, a theatrical troupe from Russian Georgia enacted an expressionist *Richard III* under the direction of Robert Sturua. Richard (Ramaz Chkhikvadze) 'appeared dressed in a Napoleonic greatcoat, with a huge head and bulging, heavy-lidded eyes'[3] that reminded many of the 'toad' and 'spider' images in the play. Acted in the Georgian language as a symbolic political allegory, this production has been influential not for its script, which most in the English-speaking audience could not understand, but for its broad, cartoonish style, portraying Richard's reign as a sort of circus from hell.

One admirer of Chkhikvadze's performance was Antony Sher, who played Richard in Bill Alexander's Royal Shakespeare Company production of 1984. R. Chris Hassel's reaction to this *Richard III* is typical of most reviews: 'Antony Sher will almost certainly be remembered as the most impressive Richard since Olivier.'[4] Sher helped enhance his place in theatrical memory by writing a book, *The Year of the King*, about his preparation for the part. As the book's diary-style narration reveals, Sher's characterisation drew inspiration from many sources, from the Third Reich to schools for the disabled. At one point Sher and his psychotherapist analysed Richard's relationship to his mother: 'Monty explains that, as Richard hasn't received love as a child, he won't be able to show any himself; hence his contempt for human life.'[5] In spite of such psychological probing of the character, however, Sher's athleticism proved to be the most striking aspect of his performance. Assuming a stance suggesting a polio victim and making inspired use of a pair of crutches, Sher hurtled across the stage like a nightmarish insect, the crutches and the long, thin drapes from his costume giving him four extra legs. Audiences were agreeably shocked by an obviously handicapped Richard who was also astonishingly mobile. 'With two strides of his crutches he could move nearly from one side of the stage to the other.'[6] The

[1] Roger Gellert, *New Statesman*, 30 August 1963, quoted by Colley, p. 228.   [2] Barton and Hall, p. 79.
[3] Colley, p. 231.   [4] Hassel, p. 145.   [5] Sher, p. 129.   [6] Colley, p. 238.

9 Antony Sher as the 'bottled spider' in the Royal Shakespeare Company's 1984 production of
Richard III

crutches also poked between Lady Anne's legs, lifted the crown from Queen
Margaret's head, sawed at the neck of the condemned Hastings and banged together
in fury at uppity little York.

After 4.2, when Richard becomes king, Sher abandoned his crutches in favour of
a sceptre, which he occasionally leaned on to take a few steps, unable to match his

former spiderlike agility. Otherwise, he was carried by bearers while he sat on his throne. Hassel praises Sher for giving up his highly theatrical mobility and much of his rapport with the audience to portray Richard's deterioration after gaining the crown. Richmond also applauds Sher and Alexander for showing Richard's weakness and his female opponents' strength in the second half of the play, but he claims the production avoided the moral issue of Richard's decline by denying the character's tragic dimension, particularly as embodied by his final battlefield heroics.[1] Richmond insists that *Richard III* is not the story of a handicapped person whose mother failed to love him, nor does it offer a simple, morality-play assurance that a benevolent providence will eventually overcome evil. Rather, it is a play about the attractiveness of evil and the need for individuals and societies to purge that attraction in order to survive.[2] While Hassel believes that Sher and Alexander achieved a nearly ideal production,[3] Richmond thinks the theatrical world is still waiting for a performance that incorporates the full complexity of Shakespeare's script.[4]

It seems likely that *Richard III* will continue to be revived regularly. Just when critics thought Antony Sher might be the last notable Richard of the century, Richard Eyre and the Royal National Theatre staged another successful production with Ian McKellen in the title role (1989). McKellen's Richard was as restrained as Sher's had been bizarre. 'One sees him in the first scene, standing in the ramrod posture of the career officer, his military cap and greatcoat a disguise against a world that would know his secrets. With a brilliant backlight streaming through an open doorway, McKellen comes forward into the shadowy foreground to speak the famous lines.'[5] Yet McKellen, too, offered his audiences physical virtuosity, displaying the almost magical dexterity of someone who has learned to do everything, from putting on his gloves to kneeling and baring his chest to Anne, with only one functioning arm and leg. The production, set in the 1930s, moved Richard steadily toward the throne through a succession of uniforms, from First World War overcoat, to formal dinner dress, to fascist blackshirt, to Elizabethan doublet and hose at his coronation. At Bosworth, Richard put on full medieval armour and fought, despite his deformity, with frenzied energy, dying in a convulsive horizontal dance reminiscent of Olivier's. The triumphant Richmond then executed a similar dance over the body; both power and corruption had passed from the old ruler to the new. McKellen's performance, tightly controlled in the first half of the play and harshly energetic in the second, inverted actors' usual approaches to the part. Refusing to charm the audience, this Richard also refused to fade away, suggesting, if not the attractiveness of evil, at least its tremendous vitality.

The Royal Shakespeare Company continues to mount impressive productions of *Richard III*, notably those of Sam Mendes in 1992, with Simon Russell Beale in the title role, and of Steven Pimlott in 1996, with David Troughton. According to Robert Smallwood, Beale 'was clearly going in a big way for the "poisonous bunch-backed toad" look', achieving it in part with 'wide-eyed goggling of the audience

---

[1] Richmond, pp. 118, 136. [2] *Ibid.*, p. 124. [3] Hassel, p. 160.
[4] Richmond, p. 124. [5] Colley, p. 258.

10   Simon Russell Beale as Richard III waits with Prince Edward (Kate Duchêne) and Buckingham (Stephen Boxer) for the young Duke of York (Royal Shakespeare Company, 1992)

in splendidly camp disbelief at the gullibility of his victims'.[1] Mendes initiated a joke widely borrowed in later productions by having Richard enter hurriedly several times to the yapping of the dogs that 'bark at me as I halt by them' (1.1.23), and most critics thought Beale aptly projected both the comedy and the horror built into the role. In his scene with the two princes (3.1), for example, Richard brought along balloons for the youngsters. When little York failed to appear, Richard was forced to wait with increasing fury, clutching his cane in one hand and York's balloon in the other. David Troughton's Richard, making his initial entrance in a jester's cap and bells, was at times more overtly the joker than Beale's. The costume suggested how Richard saw his role at the court of Edward IV 'in this weak piping time of peace' (1.1.24), as well as identifying the hunchback as the kind of 'wise fool' who manipulates others for sport. But Troughton was also more psychotic than many previous Richards. Keith Michael Ramsay described him as 'a love-deprived, insane teenager, not yet grown up, although of mature years', just the sort of person who might wear a clown suit while confiding his murderous plots to an audience.[2]

[1] Robert Smallwood, 'Shakespeare at Stratford-upon-Avon, 1992', *SQ* 44 (1993), 358.
[2] Keith Michael Ramsay, '*Richard III*' (review), *Shakespeare Bulletin* 14:1 (1996), 11.

11   David Troughton as Richard III plays jester to the court of Edward IV in the 1995 Royal Shakespeare
Company production

RECENT RICHARDS PRESERVED

Although its cinematic technique seems dated, Olivier's *Richard III* remains the
standard film version, as the memory of his theatrical performance, even after Sher,
McKellen and others, continues to influence stage tradition. The other performance
readily available to compare to Olivier's is the BBC *Richard III*, taped in 1982, two
years before the Alexander/Sher production, and directed by Jane Howell. Olivier's
movie had used the camera to good effect, especially in Richard's soliloquies and
asides. Nevertheless, it was largely conceived as a film of a stage play. The BBC production was designed for video and successfully exploits many of the features of that
medium. Like the Barton/Hall production, the BBC *Richard III* follows a *Henry VI*
series using the same actors, although Howell directed all three *Henry VI* plays,
while Barton and Hall had reduced them to two. The situations and characters of
Ron Cook as Richard, Julia Foster as Margaret, and others become familiar to viewers
who watch the tapes in order, making interpolated history lessons unnecessary. Cook
deliberately pitches his Richard in a low key, as unlike Olivier as possible. Foster's
Margaret, on the other hand, is bright, tense and clearly mad, giving Margaret the
edge in her scenes with Richard, as Howell undoubtedly intended. A final scene,
inserted by Howell after Richard's death, has proved the most controversial aspect
of the entire series. Presented with a tableau of heaped-up bodies, the audience hears

Margaret's laugh. The camera pans upward to discover the cackling Margaret sitting on top of the bodies, holding Richard in her lap as if he were the crucified Jesus. 'Our last taste', as Hassel says, 'is not of the restoration of order and good governance, but of chaos and arbitrary violence.'[1]

Less widely available than either the Olivier film or the BBC tape is the Portman Productions video of the English Shakespeare Company's *Richard III* directed by Michael Bogdanov (1990). Notable for Andrew Jarvis's energetic, contemporary Richard with bald head and pinstriped suit, the production also features Michael Pennington as a sly, intelligent Buckingham. In addition to its treatment of *Richard III* as a gloss on the 'me' decade of the 1980s, the video offers an accessible record of a modern stage production taped before a live audience.

Like Olivier and Bogdanov, McKellen saw the advantages of preserving his *Richard III* on film. Yet the resulting production, directed by Richard Loncraine in 1995, differs strikingly from McKellen's theatrical version. Loncraine embraces the conventions of the contemporary action movie, including realistic settings. Richard delivers part of his first soliloquy in a men's toilet, for example, 'relieving', as Samuel Crowl put it, 'bile and bladder at once'.[2] The screenplay, by McKellen and Loncraine, eliminates everything from Shakespeare's script that will not yield to 1930s realism, including any hint that Richard III lived in the middle ages, and nearly all dialogue not resembling contemporary English. Often successful in translating Shakespeare's verbal points into visual terms, this film is as much an adaptation in its way as Cibber's revision of 1700. Queen Margaret, who figured prominently in the Eyre/McKellen stage production, disappears from the film, although, rather oddly, Maggie Smith's Duchess of York delivers a few of Margaret's taunts to her daughter-in-law, Queen Elizabeth. Richmond appears around the edges of the court in his naval uniform, presenting a square-jawed figure for the audience to favour in an otherwise unattractive crowd of decadent aristocrats. In the end, after a chase scene in jeeps and on foot, Richard and Richmond face each other high among the steel girders of a bombed-out building:

> RICHMOND   pulls himself level with RICHARD. He prepares to fire at the sitting target, the throne only a bullet away.
> RICHARD   (smilingly challenging at RICHMOND). Let's to it pell-mell,
>   If not to Heaven, then hand-in-hand to Hell!
> RICHARD   steps calmly out into space. At exactly the same moment RICHMOND pulls the trigger.[3]

Grinning, Richard falls into the smoke and flames below, as the soundtrack plays 'I'm Sitting on Top of the World', sung by Al Jolson. Like Alan Bates's glum Crookback of 1967, this one commits suicide, but McKellen's self-destruction is jauntily performed. The ending of Loncraine's film recalls the last moments of *White Heat* (1949), when Cody Jarrett, the deranged gangster played by James Cagney, shoots it out with a

---

[1] Hassel, p. 28. See also Linda Shenk, 'Jane Howell and subverting Shakespeare: where do we draw the line?', *Shakespeare Bulletin* 13:4 (1995), 33–5.
[2] Samuel Crowl, '*Richard III*' (review), *Shakespeare Bulletin* 14:2 (1996), 38.
[3] McKellen and Loncraine, p. 287.

12   Ian McKellen as Richard III and Kristin Scott Thomas as Lady Anne in Richard Loncraine's film adaptation set in the 1930s (1995)

police agent on top of an oil tank.[1] When Jarrett is hit, his gun accidentally discharges into the tank. 'Made it, Ma', he yells as the tank explodes in flames, 'Top of the world!' 'Top of the world' had been the motto of the hoodlum's ambitious mother, who encouraged him in his crimes. In echoing *White Heat*, Loncraine implies not only that Richard is a brutal Jarrett-like gangster, but also that the two characters share psychopathic symptoms.

Looking back over the performance history of this enduringly popular Shakespearean play, one can see that extreme adaptation has been the norm almost from the start. The characters break easily into two groups, Richard and everyone else. When Richard speaks, his voice is often colloquial, confiding, earthy. Except for the two murderers and occasionally Buckingham, all the others speak a formal rhetoric of vengeance, suffering and grief. Richard is enormously entertaining, and, not surprisingly, most adaptations have chosen to maximise his part and minimise everything else. While this tradition has developed *Richard III* as a peerless vehicle for a virtuoso actor, many playgoers who know Shakespeare's script feel that they have yet to see a production of the whole play as he wrote it.

The audience in *Richard III*

Again and again the characters in *Richard III*, especially Richard and Margaret, call attention to the metadramatic situation: this is a play, and the only 'real' people are the

---

[1] I am indebted to A. R. Braunmuller for pointing out this connection.

people in the audience. The developmental path the play constructs for its spectators begins with delight in ill-doing and revenge. Playgoers are encouraged to identify with an evil protagonist who is smarter than those around him. The plot then proceeds to a series of reminders of the consequences of evil, the need for repentance and the comfort of identifying with a group (for example, the female triads) rather than with an extreme individualist (Richard). As the final confrontation looms, however, the play takes an unexpected turn. The protagonist himself recognises the possibility of repentance and salvation and turns them down. The audacity of this choice cannot be lost on an audience that has been pondering its own surprisingly positive responses to a ruthless tyrant. Richard is a kind of hero, but the very heroism for which we admire him results in the death of his soul. And all these things – Richard's villainy, his daring, his death – happen because God has determined them. Far from being a simple morality play about the purgation of evil from England by Henry Tudor, *Richard III* explores the clash between our human sympathy for self-determination and a structure of belief that affirms determinism. Rather than leaving the performance with a satisfied sense that they have got Satan behind them, the attentive audience may leave with a renewed appreciation of how difficult it is to act well in a world where they must live as if their choices were their own, all the while understanding that freedom and individualism can be destructive illusions.

Recent stage, film and critical interpretations

Like Hamlet, Richard III is a celebrity among Shakespeare's characters, a figure who often overshadows the play that gives him life. The majority of directors approach *Richard III* as a frame for a virtuoso actor rather than the concluding chapter in an English historical saga. Film treatment only seems to increase the dominance of the main character. On the Internet, where video snippets of professional performances compete for attention with clips of rehearsals, acting contests, parodies and slide presentations, Richard may be escaping his context altogether. Yet recent scholarship also reaffirms the relationship of criticism to Shakespearean texts and the central place of reading in the study of the plays. Shakespeare's *Richard III* continues to change shape in today's digital culture, but, among other things, it remains a work of literature.

STAGE AND FILM

The greater number of stage productions in Britain and the United States during the years covered here (1999–2008) followed tradition by treating *Richard III* as a star vehicle. The most prominent revival in this vein was Kenneth Branagh's 2002 interpretation at the Crucible Theatre, Sheffield, directed by Michael Grandage. This production was notable, in the first place, because Branagh is notable, perhaps the best-known Shakespearean actor of recent times. This interpretation also showed that the customary focus on the protagonist can still yield new insights into this play after 400 years. The Richard created by Branagh and Grandage was severely disabled. He began his opening soliloquy speaking slowly, strapped to a traction bed in which

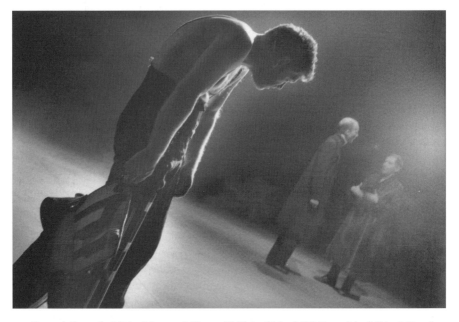

13   Kenneth Branagh, Michael Jenn and Danny Webb in *Richard III* directed by Michael Grandage (Crucible Theatre, Sheffield, 2002)

he was obliged to sleep, and only gradually became more animated as he dressed in the corset and brace that allowed him to move around during the day. Gloucester's symbolic battle with his costume at the beginning of the play found an echo in the last scene, where the king's armour resembled an artificial upper body that he had to strap on in order to fight. Even when the clothed Richard managed to appear physically unremarkable, his continuing struggle with his handicap was revealed by lightning changes of mood, as when he suddenly banged the murderers' heads together before jovially telling them, 'I like you, lads' (1.3.354). Branagh's ability to find similarities between Shakespeare's verse and the patterns of contemporary English speech added to the impression that Richard, rather than merely carrying out preconceived Machiavellian schemes, was making them up as he went along. Often, he seemed surprised at himself. Announcing his intention to 'marry Warwick's youngest daughter', for example, he abruptly exclaimed, 'What? Though I killed her husband and her father?' (1.1.155), as if unable to credit his own audacity.[1] The sense that Richard responded to events rather than simply directing them brought Branagh's performance closer to Macbeth-like character development than most. The other actors were praised by reviewers, especially Danny Webb as Buckingham and

[1] Sarah Hatchuel, 'Richard III, directed by Michael Grandage at the Crucible Theatre, Sheffield, 13 March–10 April 2002', *Etudes Epistémè* 2 (2002), 272.

Barbara Jefford as Margaret.[1] Nevertheless, the path of least resistance is always to emphasise Richard, who is so much funnier, more clever and more interesting than anyone else in the cast.[2] Grandage's Sheffield production was no exception to this rule.

Michael Boyd, on the other hand, is a director who likes to take the long view. With the Royal Shakespeare Company, he has presented all three parts of *Henry VI* and *Richard III* as a sequence twice, first in 2000–1, and again in 2007–8. In 2001, a year before Branagh's star turn in Sheffield, Boyd directed the *Henry VI* plays in Stratford, then staged the entire cycle in the United States at the University of Michigan. The tetralogy later returned to England for a run at London's Young Vic. These were athletic productions, with actors flying in on trapezes, crawling up through trap doors, climbing on ladders, and dangling from ropes, spectacular actions that underscored the spectacular chaos that engulfs England during its civil war. Among the many devices the director used to increase continuity from play to play was the persistence of supporting characters. Fiona Bell, who played Queen Margaret in all the plays, also played Joan of Arc (in a similar costume) in *1 Henry VI*. In *Richard III*, Margaret lingered past her scripted exit to watch the usurper's defeat on the battlefield. Richard's father, the Duke of York, who dies in *3 Henry VI*, made a ghostly appearance at the end of *Richard III* to remove the crown from his son's head. Aidan McArdle (after taking the role of the Dauphin in *1 Henry VI*) developed the character of Richard from its beginnings in *2 Henry VI* rather than emerging full-blown with the word 'Now', at the opening of *Richard III*. In such a context, with its emphasis on historical patterns, *Richard III* became less the tragedy of Richard and more the final chapter in a tragic national conflict.

In spite of Boyd's affinity for the epic perspective, however, the RSC did not entirely turn its back on the character-centred approach. In Stratford in 2003, Sean Holmes directed Richard Goodman, costumed as a Victorian showman, in the title role. Goodman's Richard was accompanied by a similarly-dressed page – a borrowing from Dr Evil's Mini-Me sidekick in Mike Myers's *Austin Powers* movies. But if the Mini-Me device in film underlines Dr Evil's egotism, at least one reviewer felt that its effect in Holmes's *Richard III* was to make the main character seem more childish.[3] Further underscoring Crookback's infantile side, Goodman's newly crowned king assumed an oversized throne and began his decline into tantrums the moment he was seated. Meanwhile, at the Globe in London, director Barry Kyle's *Richard III* ran concurrently with Holmes's RSC version. The unique feature of this production was an all-female cast, with Kathryn Hunter in the lead. This might have seemed more of a gimmick if not for the recent fashion of using men for all the roles in

---

[1] Stephen Brown, 'Do we like him now?' *TLS*, 5 April 2002, 24–5. Charles Spencer, Review of *Richard III*, *Daily Telegraph* (London) 12 June 2003, 18.

[2] As McKellen genially puts it in one of his many Internet appearances, 'If the part weren't any good, nor would the actors be, and the audiences wouldn't bother, either.' See 'Stagework', a website of the Royal National Theatre.

[3] Michael Dobson, 'Shakespeare performances in England, 2003', *Shakespeare Survey 57* (2004), 277.

Elizabethan plays. Male-only productions have the excuse of theatrical history – imitating the man-and-boy companies of Shakespeare's time – and the all-female experiment takes the obvious next step for our own era. Hunter, small, comic, and extravagantly handicapped – not only by her hump, but also by a twisted torso and a withered hand – was enthusiastically received as a virtuoso performer.[1]

The more a production of *Richard III* resembles a one-person show, however, the more it risks losing not only Shakespeare's sense of history, but also the political implications of the script. Directors may try to get around this problem by giving the play a contemporary setting, drawing parallels between the power politics of the Middle Ages (or the Renaissance) and those of our own time. This usually works, but only a little. The Australian director Gale Edwards, for example, tried to update the play for The Shakespeare Theatre Company of Washington, DC, in 2003. Describing *Richard III* as a 'relevant, confronting play' for the twenty-first century, Edwards attempted to make it seem so by setting it in the lobby of a modern hospital.[2] Here, with the apparent complicity of the staff, Richard systematically assassinated his victims, turning the hospital into a killing field. Sounds of explosions echoed offstage, suggesting a location in a modern war zone. But as usual, the real focus of the production was not political allegory but the sociopathic protagonist, played by Wallace Acton, whose short stature appeared to be his chief physical distinction. As one reviewer said, the production demonstrated that 'how blood gets spilled is not very different from one age to another'.[3] For most of the audience, however, it did not draw any more specific parallels between Richard's era and our own. When Michael Kahn directed the play again for the Shakespeare Theatre in 2007, he chose to give it a more-or-less medieval setting, letting audiences draw whatever contemporary parallels suggested themselves.[4]

In 2004, Peter Dinklage, who is four feet six inches tall, took the role of Richard at the Public Theatre in New York. In an interview with Dinklage, Marc Peyser offered this formulation of a question that was bound to come up: 'Doesn't [your] playing one of the most famous deformed guys in literature send a bad message about dwarfs?'[5] Unsurprisingly, Dinklage said it did not. According to the actor, the bad message was about the character, who used his restricted growth as a cover for his crimes. Director Peter DuBois chose strapping actors for most of the other male parts, an expected visual device that nevertheless proved effective in isolating Richard. Like Branagh, Hunter, and others, Dinklage interpreted Richard's deformity as a physical affliction, but unlike Branagh, this actor failed to suggest a causal relationship between the character's suffering and his terrible deeds. Another New York production, at

---

[1] See, for example, Nicholas de Jongh, 'Women liberate Richard', *Evening Standard*, 12 June 2003, on an *Evening Standard* website, www.thisislondon.co.uk, and Sheridan Morley, *New Statesman*, 30 June 2003, 48.

[2] '*Richard III*, directed by Gale Edwards, 3/25/2003 – 5/18/2003', on the website of the Shakespeare Theatre Company.

[3] Peter Marks, '*Richard III*: Rolling over the competition', *Washington Post*, 1 April 2003, C01.

[4] 'Director Michael Kahn's words at first rehearsal', *Richard III*, 2006–2007 Season, on the website of the Shakespeare Theatre Company.

[5] Marc Peyser, 'Peter Dinklage', *Newsweek*, 18 October 2004, on the *Newsweek* website.

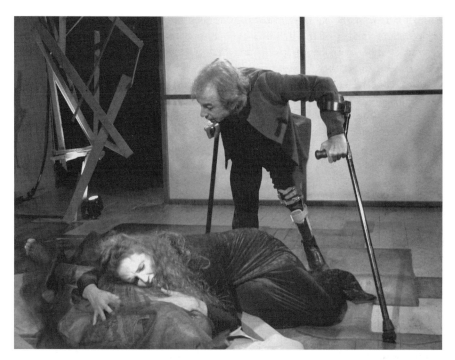

14   Amber Allison and Henry Holden in the Nicu's Spoon's production of *Richard III* directed by Heidi
Lauren Duke (Spoon Theatre, New York, 2007)

Nicu's Spoon Theatre, also featured a disabled actor, Henry Holden, who needs
crutches to walk. The programme notes from 2007 describe Richard as 'a normal
guy who has had enough and wants things that are rightfully his and will earnestly
try his best to get them – in reality the story of any disabled member of our society
even today'.[1] Here the director, Heidi Lauren Duke, really did seem to be sending a
particular message about Richard's disability, but it was hard to tell what the message
was. One source of confusion was Duke's decision to split Richard's lines between
two actors: Holden, who moved around the stage, and Andrew Hutcheson, who
stood behind a lectern. Hutcheson delivered Richard's dramatic dialogue from his
fixed position, while Holden mimed the action, speaking only when Richard had an
aside or soliloquy. This device, although striking, failed to communicate much about
either Richard's handicap or his character.

By using actors who were not conventionally 'well-formed', both these New York
productions attempted to address the question of Richard's disability – is it primarily
in his body or his mind? Yet neither managed to make a coherent bridge between
Elizabethan notions of deformity and our own. To what degree do today's audiences
still suffer from the old fear that disabled people are undergoing punishment, that the

[1] Anthony C. E. Nelson, Review of *Richard III* on www.nytheatre.com, 18 July 2007.

maimed villain might be maimed because he somehow deserves it? (Leslie Fiedler, writing about images of the disabled in literature, mentions that his grandmother referred to those with handicaps as 'the *Bestrafte*, the punished ones'.)[1] As these directors recognised, there is a real distinction between casting actors such as Anthony Sher or Kenneth Branagh, whom the audience believes to be able-bodied in real life, and Henry Holden or Peter Dinklage, whose divergences from the norm are evident both on and off stage. For Sher, playing the 'bottled spider' on crutches was a display of skill. For Holden, it was a necessity. Unfortunately, neither director appeared to know what to do with this distinction. Among recent performances, it was Branagh's that brought audiences closest to Richard's suffering and its connections to his villainy.

If there was any doubt about Michael Boyd's commitment to Shakespeare's history plays as cycles, it was dispelled by his project of staging eight history plays with a single group of actors in 2007–8. Jonathan Slinger played Richard in *2* and *3 Henry VI* and *Richard III*. In spite of the casting continuity, however, this time through the sequence, Boyd drew a line between the *Henry VI* plays and *Richard III* by jumping forward in time. The *Henry VI* trilogy took place in a generalised medieval setting, but for *Richard III*, the scene shifted to a modern totalitarian state, where assassins did their work with silencer-equipped pistols. In spite of the updated dress, however, this production seemed to lack references to specific modern possibilities such as the Nazified England portrayed in Richard Loncraine's film. Boyd's interest remained on the protagonist's development throughout the sequence; he seemed to see the tetralogy as almost arbitrarily divided into individual plays. In a video interview on the RSC website, the director explained that Richard strives for the crown for 'almost a whole play'. This 'play' was defined by Boyd as the last half of *3 Henry VI* through to the unscripted coronation scene in *Richard III*.[2] Audiences were intrigued by Slinger as Richard, but some were puzzled by the period shift after *3 Henry VI*, since it did not seem to signal any political parallels to our own time.

As if to show how to make real political allegory from *Richard III*, the RSC also presented in 2007 an Arabic-language version directed by Sulayman Al Bassam. Emir Gloucester, played by Fayez Kazak, was modelled on Saddam Hussein, while Richmond turned out to be a US Army general arriving to establish a new interim government. Nevertheless, apart from suggesting again that tyranny and takeover differ little from age to age, it was hard to see what light the production meant to shine either on Shakespeare or on modern conflicts in the Middle East. Clearly, *Richard III* lends itself to allegory, but that by itself is not a good reason to allegorise it. If the point of Al Bassam's production was to show that Saddam Hussein and others like him are murderous tyrants, most of the audience already thought so before they came to the theatre. If the point was to show that old plays depict evil just as we know it today, one is left wondering why we need old plays. Like many modern-dress

---

[1] Leslie Fiedler, *Tyranny of the Normal: Essays on Bioethics, Theology, and Myth*, 1996, 40.
[2] The website of the Royal Shakespeare Company.

productions, those at the RSC in 2007 had little to say about how we might apply the specific political insights of *Richard III* to contemporary situations.

Unlike stage directors, feature filmmakers have not been eager to take on *Richard III* in the last ten years. Since Loncraine and McKellen in 1995, there have been no large-scale works 'directly committed to reproducing a Shakespearean text in the traditional language of the narrative film', to borrow Samuel Crowl's phrase.[1] As Crowl's careful definition suggests, however, film and video have branched out into other kinds of treatments, ranging from *Looking for Richard*, Al Pacino's 1996 feature film about himself as a Shakespearean actor and director, to video clips appearing and disappearing daily on the Internet. What W. B. Worthen calls 'the diffuse connectivity of digital communications' exemplified by the Internet points to a third mode of existence for Shakespearean drama, to be added to the text, on the one hand, and the theatrical or recorded performance on the other.[2] No one claims to know the future of digitised Shakespeare, but the mixing of images on the Internet and the increasingly on-demand character of television offer hints. A search of YouTube, a website for sharing video clips, returned 770 entries for 'Richard III'. Many of these were snippets from traditional stage, film or television productions. Others included school productions, audition tapes, parodies, pastiches, animations and rehearsal clips originally shown on the websites of theatre companies such as the RSC. Although content on the web can vary from minute to minute, one other source that will probably be around long enough for readers of this book to see it is 'Wikipedia'. This site offers, at the end of a longish article on *Richard III*, a list of links that includes an interactive video interview with Ian McKellen.[3] From there, the viewer can go on to compare Sir Ian's delivery of Richard's opening speech with those of Laurence Olivier (1955) and Conrad Nelson (2006). This progression suggests a future for Shakespearean performance on the Internet as an endless series of links with ever-improving interactivity. Meanwhile, Kenneth Branagh's film of *As You Like It* first went into wide release not in theatres but on television, where it can be recorded and called up for viewing and even re-editing any time.[4] As television approaches the interactivity of the Internet and the Internet becomes more like film or television, it is easy to imagine a medium that transforms audiences into disseminators of Shakespearean performance, able to select, manipulate, and share words, images and sounds at will.

SCHOLARSHIP AND CRITICISM

Performance criticism stands out among contemporary scholarly treatments of *Richard III*. This is partly because the play is performed so often and partly because performance studies continue to loom large in Shakespeare scholarship generally. The number of stage productions of *Richard III* worldwide has grown huge, offering to those who write about live performance a wide selection of examples. (Margaret

---

[1] Samuel Crowl, *Shakespeare at the Cineplex: The Kenneth Branagh Era*, 2003, 2.
[2] W. B. Worthen, 'Performing Shakespeare in digital culture', in *The Cambridge Companion to Shakespeare and Popular Culture*, ed. Robert Shaughnessy, 2007, 244.
[3] See the 'Stagework' website.   [4] HBO, 21 August 2007.

Gurowitz, on the website of the quirky but useful Richard III Society, American Branch, maintains that *Richard III* is Shakespeare's most performed play, although she does not document the claim.)[1] Gillian Day, surveying RSC productions of *Richard III* since World War II, divides directorial approaches into three categories: the political, the psycho-social and the metatheatrical.[2] This division helps Day carve up a considerable territory – the RSC alone has mounted a production of *Richard III* roughly every three years during the period – although, as Lois Potter points out, the three approaches tend to blur into each other in practice.[3] In the absence of new full-length films or videos, critics have continued to analyse existing versions such as those of Olivier, Howell and McKellen, as well as Pacino's hybrid, with studies of the relatively contemporary Loncraine/McKellen film understandably the most numerous in the last few years. Traditional scholarly emphasis on a single medium – *Richard III* on stage or on film – has lately made more room for comparative studies of one kind or another: theatre to film, film to film, or stage and film to representations in other media. (For a useful overview of the media history of this play, see Barbara Freedman.[4]) Sarah Hatchuel, in her book on Shakespearean stage and screen adaptations, outlines what she sees as the radical transformation of the playscripts, including *Richard III*, for the medium of film.[5] Hatchuel and many others have increasingly taken interdisciplinary approaches to Shakespearean movies, bringing the ideas and techniques of film study to bear not only on feature films, but also on film adaptations, translations, modernisations, appropriations and the like.[6] The tendency to ignore (or deplore) distinctions between elite and popular culture is nowhere more evident than in performance studies of *Richard III*. 'Touchstone', an Internet research site maintained by the Shakespeare Institute Library, exemplifies this contemporary inclusiveness. Its scope includes 'professional and amateur productions, "straight" versions, ballets, operas, puppet versions, adaptations for children, apocrypha, plays which include Shakespeare as a character, plays which use Shakespearean themes. The slightest connection with Shakespeare warrants inclusion.'[7]

Like performance critics, those who study Shakespeare's texts as literature have found that the political and metatheatrical dimensions of *Richard III* can seldom be treated separately. Stephen Marche, for example, argues in an article in *Comparative Drama* that Richard's role as actor-director is inseparable from his role as a manipulator of the received political history of his time: 'the metatheatrical dimension of the

---

[1] Margaret Gurowitz, ' "Me, drunk? Ha! You should see Buckingham!" A Performance History of Shakespeare's *Richard III*', on the website of the Richard III Society, American Branch.

[2] Gillian Day, *Shakespeare at Stratford: King Richard III* (Arden Shakespeare, 2002).

[3] Lois Potter, 'Shakespeare's histories in performance', *Transactions of the Leicester Literary and Philosophical Society*, V. 96 (2002), 13–15.

[4] Barbara Freedman, 'Critical junctures in Shakespeare screen history: the case of *Richard III*', in *The Cambridge Companion to Shakespeare on Film*, ed. Russell Jackson, 2007.

[5] Sarah Hatchuel, *Shakespeare, from Stage to Screen*, 2004.

[6] Sarah Hatchuel and Nathalie Vienne-Guérin (eds.), *Shakespeare on Screen: 'Richard III'*, 2005. Especially valuable in this volume is Jose Ramon Diaz Fernandez, 'Richard III on screen: an annotated filmo-bibliography'. See also Saskia Kossak, *'Frame my face to all occasions': Shakespeare's 'Richard III' on Screen*, Austrian Studies in English 92, 2005, and Laurie E. Osborne, 'Clip Art: theorizing the Shakespearean film clip', *SQ* 53 (2002) 227–40.

[7] Touchstone website, 'Shakespeare in Performance'.

play aims squarely at the question of genre. Shakespeare's adaptation, far from eliminating the problems of history's responsibilities to the dead, brings them into clearer focus, while transforming them from problems of prose history to those of theater.'[1] The reception history of this play, as Charles Whitney and others demonstrate, has often been concerned with the political dimensions of theatre and its applications to the theatre of politics. In his *Early Responses to Renaissance Drama*, Whitney discusses Milton's use of Richard as a surrogate for Charles I (*Eikonoklastes*, 1649).[2] M. G. Aune points out that Shakespeare's *Richard III* became a vehicle for social and political commentary almost as soon as it was written, with the playwright's contemporaries drawing parallels between the crook-backed stage villain and Robert Cecil, minister to Elizabeth I and James I.[3]

Another strain of current criticism concentrates on what Day calls the 'psycho-social' aspects of *Richard III*. The continued influence of feminist criticism can be felt here, not necessarily in a narrow focus on patriarchy or female characters – although these subjects remain of interest – but in the treatment of domestic and personal themes more generally. Heather Dubrow, for instance, in her study of mourning in Shakespeare, identifies loss and recovery not only with the women in *Richard III*, but also with the protagonist, a usurper who repeatedly disrupts the normal processes of birth, death and recuperation.[4] Contemporary critics have also shown a heightened interest in the theme of Richard's deformity as it reflects basic human concerns about family, identity, childhood and the body.[5] David Overton's doctoral thesis examines the physical techniques various actors have used to represent Richard's deformity, although it does not discuss actors such as Peter Dinklage and Henry Holden, whose choices are determined partly by their own physical condition.[6] Medical professionals are also much concerned with 'otherness' and difference, and Richard III, like Hamlet, often appears in medical and psychological publications as an illustration of illness. Thus, psychiatrist Maxine K. Anderson argues that everyone encounters circumstances that 'bring out our internal Richard'.[7] Although talk about the universality of Shakespeare is out of fashion among literary critics, interdisciplinary studies such as Anderson's return us to the individual's responses

---

[1] Stephen Marche, 'Mocking dead bones: historical memory and the theater of the dead in *Richard III*', *Comparative Drama* 37 (2003–4), 41.

[2] Charles Whitney, 'Jonson and Shakespeare: living monuments and public spheres', in *Early Responses to Renaissance Drama*, 2006, 241.

[3] M. G. Aune, 'The uses of *Richard III*: from Robert Cecil to Richard Nixon', *Shakespeare Bulletin* 24:3 (2006), 23.

[4] Heather Dubrow, *Shakespeare and Domestic Loss: Forms of Deprivation, Mourning, and Recuperation*, 1999.

[5] See among others: Greta Olson, 'Richard III's animalistic criminal body', *Philological Quarterly* 82 (2003), 301–24; Joel Slotkin, 'Honeyed toads: sinister aesthetics in Shakespeare's *Richard III*', *The Journal for Early Modern Cultural Studies* 7 (2007), 5–32; Michael Torrey, ' "The plain devil and dissembling looks": ambivalent physiognomy and Shakespeare's *Richard III*', *ELR* 30 (2000), 123–53.

[6] David Overton, 'The actor's physical articulation of character text in Shakespeare's *Richard III*: performing deformity', Diss., University of Colorado, 2006.

[7] Maxine K. Anderson, 'The death of a mind: a study of Shakespeare's *Richard III*', *Journal of Analytical Psychology* 51 (2006), 701. Julio C. Avalos Jr, 'The unfinished self: Richard's gender, deformity, and personhood in *3 Henry VI* and *Richard III*', *PsyArt: An Online Journal for the Psychological Study of the Arts* (2002), article 020709.

to *Richard III* and Matthew Arnold's notion that literature is concerned with 'how to live'.

The transaction between reader and text also remains at the centre of things for Shakespearean editing and textual criticism. Yet here, too, the recent emphasis on performance continues to be evident. In his Oxford edition of *Richard III* (2001), John Jowett argues that the 1597 quarto (Q1) has 'high theatrical authority' (130) and he therefore takes Q as his control text. Acknowledging that there are disadvantages in basing a modern edition on Q – notably that the editor must relegate to an appendix the many lines that appear only in the 1623 Folio (F) – Jowett nevertheless regards it as more or less obvious that a text close to stage performance is preferable to one that may have come from an authorial draft and therefore represent an earlier phase of the playwright's thinking. To be sure, Jowett does not subscribe to the extreme version of this preference, which would accept as superior a text from any performance – including one by a company other than Shakespeare's – over an early draft. But he thinks Q *Richard III* 'retains authorial texture' (130) and probably does not derive from a memorial reconstruction by actors, so the choice is clear for him.

Partly as a result of Jowett's own work as an editor of the Oxford Shakespeare (1986), many scholars in the first years of the twenty-first century have tended to prefer Shakespearean texts that seem to derive from the stage over those more likely to have come from the study. Shakespeare, so the argument goes, was a man of the theatre who cared more about ticket sales than preserving his plays in print. The closer to performance, the closer to Shakespeare. Lately, however, Shakespeareans have begun to question this line of reasoning, and it no longer seems as obvious as it did just a few years ago that a performance text ought to trump all others. Lukas Erne, for instance, has taken up the suggestion made by E. A. J. Honigmann in 1965 that Shakespeare's lack of interest in the printing of his plays is something of a myth.[1] Jonathan Bate, general editor of *The RSC Shakespeare* (2007), vigorously endorses the use of F as control text for *Richard III* (and all the other plays), along with the general principle of 'version-based editing' – sticking to one of the early printed versions rather than conflating them.[2] For Bate, this procedure 'seems a more fitting way of approaching authors who self-consciously revised their work', not to mention authors whose work may have been revised by others (*Folio* p. 21). As Jowett argues, however, 'these are matters of choice rather than law' (129). His edition of *Richard III* offers a thorough and judicious discussion of the textual complexities of the play, as well as several useful appendices, including an index of his references to actors, directors and others involved in important productions (399 ff.).

The practices of critics and editors of *Richard III*, like those of actors and audiences, have also been affected by the recent growth of digital culture. Bate points

---

[1] Lukas Erne, *Shakespeare as Literary Dramatist*, 2003; Honigmann, *The Stability of Shakespeare's Text*, 1965.

[2] 'The case for the Folio', from the website of *The RSC Shakespeare: Complete Works*, ed. Jonathan Bate and Eric Rasmussen (Macmillan, 2007). Bate describes this Internet article as 'a more detailed account of the editorial problem in Shakespeare than that provided on pp. l–lvii of the general introduction to *The RSC Shakespeare: Complete Works*' (1).

out, for example, that scholars can now use digitised databases that in many ways supersede such venerable tools as the *Oxford English Dictionary*.[1] They and their students both have access to resources such as *The Internet Shakespeare Editions* (ISE) online, a site that plans eventually to offer new electronic editions of all the plays.[2] While the ISE site does not yet have a modern edition of *Richard III*, it does provide transcriptions of Q and F, as well as links to facsimiles of both. From the ISE's *Richard III* home page, the viewer can also link to such texts as More's life of Richard III and Holinshed's *Richard III*. And this is only one set of Shakespeare links out of hundreds. Theorists have been saying for some time that every edition is an interpretation, and unlike their counterparts fifty years ago, today's readers can easily see this for themselves by comparing editorial choices with materials closer to the source. As much as the study of Shakespeare seems to be confronting yet another technological revolution, however, Worthen reminds us 'that this transformation – if that's what it is – is barely underway' (230). We have a new venue for watching and hearing Shakespeare's plays as well as for reading and studying them. Now that we can watch a performance of *Richard III* in the same place – the computer screen – where we read the text or look up Elizabethan word usages or see an interview with the star of a current production, how will our experiences of the play be different? How will Shakespeare's work interact with this newer, faster flow of information? One thing seems sure: judging by the amount of data available about *Richard III* on the Internet at this early point in the twenty-first century, Richard is indeed 'himself again', as protean and adaptable as ever.

[1] 'The mirror of life: how Shakespeare conquered the world', *Harper's Magazine* (April 2007), 40.
[2] See the website of 'The Internet Shakespeare Editions', University of Victoria, Canada.

NOTE ON THE TEXT

This edition of *Richard III* is based on the text that appeared in the First Folio of 1623 (F). The first edition (Q) was published in quarto format twenty-six years earlier, in 1597. F differs from Q in well over a thousand readings, including several F-only passages and one substantial Q-only passage. Although the two substantive texts of *Richard III* have often been conflated by Shakespearean editors, most scholars today see them as two separate though closely related plays. (See the Textual Analysis, pp. 209–19 below, for a discussion of the relationship of F to Q and to the other five quarto editions published before 1623.) Readers may consult the first quarto text in a separate New Cambridge Shakespeare edition.

Since the present edition treats Q and F as two different plays, passages that appear only in Q, including oaths, are never incorporated into the text. In 3.7, for example, Buckingham's 'zounds ile intreat no more' and Richard's hypocritical reply 'O do not sweare my Lord of Buckingham', may (or may not) be good theatre, but like the well-known 'clock' passage of Act 4, the exchange appears only in Q and does not belong in an edition of F (see collation 4.2.99 and Appendix 1, pp. 220–1). Similarly, a word that makes sense in F is not replaced with a word from Q, even if most editors and critics have preferred the Q reading. Some past editors of *Richard III* have assumed that if any circumstance suggests quarto corruption in F – for example, when F follows one of the later quartos against a 'superior' reading in Q – then F should be emended. Emendation has also proved particularly tempting in the two sections of F – 3.1.1–167 and 5.3.50 to the end – where the number of corrections to quarto copy (apparently Q3) drops drastically. Even editions that take F as copy text often switch to Q in these two places. The present edition, however, is based on F throughout. If a passage in F is not nonsense and could have appeared in the compositor's manuscript copy, it is allowed to stand.

F introduces act and scene divisions into the play, which the quartos represent as one continuous action. The arrangement of the quartos reflects the nonstop staging practices of the 1590s. Continuous action helps explain how a play as long as *Richard III* could have had a reasonable running time. The act and scene divisions added in F suggest the changing practices of the Jacobean theatre, when pauses between acts became more common (Gurr, p. 177). F, however, is even longer than Q. If it was played uncut on the Jacobean stage, any pauses must have been short. By convention, a new scene begins whenever the stage empties and new characters enter. Probably by oversight, some of the acts in F are not divided at places where this happens, such as at the end of 3.4, where Richard's agents and Lord Hastings leave the stage, and Richard and Buckingham enter, talking about their plan to win over the citizens. Again at 3.6 and 3.7 F gives no scene divisions, and this also happens in Acts 4 and 5 (4.3, 4.4, 4.5, 5.3, 5.4 and 5.5). I have followed earlier editors in adding these divisions. I have also indicated in the headnotes to each scene corresponding passages in the chronicles of Hall and Holinshed, including locations, where they are mentioned. In most cases, the dialogue would have told an Elizabethan audience the approximate setting for the scenes in *Richard III*. For example, all of Act 1 takes place in London, as indicated by the proximity of characters to the Tower or the court. Similarly, the audience knows where the 'Baynard's Castle' scene (3.7) occurs because Richard has told Buckingham to meet him there at 3.5.98.

F *Richard III* is both a reading text and a playable one. The Folio division into acts and scenes suits this stately, rhetorical play, and the stage directions give spare but generally adequate information while leaving the details to the theatrical imagination. This edition does not try to improve F as a performance script. Except for introducing entrances and exits, for instance, it does not attempt to 'complete' the F stage directions by adding players, gestures or actions not in the original. In general, it does not interpolate stage directions from the quarto editions of the play, even where such directions make good dramatic sense. Only manifestly incomplete stage directions are emended – as when Clarence exits on his way to the Tower in 1.1, but neither F nor Q gives an exit for Brakenbury, who is guarding him. Such emended stage directions are enclosed in square brackets, and the changes are noted in the collation and the commentary. Often, readers will find information about how a scene was to be played embedded in Shakespeare's dialogue. Unlike suggestions of location, however, these implied stage directions require no special knowledge, only attentive reading. Once students of the play become accustomed to reading this way, they may find their experience enhanced by the extra dramatic dimension in the playtext itself. For similar reasons, I have not incorporated such post-1623 stage traditions as Richard's kneeling when he bares his breast to Anne's sword in 1.2.

Substantive variants in the five quarto editions published between Q and F appear in the collation when any of the six early quartos disagrees with F. These Q2–6 variants give a sense of the progressive sequence of changes that tend to be introduced in a series of editions and keep up a running reminder of the unusually large number of such editions that could have been available to the printers of F. Q7 and Q8, published after F but largely derived from the earlier quartos, are not generally collated. Press variants among existing copies of a single quarto appear in the collation if they coincide with variants among the first six quartos. A more complete collation of the early quartos has been published by Kristian Smidt in *The Tragedy of King Richard the Third: Parallel Texts of the First Quarto and the First Folio with Variants of the Early Quartos*, 1969.

Where this edition alters the arrangement of verse lines as they appear in F, the change is noted in the collation but not in the commentary, unless the rearranged lines raise unusual textual or interpretative questions. This text also uses white space to indicate that certain passages form a single line of verse split between two speakers. Such use of white space has been common in editions of Shakespeare since the eighteenth century, but it was not widely used in 1623, and split-line arrangements are seldom found in F. The decision to arrange two speeches as a split line rather than as two short lines depends on the editor's interpretation of the dramatic situation.

Such judgements are discussed in the commentary notes. Often, however, the F arrangement of a pentameter as two separate lines is retained. For example, in Act 4, Elizabeth challenges Richard's swearing by the world, by his father's death and by heaven, saying he has profaned them all, and then she asks 'What canst thou swear by now?' Richard's reply, 'The time to come', metrically completes Elizabeth's short line (4.4.391–2). The F setting of the speeches as two lines, however, suggests Richard's failing wit better than a single-line arrangement in the eighteenth-century style. By introducing a visual break in the exchange, F implies a pause, as Richard gathers his thoughts and at last produces a barely adequate response.

Speech headings have been expanded and regularised from the abbreviations used in F. Where headings have been changed for any other reason, the collation and the commentary mention the first instance. For example, Richard is 'Glocester' in the stage directions of Q and usually 'Glo.' in speech headings. After he is crowned, he is called 'King'. Q makes the same kind of temporal distinction for Anne, calling her 'La.' or 'Lady' before she marries Richard, but *'Duch. Glo.'* afterward. The usual heading in F is *'Anne'*. F commonly calls the main character *'Richard'* in stage directions and *'Rich.'* in speech headings, except in the two passages set with little correction from Q3, where he is *'Glo.'* or *'King'*. Neither text is consistent about Stanley, who is sometimes 'Stanley' and sometimes 'Darby' or 'Derby'. In stage directions, this edition attempts to regularise and modernise all proper names while keeping as much of the original as possible. Thus Stanley often carries both his names as a reminder that he was usually 'Derby' in the F stage directions. Speech headings have also been regularised and modernised. Richard, Elizabeth and Margaret are called by these names alone, while King Edward and Prince Edward are differentiated by title. Most other characters are called by shortened forms of their titles, e.g. 'Clarence' for the Duke of Clarence and 'Buckingham' for the Duke of Buckingham, or by family names, e.g. Hastings, Catesby.

Spelling, punctuation and capitalisation of the text have been modernised. Both 'then' and 'than' are usually spelled 'then' in the Folio, for instance, and I have silently changed the spelling to 'than' when it suits the modern sense. Punctuation is much lighter than in F, which uses some kind of stop at the end of almost every verse line and often marks the mid-point as well. In cases where the metre places an accent on the 'ed' form of a verb, I have marked the verb with a *grave* accent (e.g. barbèd, determinèd). I have also silently expanded some abbreviations and symbols that occur in F, such as 'and' for '&' 'thou' for 'y ^{u}' or 'that' for 'y ^{t}'. Quotations from F and Qq are modernised only by changing long *s* to modern *s* and regularising *i* and *j*. Quotations from other Shakespearean plays, unless otherwise noted, are from the Riverside edition, although Riverside spelling conventions (e.g. 'murther') have been modernised to accord with those of this edition.

King Richard III

LIST OF CHARACTERS
In order of appearance (for speaking characters)

RICHARD, DUKE OF GLOUCESTER, *later* KING RICHARD III
DUKE OF CLARENCE (*later, his* GHOST)
SIR ROBERT BRAKENBURY
LORD HASTINGS (*later, his* GHOST)
LADY ANNE (*later, her* GHOST)
TRESSEL
BERKELEY
A GENTLEMAN *attendant on Lady Anne*
QUEEN ELIZABETH
EARL RIVERS (*later, his* GHOST)
LORD GREY (*later, his* GHOST)
MARQUESS OF DORSET
DUKE OF BUCKINGHAM (*later, his* GHOST)
LORD STANLEY, EARL OF DERBY
QUEEN MARGARET
SIR WILLIAM CATESBY
Two MURDERERS
KEEPER *of the Tower*
KING EDWARD IV
SIR RICHARD RATCLIFFE
DUCHESS OF YORK
CHILDREN OF CLARENCE (BOY *and* GIRL)
Three CITIZENS
ARCHBISHOP OF YORK
DUKE OF YORK (*later, his* GHOST)
A MESSENGER (*to the Archbishop of York*)
PRINCE EDWARD (*later, his* GHOST)
LORD CARDINAL (*Archbishop of Canterbury*)
LORD MAYOR *of London*
A MESSENGER (*from Stanley to Hastings*)
A PURSUIVANT
A PRIEST
SIR THOMAS VAUGHAN (*later, his* GHOST)
BISHOP OF ELY
DUKE OF NORFOLK
LORD LOVELL
A SCRIVENER
Two BISHOPS

A PAGE (*to Richard*)
SIR JAMES TYRREL
Four MESSENGERS (*to Richard*)
A PRIEST (*Sir Christopher Urswick*)
SHERIFF
EARL OF RICHMOND, *afterwards* KING HENRY VII
EARL OF OXFORD
SIR JAMES BLUNT
SIR WALTER HERBERT
EARL OF SURREY
SIR WILLIAM BRANDON
GHOST OF PRINCE EDWARD, *son of Henry VI*
GHOST OF HENRY VI
A MESSENGER (*to Richard*)

Guards, halberdiers, gentlemen, attendant lords, citizens, servants, soldiers

Notes

RICHARD (1452–85) Eleventh child of Richard Duke of York and Cicely Neville, nick-named 'Crook-back' or 'Crouchback'. Fought bravely for his brother Edward IV against Lancastrian forces at the battles of Tewkesbury and Barnet in 1471. Appointed Protector of his nephew Edward V, Richard imprisoned the young king in 1483 and took the crown for himself. His only son, Edward, died in 1484. Defeated and killed by the forces of the Earl of Richmond (later Henry VII) at Bosworth Field, August 1485.

DUKE OF CLARENCE (1449–78) George, younger brother of Edward IV and older brother of Richard III. Married Isabel Neville, older sister of Anne Neville, Richard's queen. Joined his father-in-law, the Earl of Warwick, fighting for the deposed Henry VI against Edward IV in 1470. Deserted Warwick for Edward IV in 1471. Imprisoned in the Tower by Edward and reportedly drowned there in a butt of malmsey.

SIR ROBERT BRAKENBURY (?–1485) Appointed chief officer of the Tower of London by Richard in 1484. Reportedly refused to execute the young sons of Edward IV and relinquished his keys to Sir James Tyrrel. Fought for Richard at Bosworth in 1485 and was killed there.

LORD HASTINGS (1430?–83) William Hastings was alleged to have taken part in the mur-der of the Lancastrian Prince Edward at Tewkesbury. Created chamberlain of the royal household by Edward IV. Remained loyal to Edward's son after the king's death, refusing to participate in Richard's usurpation of the throne. Beheaded without a trial by Richard.

LADY ANNE (1456–85) Anne Neville, younger daughter of the powerful Earl of Warwick. Betrothed to Edward, son of Henry VI, in 1470. After Prince Edward was killed at Tewkesbury, Anne married Richard Duke of Gloucester (later Richard III). She was crowned with him in 1483. Died in 1485, a year after the death of her only son, Edward.

TRESSEL Sir William Tressel (or Trussel) was a supporter of Lord Hastings and may be the person Shakespeare represents as an attendant of Lady Anne at the funeral of Henry VI (1.2). Although Tressel has no lines in the play, he is distinguished by name when Anne directs him and Berkeley to leave the stage with her (1.2.225).

BERKELEY Member of a family descended from feudal lords in Gloucester. Attendant on Lady Anne at the funeral of Henry VI (1.2). Like Tressel, he does not speak, but exits with Anne.

QUEEN ELIZABETH (1437–92) Daughter of Sir Richard Woodville, the first Earl Rivers. Married Sir John Grey, who was killed fighting on the Lancastrian side in the Wars of the Roses. Married Edward IV in secret in 1464 and was crowned queen in 1465. Took sanctuary after Richard became Protector. Although her daughter married Henry VII (Richmond), she was distrusted and persecuted by the new king as she had been by Richard.

EARL RIVERS (1442?–83) Anthony Woodville, brother of Queen Elizabeth. Became the second Earl Rivers at his father's death and Lord Scales through marriage. Aided Edward IV in his wars against the Lancastrians, and was promoted by Edward to chief butler of England. When Richard became Protector, he suspected that Rivers exerted a hostile influence over the young king and had Rivers executed, probably without trial as in the play (3.3).

LORD GREY (?–1483) Richard Grey, younger son of Queen Elizabeth by her first husband and brother of the Marquess of Dorset. Grey and his uncle, Lord Rivers, were arrested by Richard of Gloucester while conducting the young king, Edward V, toward London from Ludlow Castle, near the Welsh border. Charged with alienating the prince's affections from Richard, Grey was executed at Pontefract Castle.

MARQUESS OF DORSET (1451–1501) Thomas Grey, older son of Queen Elizabeth and Sir John Grey. Fought for Edward IV at Tewkesbury and supposedly participated in the murder of Edward, son of Henry VI. Supported the Duke of Buckingham's rising against Richard III in 1484 and joined Richmond in Brittany soon after, although he did not participate in Richmond's invasion in 1485.

DUKE OF BUCKINGHAM (1454?–83) Henry Stafford, the second duke, was lord high steward of England under Edward IV. Married Catherine Woodville, sister of Queen Elizabeth. Helped Richard arrest Rivers, Vaughan and Grey after the death of Edward IV, and spoke at the Guildhall in favour of Richard's accession. Rebelled against Richard in 1483, but lost his forces to floods and was captured and beheaded at Salisbury.

LORD STANLEY (1435?–1504) Thomas Stanley married Richmond's mother, Margaret Beaufort, but served both Edward IV and Richard III until Richmond's invasion in 1485. Brought his armies to the battle of Bosworth but did not fight. Reportedly found Richard's crown and presented it to Richmond after the battle. Created first Earl of Derby by Richmond (Henry VII) in 1485.

QUEEN MARGARET (1430–82) Margaret of Anjou was the daughter of Reignier, King of Naples. Married Henry VI in 1445 and fought to restore him to the throne until she was defeated by Edward IV at the battle of Tewkesbury in 1471. In 1476 she left England for exile in France and died in poverty in Anjou in 1482. Shakespeare unhistorically represents her as alive and present in England until just before the battle of Bosworth (1485).

SIR WILLIAM CATESBY (?–1485) Made Chancellor of the Exchequer by Richard in 1483 after he helped Richard remove the previous chancellor, Lord Hastings. Never knighted, he served as speaker in the only parliament of Richard's reign (1484). Captured at Bosworth and executed.

KING EDWARD (1442–83) Son of Richard Duke of York and his duchess, Cicely Neville. Crushed the forces of Henry VI at Northampton in 1460 and became Edward IV in 1461. Defeated the Lancastrians again at Towton in 1461 and named his brothers George and Richard Dukes of Clarence and Gloucester, respectively. Married Elizabeth Grey in 1464 in the midst of negotiations for a political marriage abroad. Attacked by the Earl of Warwick, Clarence and Queen Margaret in 1470, he was reconciled with Clarence the following year, killed Warwick in battle, and captured Margaret at Tewkesbury after killing her son Edward. Imprisoned and executed his brother Clarence in 1478, but probably not because Richard urged it, as he does in the play.

SIR RICHARD RATCLIFFE (?–1485) Knighted by Edward IV at Tewkesbury, Ratcliffe became a prominent adviser to Richard during the protectorate. Responsible for arresting and executing Rivers, Grey and Vaughan at Pontefract in 1483. Died at the battle of Bosworth.

DUCHESS OF YORK (?–1495) Cicely Neville, daughter of Ralph Neville, first Earl of Westmorland, and Joan Beaufort, a daughter of John of Gaunt. Married Richard Duke of York in 1438 and saw two of her sons, Edward and Richard, become kings of England. She outlived them both.

CHILDREN OF CLARENCE Margaret (1473–1541) and Edward (1475–99) Plantagenet. Their mother died before their father, so that Clarence's death in 1478 left them orphans. Edward was imprisoned by Richard III in 1484, and remained a prisoner under Henry VII, who had him executed in 1499. Margaret was married to Sir Richard Pole by Henry VII (not by Richard as in the play). She was executed by Henry VIII.

ARCHBISHOP OF YORK (1423–1500) Thomas Rotherham (or Scott), Keeper of the Privy Seal to Edward IV, became Chancellor in 1474 and Archbishop in 1480. Surrendered the great seal to Queen Elizabeth in 1483. Imprisoned by Richard III and later released, he lived quietly away from politics for the rest of his life.

DUKE OF YORK (1472–83?) Richard, younger son of Edward IV and Queen Elizabeth. Married in 1478 at the age of six to Anne of Norfolk, also six. Taken by his mother to sanctuary at Westminster Abbey after his father died, but relinquished to Richard through the persuasions of Cardinal Bourchier. Died at the Tower with his older brother.

PRINCE EDWARD (1470–83?) Older son of Edward IV and Queen Elizabeth. Created Prince of Wales as an infant in 1471. At his father's death in 1483 he became Edward V and reigned for two months before his uncle Richard sent him to the Tower, where he died.

LORD CARDINAL (1404?–86) Thomas Bourchier, Archbishop of Canterbury, Lord Chancellor to Henry VI. A friend to both factions in the Wars of the Roses, Bourchier also served Edward IV, and persuaded Queen Elizabeth to surrender her younger son to Richard of Gloucester after her husband's death. Officiated at the coronations of both Richard III and Henry VII (Richmond). Married Henry VII to Elizabeth of York in 1486.

LORD MAYOR (?) Sir Edmund Shaw (or Shaa), a goldsmith and brother to the Dr Shaw who preached in favour of Richard in 1483 (mentioned by Richard at 3.5.103). Helped persuade the citizens of London to support Richard's accession to the throne.

SIR THOMAS VAUGHAN (?–1483) A supporter of Edward IV and afterwards of his young son Edward V. Taken prisoner by Richard together with Earl Rivers and Lord Grey and executed at Pontefract Castle.

BISHOP OF ELY (1420?–1500) John Morton, a supporter of Henry VI and Queen Margaret. Later reconciled to Edward IV, Morton became Bishop of Ely in 1479, and was imprisoned by Richard of Gloucester after Edward's death. Held in the custody of the Duke of Buckingham in Wales, he aided the duke's rebellion against Richard and then escaped to Richmond (Henry VII). Became Archbishop of Canterbury and Lord Chancellor under Henry VII. Became a cardinal in 1493. Patron to Sir Thomas More, who wrote the most influential history of Richard III.

DUKE OF NORFOLK (1430?–85) John Howard, first duke. A loyal Yorkist, he supported the accessions of both Edward IV and Richard III. Although his friends tried to persuade 'Jockey of Norfolk' to remain neutral, he commanded Richard's vanguard at Bosworth, where he was killed.

LORD LOVELL (1454–87?) Sir Francis Lovell, knighted in 1480 while serving in Richard of Gloucester's expedition against the Scots. Created viscount in 1483 and promoted to Lord Chamberlain when Richard became king. Assisted in Richard's preparations against Buckingham and Richmond and fought at Bosworth. Named in a famous rhyme for which William Collingbourne was executed: 'The Catte, the Ratte, and Lovel our dogge/Rulyth all

Englande under a Hogge.' The cat and the rat were Catesby and Ratcliffe, and the hog was Richard, whose emblem was a wild boar.

SIR JAMES TYRREL (?–1502) Knighted by Edward IV after the battle of Tewkesbury. Pardoned by Henry VII but later imprisoned and executed, he is said to have confessed before he died to supervising the murders of the young princes in the Tower.

A PRIEST, Sir Christopher Urswick (1448–1522) Confessor to Lady Margaret Beaufort, Richmond's mother. Chaplain to Richmond after he became Henry VII.

EARL OF RICHMOND (1457–1509) Henry Tudor, son of Edmund Tudor and Margaret Beaufort, great-granddaughter of John of Gaunt, from whom the Lancastrians traced their claim to the throne. Exiled to France during the reign of Edward IV, he returned in 1485 to defeat Richard III at the battle of Bosworth and become Henry VII. Married Elizabeth, daughter of Edward IV and Queen Elizabeth, in 1486. The Tudor monarchs, including Henry VII's son, Henry VIII, and his granddaughter, Elizabeth I, ruled England until 1603.

EARL OF OXFORD (1443–1513) John de Vere, the thirteenth earl. A Lancastrian in exile, Oxford joined the Earl of Richmond's forces in 1483 and commanded one wing of Richmond's army at Bosworth. Created Lord Chamberlain by Henry VII.

SIR JAMES BLUNT (?–1493) Third son of Sir Walter Blunt (or Blount), first Baron Mountjoy. Landed with Richmond at Milford Haven in 1485 and was knighted by him after the battle. As part of his reward, Blunt was given the manor of the executed Catesby.

SIR WALTER HERBERT Second son of the Earl of Pembroke and son-in-law of the Duke of Buckingham.

EARL OF SURREY (1443–1524) Thomas Howard, only son of the Duke of Norfolk, created Earl in 1483. Like his father, Surrey supported Richard III. Taken prisoner at Bosworth, he remained a captive until 1489.

SIR WILLIAM BRANDON (?–1485) Standard-bearer for the Earl of Richmond at Bosworth, where he was killed by Richard III.

GHOST OF PRINCE EDWARD (1453–71) Son of Henry VI and Queen Margaret. Killed at the battle of Tewkesbury. In *3H6*, he dies at the hands of Richard and his brothers.

GHOST OF HENRY VI (1421–71) Son of Henry V and husband of Queen Margaret. Shakespeare shows Richard murdering him in *3H6*.

THE TRAGEDY OF RICHARD THE THIRD

1.1 *Enter* RICHARD DUKE OF GLOUCESTER, *solus*

RICHARD Now is the winter of our discontent
       Made glorious summer by this son of York,
       And all the clouds that loured upon our house
       In the deep bosom of the ocean buried.
       Now are our brows bound with victorious wreaths,   5
       Our bruisèd arms hung up for monuments,
       Our stern alarums changed to merry meetings,
       Our dreadful marches to delightful measures.
       Grim-visaged war hath smoothed his wrinkled front,
       And now, instead of mounting barbèd steeds   10

Title] The Tragedy of Richard the Third: / with the Landing of Earle Richmond, and the / Battell at Bosworth Field. F *title page*; The Life & Death of Richard the Third. F *table of contents*; The Life and Death of Richard the Third. F *running titles pp. 173–200*; The Life and death of Richard the Third. F *running titles pp. 201–4*; The Tragedy of / King Richard the third. / Containing, / His treacherous Plots against his brother Clarence: / the pittiefull murther of his iunocent nephewes: / his tyrannicall vsurpation: with the whole course / of his detested life, and most deserued death. / As it hath beene lately Acted by the / Right honourable the Lord Chamber- / laine his seruants. Qq (*subst.*) Act 1, Scene 1 1.1] F (*Actus Primus. Scoena Prima.*); *not in* Qq 0 SD GLOUCESTER] Q6; *Gloster* Q2, F; *Glocester* Q, Q3–5 1 SH] *Capell (Ric.)*; *not in* F, Qq 1 our] F, Q, Q2; *not in* Q3–6 8 measures] F, Q, Q2–3; pleasures Q4–6

Title Subtitles advertising notable events in a play are common in quarto editions of Shakespeare. In F, however, such subtitles are confined to a few of the history plays, possibly those like *Richard III* whose popularity had made certain incidents or characters famous. See, for example, the F title pages of *The First Part of Henry the Fourth, with the Life and Death of Henry Sirnamed Hot-Spurre* or *The third Part of Henry the Sixt, with the death of the Good Duke Hvmfrey.*

Act 1, Scene 1
The Elizabethan audience would have known that the action takes place in London, since Clarence goes toward the Tower of London and Hastings comes from it. Elizabethan staging would have indicated location by the dialogue rather than by properties or scenery denoting London. This scene is largely a Shakespearean invention from hints in Hall and Holinshed that Richard 'long time in king Edwards life forethought to be king' (Holinshed, III, 362). Hall and Holinshed both mention Clarence's being imprisoned in the Tower because of a 'foolish prophesie' that someone whose name began with

a 'G' should reign after Edward (Holinshed, III, 346).

0 SD solus alone (Latin).

1 SH Since Richard enters alone, F and Qq allow the stage direction to designate the speaker as well. Using an entry stage direction as a surrogate speech heading is common in F.

2 son Richard's older brother, King Edward IV – a son of the house of York – adopted the sun as his badge. The pun announces a pattern of sun and shadow images that continues to the end of the play.

3 loured upon threatened. Literally, frowned on (see 9: 'wrinkled front').

6 arms armour, weapons.

6 monuments memorials, relics.

7 alarums calls to arms.

8 dreadful inspiring dread; in this case, in the enemy.

8 measures dances.

9 front forehead. War is personified as a soldier who has exchanged his warrior attributes, including his scowl, for those of a lover.

10 barbèd steeds War horses with breasts and flanks covered in armour.

To fright the souls of fearful adversaries,
He capers nimbly in a lady's chamber
To the lascivious pleasing of a lute.
But I that am not shaped for sportive tricks
Nor made to court an amorous looking-glass,   15
I that am rudely stamped and want love's majesty
To strut before a wanton ambling nymph,
I that am curtailed of this fair proportion,
Cheated of feature by dissembling nature,
Deformed, unfinished, sent before my time   20
Into this breathing world scarce half made up,
And that so lamely and unfashionable
That dogs bark at me as I halt by them,
Why, I, in this weak piping time of peace,

13 lute] F; loue Qq   14 shaped for] F; shapte for Q, Q2–3; sharpe for Q4–5; sharpe of Q6   15 Nor] F, Q, Q3–6; Not Q2
21 scarce] F, Q, Q2; *not in* Q3–6

11 **fearful** full of fear.

13 **lascivious   pleasing** lewd   attraction. Characteristically, Richard reduces the sensual appeal of music to mere arousal.

14 **sportive   tricks** playful   games.   Both 'sportive' and 'tricks' could have sexual connotations in Shakespeare's time as now, though perhaps Shakespeare himself was the first to make the connections. See *OED* Sportive *adj* 2, citing this passage as the earliest example. See also 'trick' as a term for sexual intercourse (*OED* Trick *sb* 10a and b). Compare *MM* 3.1.112–14, where Claudio questions Isabella about Angelo's interest in sex: 'If it were damnable, he being so wise, / Why would he for the momentary trick / Be perdurably fined?' Richard, of course, is certainly 'shaped for' (and 'sharpe for' as in Q4–5) tricks in the more usual sense of devices to cheat or deceive (*OED* Trick *sb* 1a).

16 **want** lack.

17 **ambling** sauntering, strolling.

18 **curtailed** cut short. In Shakespeare's time, the word was especially associated with the docking of tails (*OED* Curtail *v* 1). By evoking the association here, Richard, like his enemies, connects his birth and his body with those of a dog (see especially Margaret's speech to Richard's mother at 4.4.47–50: 'From forth the kennel of thy womb hath crept / A hell-hound that doth hunt us all to death: / That dog, that had his teeth before his eyes / To worry lambs and lap their gentle blood').

19 **feature** good form or shape (*OED* Feature *sb* 1b).

19 **dissembling** deceiving; disguising.

20 **before my time** Earlier stories (Rous, More, Hall) of Richard's abnormal gestation usually had him spending too much time in the womb rather than too little. Although Shakespeare adopts many of the other omens and signs that his sources associate with Richard's nativity, including a full set of teeth, he makes the birth premature rather than late, confining delay to the mother's difficult labour. See the Duchess's remark: 'Art thou so hasty? I have stayed for thee, / God knows, in torment and in agony' (4.4.163–4). Compare King Henry's similar description of Richard's birth in *3H6* 5.6.44–56. Throughout this scene, Richard continues to remind the audience of his unnatural birth by harping on the word 'delivery'.

22 **unfashionable** not   good-looking   or stylish; not properly fashioned or shaped. See *OED* Fashion *v* 1.

23 **halt** limp. Just how lame Richard is and how much deformity he reveals vary from production to production. Laurence Olivier (film version, 1955) displayed both a pronounced hobble and a monkey-like agility. Some recent Richards such as Ron Cook (BBC, 1983) and Antony Sher (Royal Shakespeare Company, 1984) followed Olivier in emphasising the limp. Others, such as Ian McKellen (Royal National Theatre, 1989), showed Richard successfully disguising or compensating for his limp and deformed arm most of the time.

24 **piping** sounding like a pipe or wind instrument. *OED* cites this as the earliest use in English

Have no delight to pass away the time,   25
Unless to see my shadow in the sun
And descant on mine own deformity.
And therefore, since I cannot prove a lover
To entertain these fair well-spoken days,
I am determinèd to prove a villain   30
And hate the idle pleasures of these days.
Plots have I laid, inductions dangerous,
By drunken prophecies, libels, and dreams
To set my brother Clarence and the king
In deadly hate the one against the other.   35
And if King Edward be as true and just
As I am subtle, false, and treacherous,
This day should Clarence closely be mewed up
About a prophecy which says that 'G'
Of Edward's heirs the murderer shall be.   40

---

26 see] F; spie Qq   29 well-spoken] F3; well spoken F, Qq   39, 55, 56 58 'G'] F3 (G); G F, Qq   40 murderer] F, Q3–6 (murtherer); murtherers Q, Q2

of the meaning 'Characterized by piping, i.e. the music of pastoral pipe (as distinguished from the martial fife, trumpet, etc.)' (*OED* Piping *ppl a* 1b). The combination with 'weak' suggests that Richard contrasts the shrill, effeminate pipe of peace not to the fife but to the drum, as does Coriolanus: 'My throat of war be turned, / Which quiered with my drum, into a pipe / Small as an eunuch, or the virgin voice / That babies lull asleep' (*Cor.* 3.2.112–15).

25 delight source of pleasure.

26 Having expressed his hatred of the 'glorious summer' brought in by the son/sun of York, Richard now says his only use for the sun is to see his own shadow. This indirect way of looking at himself contrasts him both with the sun itself – a metaphor for his older brother – and with the well-proportioned courtier who enjoys regarding himself directly in an 'amorous looking-glass' (15). These metaphors help establish Richard's contrariness, but not yet his stealth.

26 see Most eclectic modern editions prefer Qq's 'spie' (spy) as the more vivid word. Wilson, for example, says 'spie' gives 'just the sense of stealthy observation which the context demands' (p. 153). Without 'spie', however, there is no suggestion of secrecy in the immediate context. In fact, Richard has just finished saying that he is conspicuous enough to set dogs barking.

27 descant comment (*OED* Descant *v* 2, citing this passage). In music, to sing in harmony with a fixed theme (*OED* Descant *v* 1).

29 entertain spend pleasantly.

30 determinèd decided, resolved; foreordained or predestined. Compare Richard's words as he murders Henry VI: 'I'll hear no more; die, prophet, in thy speech: / For this, amongst the rest, was I ordained' (*3H6* 5.6.56–7). See pp. 1–16 above.

32 inductions initial steps (*OED* Induction 3c); introductions, as to books or plays (*OED* Induction 3b). Richard's opening soliloquy resembles an induction such as those spoken by the Prologue in *H5* and Rumour in *2H4*. In addition, many of his schemes have a staged quality that makes the theatrical meaning of 'induction' appropriate here.

33 dreams Probably Richard's interpretations of his own dreams, perhaps of Edward's dreams as well.

35 the one against the other Like most of Shakespeare's villains, Richard seems to make up his plots as he goes along. Here he says he plans to turn his two brothers against one another, but at 63 he seems to take pains not to set Clarence against the king, assuring him that the queen alone is his enemy.

38 mewed up put in a 'mew' or cage, as a hawk (*OED* Mew *v²* 3b). Compare 133.

Dive, thoughts, down to my soul, here Clarence comes.

Enter CLARENCE *and* BRAKENBURY, *guarded*

Brother, good day. What means this armèd guard
That waits upon your grace?
CLARENCE   His majesty,
Tend'ring my person's safety, hath appointed
This conduct to convey me to the Tower.   45
RICHARD Upon what cause?
CLARENCE   Because my name is George.
RICHARD Alack, my lord, that fault is none of yours.
He should for that commit your godfathers.
Oh, belike his majesty hath some intent
That you should be new christened in the Tower.   50
But what's the matter, Clarence? May I know?
CLARENCE Yea, Richard, when I know, but I protest
As yet I do not. But as I can learn,
He hearkens after prophecies and dreams,
And from the cross-row plucks the letter 'G',   55

41] F; Dive . . . soule, / Heere . . . comes, Qq   **41** SD *and* BRAKENBURY] F; *not in* Qq   **41** SD *guarded*] F; *with a gard of men.* Qq (*subst.*)   **42** day] F; dayes Qq (*subst.*)   **43–5** His . . . Tower] *Pope*; His . . . safety, / Hath . . . Tower F; His . . . ap-po nted / This . . . tower. Q (appointed Q2–6)   **45** the Tower] Qq; th'Tower F   **46** SH RICHARD] F (*Rich.*); *Glo* Qq *throughout*   **46**] *Steevens*; Upon . . . cause? / Because . . . George. F, Qq   **48** godfathers] F, Q, Q2–3; good fathers Q4–6   **50** should] F; shall Qq (*subst.*)   **51** what's] F, Q, Q2 (*subst.*); what is Q3–6   **52** know] F, Q, Q2–5; doe know Q6   **52** but] F; for Qq

41 SD *guarded* surrounded by guards. F places Clarence's entrance after Richard's 'Dive, thoughts', while the typography of Q suggests that the line and the entrance are simultaneous.

43, 46 Clarence's ironic responses in these lines suggest the same familiarity between the two brothers that they display in *3H6* 3.2, commenting on Edward's courtship of Lady Grey (Queen Elizabeth in this play). The split lines reinforce this sense of apparent intimacy, although it is a false sense from Clarence's point of view.

44 Tend'ring Caring for tenderly. F's elision may reflect the underlying manuscript, implying that these lines were to be set as verse.

45 conduct escort.

45 Tower The Tower of London, both a royal residence and a state prison. It had become an ominous symbol by Shakespeare's time, not only because of the little princes portrayed in this play, but also for such later inmates as Anne Boleyn. The Tower was said to stand on the site of a fort built by Julius Caesar (see 3.1.68–9).

46 SH RICHARD Qq use the SH *Glo.* for Richard until 4.2.1, his first entrance as king. After that, his SH is *King*. F usually gives him the SH *Rich.* or the equivalent (*Ric.*, *Ri.*) except at 3.1.63–183, where he is *Glo.*, and at 5.3.72, where he is *King*. F uses *King.* intermittently in the final scenes of the play, after Richard awakens from his nightmare.

48 godfathers In Christian churches, those who sponsor a child at baptism, which usually includes naming.

49 belike perhaps, probably.

50 christened named; baptised. An ironic foreshadowing of Clarence's fatal immersion in a butt of wine.

51 the matter the real substance (of the king's displeasure), as distinguished from Clarence's earlier flippant answer.

55–9 These rhyming lines may suggest Richard's contempt for such superstitions.

55 cross-row alphabet. From the child's hornbook, where the alphabet was marked with a Maltese cross.

And says a wizard told him that by 'G'
His issue disinherited should be.
And for my name of George begins with 'G',
It follows in his thought that I am he.
These, as I learn, and suchlike toys as these   60
Hath moved his highness to commit me now.

RICHARD Why, this it is when men are ruled by women.
'Tis not the king that sends you to the Tower.
My lady Grey, his wife, Clarence, 'tis she
That tempts him to this harsh extremity.   65
Was it not she and that good man of worship,
Anthony Woodville, her brother there,
That made him send Lord Hastings to the Tower,
From whence this present day he is delivered?
We are not safe, Clarence, we are not safe.   70

CLARENCE By heaven, I think there is no man secure
But the queen's kindred and night-walking heralds
That trudge betwixt the king and Mistress Shore.
Heard you not what an humble suppliant
Lord Hastings was for her delivery?   75

59 follows] F, Q, Q2–4, Q6; fellowes Q5   61 Hath] F; haue Qq   65 tempts . . . harsh extremity] F; tempers . . . extremity Q; tempts . . . extremitie Q2, Q4–6 (*subst.*); temps . . . extremitie Q3   67 Woodville] F2; Woodeulle F; Wooduile Qq; Woodeville *Capell*   71 secure] F; is securde] F; is securde Q, Q2–3; securde Q4–6 (*subst.*)   75 for her] F; to her for his Qq; for his F2

60 toys trifles.

61 Hath Shakespeare often uses 'hath' with plural subjects (see Abbott 334).

65 tempts . . . harsh extremity Many editors have preferred the Q line as verse, and have conjectured that F was a compositor's attempt to repair the metre of his quarto copy. Oxford argues, however, that Q3 was copy at this point, and that the series of changes postulated for the F compositor – first emending 'temps', then adding 'harsh' is unlikely (Wells and Taylor, pp. 232–3).

66 worship honour.

67 Woodville Editors often adopt Capell's spelling because it suggests, as F's 'Woodeulle' may also, a trisyllabic pronunciation. F has 'Wooduill' at TLN 1193, where the metre requires a disyllable. A modern actor would probably stress the name slightly rather than pronouncing it as three distinct syllables.

67 her brother there her brother who influences her at court (?). In Olivier's film, Richard, who is lurking above the court rooms, gestures to the figure of Rivers below as he speaks this line. 'There' may also indicate Richard's contempt for Rivers (see *OED* There *adv* 3b).

71 secure The changes made by later quartos to Q's reading, probably the work of compositors, show how coincidental correction as well as error may creep into derivative editions.

72 night-walking heralds secret messengers. 'Night-walking' in Shakespeare's period implied both criminal intent (*OED* Night-walker 1a) and prostitution (*OED* Night-walker 1b).

73 trudge walk laboriously.

73 Mistress Shore Jane Shore, wife of a London goldsmith and mistress of Edward IV. She was a notable figure in most stories of Richard III, but not in Shakespeare's. According to More, Shore became Hastings's mistress after Edward's death. Shakespeare also excludes this episode, although it is often represented on stage even today, with Shore most likely to be present (silently) in 3.2, when the messenger comes to warn Hastings in the middle of the night.

75 her delivery Mistress Shore's delivery of Hastings from prison. Qq's 'his delivery' is the more common expression, but F is not as awkward as many editors have insisted (see Thompson, Wilson). Richard seldom misses a

RICHARD Humbly complaining to her deity
    Got my Lord Chamberlain his liberty.
    I'll tell you what, I think it is our way,
    If we will keep in favour with the king,
    To be her men and wear her livery.   80
    The jealous, o'er-worn widow and herself,
    Since that our brother dubbed them gentlewomen,
    Are mighty gossips in our monarchy.
BRAKENBURY I beseech your graces both to pardon me;
    His majesty hath straitly given in charge   85
    That no man shall have private conference,
    Of what degree soever, with your brother.
RICHARD Even so. And please your worship, Brakenbury,
    You may partake of any thing we say.
    We speak no treason, man. We say the king   90
    Is wise and virtuous, and his noble queen
    Well struck in years, fair, and not jealous.
    We say that Shore's wife hath a pretty foot,
    A cherry lip, a bonny eye, a passing pleasing tongue,
    And that the queen's kindred are made gentlefolks.   95

---

76 Humbly] F, Q, Q2–4; Humble Q5–6   83 our] F; this Qq   84 BRAKENBURY] F; *Brokenbury* Qq *throughout*   87 your] F; his Qq

chance to sneer at women and their functions; the usage 'her delivery' in connection with Mistress Shore hints at childbirth, where the child is released from confinement but the delivery is usually said to be the woman's (*OED* Delivery 2a).

76 complaining to her deity complaining to Mistress Shore as if she were a god.

77 Lord Chamberlain Hastings.

80 livery badge of servitude; often a distinguishing suit of clothes or uniform worn by servants (*OED* Livery *sb* 2a).

81 widow Queen Elizabeth, the former Lady Grey. Shakespeare portrays Edward's courtship and marriage of the widow, and his brothers' animosity toward her, in *3H6*.

82 dubbed them gentlewomen Elizabeth Woodville, Lady Grey, was a gentlewoman. Jane Shore was not; Richard lumps them together as mere creatures of his brother.

83 mighty gossips The idea seems to be that women in general are gossips, a trivial occupation (*OED* Gossip *sb* 3), but that these particular women have been unsuitably promoted to

'mighty gossips' through King Edward's favour.

84 SH Qq's Brokenbury takes the lines of F's Brakenbury and also of the Keeper in 4.1.

85 straitly strictly.

87 Of what degree soever Of whatever rank. Brakenbury acknowledges Richard's high station while enforcing the king's prohibition.

87 your brother Qq's 'his brother' is probably intended to refer to 'His majesty' at 85.

88 And please your worship If it may please your honour. As a duke, Richard ironically defers to Brakenbury, who is only a knight, by calling him 'your worship'. Compare Richard's contemptuous 'fellow' (98) and 'knave' (102).

92 Well struck in years Usually, well along in years (*OED* Stricken A). Used by Richard here as an ironic compliment.

92 jealous F's 'iealious' may indicate that someone – the typesetter? the author? – thought the word should be trisyllabic to fit the metre. The same compositor (B) uses 'iealous' at 81, where the metre requires two syllables. See 67n.

94 passing surpassingly, exceptionally.

How say you, sir? Can you deny all this?
BRAKENBURY With this, my lord, myself have nought to do.
RICHARD Naught to do with Mistress Shore? I tell thee, fellow,
He that doth naught with her (excepting one)
Were best to do it secretly alone.   100
BRAKENBURY What one, my lord?
RICHARD Her husband, knave. Wouldst thou betray me?
BRAKENBURY I do beseech your grace to pardon me, and withal
Forbear your conference with the noble duke.
CLARENCE We know thy charge, Brakenbury, and will obey.   105
RICHARD We are the queen's abjects and must obey.
Brother, farewell. I will unto the king,
And whatsoe'er you will employ me in,
Were it to call King Edward's widow 'sister',
I will perform it to enfranchise you.   110
Meantime, this deep disgrace in brotherhood
Touches me deeper than you can imagine.
CLARENCE I know it pleaseth neither of us well.
RICHARD Well, your imprisonment shall not be long.
I will deliver you or else lie for you.   115
Meantime, have patience.
CLARENCE I must perforce. Farewell.
                Exeunt Clarence[, Brakenbury, and guards]

---

97 nought] F, Q, Q6; naught Q2–5 98–100] Qq; Naught . . . Shore? / I . . . her / (Excepting . . . alone. F 100 to] F;
he Qq 101–2] F, Q2–6; *not in* Q 103–4] Capell; I . . . forbeare / Your . . . Duke. Qq; I . . . Grace / To . . . forbeare /
Your . . . Duke. F 103 do] F; *not in* Qq 108 whatsoe'er] F; whatsoeuer Qq 109 'sister'] Capell (–*Sister*–); Sister F;
sister Qq 115 or else] F; or Qq 117 SD] Capell; *Exit Clar.* F, Qq

97 **nought** nothing.
98 **Naught** Naughtiness, especially sexual
(*OED* Naught *sb* 2). Both F and Q make
the nought/naught pun clear through spelling,
although some later editions muddle it.
101–2 Scholars assume that the appearance of
these two lines in Q2 but not in Q means that
the lines were printed in some copies of Q. Q2
was presumably set from one of these corrected
copies. See Textual Analysis, p. 220 below, n. 1.
103 **do** F's additional word helps regularise the
iambic pattern, but the line is even more hyper-
metrical than in Q.
103 **withal** besides.
106 **abjects** abject servants. The usual term
would be 'subjects', which Richard suggests
is not strong enough to describe the queen's
oppressive rule.

110 **enfranchise** liberate.
115 Clarence is meant to understand that
Richard will either deliver him from prison or
take his place – 'lie for you'. Richard actually
means that he will either get Clarence out of
prison or else tell lies about him, with the latter as
his real intention. The line recalls Richard's earlier play on 'delivery' (75), and suggests further
word-play at the expense of women: if Richard
cannot deliver Clarence, he will labour to do so –
'lie for you'. (Compare Clarence's exclamation
to the murderers at 1.4.234–6: 'It cannot be, for
he bewept my fortune, / And hugged me in
his arms, and swore with sobs / That he would
labour my delivery.')
117 **perforce** 'Patience perforce' was proverbial for a condition without remedy. See Tilley
P111.

RICHARD   Go, tread the path that thou shalt ne'er return.
Simple, plain Clarence, I do love thee so
That I will shortly send thy soul to heaven,   120
If heaven will take the present at our hands.
But who comes here? The new-delivered Hastings?

Enter LORD HASTINGS

HASTINGS   Good time of day unto my gracious lord.
RICHARD   As much unto my good Lord Chamberlain.
Well are you welcome to this open air.   125
How hath your lordship brooked imprisonment?
HASTINGS   With patience, noble lord, as prisoners must.
But I shall live, my lord, to give them thanks
That were the cause of my imprisonment.
RICHARD   No doubt, no doubt, and so shall Clarence too,   130
For they that were your enemies are his
And have prevailed as much on him as you.
HASTINGS   More pity that the eagles should be mewed
While kites and buzzards play at liberty.
RICHARD   What news abroad?   135
HASTINGS   No news so bad abroad as this at home:
The king is sickly, weak, and melancholy,
And his physicians fear him mightily.
RICHARD   Now by Saint John, that news is bad indeed.
Oh, he hath kept an evil diet long   140
And over-much consumed his royal person.

122 new-delivered] *Pope*; new deliuered F, Qq   125 this] F, Q3–6; the Q, Q2   133 eagles] F; Eagle Qq   134 While]; Qq
Whiles F   134 play] F; prey Qq   139 Saint John] F (S. Iohn); Saint Paul Qq (*subst.*)   139 that] F; this Qq

122 new-delivered Merely by repeating the
word, Richard has made 'delivered' into a kind of
ironic insult. Here he aims it at the approaching
Hastings and at his supposed deliverer, Mistress
Shore.
  126 brooked endured.
  128 give them thanks revenge myself on
them.
  133 eagles should be mewed Hastings compares himself and Clarence to eagles and their
imprisonment to the 'mewing up' or caging of
hunting birds (compare 38).
  134 kites and buzzards inferior birds of
prey. Compare this to Richard's image of
Clarence as a soon-to-be-imprisoned hawk
(38).

  134 play Most editors prefer Qq's 'prey'
because it fits the birds-of-prey metaphor. Both
speakers stress the birds' associations with freedom and imprisonment, however, rather than
with predation. In addition, F's image of Hastings's enemies as kites and buzzards at 'play'
adds a dimension of scorn to his lines that is not
present in Q.
  138 fear him fear for him, fear for his life.
  139 Saint John Many editors have adopted
Qq's 'Saint Paul' because it is Richard's usual
oath. Even in the quartos, however, he does not
swear exclusively by Paul. See 'by God's holy
mother' (1.3.306).
  140 diet way of life (*OED* Diet *sb*[1] 1). Richard
alludes to Edward's sexual promiscuity.

'Tis very grievous to be thought upon.
Where is he, in his bed?
HASTINGS He is.
RICHARD Go you before, and I will follow you.   145

                                        Exit Hastings

He cannot live, I hope, and must not die
Till George be packed with post-horse up to heaven.
I'll in to urge his hatred more to Clarence
With lies well steeled with weighty arguments,
And if I fail not in my deep intent,   150
Clarence hath not another day to live:
Which done, God take King Edward to his mercy
And leave the world for me to bustle in!
For then I'll marry Warwick's youngest daughter.
What though I killed her husband and her father?   155
The readiest way to make the wench amends
Is to become her husband and her father,
The which will I, not all so much for love
As for another secret close intent
By marrying her which I must reach unto.   160
But yet I run before my horse to market.
Clarence still breathes, Edward still lives and reigns;
When they are gone, then must I count my gains.   *Exit*

---

143 Where] F; What Qq   147 post-horse] F, Qq (post horse); post-haste *Oxford*; posthaste *Collier²*

147 post-horse A horse kept ready at an inn for the next stage of a journey; hence, a fresh, fast horse.

149 steeled fortified.

150 deep profoundly crafty; subtle (*OED* Deep *a* 17).

153 bustle be active. Compare 5.3.291.

154 Warwick's youngest daughter Anne Neville, daughter of Richard, Earl of Warwick ('the Kingmaker'), who had fought for, then against, the house of York in the Wars of the Roses.

155 her father her father-in-law (in the play), Henry VI. In a way, Richard killed both Anne's father-in-law and her father, since Warwick died fighting Richard's forces, but Shakespeare attributes only the murder of Henry VI directly to Richard (see *3H6* 5.2 and 5.6).

156 wench girl. Often in Shakespeare 'wench' is simply an endearing or familiar form of address (*OED* Wench *sb* 1c), but Richard may also intend to imply wantonness (*OED* Wench *sb* 2).

157 and her father Note that the iambic rhythm of the line stresses 'and'. Paternalistic notions of the husband's role were commonplace in Shakespeare's time, as in Richard's.

159 secret close intent Richard's motive for courting Anne remains obscure. Marriage to the widow of Henry VI's son, as she is in the play, would probably add legitimacy to a bid for the crown, but Richard's desire for the crown is no secret, at least not to the audience.

161 before my horse Tilley cites 'I will not go (run) before my mare to market' as an English proverb, giving this line as his earliest instance (M649). Even if Shakespeare invented this saying, which seems unlikely, it resembles 'To set the cart before the horse', already an old saying in 1590 (Tilley C103).

1.2 *Enter the corpse of Henry the Sixth with Halberds to guard it,* LADY
ANNE *being the mourner* [*attended by* TRESSEL, BERKELEY, *and other*
GENTLEMEN]

ANNE Set down, set down your honourable load,
  If honour may be shrouded in a hearse,
  Whilst I awhile obsequiously lament
  Th'untimely fall of virtuous Lancaster.
  Poor key-cold figure of a holy king,   5
  Pale ashes of the house of Lancaster,
  Thou bloodless remnant of that royal blood,
  Be it lawful that I invocate thy ghost
  To hear the lamentations of poor Anne,
  Wife to thy Edward, to thy slaughtered son,   10

Act 1, Scene 2 1.2] F (*Scena Secunda.*); *not in* Qq 0 SD] *Hammond; Enter the Coarse of Henrie the sixt with Halberds to guard it, Lady Anne being the Mourner.* F; *Enter Lady Anne with the hearse of Harry the 6.* Qq 1 SH] F; *Lady An. / later / La.* (*subst.*) Qq 1 Set . . . set] F, Q, Q3–6; *Sit . . . sit* Q2 1 load] F; lo Q; lord Q2–6 (*subst.*)

Act 1, Scene 2

The action is continuous with 1.1. Shakespeare's chronicle sources do not show Anne accompanying the body of Henry VI, which Holinshed says was carried from the Tower to Saint Paul's where the corpse 'in presence of the beholders did bleed; where it rested the space of one whole daie. From thense he was carried to the Blackfriers, and bled there likewise: and on the next daie after, it was conueied in a boat, without priest or clerke, torch or taper, singing or saieng, vnto the monasterie of Chertseie, distant from London fifteene miles, and there was it first buried' (Holinshed, III, 324).

0 SD *Halberds* Halberdiers, guards carrying halberds. A halberd was a combination spear and battle-axe mounted on a long handle. As Hammond points out (1.2.136n.), the funeral procession requires a minimum of nine actors: four gentleman pallbearers, Tressel and Berkeley, who must exit with Anne at 228 SD, and at least two halberdiers.

1 SH In this scene, F uses the speech heading *Anne.* or *An.* Q has *Lady An.* at first, then *La.,* *Lad.* or *Lady.* The quarto's usage is in keeping with its practice of identifying characters by their titles or roles at particular points in the plot rather than by single character names throughout (see Note on the Text, p. 44 above).

1 load Here F corrects a typographical error begun in Q and augmented in subsequent quarto editions. As is often the case, F's correction had no influence on Q7 and Q8, which follow the quartos printed before F.

2 hearse Probably not a closed box, but a

frame holding a cloth or pall above the dead body, which rests on a litter (see *OED* Hearse *sb* 3). Anne wonders 'if honour may be shrouded in a hearse', suggesting that the hearse is either such a frame or perhaps the cloth (shroud) itself (*OED* Hearse *sb* 4).

3 obsequiously as one who carries out funeral rites (*OED* Obsequy).

4 fall of virtuous Lancaster Henry VI belonged to the house of Lancaster, and his death marked the downfall of that family as well as of the virtuous king himself.

5–6 key-cold . . . Pale ashes Keys were proverbially cold, as ashes were pale (see Tilley K23 and A339). Anne's proverbial language enhances the impression of a ritualised lament.

5 figure form, shape.

8 Be it Let it be. (See Abbott 365 on the optative use of the subjunctive.) Anne seems a bit tentative at the beginning of this scene, twice expressing doubt about the proper forms of lamentation. Is the dead Henry VI 'honourable', or is honour an attribute only of the living? May Anne appeal to his ghost and still be obedient to church law? In Shakespeare's time, one source of the second doubt would have been the Protestant ban on prayers for the dead or to saints. But the play is set in the fifteenth century, when England was a Roman Catholic country, so Anne may be wondering if she may invoke Henry as a saint even before he is canonised.

10 Wife to thy Edward Historically, Anne was betrothed but not married to Edward, son of Henry VI.

Stabbed by the selfsame hand that made these wounds.
Lo, in these windows that let forth thy life,
I pour the helpless balm of my poor eyes.
Oh, cursèd be the hand that made these holes,
Cursed the heart that had the heart to do it,   15
Cursed the blood that let this blood from hence.
More direful hap betide that hated wretch
That makes us wretched by the death of thee
Than I can wish to wolves, to spiders, toads,
Or any creeping venomed thing that lives.   20
If ever he have child, abortive be it,
Prodigious, and untimely brought to light,
Whose ugly and unnatural aspèct
May fright the hopeful mother at the view,
And that be heir to his unhappiness.   25
If ever he have wife, let her be made
More miserable by the death of him

---

11 hand] F; hands Qq   11 wounds] F; holes Qq   12 these] F; those Qq   14] F; Curst . . . these fatall holes, Q, Q2;
Curst . . . the fatall holes, Q3–6   15 Cursed] F; Curst be Qq   16] F; *not in* Qq   19 wolves, to spiders] F; adders, spiders
Qq   25] F; *not in* Qq   26 made] F, Q, Q2–5; mad: Q6   27 More] F; As Qq

---

11 **selfsame hand** In *3H6*, Shakespeare
shows all three York brothers – Edward, Richard
and George – stabbing the young Prince of
Wales after the battle of Tewkesbury (5.5.37–
40). Memory of this scene may have suggested
Qq's 'hands'. At the end of that play, however,
Richard alone kills Henry VI, and Anne appears
to be thinking of Richard's as the single murdering hand (compare 14).

12 **windows** The holes in Henry's body, his
wounds. Compare *Lear* 3.4.31, 'Your looped and
windowed raggedness'. Honigmann refers to 'the
custom of opening the windows to allow a dying
soul to pass.'

16 Wilson (p. 174) thinks this line 'clearly'
should have been inserted before 15 in F. Walker
had said 'Possibly' (p. 32). In the Folio the
metaphor in 14–16 progresses from 'hand' to
'heart' to 'blood', a movement from the outside
to the inside of the body and also from the literal
to the figurative. The line does not appear in Q.

17 **hap** chance, luck.

17 **betide** befall.

19 **wolves** Many editors prefer Qq's 'adders',
since a wolf is not a 'venomed thing'.

21 **abortive** premature (*OED* Abortive *adj*
1a).

22 **Prodigious** Monstrous (*OED* Prodigious
a 3); unnatural, abnormal (*OED* Prodigious *a* 2);
ominous, portentous (*OED* Prodigious *a* 1).

22 **untimely** too early, prematurely, an echo
of 'abortive' at 21. Compare Macduff, who was
'untimely ripped' from his mother's womb (*Mac.*
5.8.16).

23 **aspèct** appearance (*OED* Aspect *sb* 11).
The sense of countenance or face is also relevant here (*OED* Aspect *sb* 10). See Richard's use
of the word at 159. In both lines, the word is
accented on the second syllable.

24 **at the view** on sight (see *OED* View *sb*,
esp. 14 and 15).

25 **unhappiness** Anne wishes Richard's
issue – 'that' monstrous child she has just finished describing – to inherit his unhappy delivery as well as the unhappiness he brought into
the world. Her curse parallels Richard's account
of his own birth in 1.1. As Shakespeare's audience may have known, Richard III and Queen
Anne did have a child, Edward, who died at
the age of ten, about a year before Richard's
defeat at Bosworth. Shakespeare's Richard has no
child.

27 **by the death** Following Wilson, many
recent editors change 'death' to 'life', because
the death of Richard would presumably make
his wife happy, not miserable. When Anne later
recalls this scene, she quotes herself as having
said 'And be thy wife, if any be so mad, / More
miserable by the life of thee / Than thou hast
made me by my dear lord's death' (4.1.75–7).

> Than I am made by my young lord and thee.
> Come now towards Chertsey with your holy load,
> Taken from Paul's to be interrèd there.   30
> And still as you are weary of this weight,
> Rest you while I lament King Henry's corpse.

Enter RICHARD DUKE OF GLOUCESTER

RICHARD Stay, you that bear the corpse, and set it down.
ANNE What black magician conjures up this fiend
> To stop devoted charitable deeds?   35
RICHARD Villains, set down the corpse, or by Saint Paul,
> I'll make a corpse of him that disobeys.
GENTLEMAN My lord, stand back and let the coffin pass.
RICHARD Unmannered dog, stand thou when I command.
> Advance thy halberd higher than my breast,   40
> Or by Saint Paul, I'll strike thee to my foot
> And spurn upon thee, beggar, for thy boldness.
ANNE What, do you tremble? Are you all afraid?
> Alas, I blame you not, for you are mortal,
> And mortal eyes cannot endure the devil.   45
> Avaunt, thou dreadful minister of hell.
> Thou hadst but power over his mortal body;
> His soul thou canst not have. Therefore be gone.
RICHARD Sweet saint, for charity, be not so curst.

28 Than] F (Then); As Qq   28 young] F; poore Qq   31 weary] F, Q, Q2, Q6; awearie Q3; a wearie Q4–5   31 this] F; the
Qq   33 SD] F; *Enter Glocester.* Qq   36 Villains] F; Villaine Qq   38 SH] F (*Gen.*), Qq (*subst.*)   38 My lord] F, Q, Q2–5
(*subst.*); *not in* Q6   39] Qq; Vnmanner'd Dogge, / Stand'st . . . commaund: F

But whatever she later remembers, Anne is
speaking here of her misery at the deaths of
Henry VI and Prince Edward, and wishing the
same misery – the death of a loved one –
on anyone foolish enough to marry Richard.
(McKellen sees Anne's grief in this scene as
partly a longing for lost privilege. He compares
her acceptance of Richard to 'the youthful widow
Jackie Kennedy's marriage to Aristotle Onassis'
(p. 72).)
  28 thee the corpse.
  29 Chertsey Monastery in Surrey, south-
west of London, where Henry VI was eventually
buried.
  30 Paul's St Paul's Cathedral in London.
  31 still as whenever. When the bearers get
tired, the procession will stop, and Anne will
resume her lament.
  38 SH Hammond says that the 'gentleman'
who speaks cannot be the same person whom
Richard calls an 'unmannered dog' in the next

line, but Richard has already called Brakenbury
'knave' (1.1.102), and clearly does not use low
language only to low persons. On the other
hand, perhaps a guard lowers his halberd toward
Richard's chest as the gentleman is speaking,
and Richard turns on the halberdier rather than
responding to the gentleman.
  38 coffin Possibly a bier or stretcher rather
than a casket (*OED* Coffin *sb* 3b).
  42 spurn trample.
  45 This belief explains why the devil has not
been seen.
  46 Avaunt Begone, go away.
  46 minister agent (*OED* Minister *sb* 2a).
  47 but only.
  49 curst shrewish, with a pun on 'curse'.
  49–50 Anne's rhetorical response counters
Richard's 'Sweet' with 'Foul' and his 'saint' with
'devil'. This exchange establishes a pattern for
the verbal duel that makes up most of the rest of
the scene.

ANNE Foul devil, for God's sake hence, and trouble us not,   50
      For thou hast made the happy earth thy hell,
      Filled it with cursing cries and deep exclaims.
      If thou delight to view thy heinous deeds,
      Behold this pattern of thy butcheries.
      O gentlemen, see, see, dead Henry's wounds   55
      Open their còngealed mouths and bleed afresh.
      Blush, blush, thou lump of foul deformity,
      For 'tis thy presence that exhales this blood
      From cold and empty veins where no blood dwells.
      Thy deeds inhuman and unnatural   60
      Provokes this deluge most unnatural.
      O God, which this blood mad'st, revenge his death.
      O earth, which this blood drink'st, revenge his death.
      Either heav'n with lightning strike the murd'rer dead,
      Or earth gape open wide and eat him quick,   65
      As thou dost swallow up this good king's blood,
      Which his hell-governed arm hath butcherèd.
RICHARD Lady, you know no rules of charity,
      Which renders good for bad, blessings for curses.
ANNE Villain, thou know'st nor law of God nor man.   70
      No beast so fierce but knows some touch of pity.
RICHARD But I know none, and therefore am no beast.
ANNE Oh, wonderful, when devils tell the truth!
RICHARD More wonderful, when angels are so angry.
      Vouchsafe, divine perfection of a woman,   75
      Of these supposèd crimes to give me leave
      By circumstance but to acquit myself.

50] Qq; Foule Diuell, / For . . . not, F   60 deeds] F; deed Qq   66 dost] F, Q, Q2–5 (*subst.*); didst Q6   70 know'st] F; knowest Qq   70 nor law] F; no law Qq   76 crimes] F; euils Qq

50 hence go hence, go away.
54 pattern typical example.
55–6 Henry's wounds . . . bleed afresh. It was believed that a victim's body would bleed again in the presence of the murderer.
58 exhales draws out. *OED* Exhale *v* 2b cites this line as the first use in the sense of causing blood or tears to flow.
60 deeds Q's 'deed' agrees with the singular verb 'Prouokes'. According to Abbott, however, a plural subject paired with an apparently singular verb 'is extremely common in the Folio' (e.g. 2.3.37, 'Untimely storms makes men expect a dearth'). The Folio practice may reflect Shakespeare's use of old, third-person-plural verb endings (Abbott 333).

65 quick alive.
69 Compare Matt. 5.44: 'Blesse them that curse you: do good to them that hate you, praye for them which hurt you.'
70 nor . . . nor Shakespeare often uses 'nor . . . nor' in place of 'neither . . . nor' (see *OED* Nor *conj*[1] 2b). Compare 1.3.55: 'To thee, that hast nor honesty nor grace'.
73 devils tell the truth Dent cites a proverb derived from John 8.44: 'The Devil is a liar and the father of lies' (D 241.1). Anne implies that Richard is neither a man nor a beast because he is a devil.
75 Vouchsafe Grant.
77 circumstance detailed proof, circumstantial evidence.

ANNE Vouchsafe, diffused infection of man,
    Of these known evils but to give me leave
    By circumstance to curse thy cursèd self.   80

RICHARD Fairer than tongue can name thee, let me have
    Some patient leisure to excuse myself.

ANNE Fouler than heart can think thee, thou canst make
    No èxcuse current but to hang thyself.

RICHARD By such despair I should accuse myself.   85

ANNE And by despairing shalt thou stand excused
    For doing worthy vengeance on thyself,
    That didst unworthy slaughter upon others.

RICHARD Say that I slew them not.

ANNE Then say they were not slain.   90
    But dead they are, and, devilish slave, by thee.

RICHARD I did not kill your husband.

ANNE Why, then he is alive.

RICHARD Nay, he is dead, and slain by Edward's hands.

ANNE In thy foul throat thou liest. Queen Margaret saw   95
    Thy murd'rous falchion smoking in his blood,
    The which thou once didst bend against her breast,
    But that thy brothers beat aside the point.

RICHARD I was provokèd by her sland'rous tongue,

---

78 man] F; a man Qq   79 Of] F; For Qq   83–4] Qq; Fouler . . . thee, / Thou . . . currant, / But . . . selfe, F   86 shalt] F; shouldst Qq   88 That] F; Which Qq   90] F; Why then they are not dead, Qq   94 hands] F; hand Qq   95] Qq; In . . . Ly'st, / Queene . . . saw F   96 murd'rous] F; bloudy Qq (*subst.*)   98 brothers] F, Q, Q2; brother Q3–6   99 sland'rous] F; slaunderous Qq (*subst.*)

78 diffused dispersed, distributed widely.

78 infection of man In keeping with Anne's argument that Richard is the devil, F has her calling him not *an* infection but *the* infection, the fundamental infection of humankind. Anne may also be sneering at Richard's pronunciation, since he would have to elide a syllable of 'perfection' to fit his line to the metre, while her line allows her to pronounce all four syllables of 'infection'.

80 Several recent editors (Riverside, Hammond, Oxford) have substituted 't'accuse' for 'to curse', to strengthen the parallels with Richard's speech. Certainly 'curse thy cursèd self' could be wittier, but the point may be that Anne is already starting to tire in her rhetorical contest with Richard. See 27n.

84 no èxcuse current no genuine release from responsibility (*OED* Excuse *sb* 1c; *OED* Current *a* 5). The association of 'currency' with authenticity survives in such expressions as 'the rumour gained currency'.

86–8 Anne sacrifices theology for word-play here, suggesting that Richard would be forgiven the sins of despair and suicide because he would be avenging his own crimes by killing himself. Her argument is weak both as persuasion and as logic, and Richard brushes it aside. Yet this dialogue seems to have delayed emotional effects. In the ghost scene (5.3), when Richard is actually tempted to despair, Anne's theme returns to haunt him: 'Is there a murderer here? No. Yes, I am. / Then fly. What, from myself? Great reason why: / Lest I revenge. What, myself upon myself?' (5.3.187–9).

94 Edward's hands This is a typical equivocation. Edward's hands were involved in the murder, but so were Richard's.

95 throat 'To lie in one's throat' was a proverbial expression for a gross lie (see Tilley T 268).

96 falchion sword (*OED* Falchion 1).

96 smoking in steaming with – that is, still hot from the killing.

That laid their guilt upon my guiltless shoulders.   100
ANNE Thou wast provokèd by thy bloody mind,
    That never dream'st on aught but butcheries.
    Didst thou not kill this king?
RICHARD I grant ye.
ANNE Dost grant me, hedgehog? Then God grant me too   105
    Thou mayst be damnèd for that wicked deed.
    Oh, he was gentle, mild, and virtuous.
RICHARD The better for the king of heaven that hath him.
ANNE He is in heaven, where thou shalt never come.
RICHARD Let him thank me, that holp to send him thither,   110
    For he was fitter for that place than earth.
ANNE And thou unfit for any place but hell.
RICHARD Yes, one place else, if you will hear me name it.
ANNE Some dungeon.
RICHARD Your bedchamber.   115
ANNE Ill rest betide the chamber where thou liest.
RICHARD So will it, madam, till I lie with you.
ANNE I hope so.
RICHARD I know so. But gentle Lady Anne,
    To leave this keen encounter of our wits   120
    And fall something into a slower method,
    Is not the causer of the timeless deaths
    Of these Plantagenets, Henry and Edward,
    As blameful as the executioner?
ANNE Thou wast the cause and most accursed effect.   125
RICHARD Your beauty was the cause of that effect:
    Your beauty, that did haunt me in my sleep
    To undertake the death of all the world,

---

100 That] F; Which Qq   102 That . . . dream'st] F; Which . . . dreamt Qq.   103–4] F; Did'st . . . King. *Glo.* I grant yea Q, Q2; Did'st . . . king? *Glo.* I grant yee Q3–6 (*subst.*)   105] Qq; Do'st . . . Hedge-hogge, / Then . . . too F   108 better] F; fitter Qq   114–15] F; *as one line* Qq   120 keen] F, Q; kinde Q2–6 (*subst.*)   121 something] F; somewhat Qq   122 timeless] F, Q, Q2–3, Q5–6; teem-lesse Q4   125 wast] F; art Qq   127 that] F; which Qq

102 **aught** anything.
105 **hedgehog** An insult derived from Richard's badge, the wild boar.
110 **holp** helped.
116 **betide** befall.
122 **timeless** untimely. The play emphasises prematurity of both birth and death.
125 **effect** Editors have worried over whether Anne can possibly mean that Richard was the 'effect' of his own murders. The debate between Richard and Anne, however, represents a parody of medieval hair-splitting. Richard has just drawn a distinction between the 'causer' of the deaths and the 'executioner'. In Aristotelian terms, he differentiates the final cause or purpose of the murder from the efficient cause, the immediate carrying out of the purpose. Anne responds that he is both kinds of cause, using 'effect' in the sense of fulfilment (*OED* Effect *sb* 7a). Richard, as Hammond points out, immediately shifts the ground of the debate by using 'effect' in the usual sense of 'result' (*OED* Effect *sb* 1a).

So I might live one hour in your sweet bosom.

ANNE If I thought that, I tell thee, homicide,   130
These nails should rend that beauty from my cheeks.

RICHARD These eyes could not endure that beauty's wrack.
You should not blemish it if I stood by.
As all the world is cheerèd by the sun,
So I by that. It is my day, my life.   135

ANNE Black night o'ershade thy day, and death thy life.

RICHARD Curse not thyself, fair creature; thou art both.

ANNE I would I were, to be revenged on thee.

RICHARD It is a quarrel most unnatural
To be revenged on him that loveth thee.   140

ANNE It is a quarrel just and reasonable
To be revenged on him that killed my husband.

RICHARD He that bereft thee, lady, of thy husband
Did it to help thee to a better husband.

ANNE His better doth not breathe upon the earth.   145

RICHARD He lives that loves thee better than he could.

ANNE Name him.

RICHARD   Plantagenet.

ANNE   Why, that was he.

RICHARD The selfsame name, but one of better nature.

ANNE Where is he?

RICHARD   Here.

                    [*She*] *spits at him*
                    Why dost thou spit at me?

ANNE Would it were mortal poison for thy sake.   150

RICHARD Never came poison from so sweet a place.

ANNE Never hung poison on a fouler toad.
Out of my sight. Thou dost infect mine eyes.

---

129 live] F; rest Qq   129 one] F, Q, Q2–4; that Q5–6   131 my] F, Q, Q2–5; their Q6   132 not . . . that] F; neuer . . .
sweet Qq   133 it] F; them Qq   134 sun] F, Q3–6; sonne Q, Q2   137] Qq; Curse . . . Creature, / Thou . . . both.
F   138 were,] F; were Qq   140 thee] F; you Qq   142 killed] F; slew Qq   143 thee] F (the), Qq   146 He] F; Go to, he Qq
(*subst.*)   146 thee] F; you Qq   147] *Steevens*; Name him. / *Rich.* Plantagenet. / *An.* Why . . . he. F; Name him. *Glo.*
Plantagenet. / *La.* Why . . . hee. Q   147 that was he] F, Q, Q2 (*subst.*); what was he? Q3–6 (*subst.*)   149] *Steevens*;
Where is he? / *Rich.* Heere: / Why . . . me. F, Qq (*subst.*)   149 SD] Qq (*Shee spitteth at him*.); *Spits at him* F   153 mine]
F; my Qq

---

131 **rend** tear.
132 **wrack** wreck.
134 **sun** Richard, of course, is not cheered by
the sun, as he told the audience in 1.1.
146 **He lives** There is a man.
147 **that was he** Like Richard, Anne's 'husband' Edward traced his descent from the Plan-

tagenet rulers of England.
147 The two shared lines, 147 and 149, show
not only opposition between the disputants, but
also involvement. Richard manages to transform
Anne's intensity into pity in his 'salt tears' speech
which follows.
148 **nature** character, disposition.

RICHARD Thine eyes, sweet lady, have infected mine.
ANNE Would they were basilisks', to strike thee dead.   155
RICHARD I would they were, that I might die at once,
      For now they kill me with a living death.
      Those eyes of thine from mine have drawn salt tears,
      Shamed their aspècts with store of childish drops.
      These eyes, which never shed remorseful tear,   160
      No, when my father York and Edward wept
      To hear the piteous moan that Rutland made
      When black-faced Clifford shook his sword at him,
      Nor when thy warlike father, like a child,
      Told the sad story of my father's death   165
      And twenty times made pause to sob and weep,
      That all the standers-by had wet their cheeks
      Like trees bedashed with rain. In that sad time
      My manly eyes did scorn an humble tear.
      And what these sorrows could not thence exhale   170
      Thy beauty hath, and made them blind with weeping.
      I never sued to friend nor enemy.
      My tongue could never learn sweet smoothing word.
      But now thy beauty is proposed my fee,
      My proud heart sues and prompts my tongue to speak.   175
               She looks scornfully at him
      Teach not thy lip such scorn, for it was made
      For kissing, lady, not for such contempt.
      If thy revengeful heart cannot forgive,

---

157 they] F, Q, Q2–4, Q6; thy Q5   159 aspècts] F; aspect Qq   160–71] F; *not in* Qq   167 standers-by] *Rowe*; standers by F   172 friend] F, Q, Q2–5; friends Q6   173 smoothing] F; soothing Qq   173 word] F; words Qq   176 SD] F; *not in* Qq   176 lip] F; lips Qq   176 it was] F; they were Qq

154 infected smitten (with love).

155 basilisks The basilisk, also called a 'cockatrice', was a fabled 'king' serpent or monster whose glance was supposedly fatal.

159 Shamed their aspècts Richard claims his tears spoiled the appearance of his eyes – their 'aspects' or faces – and also shamed the function of his eyes, their gaze (*OED* Aspect *sb* 1).

160–71 Pope called these 'beautiful lines'. The passage, which occurs only in F, represents the rhetorical climax of the scene, although its effect is seen by the audience only when Anne refuses to stab Richard.

160 remorseful pitying.

162 Rutland Richard's brother, the Earl of Rutland. Shakespeare portrays his death as a child-murder in *3H6* (1.3). 'To hear the piteous moan' probably means to hear about it, since York and Edward were not present at the death of Rutland, at least in Shakespeare's version.

163 black-faced darkly angry, terrifying.

164 thy warlike father The Earl of Warwick. Richard puns on the name.

170 exhale draw out.

172 sued appealed.

173 smoothing complimentary, flattering. Unusually, Q7 and Q8 also read 'smoothing', against the earlier quartos.

174 is proposed is proposed as. Richard uses the passive, 'is proposed', making it sound as if someone is proposing to him rather than the other way around.

Lo, here I lend thee this sharp-pointed sword,
Which if thou please to hide in this true breast   180
And let the soul forth that adoreth thee,
I lay it naked to the deadly stroke
And humbly beg the death upon my knee.
He lays his breast open[;] *she offers at with his sword*
Nay, do not pause, for I did kill King Henry,
But 'twas thy beauty that provokèd me.   185
Nay, now dispatch; 'twas I that stabbed young Edward,
But 'twas thy heavenly face that set me on.
                    She falls the sword
Take up the sword again, or take up me.
ANNE Arise, dissembler; though I wish thy death,
I will not be thy executioner.   190
RICHARD Then bid me kill myself, and I will do it.
ANNE I have already.
RICHARD   That was in thy rage.
Speak it again, and even with the word,
This hand, which for thy love did kill thy love,
Shall for thy love kill a far truer love.   195
To both their deaths shalt thou be àccessary.
ANNE I would I knew thy heart.
RICHARD 'Tis figured in my tongue.
ANNE I fear me both are false.
RICHARD Then never man was true.   200
ANNE Well, well, put up your sword.
RICHARD Say then my peace is made.

---

180 this true] F, Q, Q2, Q4–6; true this Q3 180 breast] F; bosome Qq 182 the] F, Q, Q2–5; thy Q6 184 SD] F; *not in* Qq 184 for I did kill King Henry] F; twas I that kild your husband Qq (*subst.*) 186 stabbed young Edward] F; kild King Henry Qq 188 SD She falls] F; Here she lets fall Qq 190 thy] F; the Qq 192] *Steevens*; I . . . already. / *Rich.* That . . . rage: F; I . . . already. / *Glo.* Tush that . . . rage: Qq 192 thy] F, Q, Q2; the Q3–6 194 This] F; That Qq 196 shalt thou] F, Q; thou shalt Q2–6 196 be] F, Q, Q2–5; by Q6 200 man was] F, Q3–6; was man Q, Q2

183 upon my knee Editors often add here a direction for Richard to kneel, but the dialogue makes such added direction unnecessary. Richard describes himself as on his knee at 183, and Anne bids him rise at 189.

183 SD *lays his breast open* opens his shirt.

183 SD *offers at* aims (*OED* Offer *v* 5c).

184, 186 Nay Richard's prompt acts as a stage direction, showing that Anne has hesitated.

188 SD *falls* lowers.

196 àccessary participating or sharing in a crime (*OED* Accessary *adj* 1).

197 would wish.

198 figured represented; adorned with rhetorical figures.

201 put up raise, put away. Richard has probably been pointing the sword at his own breast.

202 peace reconciliation; also, the ratification of a treaty between warring parties (*OED* Peace *sb* 1b). In this case, the treaty includes Anne's admission of Richard's love suit.

ANNE That shalt thou know hereafter.

RICHARD But shall I live in hope?

ANNE All men, I hope, live so.   205

RICHARD Vouchsafe to wear this ring.
    Look how my ring encompasseth thy finger.
    Even so thy breast encloseth my poor heart.
    Wear both of them, for both of them are thine.
    And if thy poor devoted servant may   210
    But beg one favour at thy gracious hand,
    Thou dost confirm his happiness forever.

ANNE What is it?

RICHARD That it may please you leave these sad designs
    To him that hath most cause to be a mourner   215
    And presently repair to Crosby House,
    Where, after I have solemnly interred
    At Chertsey monast'ry this noble king
    And wet his grave with my repentant tears,
    I will with all expedient duty see you.   220
    For divers unknown reasons, I beseech you,
    Grant me this boon.

ANNE With all my heart, and much it joys me, too,
    To see you are become so penitent.
    Tressel and Berkeley, go along with me.   225

RICHARD Bid me farewell.

ANNE   'Tis more than you deserve,
    But since you teach me how to flatter you,
    Imagine I have said farewell already.
                  Exeunt two with Anne

GENTLEMAN Towards Chertsey, noble lord?

RICHARD No, to Whitefriars; there attend my coming.   230
         Exeunt [all but Richard with the] corpse

203 shalt thou] F; shall you Qq   204 shall I] F, Q; I shall Q2–6   206 SH] Qq (*Glo.*); *not in* F   206] F; Voutsafe . . . ring. / *La*. To take is not to giue. Qq   207 my] F; this Qq   208 my] F, Q, Q2–4; me Q5–6   209 Wear] F, Q, Q2–3; Were Q4–6   210 devoted] F, Q; *not in* Q2–6   210 servant] F; suppliant Qq   214 may] F; would Qq   214 you] F; thee Qq   215 most] F; more Qq   216 House] F; place Qq   218 monast'ry] F; monastery Qq   226] *Steevens*; Bid . . . farwell. / *An*. 'Tis . . . deserue; F, Qq (*subst.*)   228 SD] F (*Exit two with Anne.*); *Exit*. Qq   229] F; *Glo*. Sirs take vp the corse. / *Ser*. Towards . . . Lord. Qq (*subst.*)   229 SH] F (*Gent.*); *Ser*. Qq   230 SD *all but Richard with the*] *This edn*; *Exit Coarse* F; *Exeunt. manet Gl*. Qq (*subst.*)

205 **All men** Anne's evasion draws on the Christian commonplace that everyone lives in hope of heaven, probably suggested by her word 'hereafter' (203).

206 Anne's silent assent in F implies a more complete defeat than her rather weak reservation in Q.

206 **Vouchsafe** Agree.

216 **presently** immediately.
216 **repair** withdraw.
216 **Crosby House** Richard's house in London, also called Crosby Place.
221 **unknown** secret.
230 **Whitefriars** The Carmelite religious house in Fleet Street, London. Holinshed says

Was ever woman in this humour wooed?
Was ever woman in this humour won?
I'll have her, but I will not keep her long.
What, I that killed her husband and his father,
To take her in her heart's extremest hate,   235
With curses in her mouth, tears in her eyes,
The bleeding witness of my hatred by,
Having God, her conscience, and these bars against me,
And I no friends to back my suit withal
But the plain devil and dissembling looks?   240
And yet to win her, all the world to nothing!
Ha!
Hath she forgot already that brave prince,
Edward, her lord, whom I some three months since
Stabbed in my angry mood at Tewkesbury?   245
A sweeter and a lovelier gentleman,
Framed in the prodigality of nature,
Young, valiant, wise, and (no doubt) right royal,
The spacious world cannot again afford.
And will she yet abase her eyes on me,   250
That cropped the golden prime of this sweet prince
And made her widow to a woeful bed?
On me, whose all not equals Edward's moiety?
On me, that halts and am misshapen thus?

---

234 his] F, Q, Q2; her Q3–6   235 hate] F, Q; heate Q2–6   237 my] F; her Qq   239 no friends] F; nothing Qq   239
withal] F, Q3–6 (*subst.*); at all Q, Q2   241–2] F; *as one line* Qq   250 abase] F; debase Qq   254 halts] F; halt Qq   254
misshapen] F; vnshapen Qq

the body was taken to Blackfriars, the Domini-
can monastery on the Thames. The detail
here, apparently invented by Shakespeare, shows
Richard's peremptory habits. He contradicts,
evidently just for the sake of contradiction, what
he told Anne he would do (218).
   234 his father See 1.1.155 n.
   237 bleeding witness The bleeding body of
Henry VI.
   237 by nearby.
   238 bars The obstacles he has just mentioned.
   239 I no friends I having no friends; 'having'
is understood from 238.
   239 withal with (*OED* Withal *prep*), besides
(*OED* Withal *adv* 1). Both meanings apply.
   241 all the world to nothing with everything against me and nothing for me.

   245 mood fit of temper.
   245 Tewkesbury Shakespeare represents the
battle of Tewkesbury (1471) in *3H6*.
   247 Framed Created, formed.
   247 prodigality lavishness, abundance.
   248 right properly, completely (see *OED*
Right *adv*).
   250 abase her eyes degrade herself by looking favourably.
   251 cropped cut short. The language suggests a premature harvesting of the 'golden' and
'sweet' young prince, a reminder of Richard's
association with winter.
   253 whose . . . moiety whose whole worth
doesn't equal half of Edward's.
   254 halts limps.

My dukedom to a beggarly denier,   255
I do mistake my person all this while.
Upon my life, she finds (although I cannot)
Myself to be a marv'lous proper man.
I'll be at charges for a looking-glass
And entertain a score or two of tailors   260
To study fashions to adorn my body.
Since I am crept in favour with myself,
I will maintain it with some little cost.
But first I'll turn yon fellow in his grave
And then return lamenting to my love.   265
Shine out, fair sun, till I have bought a glass,
That I may see my shadow as I pass.   *Exit*

1.3 *Enter the* QUEEN MOTHER [ELIZABETH], LORD RIVERS *and*
LORD GREY [*and the* MARQUESS OF DORSET]

RIVERS Have patience, madam. There's no doubt his majesty
        Will soon recover his accustomed health.
GREY In that you brook it ill, it makes him worse.

---

255 to] F, Q, Q2–4; to be Q5–6   258 marv'lous] F (maru'llous); merueilous Qq (*subst.*)   260 a] F some Qq   261 adorn]
F, Q, Q2; adore Q3–6   263 some] F, Q, Q2; a Q3–6   264 yon] F, Q, Q2–3; you Q4–6   266 out] F, Q, Q2–5; our
Q6   Act 1, Scene 3   1.3] F (*Scena Tertia.*); *not in* Qq   0 SD *and the Marquess of* DORSET] Hanmer; *Enter the Queene
Mother, Lord Riuers, and Lord Gray.* F; *Enter Queene, Lord Riuers, Gray.* Qq (*subst.*)   1 SH] F (*Riu*), Qq (*Ri. / or / Ry. /
later/ Riu. / or / Ryu.*)

255 **denier** A very small sum. The denier was
a minute French coin, the equivalent of a fraction
of a penny (*OED* Denier[3] 1).
    259 **be at charges for** go to the expense of.
    260 **entertain** employ.
    262 Now that I know I'm so handsome.
    264 **yon fellow** the corpse. Richard's casual
reference to the deceased king as 'fellow' is a
mark of his disrespect.
    266 **glass** mirror.
    266–7 Echoing the sun/shadow imagery of the
first scene, Richard mocks the 'fair sun' and fair
courtiers who 'court an amorous looking-glass'
(1.1.15). As before, he associates himself with
shadows.

Act 1, Scene 3

Thomas More and the chroniclers who borrow from him describe the animosity between
the queen's family and the king's nobles, especially Lord Hastings. Shakespeare adds Queen

Margaret as the voice of older grievances from
the Wars of the Roses.
    0 SD QUEEN MOTHER Widow of the king and
mother of the current monarch. At this point,
Elizabeth is not actually the Queen Mother, but
the Queen Consort, the wife of the king. Whoever wrote this stage direction may have been
thinking of Elizabeth's role in the play, which is
far more that of mother than of queen.
    0 SD DORSET Neither F nor Q gives Dorset an
entrance here, so he could be brought on nearer
his first line (184). The interruption of a separate entrance seems unjustified, however, and as
Hammond observes, Dorset's arrival with one of
his adversaries – either Buckingham or Richard –
is 'dramatically unlikely' (1.3.0 SD n.). Like
Rivers's, Dorset's significance in this scene is not
primarily in what he says but in his presence. He
helps swell out two distinct factions – the relatives of Elizabeth and the enemies of Margaret.
    3 **brook** take.

Therefore, for God's sake, entertain good comfort,
And cheer his grace with quick and merry eyes.   5
ELIZABETH If he were dead, what would betide on me?
GREY No other harm but loss of such a lord.
ELIZABETH The loss of such a lord includes all harms.
GREY The heavens have blessed you with a goodly son
   To be your comforter when he is gone.   10
ELIZABETH Ah, he is young, and his minority
   Is put unto the trust of Richard Gloucester,
   A man that loves not me nor none of you.
RIVERS Is it concluded he shall be Protector?
ELIZABETH It is determined, not concluded yet,   15
   But so it must be if the king miscarry.

Enter BUCKINGHAM *and* [STANLEY EARL OF] DERBY

GREY Here come the lords of Buckingham and Derby.
BUCKINGHAM Good time of day unto your royal grace.
STANLEY God make your majesty joyful, as you have been.
ELIZABETH The Countess Richmond, good my lord of Derby,   20

---

5 with quick] F, Q2–6; quick Q   5 eyes] F; words QQ   6 on] F; of QQ   6] F *repeats this line at the top of a new page*   7
SH] F (Gray); *Ry.* Q; *Ri.* Q2–6   8 harms] F; harme QQ   11 Ah] F; Oh QQ   12 Richard Gloucester] F (Glouster); Rich.
Glocester QQ   14 Is it] F, Q, Q2–5; It is Q6   16 SD] *Theobald (Enter Buckingham and Stanley.); Enter Buckingham and
Derby.* F; *Enter Buck. Darby* QQ   17 come the lords] Q, Q2 (Lords); comes the Lords Q3–6; comes the Lord F   19 SH]
Theobald (and throughout); Der. F; *Dar.* QQ   20 lord] Q5–6; L. F; Lo Q, Q2–4

---

4 entertain . . . comfort be comforted, cheer up.

5 eyes Q's 'quick and mery words' contrasts sharply to Elizabeth's first line, which is anything but merry. In neither version does she pay any attention to Grey's efforts to cheer her.

6 betide on become of.

6 The catchword printed at the bottom of the previous page is 'Gray', suggesting that F repeated this line accidentally.

7 The quartos give this line to Rivers, which changes the dialogue from a two- to a three-way conversation.

9 Grey continues the word-play on son/sun begun by Richard in 1.1. Prince Edward, of all the queen's sons, is a blessing from heaven because he is heir to the throne. Lord Grey was also Elizabeth's son, although Shakespeare may have been uncertain about the relationship. See 37n.

12 Richard has been appointed the young prince's guardian or Protector to help him rule until he comes of age.

15 determined, not concluded decided, but not finally approved. In the sixteenth century, as

now, the words were virtual synonyms (*OED* Conclude *v* IV). By forcing them to mean different things here, Shakespeare recalls the play's thematic exploration of determinism and free will. Compare the ambiguity of Richard's 'I am determinèd to prove a villain' at 1.1.30, which implies that he has both decided and is predestined to do evil. Like Macbeth, Richard draws no distinction between fate and his own decisions.

16 miscarry die. Elizabeth's use of the word here also suggests prematurity, as in the miscarriage of a child. For the king to 'miscarry' in this context would be for him to die before his time – that is, before his son grows up.

16 SD DERBY The spelling in Q, 'Darby', indicates the pronunciation. This character is called by his family name, 'Stanley', rather than by his (later) title, Earl of Derby. This edition uses 'Stanley' as a speech heading throughout.

20 Countess Richmond The countess was Stanley's wife and the mother, by her first marriage, of Henry Tudor, Earl of Richmond. Richmond becomes Henry VII at the end of this play.

To your good prayer will scarcely say amen.
Yet Derby, not withstanding she's your wife
And loves not me, be you, good lord, assured
I hate not you for her proud arrogance.

STANLEY I do beseech you, either not believe   25
The envious slanders of her false accusers,
Or if she be accused on true report,
Bear with her weakness, which I think proceeds
From wayward sickness and no grounded malice.

ELIZABETH Saw you the king today, my lord of Derby?   30
STANLEY But now the Duke of Buckingham and I
Are come from visiting his majesty.
ELIZABETH What likelihood of his amendment, lords?
BUCKINGHAM Madam, good hope. His grace speaks cheerfully.
ELIZABETH God grant him health. Did you confer with him?   35
BUCKINGHAM Ay, madam. He desires to make atonement
Between the Duke of Gloucester and your brothers,
And between them and my Lord Chamberlain,
And sent to warn them to his royal presence.
ELIZABETH Would all were well, but that will never be.   40
I fear our happiness is at the height.

---

21 prayer] F; praiers Qq (*subst.*)   24 arrogance] F, Q, Q2; arrogancie Q3–6 (*subst.*)   25 do] F, Q, Q2; *not in* Q3–6   26 false] F, Q, Q2; *not in* Q3–6   27 on] F; in Qq   30 SH] F (*Qu.*); *Ry.* Qq (*subst.*)   30 of Derby] F, Q, Q2–5 (*subst.*); Darby Q6   32 Are come] F; Came Qq   33 What] F, Q3–6; With Q, Q2   34 speaks] F, Q, Q2, Q5–6 (*subst.*); speaketh Q3   36 Ay, madam] F (*subst.*); Madame we did Qq (*subst.*)   36 to make] F, Q, Q2–3, Q5–6; make Q4   37 Between] F; Betwixt Qq   38 between] F; betwixt Qq   39 to his] F, Q, Q2–5; ot his Q6   41 height] F; highest Qq (*subst.*)

---

29 wayward obstinate, not yielding to treatment (*OED* Wayward *a* 1e). Stanley's dithering equivocation in this speech suggests that the 'wayward sickness' is the countess's own obstinate will.

31 But Just.

33 amendment recovery.

36 atonement reconciliation.

37 brothers Of the characters in this play, only Lord Rivers was actually Elizabeth's brother, but Shakespeare seems to think of her grown son Grey as another. At 3.1.6, for example, young Prince Edward says he wants 'more uncles here to welcome me', apparently meaning Rivers and Grey, whom Richard has imprisoned.

38 Lord Chamberlain Hastings. In other words, the king wants to make peace between Richard and Hastings, on the one hand, and the relatives of the queen, on the other. Buckingham's rather roundabout way of saying it allows him to identify each group of characters for the audience.

39 warn summon.

40–1 Shakespeare often links impending disaster to a wish or statement that all will be well. Compare Elizabeth's remark here to that of the Third Citizen at 2.3.38–9: 'All may be well, but if God sort it so, / 'Tis more than we deserve or I expect.' In later tragedies, the Shakespearean 'all's well' becomes increasingly ironic. See Capulet's lines just before Juliet's supposed suicide: 'Tush, I will stir about, / And all things shall be well, I warrant thee, wife' (*Rom.* 4.2.39–40), and Iago's false comfort to Desdemona: 'Go in, and weep not; all things shall be well' (*Oth.* 4.2.171). Sixteenth-century expressions often associate the word 'well' with death. Ross assures Macduff that his murdered wife and children are 'well' (*Mac.* 4.3.177), and Cleopatra tells the messenger, 'we use / To say the dead are well' (*Ant.* 2.4.33).

Enter RICHARD [*and* HASTINGS]

RICHARD They do me wrong, and I will not endure it.
　　　　Who is it that complains unto the king
　　　　That I, forsooth, am stern and love them not?
　　　　By holy Paul, they love his grace but lightly   45
　　　　That fill his ears with such dissentious rumours.
　　　　Because I cannot flatter and look fair,
　　　　Smile in men's faces, smooth, deceive, and cog,
　　　　Duck with French nods and apish courtesy,
　　　　I must be held a rancorous enemy.   50
　　　　Cannot a plain man live and think no harm,
　　　　But thus his simple truth must be abused
　　　　With silken, sly, insinuating jacks?
GREY To who in all this presence speaks your grace?
RICHARD To thee, that hast nor honesty nor grace.   55
　　　　When have I injured thee? When done thee wrong?
　　　　Or thee? Or thee? Or any of your faction?
　　　　A plague upon you all. His royal grace,
　　　　Whom God preserve better than you would wish,
　　　　Cannot be quiet scarce a breathing while   60
　　　　But you must trouble him with lewd complaints.
ELIZABETH Brother of Gloucester, you mistake the matter.
　　　　The king, on his own royal disposition,
　　　　And not provoked by any suitor else,
　　　　Aiming, belike, at your interior hatred,   65
　　　　That in your outward action shows itself

---

41 SD *and* HASTINGS] *Hanmer; Enter Richard.* F; *Enter Glocester.* Qq   43 is it] F; *are they* Qq   44 and] F, Q, Q2–5; *not in* Q6   47 look] F; *speake* Qq   52 his] F, Q, Q2–4; *in* Q5–6   53 With] F; *By* Qq   54 SH] F; *Ry.* Q; *Ri.* Q2–6   54 who] F; *whom* Q, Q2–5; *home* Q6   54 all] F, Q, Q2–5; *not in* Q6   55 hast nor] F, Q, Q2–3, Q5–6; *hast not* Q4   58 grace] F; *person* Qq   63 on] F; *of* Qq   66 That] F; *Which* Qq   66 action] F; *actions* Qq

44 forsooth in truth. Used ironically, as often in Shakespeare's time and always today (see *OED* Forsooth *sb* 1b).

47 look fair put on a charming appearance. Q's 'speake', like its 'words' in 5, shifts the emphasis from the visual to the verbal.

48 smooth compliment.

48 cog cheat, trick (*OED* Cog *v* 3). Like Richard's assertion in his opening speech that he cannot play 'sportive tricks' (1.1.14), this line reminds the audience of how tricky he really is.

49 Duck . . . nods Bow in the affected French way.

51 plain open, honest.

53 silken smooth, glib.

53 jacks commoners, ill-bred persons (*OED* Jack *sb¹* 2a). Richard associates low-class origins with courtly manners by way of insult to Elizabeth and her family. See 71–2.

55 nor . . . nor neither . . . nor.

60 a breathing while long enough to take a breath.

61 lewd common, vulgar (*OED* Lewd 3). Another class slur.

63 on . . . disposition of his own will as king.

65 belike probably.

Against my children, brothers, and myself,
Makes him to send, that he may learn the ground.
RICHARD I cannot tell. The world is grown so bad
    That wrens make prey where eagles dare not perch.   70
    Since every jack became a gentleman,
    There's many a gentle person made a jack.
ELIZABETH Come, come, we know your meaning, brother Gloucester.
    You envy my advancement and my friends'.
    God grant we never may have need of you.   75
RICHARD Meantime, God grants that I have need of you.
    Our brother is imprisoned by your means,
    My self disgraced, and the nobility
    Held in contempt, while great promotions
    Are daily given to ennoble those   80
    That scarce some two days since were worth a noble.
ELIZABETH By Him that raised me to this careful height
    From that contented hap which I enjoyed,
    I never did incense his majesty
    Against the Duke of Clarence, but have been   85
    An earnest advocate of plead for him.
    My lord, you do me shameful injury
    Falsely to draw me in these vile suspècts.
RICHARD You may deny that you were not the mean
    Of my Lord Hastings' late imprisonment.   90
RIVERS She may, my lord, for –
RICHARD She may, Lord Rivers, why, who knows not so?
    She may do more, sir, than denying that.

---

67 children] F; kindred Qq (*subst.*)   67 brothers] F; brother Qq   68 that he may learn the ground.] F; that thereby he may gather / The ground of your ill will and to remoue it. Qq (grounds Q6)   70 make prey] F, Q2; make pray Q; may prey Q3–6   71 jack] Qq (Iacke); Iaeke F   74 envy my] F, Q; enuy mine Q2–6 (*subst.*)   76 grants] F, Q, Q2; grant Q3–6   76 I] F; we Qq   79 while great] F; whilst many faire Qq   89 mean] F; cause Qq   91 lord, for] F; Lord Qq

67 children, brothers Elizabeth has only one brother, Rivers, in this play, although Grey seems to function as an all-purpose relative (see 37n). Her children are Grey, Dorset, the two young princes and their older sister, Elizabeth of York, who is discussed but does not appear.
68 Makes . . . send Causes him to send for you.
69 cannot tell do not really know.
70 wrens make prey Theobald notes the similarity to Hastings's speech at 1.1.133–4: 'More pity that the eagles should be mewed / While kites and buzzards play at liberty.' To Theobald, the correspondence suggests that Qq's 'prey' must be the correct reading for Hastings's line.

74 friends' family's. 'Friends' often means kindred in Shakespeare.
76 have need of you am lacking something because of you. Richard explains what he 'needs' in the next line. He is not asking Elizabeth for favours, but playing his customary rhetorical games.
77 Our brother Clarence, brother to both Richard and the king.
81 noble Coin worth less than half a pound.
82 careful full of care.
83 hap fortune.
88 suspècts suspicions.
89 mean means.

She may help you to many fair preferments,
And then deny her aiding hand therein,   95
And lay those honours on your high desert.
What may she not? She may, ay, marry, may she.

RIVERS What, marry, may she?

RICHARD What, marry, may she? Marry with a king,
A bachelor, and a handsome stripling too.   100
I wis your grandam had a worser match.

ELIZABETH My lord of Gloucester, I have too long borne
Your blunt upbraidings and your bitter scoffs.
By heaven, I will acquaint his majesty
Of those gross taunts that oft I have endured.   105
I had rather be a country servant maid
Than a great queen with this condition,
To be so baited, scorned, and stormèd at.
Small joy have I in being England's queen.

Enter old QUEEN MARGARET

MARGARET [*Aside*] And lessened be that small, God I beseech him.   110
Thy honour, state, and seat is due to me.

RICHARD What? Threat you me with telling of the king?
I will avouch't in presence of the king.

---

96 desert] F; deserts Qq   97 ay] F (I); yea Qq   100 and] F; *not in* Qq   101 I wis] F, Q4–6; Iwis Q, Q2–3   101 a worser] F, Q, Q2, Q4, Q6; aworser Q3; worser Q5   105 Of] F; With Qq   105 that oft I] F; I often Qq   108 so baited, scorned, and stormèd] F; thus, taunted, scorned, and baited Qq   109 SD] F; *Enter Qu. Margaret.* Qq (*at 108*); *Enter Queen MARGARET, at a Distance.* / *Capell*   110, 116, 124, 132, 135, 141, 153 SD] *Collier*; *not in* F, Qq   110 him] F; thee Qq   112] F; What . . . King, / Tell him and spare not, looke what I haue said Q, Q2; I sayd Q3–6 (*subst.*)   112 of] F, Q, Q3–5; or Q2; *not in* Q6   113 avouch't] F; auouch Qq

96 **desert** deserving.
97 **marry** indeed. This is a mild oath meaning 'by the Virgin Mary'.
100 **stripling** youth.
101 **I wis** 'Iwis' means 'certainly'. F splits the word, a common usage perhaps derived from the misapprehension that it means 'I know' (see *OED* Iwis).
108 **baited** tormented, as in bear-baiting.
109 SD Margaret is the widow of Henry VI. Her Qq entrance comes one line earlier than in F, a position preferred by many editors because it gives the audience time to see her listening to Elizabeth's lament before she speaks. Although the F stage directions do not mention it, the dialogue makes clear that Margaret continues to listen and respond unnoticed by the others until she speaks aloud at 156. Historically, Queen Margaret was imprisoned after the battle of

Tewkesbury in 1471 (dramatised in *3H6*) and then exiled to France. Shakespeare brings her back as a kind of spirit of Lancastrian vengeance.
110 SH Both F and Qq have trouble with Margaret's speech headings in this scene, since both Margaret and Elizabeth are queens. F tends generally to use proper names rather than titles, and finally settles on *Mar*. The quartos usually employ some variant of *Qu. Mar.*
110 **God . . . him** I beseech God.
111 **state** rank.
111 **seat** throne.
112 The extra line inserted in Qq breaks up F's repeated phrase 'of the King'. In F, the repetition of the same phrase at the ends of two lines (the rhetorical figure, epistrophe) stresses Richard's audacity. Not only does he not care if Elizabeth tells the king what he has said, but he will say it again in the presence of the king.

I dare adventure to be sent to th'Tower.

'Tis time to speak. My pains are quite forgot.   115

MARGARET [*Aside*] Out, devil. I do remember them too well.

Thou kill'dst my husband, Henry, in the Tower,

And Edward, my poor son, at Tewkesbury.

RICHARD Ere you were queen, ay, or your husband king,

I was a pack-horse in his great affairs,   120

A weeder-out of his proud adversaries,

A liberal rewarder of his friends.

To royalise his blood I spent mine own.

MARGARET [*Aside*] Ay, and much better blood than his or thine.

RICHARD In all which time, you and your husband Grey   125

Were factious for the house of Lancaster,

And, Rivers, so were you. Was not your husband

In Margaret's battle at Saint Albans slain?

Let me put in your minds, if you forget,

What you have been ere this, and what you are;   130

Withal, what I have been, and what I am.

MARGARET [*Aside*] A murderous villain, and so still thou art.

RICHARD Poor Clarence did forsake his father Warwick,

Ay, and forswore himself, which Jesu pardon.

MARGARET [*Aside*] Which God revenge.   135

RICHARD To fight on Edward's party for the crown.

114] F; *not in* Qq   115] Qq; 'Tis . . . speake, / My . . . forgot. F   115 My] F, Q, Q2–5; when Q6   116] Qq; Out Diuell, /
I . . . well: F   116 do remember] F; remember Qq   117 kill'dst] F; slewest Qq   119] Qq; Ere . . . Queene, / I . . . King:
F   119 ay] F (I); yea Qq   119 or] F, Qq; of Q2 (*Trinity College, Cambridge, copy*)   121 weeder-out] Capell; weeder out F,
Qq   123 spent] F; spilt Qq   124] Qq; I . . . blood / Then . . . thine. F   124 Ay] F (I); Yea Qq   129 minds] F, Q, Q2–4
(*subst.*); minde Q5; mind Q6   129 you] F; yours Qq   130 this] F; now Qq   134 Ay] F; Yea Qq

114 **adventure to be** risk being.

115 **My . . . forgot** Edward has forgotten the
trouble I took (to make him king).

116 **Out** An expression of anger (*OED* Out
int 2).

116 **remember them** Margaret turns
Richard's mention of the 'pains' he took for
Edward into a reminder of the 'pains' he caused
her. Although Richard does not yet hear her,
Margaret has already scored a point in their
rhetorical battle.

119 **ay** The fact that only one surviving copy
of Q2 contains 'of' instead of 'or' in this line suggests a stop-press correction in the midst of the
print run.

123 **spent** The historical Richard was too
young to help 'royalise' his brother, and Shakespeare's character, who does fight in Edward's
wars (*3H6*), is not injured. He means that he

exhausted himself – 'spent' his blood – rather
than 'spilt' it as in Qq. Margaret turns his own
word against him again in the next line, implying
that 'spent' means 'wasted'.

125–8 In *3H6* (3.2), Shakespeare represents
Elizabeth's first husband as a Yorkist. Histori-
cally, he died fighting on the Lancastrian side, as
Richard says here.

126 **Were factious for** Were on the side of.

128 **Margaret's battle** The battle Margaret
fought (in *3H6* she acts as political head of the
army) and also the main body of her army.

131 **Withal** Additionally.

133 **his father Warwick** His father-in-law,
the same Earl of Warwick whose daughter Anne
marries Richard in this play. Clarence and
Warwick deserted the Yorkist side to fight for
the house of Lancaster, but Clarence later turned
again and fought for his brother.

And for his meed, poor lord, he is mewed up.
I would to God my heart were flint, like Edward's,
Or Edward's soft and pitiful, like mine.
I am too childish-foolish for this world.   140
MARGARET [*Aside*] Hie thee to hell for shame, and leave this world,
    Thou cacodemon. There thy kingdom is.
RIVERS My lord of Gloucester, in those busy days
    Which here you urge to prove us enemies,
    We followed then our lord, our sovereign king.   145
    So should we you, if you should be our king.
RICHARD If I should be? I had rather be a pedlar.
    Far be it from my heart, the thought thereof.
ELIZABETH As little joy, my lord, as you suppose
    You should enjoy were you this country's king,   150
    As little joy you may suppose in me
    That I enjoy, being the queen thereof.
MARGARET [*Aside*] A little joy enjoys the queen thereof,
    For I am she, and altogether joyless.
    I can no longer hold me patient –   155
    Hear me, you wrangling pirates, that fall out
    In sharing that which you have pilled from me.
    Which of you trembles not that looks on me?
    If not that I am queen, you bow like subjects,
    Yet that by you deposed, you quake like rebels.   160
    Ah, gentle villain, do not turn away.

---

140 childish-foolish] *Theobald*; childish foolish F, Q3–6; childish, foolish Q, Q2   141 this] F; the Qq   145 sovereign] F; lawfull Qq   146 we you] F, Q, Q2–5; we now Q6   147 If I] F, Q, Q2–5; If Q6   148 thereof] F; of it Qq   149 SH] F, Q, Q2 (*Qu.*); *Qu. M.* Q3–4; *Qu. Nar.* Q5; *Qu. Mar.* Q6   151 you may] F; may you Qq   156] F, Qq; *Capell adds* SD *advancing*   157 sharing] F, Q; sharing out Q2–6   158 looks] F, Q, Q2–4; looke Q5–6   159 am] F; being Qq   160 by you] F, Q, Q2, Q5–6; byou Q3; by on Q4   161 Ah] F; O Qq

137 **meed** reward.
137 **mewed up** imprisoned.
141 **Hie** Hurry.
142 **cacodemon** evil spirit.
144 **urge** bring up.
153 **A little joy** Despite the agreement of all texts on this reading, editors have usually emended to 'As little joy', for parallelism with 149 and 151. Oxford reads 'Ah', claiming that 'As Margaret says she is "altogether joyless" in the next line, it would be preposterous for her to claim here that she "enjoys a little joy" (Wells and Taylor, p. 234). But Margaret's point – another of her rhetorical tricks – is that the 'little

joy' enjoyed by the queen is even smaller than Elizabeth thinks, because it is Margaret's, and therefore no joy at all.
157 **pilled** pillaged.
159–60 If you do not bow because I am the queen and you are my subjects, then at least you tremble because you deposed me and you know you are rebels.
161 **gentle villain** well-born villain. Since 'villain' means a lowly person (*OED* Villain *sb* 1), Margaret's insult to Richard is the inverse of his slurs on Elizabeth and her family for being low-born royalty.

RICHARD Foul wrinkled witch, what mak'st thou in my sight?
MARGARET But repetition of what thou hast marred,
        That will I make before I let thee go.
RICHARD Wert thou not banishèd on pain of death?   165
MARGARET I was. But I do find more pain in banishment
        Than death can yield me here by my abode.
        A husband and a son thou ow'st to me –
        And thou a kingdom – all of you allegiance.
        This sorrow that I have by right is yours,   170
        And all the pleasures you usurp are mine.
RICHARD The curse my noble father laid on thee
        When thou didst crown his warlike brows with paper
        And with thy scorns drew'st rivers from his eyes,
        And then to dry them gav'st the duke a clout   175
        Steeped in the faultless blood of pretty Rutland –
        His curses then, from bitterness of soul
        Denounced against thee, are all fall'n upon thee,
        And God, not we, hath plagued thy bloody deed.
ELIZABETH So just is God, to right the innocent.   180
HASTINGS Oh, 'twas the foulest deed to slay that babe,
        And the most merciless, that e'er was heard of.
RIVERS Tyrants themselves wept when it was reported.
DORSET No man but prophesied revenge for it.
BUCKINGHAM Northumberland, then present, wept to see it.   185
MARGARET What? Were you snarling all before I came,
        Ready to catch each other by the throat,

165–7] F; *not in* Qq   168 to] F, Q, Q2–5; vnto Q6   170 This] F; The Qq   171 are] F, Q, Q2; is Q3–6   172 my] F, Q,
Q2–5; me Q6   174 scorns] F; scorne Qq   176 faultless] F, Q, Q2; *not in* Q3–6   178 all fall'n] F, Q, Q2; fallen Q3–6

162 witch Margaret is typical of women likely
to be accused of witchcraft: old, solitary, angry,
and vengeful. Belief in witchcraft was widespread
in Shakespeare's England.
  162–3 what mak'st . . . marred what are
you doing? Only repeating your evil deeds. To
'make and mar' was proverbial and a frequent
expression in Shakespeare (see Tilley M48, Dent
M48).
  164 That That repetition.
  169 And thou a kingdom Spoken to Elizabeth. Margaret addresses first Richard (168),
then Elizabeth, then the whole group.
  172–5 For Margaret's mocking of the captured
York and his curse – that she will find as little

comfort as she gives him – see *3H6* 1.4.
  175 clout cloth.
  178 Denounced Angrily proclaimed.
  181 babe Historically, Rutland was one of
Richard's older brothers, but Shakespeare makes
him a child, roughly the same age as the young
princes in this play.
  184 No man but A double negative – no man
didn't (that is, every man did) prophesy revenge.
  185 Northumberland The third Earl of
Northumberland, an enemy of the house of York
in *3H6*. Not present at the death of Rutland,
Northumberland is shown moved to tears by the
Duke of York's grief for his son (*3H6* 1.4.150–1).

And turn you all your hatred now on me?
Did York's dread curse prevail so much with heaven
That Henry's death, my lovely Edward's death,   190
Their kingdom's loss, my woeful banishment,
Should all but answer for that peevish brat?
Can curses pierce the clouds, and enter heaven?
Why then, give way, dull clouds, to my quick curses.
Though not by war, by surfeit die your king,   195
As ours by murder to make him a king.
Edward thy son, that now is Prince of Wales,
For Edward our son, that was Prince of Wales,
Die in his youth by like untimely violence.
Thyself a queen, for me that was a queen,   200
Outlive thy glory, like my wretched self.
Long mayst thou live to wail thy children's death
And see another, as I see thee now,
Decked in thy rights, as thou art stalled in mine.
Long die thy happy days before thy death,   205
And after many lengthened hours of grief,
Die neither mother, wife, nor England's queen.
Rivers and Dorset, you were standers-by,
And so wast thou, Lord Hastings, when my son
Was stabbed with bloody daggers. God I pray him,   210
That none of you may live his natural age,
But by some unlooked accident cut off.

RICHARD   Have done thy charm, thou hateful, withered hag.

MARGARET   And leave out thee? Stay, dog, for thou shalt hear me.
If heaven have any grievous plague in store   215
Exceeding those that I can wish upon thee,
Oh, let them keep it till thy sins be ripe

188 all . . . now] F, Q; now . . . all Q2–6   192 Should] F; Could Qq   195 Though] F; If Qq   195 king,] F, Q, Q2, Q6; king? Q3–5   196 ours] F, Q, Q2; our Q3, Q5–6; out Q4   197 that] F; which Qq   198 our] F; my Qq   198 that] F; which Qq   199 violence] F, Q, Q2–5; violences Q6   202 death] F; losse Qq   204 rights] F, Q; glorie Q2–6   208 standers-by] *Rowe*; standers by F, Qq   209 wast] F, Q, Q2; was Q3–6   211 his] F; your Qq   214 thee?] F, Q3–6; the Q, Q2

192 **but answer for** only equal.
192 **peevish** fretful.
194 **quick** sharp, lively; the opposite of 'dull'.
195 **surfeit** over-indulgence. Compare Richard's observation that Edward 'hath kept an evil diet long' (1.1.140). Edward IV is described in Shakespeare's sources as intemperate.
204 **Decked** Draped, dressed.
204 **stalled** installed; but also with suggestions that Elizabeth is stopped and confined in her undeserved position.

211 **natural age** normal life span.
212 **But** But be.
212 **unlooked** unlooked-for, unanticipated.
217 **till . . . ripe** until your sins are as great as possible. Compare Margaret's imagery of ripening and rotting at 4.4.1–2: 'So now prosperity begins to mellow / And drop into the rotten mouth of death.' If the winter of discontent is Richard's natural season, the autumn of overripe revenge is Margaret's.

And then hurl down their indignation
On thee, the troubler of the poor world's peace.
The worm of conscience still begnaw thy soul.   220
Thy friends suspect for traitors while thou liv'st,
And take deep traitors for thy dearest friends.
No sleep close up that deadly eye of thine,
Unless it be while some tormenting dream
Affrights thee with a hell of ugly devils.   225
Thou elvish-marked, abortive, rooting hog,
Thou that wast sealed in thy nativity
The slave of nature and the son of hell.
Thou slander of thy heavy mother's womb,
Thou loathèd issue of thy father's loins,   230
Thou rag of honour, thou detested –
RICHARD   Margaret.
MARGARET Richard.
RICHARD Ha?
MARGARET I call thee not.
RICHARD I cry thee mercy then, for I did think   235
       That thou hadst called me all these bitter names.
MARGARET Why so I did, but looked for no reply.
       Oh, let me make the period to my curse.
RICHARD 'Tis done by me, and ends in 'Margaret'.
ELIZABETH Thus have you breathed your curse against yourself.   240
MARGARET Poor painted queen, vain flourish of my fortune,

---

221 while] F, Q, Q2–5; whilst Q6   222 for thy] F, Q, Q2–3, Q5–6; forth Q4   224 while] F; whilest Q, Q2–5; whilst Q6   226 elvish-marked] *Rowe*; eluish mark'd F, Qq (*subst.*)   229 heavy mother's] F; mothers heauy Qq   231 detested –] F; detested, &c. Qq   234 thee] F, Q, Q2–5; the Q6   235 I cry thee mercy then] F; Then I crie thee mercy Qq (*subst.*)   235 did think] F; had thought Qq   236 That] F, Q; *not in* Q2–6   237 looked] F, Q, Q2–5 (*subst.*); looke Q6   239 in] F, Q, Q2–5; by Q6   239 'Margaret'] F (*italics*); Margaret Qq

220 still constantly. Although the play fulfils many of Margaret's curses, it does not show Richard much troubled by conscience until near the end (5.3). Certainly he is not constantly gnawed by conscience, although Anne testifies that he has bad dreams (4.1.85).

226 elvish-marked, abortive, rooting hog Children with birth defects were said to be marked by elves. 'Abortive' carries on the theme of prematurity and damage associated with Richard's infancy. He is a 'hog' both because of his destructive selfishness and because of his heraldic emblem, a wild boar.

228 slave of nature unworthy by nature.

229 heavy mother's womb 'Heavy' does double duty here, suggesting both the mother's metaphorically heavy (sad, mournful) spirit and her literally heavy womb during pregnancy.

231 rag shred, leftover scrap.

232–3 Printed in F (TLN 704), very unusually, as a single line split between two speakers.

235 cry thee mercy beg your pardon.

238 period conclusion.

241 painted imitation.

241 vain flourish of my fortune worthless decoration or trivial ornament adorning a life that properly belongs to me.

Why strew'st thou sugar on that bottled spider
Whose deadly web ensnareth thee about?
Fool, fool, thou whet'st a knife to kill thyself.
The day will come that thou shalt wish for me   245
To help thee curse this poisonous bunch-backed toad.

HASTINGS False-boding woman, end thy frantic curse,
    Lest to thy harm thou move our patience.

MARGARET Foul shame upon you. You have all moved mine.

RIVERS Were you well served, you would be taught your duty.   250

MARGARET To serve me well, you all should do me duty,
    Teach me to be your queen, and you my subjects;
    Oh, serve me well and teach yourselves that duty.

DORSET Dispute not with her. She is lunatic.

MARGARET Peace, master marquess, you are malapert.   255
    Your fire-new stamp of honour is scarce current.
    Oh, that your young nobility could judge
    What 'twere to lose it and be miserable.
    They that stand high have many blasts to shake them,
    And if they fall, they dash themselves to pieces.   260

RICHARD Good counsel, marry. Learn it, learn it, marquess.

DORSET It touches you, my lord, as much as me.

RICHARD Ay, and much more. But I was born so high.
    Our aerie buildeth in the cedar's top,
    And dallies with the wind and scorns the sun.   265

MARGARET And turns the sun to shade, alas, alas.
    Witness my son, now in the shade of death,
    Whose bright out-shining beams thy cloudy wrath
    Hath in eternal darkness folded up.

---

245 day] F; time Qq   **245** that] F, Q; when Q2–6   **246** this] F; that Qq   **246** poisonous] F, Q (*subst.*); poisoned Q2–6 (*subst.*)   **247** False-boding] *Theobald*; False boding F, Qq   **259** blasts] F, Q2–6; blast Q   **262** touches] F; toucheth Qq   **263** Ay] F (I); Yea Qq   **267** son] F, Q, Q2–4 (*subst.*); sunne Q5–6

242 bottled shaped like a bottle; an allusion to the form of a spider's body and to Richard's deformity, at least as seen by Margaret.

246 bunch-backed hunch-backed.

247 False-boding Falsely predicting (but also, ironically, Margaret is 'false-boding' in that she predicts Richard's falsity to Hastings, Buckingham and the others).

252 Teach me to be Show me that I am.

255 master A title for a young boy, therefore an insult to the adult Dorset.

255 malapert impertinent.

256 Your new title is like a coin fresh from the mint, hardly yet legal.

257 young newly acquired.

263 born so high noble by birth.

264 aerie Either an eagle's nest or the young eagles in the nest. Richard and Margaret reprise the images of birds, sun and shadow from 1.1.

264 cedar A tree noted for its height and long life, hence an emblem of nobility.

267 shade darkness; with an echo of the biblical 'shadow of death' (see Ps. 23 and *OED* Shadow *sb* 1b).

Raheny Library
Dublin City Libraries
Borrowed Items

Customer name: Morrissey, Niamh

Title: King Richard III / William Shakespeare ;
edited by Janis Lull.
ID: DCPL000016583 4
Due: 11-10-18

Total items: 1
Total fines: €0.10
20/09/2018 19:32
On Loan: 1
Overdue: 0
Reserves: 0
Ready for Collection: 0

Thank you for using the self service system
please keep this receipt for the due dates.
Visit us on line at www.dublincitylibraries.ie
(4)

Your aerie buildeth in our aerie's nest.   270
O God that seest it, do not suffer it;
As it is won with blood, lost be it so.
BUCKINGHAM Peace, peace, for shame, if not for charity.
MARGARET Urge neither charity nor shame to me.
      Uncharitably with me have you dealt,   275
      And shamefully my hopes by you are butchered.
      My charity is outrage, life my shame,
      And in that shame still live my sorrow's rage.
BUCKINGHAM Have done, have done.
MARGARET O princely Buckingham, I'll kiss thy hand   280
      In sign of league and amity with thee.
      Now fair befall thee and thy noble house.
      Thy garments are not spotted with our blood,
      Nor thou within the compass of my curse.
BUCKINGHAM Nor no one here, for curses never pass   285
      The lips of those that breathe them in the air.
MARGARET I will not think but they ascend the sky
      And there awake God's gentle sleeping peace.
      O Buckingham, take heed of yonder dog.
      Look when he fawns, he bites; and when he bites,   290
      His venom tooth will rankle to the death.
      Have not to do with him; beware of him.
      Sin, death, and hell have set their marks on him,
      And all their ministers attend on him.
RICHARD What doth she say, my lord of Buckingham?   295
BUCKINGHAM Nothing that I respect, my gracious lord.
MARGARET What, dost thou scorn me for my gentle counsel
      And soothe the devil that I warn thee from?

272 is] F; was Qq   273 Peace, peace] F; Haue done Qq   276 my hopes by you] F; by you my hopes Qq   278 that] F; my Qq   278 still] F, Q, Q2–5; shall Q6   279 Have done, have done] F; Haue done Qq   280 SH] F (*Mar.*); *Q. M.* Q, Q2; *Q. Mar.* Q3–4; *Q. Mary* Q5–6   280 princely] F, Q, Q2–3, Q5–6; pricely Q4   280 I'll] F (Ile); I will Qq   282 noble] F; Princely Qq (*subst.*)   286 those] F, Q, Q2–5; them Q6   287 I will not think] F; Ile not beleeue Qq   289 take heed] F; beware Qq   291 rankle] F, Q2–6; rackle Q   291 to the] F; thee to Qq   297] Qq; What . . . me / For . . . counsell? F   298 soothe] Q3, Q5; sooth Q, Q2, Q4, F; soothd Q6

274–8 These lines seem to be addressed to the assembly rather than to Buckingham in particular. Margaret still thinks of him as a friend, as seen at 280–4; perhaps here she has not yet distinguished him from the group.
282 fair good fortune.
284 compass range.
285 pass get any farther than.
287 will not think but will only believe that.

290 Look Expect that.
291 venom envenomed, poisonous.
291 rankle infect.
295 What doth she say Margaret may have been whispering to Buckingham, or perhaps Richard is simply suggesting that people who matter – especially Richard – have stopped listening to her.

> Oh, but remember this another day,
> When he shall split thy very heart with sorrow,   300
> And say poor Margaret was a prophetess.
> Live each of you the subjects to his hate,
> And he to yours, and all of you to God's.   *Exit*

BUCKINGHAM My hair doth stand on end to hear her curses.

RIVERS And so doth mine. I muse why she's at liberty.   305

RICHARD I cannot blame her, by God's holy mother,
> She hath had too much wrong, and I repent
> My part thereof that I have done to her.

ELIZABETH I never did her any to my knowledge.

RICHARD Yet you have all the vantage of her wrong.   310
> I was too hot to do somebody good
> That is too cold in thinking of it now.
> Marry, as for Clarence, he is well repaid;
> He is franked up to fatting for his pains.
> God pardon them that are the cause thereof.   315

RIVERS A virtuous and a Christian-like conclusion,
> To pray for them that have done scathe to us.

RICHARD So do I ever, being well advised.
> (*Speaks to himself*) For had I cursed now, I had cursed myself.

Enter CATESBY

CATESBY Madam, his majesty doth call for you,   320
> And for your grace, and you, my gracious lord.

---

302 to] F; of Qq   303 yours] F; your Q, Q2; you Q3–6   304 SH] F; *Hast.* Qq   304 on] Qq; an F   305 muse why] F; wonder Qq   308 to her] F; *not in* Qq   309 SH] Q, Q2–5 (*Qu.*); *Hast.* Q6; *Mar.* F   310 Yet] F; But Qq   310 her] F; this Qq   315 thereof] F; of it Qq   319 SD.1 *Speaks to himself*] F; *not in* Qq   320 SD.2 *Enter* CATESBY] F; *not in* Qq   321 grace] F, Q, Q2; noble Grace Q3–6   321 you] Qq; yours F   321 gracious] F; noble Qq

---

305 **muse** wonder.

306 **by God's holy mother** If 'marry' counts as an oath (see 97, 313), Richard swears by the Virgin as often as by St Paul. In this, as in much else, his young nephew Richard of York resembles him (see 2.4.27–30, 3.1.102–32).

309 F probably assigns this line to Margaret because the Q copy had the speech heading *Qu.*, and the F compositor became confused about which queen was which.

310 **vantage** benefits.

311 **somebody** that is, King Edward.

314 **franked up to fatting** penned up like an animal to be fattened (and then killed).

316–17, 334–5 Compare 1.2.69. The Christian Bible includes several injunctions to pray for enemies. See Matt. 5.44, Luke 6.28, Rom. 12.14. On returning good for evil, see also Rom. 12.21, 1 Thess. 5.15.

317 **scathe** harm.

318 **well advised** cautious (*OED* Advised 2 and 3).

319 SD Most editors place this direction in the previous line, after 'So do I ever'. The change works well enough, but so does the F version as it is. Richard gives nothing away by saying 'being well advised' out loud.

321 The Qq version of this summons includes everyone if 'Lo:' in Q and Q2 is taken as an abbreviated form of 'lords' (although the Q3 compositor did not take it so). Catesby's 'your grace' is probably addressed to Richard. As a member of

ELIZABETH Catesby, I come. Lords, will you go with me?
RIVERS We wait upon your grace.

Exeunt all but Gloucester

RICHARD I do the wrong, and first begin to brawl.
　　The secret mischiefs that I set abroach   325
　　I lay unto the grievous charge of others.
　　Clarence, who I indeed have cast in darkness,
　　I do beweep to many simple gulls,
　　Namely to Derby, Hastings, Buckingham,
　　And tell them 'tis the queen and her allies   330
　　That stir the king against the duke my brother.
　　Now they believe it, and withal whet me
　　To be revenged on Rivers, Dorset, Grey.
　　But then I sigh, and with a piece of scripture
　　Tell them that God bids us do good for evil.   335
　　And thus I clothe my naked villainy
　　With odd old ends stol'n forth of holy writ,
　　And seem a saint when most I play the devil.

Enter two MURDERERS

　　But soft, here come my executioners –
　　How now, my hardy, stout, resolvèd mates,   340
　　Are you now going to dispatch this thing?
FIRST MURDERER We are, my lord, and come to have the warrant
　　That we may be admitted where he is.
RICHARD Well thought upon, I have it here about me.

322 I . . . me] F; we . . . vs Qq   323 We wait upon] F; Madame we will attend Qq (*subst.*)   323 SD] F; *Exeunt man.
Ri.* Q; *Exeunt. man. Ri.* Q2; *Exeunt. ma. Clo.* Q3; *Exeunt. ma. Glo.* Q4; *Exeunt ma. Clo.* Q5; *Exeunt Ma. Glo.* Q6   324
the] F, Q, Q2–3; thee Q4–6   324 begin] F; began Qq   325 mischiefs] F, Q, Q2; mischiefe Q3–6   327 who] F; whom
Qq (*subst.*)   327 cast] F; laid Qq   329 Derby, Hastings] F; Hastings, Darby Qq   330 tell them 'tis] F; say it is Qq   332
it] F; me Qq   333 Dorset] F; Vaughan Qq   334 I] F, Q, Q2, Q4; *not in* Q3, Q5–6   335 do] F, Q, Q2–4 (*subst.*); to do
Q5–6   337 odd old] F; old odde Qq (*subst.*)   337 forth] F; out Qq   339 SD] F; *Enter Executioners.* Qq   339 come] F, Q;
comes Q2–6   341 you] F, Q, Q2; ye Q3–6   341 now] F, Q, Q2–5; *not* Q6   341 thing] F; deede Qq   342 SH] Capell (*1.
M.*); *Vil.* F; *Execu.* Qq (*subst.*)   344 Well] F; It was well Qq

the royal family, he outranks Buckingham,
though both are dukes.

　325 **set abroach** started.
　328 **gulls** fools, dupes.
　332 **withal** in addition.
　332 **whet** incite.
　335 **good for evil** This is evidently one of
Richard's stock arguments. He uses it on Anne
in the wooing scene (1.2.68–9).
　337 **ends** scraps.
　339 **executioners** doers; also those who will
execute Clarence.

　342 SH F and Qq are unclear about whether
one murderer or both do the talking in their brief
appearance here. F uses the ambiguous speech
heading *Vil.* (probably for 'Villain'), although in
1.4 it distinguishes the murderers by number.
Most editors allocate all the lines in this scene
to the First Murderer, but Hammond's emendations at 350 and 355 allow both to speak, once in
unison.

　344 **I . . . me** I have it here somewhere. Since
Richard also carries Edward's warrant revoking

When you have done, repair to Crosby Place.   345
But, sirs, be sudden in the execution,
Withal obdurate. Do not hear him plead,
For Clarence is well spoken and perhaps
May move your hearts to pity if you mark him.
SECOND MURDERER Tut, tut, my lord, we will not stand to prate;   350
Talkers are no good doers. Be assured
We go to use our hands and not our tongues.
RICHARD Your eyes drop millstones when fools' eyes fall tears.
I like you, lads. About your business straight.
Go, go, dispatch.   355
MURDERERS   We will, my noble lord.

                                                        Exeunt

1.4 *Enter* CLARENCE *and* KEEPER

KEEPER Why looks your grace so heavily today?
CLARENCE Oh, I have passed a miserable night,
So full of fearful dreams, of ugly sights,
That as I am a Christian faithful man,
I would not spend another such a night   5
Though 'twere to buy a world of happy days,
So full of dismal terror was the time.
KEEPER What was your dream, my lord? I pray you, tell me.

---

350 SH] *Hammond (2M.); Vil.* F; *Exec.* Qq   350 Tut, tut] F; Tush feare not Qq (*subst.*)   352 go] F; come Qq   353 fall] F; drop Qq   354 straight] F; *not in* Qq   355] F (Go . . . dispatch. / *Vil.* We . . . Lord.); *not in* Qq   355 SH] *Hammond (Both); Vil.* F   355 SD] Qq (*after 354*); *not in* F   **Act 1, Scene 4**   1.4] F (*Scena Quarta.*); *not in* Qq   0 SD] F; *Enter Clarence, Brokenbury.* Qq   1 SH] F; *Brok.* Qq (*subst.*) *and throughout*   3 fearful dreams] F; vgly sights Qq   3 ugly sights] F; gastly dreames Qq   8 my lord] F; *not in* Qq   8 I pray you, tell me] F; I long to heare you tell it. Qq

---

the execution of Clarence (see 2.1.89–92), he must be careful to give the murderers the right one.

345 Crosby Place Is Anne still waiting for Richard at Crosby Place? (See 1.2.216.) It would be like Richard to carry on his wooing and pay off his murderers at the same time.

347 obdurate hard-hearted.

350 prate prattle.

351 Talkers . . . doers Proverbial. See Tilley T 58, T 64.

353 millstones huge stones (like those used at a mill). Richard suggests that the murderers are so hard that if they were to weep, they would weep stones rather than water-drops. In addition, of course, falling millstones would kill anyone in the way.

353 fall drip.

Act 1, Scene 4

Shakespeare developed the murder scene from brief descriptions in the chronicles. Holinshed says, '[F]inallie the duke was cast into the Tower, and therewith adiudged for a traitor, and priuilie drowned in a butt of malmesie' (Holinshed, III, 346).

1 SH In F this scene contains two Tower officials, the keeper or jailer, and Brakenbury, the Lieutenant of the Tower, who enters after 75. In the quartos, there is only one official, called Brokenbury, who speaks both the keeper's speeches and the lines given to Brakenbury in F.

5 another such a such another.

CLARENCE Methoughts that I had broken from the Tower,
   And was embarked to cross to Burgundy,   10
   And in my company my brother Gloucester,
   Who from my cabin tempted me to walk
   Upon the hatches. There we looked toward England
   And cited up a thousand heavy times
   During the wars of York and Lancaster   15
   That had befall'n us. As we paced along
   Upon the giddy footing of the hatches,
   Methought that Gloucester stumbled, and in falling
   Struck me, that thought to stay him, overboard
   Into the tumbling billows of the main.   20
   O Lord, methought what pain it was to drown,
   What dreadful noise of water in mine ears,
   What sights of ugly death within mine eyes.
   Methoughts I saw a thousand fearful wracks,
   A thousand men that fishes gnawed upon,   25
   Wedges of gold, great anchors, heaps of pearl,
   Inestimable stones, unvalued jewels,
   All scattered in the bottom of the sea.
   Some lay in dead men's skulls, and in the holes
   Where eyes did once inhabit there were crept,   30
   As 'twere in scorn of eyes, reflecting gems,
   That wooed the slimy bottom of the deep
   And mocked the dead bones that lay scattered by.
KEEPER Had you such leisure in the time of death
   To gaze upon these secrets of the deep?   35
CLARENCE Methought I had, and often did I strive

---

9 Methoughts] F, Q, Q2–3; Me thought Q4–6 9 that I had broken from the Tower] F; I was imbarkt for Burgundy Qq
(*subst.*) 13 There] F, Q6; thence Q, Q2–5 13 toward] F, Q, Q2–5; towards Q6 14 heavy] F; fearefull Qq 18 falling]
F; stumbling Qq 21 O Lord] F; Lord, Lord Qq 22 water] F, Q6; waters Q, Q2–5 22 mine] F, Q2–6; my Q 23 sights
of ugly] F; vgly sights of Qq 23 mine] F, Q2–6; my Q 24 Methoughts] F (Me thoughts); Me thought Qq 25 A] F; Ten
Qq 28] F; *not in* Qq 29 lay in] F, Q, Q2–3, Q5–6; lay Q4 29 the] F; those Qq 32 That wooed] F; Which woed Q,
Q2–3; Which weod Q4; Which wade Q5–6 35 these] F; the Qq 36–7 and . . . ghost] F; *not in* Qq

 10 Burgundy As boys, Richard and Clarence
were sent for safety to Burgundy after their
father, the Duke of York, was killed fighting Henry VI. Later, Clarence turned against
his brothers, and Richard escaped again to
Burgundy, this time with Edward.
 12 tempted persuaded.
 13 hatches decks.
 14 heavy difficult, trying.
 17 giddy unsteady.

 19 stay hold.
 20 main ocean.
 24 fearful inspiring fear.
 24 wracks wrecks.
 26 Wedges Bars.
 27 Inestimable Impossible to count or to
value.
 27 unvalued priceless.
 31 in scorn of in imitation of, mocking.
 32 wooed addressed, sought intimacy with.

To yield the ghost; but still the envious flood
Stopped in my soul and would not let it forth
To find the empty, vast, and wandering air,
But smothered it within my panting bulk,   40
Who almost burst to belch it in the sea.

KEEPER Awaked you not in this sore agony?

CLARENCE No, no, my dream was lengthened after life.
Oh, then began the tempest to my soul.
I passed, methought, the melancholy flood,   45
With that sour ferryman which poets write of,
Unto the kingdom of perpetual night.
The first that there did greet my stranger-soul
Was my great father-in-law, renownèd Warwick,
Who spake aloud, 'What scourge for perjury   50
Can this dark monarchy afford false Clarence?'
And so he vanished. Then came wandering by
A shadow like an angel, with bright hair
Dabbled in blood, and he shrieked out aloud,
'Clarence is come: false, fleeting, perjured Clarence,   55
That stabbed me in the field by Tewkesbury.
Seize on him, furies, take him unto torment.'
With that, methought, a legion of foul fiends
Environed me, and howlèd in mine ears
Such hideous cries that with the very noise   60
I trembling waked, and for a season after

---

37 but] F; for Qq   38 Stopped] F; Kept Qq   39 find] F; seeke Q, Q2; keepe Q3–6   41 Who] F; Which Qq   42 in] F; with Qq   43 No, no] F; O no Qq   44 to] F, Q, Q2–5; of Q6   45 I] F; Who Qq   46 sour] F; grim Qq   48 stranger-soul] F; stranger soule Qq   50 spake] F; cried Qq   50–1 'What . . . Clarence'] *Rowe* (–What . . . *Clarence*); *no quotation marks in* F, Qq   53 with] F; in Qq   54 Dabbled] F, Q, Q2–5 (*subst.*); Dadled Q6   54 shrieked] F; squakt Q; squeakt Q2–3, Q5–6; squeakt Q4   55–7 'Clarence . . . torment'] *Rowe* (– Clarence . . . Torment–); *no quotation marks in* F, Qq   57 unto torment] F; to your torments Qq   58 methought] F, Q2–6 (me thought); me thoughts Q   59 me] F; me about Qq

---

37 **yield the ghost** die, release the soul from the body.

37 **envious flood** spiteful water.

38 **Stopped** Held.

40 **panting bulk** gasping body. Giving up offers relief from suffocation.

45 **melancholy flood** The River Styx. In classical mythology, Charon, the 'sour ferryman' (46), ferried souls across the Styx to Hades, the underworld.

47 **perpetual night** Everlasting night was a classical image for the afterlife. Compare 2.2.46.

48 **stranger-soul** soul newly arrived in the underworld.

49 **father-in-law** Clarence married Warwick's older daughter, Isabel. Lady Anne was Warwick's younger daughter.

50 **scourge** punishment.

51 **afford** provide.

53 **shadow** ghost. The 'angel' is Edward, Prince of Wales, son of Queen Margaret and Henry VI and, in Shakespeare, the husband of Anne.

54 **Dabbled** Daubed, smeared.

55 **fleeting** fickle.

58 **legion** multitude.

59 **Environed** Surrounded.

61 **season** while.

Could not believe but that I was in hell,
Such terrible impression made my dream.
KEEPER   No marvel, lord, though it affrighted you.
I am afraid, methinks, to hear you tell it.   65
CLARENCE   Ah keeper, keeper, I have done these things
That now give evidence against my soul
For Edward's sake, and see how he requites me.
O God, if my deep prayers cannot appease thee,
But thou wilt be avenged on my misdeeds,   70
Yet execute thy wrath in me alone.
Oh, spare my guiltless wife and my poor children.
Keeper, I prithee sit by me awhile.
My soul is heavy, and I fain would sleep.
KEEPER   I will, my lord. God give your grace good rest.   75

Enter BRAKENBURY, *the Lieutenant*

BRAKENBURY   Sorrow breaks seasons and reposing hours,
Makes the night morning and the noontide night.
Princes have but their titles for their glories,
An outward honour for an inward toil,
And for unfelt imaginations   80
They often feel a world of restless cares;
So that between their titles and low name
There's nothing differs but the outward fame.

---

63 my] F; the Qq   64 lord] F; my Lo: Q, Q2–5 (*subst.*); my Lord Q6   65 am] F; promise you, I am Qq   65 methinks]
F; *not in* Qq   66 Ah keeper, keeper] F; O Brokenbury Qq (*subst.*)   66 these] F; those Qq   67 That now give] F; Which
now beare Qq   69–72] F; *not in* Qq   73] F; I pray thee gentle keeper stay by me Qq   75 SD] F; *not in* Qq   76 SH] F; *in*
Qq *Keeper's speech continues*   76 breaks] F, Q2–6; breake Q   80 imaginations] F; imagination Qq   82 between] F; betwixt
Qq   82 their] F, Q, Q2; your Q3–6   82 name] F; names Qq

62 **hell** Clarence dreams himself in a place
that is hell for him, perhaps only purgatory for
the angel prince.
63 **impression** imprint, image in memory.
64 **though** that.
72 **wife . . . children** Clarence's wife does not
appear in the play. (Historically, she had already
died.) Clarence's son and daughter have speaking parts in 2.2, and the daughter has a silent
appearance in 4.1.
74 **fain** gladly.
75 SD Many editors add a stage direction indi-
cating that Clarence sleeps, which the dialogue
strongly implies.
76 **breaks seasons** disrupts normal sched-
ules.
76 **reposing hours** hours for sleeping.

78–83 Compare Brakenbury's monologue to
the 'ceremony' soliloquy of Henry V: 'What
infinite heart's ease must kings neglect / That
private men enjoy? / And what have kings
that privates have not too, / Save ceremony,
save general ceremony?' (*H5* 4.1.209–12). Both
Brakenbury and King Henry V argue that only
burdens and superficial glories (titles, cere-
monies) distinguish royalty from commoners.
80 **unfelt imaginations** illusory honours;
glories imagined but not experienced. The metre
requires 'imaginations' to be pronounced with six
syllables.
81 **restless** unsettling, worrying.
82 **low name** the status (title) of ordinary
citizen.
83 **fame** report, public estimation.

Enter two MURDERERS

FIRST MURDERER Ho, who's here?

BRAKENBURY What wouldst thou, fellow? And how cam'st thou   85
hither?

SECOND MURDERER I would speak with Clarence, and I came hither
on my legs.

BRAKENBURY What, so brief?

FIRST MURDERER 'Tis better, sir, than to be tedious.   90
Let him see our commission, and talk no more.

[Brakenbury] reads

BRAKENBURY I am in this commanded to deliver
The noble Duke of Clarence to your hands.
I will not reason what is meant hereby,
Because I will be guiltless from the meaning.   95
There lies the duke asleep, and there the keys.
I'll to the king and signify to him
That thus I have resigned to you my charge.

Exeunt [Brakenbury and Keeper]

FIRST MURDERER You may, sir, 'tis a point of wisdom. Fare you well.

SECOND MURDERER What, shall we stab him as he sleeps?   100

FIRST MURDERER No. He'll say 'twas done cowardly, when he wakes.

SECOND MURDERER Why, he shall never wake until the great judgement day.

FIRST MURDERER Why, then he'll say we stabbed him sleeping.

---

83 SD] F (*Murtherers*); *The murtherers enter.* Qq   84] F; *not in* Qq   84 SH] F (*1. Mur.*); *not in* Qq   85 What wouldst thou,
fellow] F; In Gods name what are you Qq   85 cam'st thou] F; came you Qq   87 SH] F (*2. Mur.*); *Execu.* Qq   89 What]
F; Yea, are you Q, Q2; Yea, are ye Q3–6   90 SH] F (*1.*); *2 Exe.* Qq   90 'Tis better, sir] F; O sir, it is better Qq   90 than]
to be] F; to be briefe then Q, Q2; be briefe then Q3–6   91 Let him see] F; Shew him Qq   91 and] F; *not in* Qq   92 SD]
F (*Reads.*); *He readeth it.* Qq   94 hereby] F, Q, Q2; thereby Q3–6   95 from] F; of Qq   96] F; Here are the keies, there
sits the Duke a sleepe Qq (*subst.*)   97 the king] F; his Maiesty Qq   97 signify to him] F; certifie his Grace Qq (*subst.*)   98
to you my charge] F; my charge to you Q, Q2; my place to you Q3–6   98 SD] *Riverside (Exit Brakenbury with Keeper.*);
Exit F; *not in* Qq   99 SH] F (*1*) (*and subsequently until 266*); *Exe.* Qq   99 You may, sir, 'tis] F; Doe so, it is Qq   99 Fare
you well] F (*Far*); *not in* Qq   100 SH] F (*2*) (*and subsequently until 263*); *Exe.* Qq, Q3–6; I Q, Q2   101–37]
F; *as verse* Qq   101 He'll] F; then he will Qq   102–3] F; When he wakes, / Why . . . day. Qq   102 Why] F; Why foole
Qq   102 until the great] F; till the Qq   104 he'll] F (*hee'l*); he will Qq

---

89 **brief** abrupt, rude.

92 **deliver** Perhaps the most ironic use of this
complex word so far (see 1.1.75, 115, 122).

94 **reason** debate; question.

95 **will be** want to be.

98 SD Many editors place Brakenbury's exit
after 99, so he can hear the Murderer's reply.

102–37 Some of the Murderers' verse here
is rough, and they soon lapse into prose, only

to return to verse as they speak to Clarence.
Rough verse or not, F appears to make a deliberate distinction between the verse and prose
portions of this exchange, and setting the whole
passage as prose seems unwarranted.

102–3 **judgement day** In Christianity, the
last day of the world in its present condition, on
which Christ will return to earth to pronounce
final sentence on humanity.

SECOND MURDERER The urging of that word judgement hath bred a   105
     kind of remorse in me.

FIRST MURDERER What? Art thou afraid?

SECOND MURDERER Not to kill him, having a warrant,
                But to be damned for killing him, from the which
                No warrant can defend me.   110

FIRST MURDERER I thought thou hadst been resolute.

SECOND MURDERER So I am, to let him live.

FIRST MURDERER I'll back to the Duke of Gloucester and tell him so.

SECOND MURDERER Nay, I prithee stay a little.
                I hope this passionate humour of mine will change.   115
                It was wont to hold me but while one tells twenty.

FIRST MURDERER How dost thou feel thyself now?

SECOND MURDERER Some certain dregs of conscience are yet within
     me.

FIRST MURDERER Remember our reward when the deed's done.   120

SECOND MURDERER Come, he dies. I had forgot the reward.

FIRST MURDERER Where's thy conscience now?

SECOND MURDERER Oh, in the Duke of Gloucester's purse.

FIRST MURDERER When he opens his purse to give us our reward, thy
     conscience flies out.   125

SECOND MURDERER 'Tis no matter; let it go. There's few or none will
     entertain it.

FIRST MURDERER What if it come to thee again?

SECOND MURDERER I'll not meddle with it; it makes a man a coward.
                A man cannot steal but it accuseth him. A man cannot swear but it   130

108–16] F; *as prose* Qq   **108** warrant] F; warrant for it Qq   **109** the which] F; which Qq   **110** me] F; vs Qq   **111–12**] F; *not in* Qq   **113** I'll back] F; Backe Qq   **113** and tell] F; tell Qq   **114** Nay] F; *not in* Qq   **114** prithee] F (prythee); pray thee Qq   **114** little] F; while Qq   **115** this passionate humour of mine] F; my holy humor Qq (*subst.*)   **116** It was] F; twas Qq   **116** tells twenty] F; would tel xx Qq (*subst.*)   **118** Some] F; Faith some Qq   **120** deed's] F; deede is Qq   **121** Come] F; Zounds Qq   **122** Where's] F; Where is Qq   **123** Oh, in] F; In Qq   **124** When] F; So when Qq   **126** 'Tis no matter] F; *not in* Qq   **126** it] F, Q, Q3–6; vs Q2   **128** What] F; How Qq   **129** it; it] F; it, it is a dangerous thing, / It Qq   **130** A man cannot swear] F; he cannot sweare Q, Q2; he cannot steale Q3–6

---

106 remorse pity.

108–10 The Second Murderer draws a distinction between human law, under which a warrant will protect him from punishment, and divine law, under which he knows killing Clarence is wrong.

115 passionate humour emotional state of mind. 'Passion' may mean suffering (*OED* Passion *sb*1). In this case, the Second Murderer suffers from fear of divine vengeance rather than from pity for Clarence. In his concern with damnation (109) and the cowardly attributes of conscience (129 ff.), this Murderer anticipates

Hamlet's 'To be or not to be' soliloquy (*Ham.* 3.1.55–87). Also compare these sentiments to Richard's at 5.3.181–2: 'Have mercy, Jesu! Soft, I did but dream. / O coward conscience, how dost thou afflict me?'

116 wont accustomed.

116 tells counts.

127 entertain welcome, shelter. The Murderer justifies ignoring his conscience by observing that everybody does it.

130–2 Stealing, swearing and adultery are three of the fundamental sins prohibited by the biblical ten commandments (see Ex. 20).

checks him. A man cannot lie with his neighbour's wife, but it
detects him. 'Tis a blushing, shamefaced spirit that mutinies in a
man's bosom. It fills a man full of obstacles. It made me once restore
a purse of gold that by chance I found. It beggars any man that
keeps it. It is turned out of towns and cities for a dangerous thing,   135
and every man that means to live well endeavours to trust to
himself and live without it.

FIRST MURDERER 'Tis even now at my elbow, persuading me not to
kill the duke.

SECOND MURDERER Take the devil in thy mind, and believe him not.   140
He would insinuate with thee but to make thee sigh.

FIRST MURDERER I am strong framed, he cannot prevail with me.

SECOND MURDERER Spoke like a tall man that respects thy reputation. Come, shall we fall to work?

FIRST MURDERER Take him on the costard with the hilts of thy sword,   145
and then throw him into the malmsey butt in the next room.

SECOND MURDERER Oh, excellent device. And make a sop of him.

FIRST MURDERER Soft, he wakes.

SECOND MURDERER Strike!

FIRST MURDERER No, we'll reason with him.   150

---

131 A man] F; he Qq   132 'Tis] F; It is Qq   133 a man] F; one Qq   134 by chance] F; *not in* Qq   135 of] F; of all Qq   136 trust to] F, Q2–6; trust to / To Q   137 live] F; to live Qq   138 'Tis] F; Zounds it is Qq   141 but] F; *not in* Qq   142 I] F; Tut, I Qq   142 framed] F; in fraud Qq   142 me] F; me, I warrant thee Qq   143 Spoke] F, Q, Q2–3; Soode Q4; Stood Q5–6   143 man] F; fellow Qq   143 thy] F; his Qq   144 fall to work] F; to this geere Qq (*subst.*)   145 on] F; ouer Qq   145 thy] F, Q, Q2; my Q3–6   146 throw him into] F; we wil chop him in Qq (*subst.*)   147 And make] F; make Qq   147 sop] F, Q, Q2; scoope Q3; soppe Q4–6   148–9] F; *1* Harke he stirs, shall I strike. Qq   150 SH] F; *2* Qq   150 we'll] F; first lets Qq   150 him.] F, Q, Q2; him. *Cla. awaketh.* Q3–6

---

131 **checks** stops.

132 **detects** notices, catches.

140 This seems to mean 'accept the devil into your mind and don't believe your conscience'. The phrase alludes to the ancient image of a sinner's interior debate as a contest between a devil and an angel. Compare Lancelot Gobbo's dilemma in *MV*: 'The fiend is at mine elbow and tempts me, saying to me, "Gobbo, Launcelot Gobbo, good Launcelot", or "good Gobbo", or "good Launcelot Gobbo, use your legs, take the start, run away." My conscience says, "no; take heed, honest Launcelot, take heed, honest Gobbo" or as aforesaid, "honest Launcelot Gobbo, do not run, scorn running with thy heels"' (2.2.2–9). Like the Murderer here, Gobbo takes the fiend's advice.

141 **insinuate with thee** make friends with you.

141 **but to** only to.

143 **tall** brave.

145 **Take** Hit.

145 **costard** head. The primary meaning is 'apple' (*OED* Costard).

146 **malmsey butt** Keg of malmsey, a sweet wine.

147 **sop** A piece of bread soaked in wine before being eaten (*OED* Sop *sb¹* I).

150 SH Both F and Qq assign the murderer-passages more or less alternately to the two Murderers. Since the quartos have 148–9 as a single line, the Qq alternation here gets out of synchrony with that of F. In F, the First Murderer appears to be the leader; he is tougher and pushier than his accomplice – at one point he even takes over a conversation that the Second Murderer has just begun with Clarence (154). Although the First Murderer seems to experience an attack of conscience at 138–44, he may just be testing the wavering resolve of his companion. Even if he really does feel his better angel at his elbow for a moment, he still appears the more vicious of the two.

150 **reason** talk.

CLARENCE Where art thou, keeper? Give me a cup of wine.

SECOND MURDERER You shall have wine enough, my lord, anon.

CLARENCE In God's name, what art thou?

FIRST MURDERER A man, as you are.

CLARENCE But not, as I am, royal.   155

FIRST MURDERER Nor you, as we are, loyal.

CLARENCE Thy voice is thunder, but thy looks are humble.

FIRST MURDERER My voice is now the king's, my looks mine own.

CLARENCE How darkly and how deadly dost thou speak!
  Your eyes do menace me. Why look you pale?   160
  Who sent you hither? Wherefore do you come?

SECOND MURDERER To, to, to –

CLARENCE To murder me?

BOTH   Ay, ay.

CLARENCE You scarcely have the hearts to tell me so,   165
  And therefore cannot have the hearts to do it.
  Wherein, my friends, have I offended you?

FIRST MURDERER Offended us you have not, but the king.

CLARENCE I shall be reconciled to him again.

SECOND MURDERER Never, my lord. Therefore prepare to die.   170

CLARENCE Are you drawn forth among a world of men
  To slay the innocent? What is my offence?
  Where is the evidence that doth accuse me?
  What lawful quest have given their verdict up
  Unto the frowning judge? Or who pronounced   175
  The bitter sentence of poor Clarence' death
  Before I be convìct by course of law?
  To threaten me with death is most unlawful.
  I charge you, as you hope for any goodness,

---

152 SH] F; *1* Qq   154 SH] F; *2* Qq   156 SH] F, Q5–6; *2* Q, Q2–4   158 SH] F; *2* Q, Q2–4   159 speak] F, Q, Q2, Q5–6; spake Q3–4   160] F; *not in* Qq   161] F; Tell me who are you, wherefore come you hither? Qq   162 SH] F; *Am.* Qq   164 SH] F; *Am.* Qq   164 Ay, ay] F (I, I); I Qq   165 hearts] F, Q, Q2–5; heart Q6   166 hearts] F, Q, Q2–5; heart Q6   171 drawn forth among] F; cald foorth from out Qq (*subst.*)   173 is . . . that doth] F; are . . . that do Q, Q2 (*subst.*); are . . . to Q3–6   178 threaten] F, Q, Q2; thteaten Q3; thereaten Q4–6   179 charge] F, Q, Q2–3, Q5–6; carge Q4   179 for any goodness] F; to haue redemption / By Christs deare blood shed for our grieuous sinnes Qq

152 **anon** shortly.

159 **darkly** threateningly; obscurely, with hidden meaning (*OED* Darkly).

171 Have you been picked out from everyone in the world.

174 **lawful quest** Body of persons holding a judicial inquiry (*OED* Quest *sb*¹ 2).

177 Clarence implies that even the king cannot lawfully sentence him to death without due process.

177 **convìct** convicted (on Shakespeare's omission of *-ed* after *d* and *t*, see Abbott 342). See 3.7.178, 'first was he contràct to Lady Lucy'.

179 **as . . . goodness** as you hope to achieve salvation.

That you depart and lay no hands on me.   180
The deed you undertake is damnable.
FIRST MURDERER What we will do, we do upon command.
SECOND MURDERER And he that hath commanded is our king.
CLARENCE Erroneous vassals! The great King of kings
    Hath in the table of his law commanded   185
    That thou shalt do no murder. Will you then
    Spurn at his edict and fulfil a man's?
    Take heed, for he holds vengeance in his hand
    To hurl upon their heads that break his law.
SECOND MURDERER And that same vengeance doth he hurl on thee   190
    For false forswearing and for murder, too.
    Thou didst receive the sacrament to fight
    In quarrel of the house of Lancaster.
FIRST MURDERER And, like a traitor to the name of God,
    Didst break that vow, and with thy treacherous blade   195
    Unripped'st the bowels of thy sovereign's son.
SECOND MURDERER Whom thou wast sworn to cherish and defend.
FIRST MURDERER How canst thou urge God's dreadful law to us
    When thou hast broke it in such dear degree?
CLARENCE Alas! For whose sake did I that ill deed?   200
    For Edward, for my brother, for his sake.
    He sends you not to murder me for this,
    For in that sin he is as deep as I.
    If God will be avengèd for the deed,
    Oh, know you yet, he doth it publicly.   205
    Take not the quarrel from his powerful arm.

---

183 our] F; the Qq   184 vassals] F; Vassaile Qq (*subst.*)   185 the table] F; the tables Q, Q2; his Tables Q3–6   186 Will you] F; and wilt thou Qq   188 hand] F; hands Qq   190 hurl] F; throw Qq   192–3 sacrament to fight / In] F; holy sacrament, / To fight in Qq   197 wast] F; wert Qq   199 such] F; so Qq   202 He] F; Why sirs, he Qq   202 you] F; ye Qq   203 that] F; this Qq   204 avengèd] F; reuenged Qq   204 the] F; this Qq   205] F; *not in* Qq

182 The First Murderer offers a variant of the 'only following orders' defence, but by using 'will' instead of 'shall', he implies that the Murderers' inclinations are in accord with their instructions.

184 vassals servants, underlings.

184 King of kings God.

185 table of his law Tablets carrying the ten commandments.

188 he . . . hand Clarence alludes here and at 206 to the biblical injunction to leave vengeance to God (see Deut. 32.35 and Rom. 12.19).

192 receive the sacrament swear solemnly at mass, taking communion to seal the vow. Shakespeare shows Clarence forsaking his brothers to fight for the house of Lancaster in *3H6* 4.2, then returning to his brothers in *3H6* 5.1.

196 sovereign's son Edward, son of Henry VI.

199 dear high, costly.

205 yet still. The whole phrase, 'know you yet', means 'remember'.

He needs no indirect or lawless course
To cut off those that have offended him.

FIRST MURDERER Who made thee, then, a bloody minister
When gallant-springing brave Plantagenet,   210
That princely novice, was struck dead by thee?

CLARENCE My brother's love, the devil, and my rage.

FIRST MURDERER Thy brother's love, our duty, and thy faults
Provoke us hither now to slaughter thee.

CLARENCE If you do love my brother, hate not me.   215
I am his brother, and I love him well.
If you are hired for meed, go back again,
And I will send you to my brother Gloucester,
Who shall reward you better for my life
Than Edward will for tidings of my death.   220

SECOND MURDERER You are deceived. Your brother Gloucester hates
you.

CLARENCE Oh, no, he loves me, and he holds me dear.
Go you to him from me.

FIRST MURDERER Ay, so we will.

CLARENCE Tell him, when that our princely father York   225
Blessed his three sons with his victorious arm,
He little thought of this divided friendship.
Bid Gloucester think on this, and he will weep.

FIRST MURDERER Ay, millstones, as he lessoned us to weep.

CLARENCE Oh, do not slander him, for he is kind.   230

FIRST MURDERER Right, as snow in harvest.
Come, you deceive yourself,

---

207 or] F; nor Qq   207 lawless] F, Q; lawfull Q2–6   210 gallant-springing] *Pope*; gallant springing F, Q; gallant spring Q2–6   211 That] F, Q, Q2–5; The Q6   213 our duty] F; the diuell Qq (*subst.*)   213 faults] F; fault Qq   214 Provoke] F; Haue brought Qq   214 slaughter] F; murder Q (*subst.*)   215 If you do] F; Oh, if you Qq   215 my] F, Q, Q2–3; *not in* Q4–6   217 are] F; be Qq   217 meed] F, Q; need Q2–6 (*subst.*)   219 shall] F; will Qq   221] *As one line* F; *two lines divided after* deceived. Qq   223–4] F, Qq   224 SH] F; *Am.* Qq   226–7 arm, / He] F; arme: / And charg'd vs from his soule, to loue each other, / He Qq   228 on] F, Q6; of Q, Q2–5   229 SH] F; *Am.* Qq   231–2] F; *as one line* Qq   232 Come, you deceiu'st thy self Qq

---

207 **indirect** devious, secret.
209 **minister** agent, deputy.
210 **gallant-springing** gallant and young.
210 **Plantagenet** Henry VI's son.
211 **novice** beginner (in warfare and in life).
217 **meed** reward.
222 **holds me dear** loves me; thinks I am worth a high price.
225–8 This blessing does not appear in *3H6*, where York is slain by Margaret's faction in the

scene immediately following the death of his young son Rutland (1.4). York has no victorious leisure in which to bless his three remaining sons, Edward, Clarence and Richard.
230 **kind** benevolent; natural.
231 **as snow in harvest** The First Murderer intuitively links Richard to winter. Until near the end, the play consistently associates harvest imagery with death rather than with fruition.

'Tis he that sends us to destroy you here.

CLARENCE It cannot be, for he bewept my fortune,
And hugged me in his arms, and swore with sobs   235
That he would labour my delivery.

FIRST MURDERER Why, so he doth, when he delivers you
From this earth's thraldom to the joys of heaven.

SECOND MURDERER Make peace with God, for you must die, my lord.

CLARENCE Have you that holy feeling in your souls   240
To counsel me to make my peace with God,
And are you yet to your own souls so blind
That you will war with God by murdering me?
O sirs, consider, they that set you on
To do this deed will hate you for the deed.   245

SECOND MURDERER What shall we do?

CLARENCE   Relent, and save your souls.
Which of you, if you were a prince's son,
Being pent from liberty, as I am now,
If two such murderers as yourselves came to you,
Would not entreat for life as you would beg,   250
Were you in my distress?

FIRST MURDERER Relent? No. 'Tis cowardly and womanish.

233 that sends] F; hath sent Q, Q2; that sent Q3–6   233 to destroy you here] F; hither now to slaughter thee Q; hither now to murder thee Q2–6 (*subst.*)   234 he bewept my fortune] F; when I parted with him Qq   235 And] F; He Qq   237 SH] F (*1*); *2* Qq   237 when] F; now Qq   237 you] F; thee Qq   238 earth's] F; worlds Qq   239 SH] F (*2*); *1* Qq   239 Make] F, Q2–6; Makes Q   239 lord] F; Lo: Q, Q2; Lord Q3–6   240 Have you . . . your souls] F; Hast thou . . . thy soule Qq   242 are you . . . your . . . souls] F; art thou . . . thy . . . soule Qq   243 you will] F; thou wilt Qq   243 by] F, Q, Q2; for Q3–6   244 O] F; Ah Qq   244 they] F; he Qq   245 the] F; this Qq   246] *Steevens*; What . . . do? / Relent . . . soules: F, Qq   247–51] F; *not in* Qq   252 No] F; *not in* Qq

234–6 Perhaps Richard behaves like this in 1.1 (Hammond inserts an explicit stage direction), or perhaps Clarence's desperate memory invents these tokens of sincerity.

236 Another suggestion that Clarence has misinterpreted Richard. Compare Richard's promise at 1.1.115: 'I will deliver you or else lie for you.' The First Murderer reiterates Richard's joke about delivering Clarence to heaven, but neither villain seems to notice the ironic use of birth imagery in connection with Richard's murder plots.

238 thraldom captivity.

244–5 they . . . you Compare this remark to Bolingbroke's sentiment when he banishes the murderer of Richard II: 'They love not poison that do poison need, / Nor do I thee. Though I did wish him dead, / I hate the murderer, love him murdered' (*R2* 5.5.38–40). Richard, by contrast, seems to like the company of murderers, both before and after their crimes. In Act 1, he

exclaims to the Murderers, 'I like you, lads,' and in Act 4, he looks forward to chatting with Tyrrel about the murdered princes (4.3.31–2).

247–51 Many editors (see Variorum, pp. 144–6) have believed that these F-only lines were somehow misplaced and should have been inserted after the First Murderer's 'Relent? No. 'Tis cowardly and womanish' (252), but the sequence in F makes both rhetorical and dramatic sense without emendation.

248 pent from liberty penned up, imprisoned.

250 as you would beg as if you were begging. Some editors (e.g. Oxford, Hammond) emend this line, starting a new sentence at 'as'.

252 womanish Shakespearean villains often associate pity or compassion with women. Similarly, Richard describes his eyes as 'manly' because they did not weep at the death of his father (1.2.169).

CLARENCE Not to relent is beastly, savage, devilish.
    My friend, I spy some pity in thy looks.
    Oh, if thine eye be not a flatterer,   255
    Come thou on my side and entreat for me;
    A begging prince, what beggar pities not?
SECOND MURDERER Look behind you, my lord.
FIRST MURDERER Take that, and that.
                        (*Stabs him*)
                              If all this will not do,
    I'll drown you in the malmsey butt within.   260
                          Exit [with Clarence's body]
SECOND MURDERER A bloody deed, and desperately dispatched.
    How fain, like Pilate, would I wash my hands
    Of this most grievous murder.

                Enter FIRST MURDERER

FIRST MURDERER How now? What mean'st thou that thou help'st
    me not?
    By heaven, the duke shall know how slack you have been.   265
SECOND MURDERER I would he knew that I had saved his brother.
    Take thou the fee, and tell him what I say,
    For I repent me that the duke is slain.   *Exit*
FIRST MURDERER So do not I. Go, coward as thou art.
    Well, I'll go hide the body in some hole   270
    Till that the duke give order for his burial;
    And when I have my meed, I will away,
    For this will out, and then I must not stay.   *Exit*

---

253 devilish] F, Q; and devilish Q2–6 (*subst.*) 254 thy] F, Q, Q2–5; your Q6 255 thine] F; thy Qq 258] F; *not in* Qq 259] F; I thus, and thus: if this will not serue Qq (*subst.*) 259 SD] F (*after* do); *He stabs him*. Qq 260 drown you] F; chop thee Qq 260 within] F; in the next roome Qq 260 SD *with Clarence's body*] Malone (*with the body*); *Exit* F; *not in* Qq 261 dispatched] F; performed Qq 262 hands] F; hand Qq 263 grievous murder] F; grieuous guilty murder done Qq 263 SD] F; *not in* Qq 264] F (*as prose*); Why doest thou not helpe me Qq 265 heaven] F, Q6; heauens Q, Q2–5 265 you have been] F; thou art Qq 266 SH] F (*2. Mur.*); 2 Qq 269 SH] F (*1. Mur.*); 1 Qq 270 Well, I'll go] F; Now must I Qq 271 Till that . . . give] F; Vntill . . . take Qq 273 will] F; must Qq 273 then] F; here Qq 273 SD] F; *Exeunt.* Qq

260 SD This SD, which does not appear in F or Qq, is suggested by the First Murderer's statement that he will drown Clarence 'in the malmsey butt within'. On the other hand, perhaps he leaves Clarence's body on stage as he exits, expecting the Second Murderer to do the heavy lifting, and then returns to chide him when he does not (264–5). If the body does not leave the stage at 260, the First Murderer will probably take it with him at the end of the scene.

262 fain gladly.

262 Pilate Pontius Pilate, the Roman governor who ordered the crucifixion of Jesus. In an attempt to dissociate himself from the guilt of Jesus's death, Pilate symbolically washed his hands in public before letting the execution proceed (see Matt. 27.24).

2.1 *Flourish. Enter the King* [EDWARD] (*sick*), *the Queen* [ELIZABETH],
LORD MARQUESS DORSET, RIVERS, HASTINGS, CATESBY,
BUCKINGHAM [*and others*]

KING EDWARD Why, so. Now have I done a good day's work.
    You peers, continue this united league.
    I every day expect an embassage
    From my redeemer to redeem me hence.
    And more to peace my soul shall part to heaven,   5
    Since I have made my friends at peace on earth.
    Rivers and Hastings, take each other's hand.
    Dissemble not your hatred; swear your love.
RIVERS By heaven, my soul is purged from grudging hate,
    And with my hand I seal my true heart's love.   10
HASTINGS So thrive I, as I truly swear the like.
KING EDWARD Take heed you dally not before your king,

Act 2, Scene 1   2.1] F (*Actus Secundus. Scoena Prima.*) *not in* Qq   0 SD. 3 *and others*] Capell (*Grey and Others*); *Flourish.*
Enter the King sicke, the Queene, Lord Marquesse Dorset, Riuers, Hastings, Catesby, Buckingham, Wooduill. F; *Enter King,*
Queene, Hastings, Ryuers, Dorcet, & c. Q, Q2; *Enter King, Queene, Hastings, Riuers, & c.* Q3–6   1 Why, so] F; So Qq   1
have I] F; I have Qq   5 more to] F; now in Qq   5 to heaven] F, Q (*Bodleian, Folger, Yale copies*), Q3–6; from heauen Q
(*British Library, Huntington copies*), Q2   6 made] F; set Qq   6 friends] F, Q, Q2–5; friend Q6   7 Rivers and Hastings] Qq;
Dorset and Riuers F   9 soul] F; heart Qq   10 heart's] F, Q, Q2–5; hears Q6   11 truly] F, Q, Q2; *not in* Q3–6

Act 2, Scene 1

Thomas More describes King Edward reconciling the nobles while propped up on his death bed, 'vndersette with pillowes' (p. 11). Hall's account is explicitly set at Westminster Palace in London, where the king lies ill. The chronicles also mention Edward's repenting for the death of Clarence, to which he had previously consented. Holinshed says that 'when anie person sued to him for the pardon of malefactors condemned to death, he would accustomablie saie, & openlie speake: "Oh infortunate brother, for whose life not one would make sute!" ' (Holinshed, III, 346).

0 SD *Flourish* Trumpet fanfare announcing the approach of distinguished persons.

0 SD F shows some perplexity about the relatives of Queen Elizabeth. 'Wooduill' is the same person as Rivers, yet they are listed in the F stage directions as if they were separate characters. Perhaps 'Wooduill' was meant (wrongly) to designate Elizabeth's son Lord Grey, who, although he does not speak, probably appears in this scene. Like Catesby, who also has no lines, Grey helps fill out one of the quarrelling factions. At 69, Richard speaks to 'Dukes, earls, lords, gentlemen', suggesting a more crowded

scene than explicitly called for in the stage directions.

2 peers lords.

4 redeemer God or Christ, regarded by Christians as saving humanity from sin or its effects (*OED* Redeemer 1).

5 This line, with its two 'to' phrases, has bothered many editors, who have often adopted 'in peace' from the quarto's 'now in peace'. Since Edward is not giving up the ghost 'now', the quarto phrase does not fit the context, and may itself represent an early attempt to 'correct' the line. The Folio line needs no correction, however; it makes sense as it stands.

7 Rivers and Hastings The F reading asks Dorset and Rivers to be reconciled, but both are relatives of Queen Elizabeth and already on the same side. The subsequent dialogue shows that Rivers and Hastings were intended, as the Q reading confirms.

8 Dissemble Disguise. Edward urges true affection rather than hatred temporarily disguised as love.

11 So . . . swear May I thrive according to the truth of my swearing. Hastings and Elizabeth express similar sentiments at 16 and 24.

12 dally pretend, counterfeit.

Lest he that is the supreme King of kings
Confound your hidden falsehood and award
Either of you to be the other's end.   15

HASTINGS So prosper I, as I swear perfect love.

RIVERS And I, as I love Hastings with my heart.

KING EDWARD Madam, yourself is not exempt from this,
Nor you, son Dorset, Buckingham, nor you;
You have been factious one against the other.   20
Wife, love Lord Hastings, let him kiss your hand,
And what you do, do it unfeignedly.

ELIZABETH There, Hastings, I will never more remember
Our former hatred, so thrive I and mine.

KING EDWARD Dorset, embrace him. Hastings, love lord marquess.   25

DORSET This interchange of love, I here protest,
Upon my part shall be inviolable.

HASTINGS And so swear I.

KING EDWARD Now, princely Buckingham, seal thou this league
With thy embracements to my wife's allies,   30
And make me happy in your unity.

BUCKINGHAM Whenever Buckingham doth turn his hate
Upon your grace, but with all duteous love
Doth cherish you and yours, God punish me
With hate in those where I expect most love.   35
When I have most need to employ a friend,

18 is . . . from] F; are . . . in Qq 19 you, son] F; your son Qq 23 There] F; Here Qq 25] *Rowe; Dorset . . . him:* /
Hastings . . . Marquesse. F; *not in* Qq 26 This] F, Q; Thus Q2–6 27 inviolable] F; vnuiolable Qq 28 I] F; I my Lord
Qq 30 embracements] F, Q, Q2–5; embracement Q6 33 Upon your grace] F; On you or yours Qq

13 **King of kings** God.
14 **Confound** Overthrow.
14 **award** bestow.
15 Each of you to be the death of the other.
19 **son** stepson.
20 **factious** inclined to form factions or parties.
23 **There** A clear example of a stage direction embedded in the dialogue. As the queen says 'There,' she gives Hastings her hand.
24 **so thrive I and mine** as I hope to see my family thrive. Elizabeth, like Hastings and the others, links her dearest wishes to her pledge of friendship and peace. Unlike the others, she appears to be sincere.
25 The italic *Hastings* at the start of a short line in F suggests a misunderstanding by the F compositor, who may have taken the name for a speech heading and so begun a new line.

25 **embrace him** An implied stage direction.
26 **protest** assert, swear.
29 **princely** The king alludes to Buckingham's noble birth, perhaps to flatter him a bit before asking him to reconcile with the queen's less well-born relatives. Buckingham was a descendant of Thomas of Woodstock, one of Edward III's seven sons (see *R2* 1.2.11 ff.).
29 **league** alliance.
32–5 Buckingham's syntax is convoluted, even for him, but the general sense of what he says comes through: 'If I ever turn my hate on you or yours instead of cherishing you with all duteous love, let God punish me with the hatred of those from whom I expect most love.'
33 **but** unless.

And most assurèd that he is a friend,
Deep, hollow, treacherous, and full of guile
Be he unto me. This do I beg of heaven,
When I am cold in love to you or yours.   40
                              Embrace
KING EDWARD A pleasing cordial, princely Buckingham,
          Is this thy vow unto my sickly heart.
          There wanteth now our brother Gloucester here
          To make the blessèd period of this peace.
BUCKINGHAM And in good time,   45
          Here comes Sir Richard Ratcliffe and the duke.

                    Enter RATCLIFFE *and* RICHARD

RICHARD Good morrow to my sovereign king and queen;
          And princely peers, a happy time of day.
KING EDWARD Happy indeed, as we have spent the day.
          Gloucester, we have done deeds of charity,   50
          Made peace of enmity, fair love of hate,
          Between these swelling wrong-incensèd peers.
RICHARD A blessèd labour, my most sovereign lord.
          Among this princely heap, if any here
          By false intelligence or wrong surmise   55
          Hold me a foe; if I unwillingly or in my rage

---

39 heaven] F; God Qq   40 love] F; zeale Qd   40 SD] F; *not in* Qq   44 blessèd] F; perfect Qq   45–6] F; And in good time here comes the noble Duke. Qq   46 SD] F; *Enter Glocest.* Qq (*subst.*) (*after 44*)   50 Gloucester] F; Brother Qq   52 wrong-incensèd] *Pope*; wrong insenced F, Qq (*subst.*)   53 my most] F, Q, Q2; most Q3–6   54 Among] F; Amongst Qq   56 unwillingly] F; unwittingly Qq

38 **Deep** Mysterious, secretive.
39 **heaven** Some commentators find evidence of Folio censorship in the difference between 'I beg of God' in the quartos and 'I beg of heaven' in F, which was printed after the statute of 1606 forbidding profanity on stage. If so, such censorship was spotty at best. Compare, for example, 34, which reads 'God punish me' in all texts.
41 **cordial** tonic, medicine for the heart.
43 **wanteth** is missing. Edward seems to feel that Richard's presence is the only thing lacking for complete peace (as suggested by the quartos' 'perfect period' in the next line). Only Elizabeth remembers Clarence (76–7).
44 **period** conclusion.
46 **Sir Richard Ratcliffe** Ratcliffe has no lines and does not appear in the quartos. Like Catesby and Grey, he is nevertheless useful in establishing factions and alliances for the audience.
46 SD Many editors prefer the quarto placing of Richard's entrance before Buckingham's lines. In the Folio version, Buckingham's announcement conveys information to the audience, since he can see the approaching figures while they cannot. Buckingham more than once takes note of the pat arrival of characters on cue, as at 3.1.24, when he announces Hastings: 'And in good time, here comes the sweating lord.'
50 **charity** love.
52 **swelling** with hostility.
54 **princely heap** high-born group. 'Heap' appears designed to leave the assembled nobles wondering if they have been flattered or insulted.
55 **intelligence** information.

Have aught committed that is hardly borne
To any in this presence, I desire
To reconcile me to his friendly peace.
'Tis death to me to be at enmity;   60
I hate it and desire all good men's love.
First, madam, I entreat true peace of you,
Which I will purchase with my duteous service;
Of you, my noble cousin Buckingham,
If ever any grudge were lodged between us;   65
Of you and you, Lord Rivers, and of Dorset,
That all without desert have frowned on me;
Of you, Lord Woodville, and Lord Scales, of you;
Dukes, earls, lords, gentlemen, indeed of all.
I do not know that Englishman alive   70
With whom my soul is any jot at odds
More than the infant that is born tonight.
I thank my God for my humility.
ELIZABETH A holy day shall this be kept hereafter.
I would to God all strifes were well compounded.   75
My sovereign lord, I do beseech your highness
To take our brother Clarence to your grace.
RICHARD Why, madam, have I offered love for this,
To be so flouted in this royal presence?

---

58 To] F; By Qq   59 his] F, Q, Q3–6; this Q2   62 true peace] F, Q, Q2; peace Q3–6   63 will purchase] F, Q, Q2; purchase Q3–6   66] F; Of you Lo: Riuers, and Lord Gray of you Qq   68] F; *not in* Qq   76 lord] F; liege Qq   76 your highness] F; your Maiesty Q, Q2–5; you Maiestie Q6   79 so flouted] F; thus scorned Qq (*subst.*)

57–8 is . . . presence conveys hurt to anyone here.

60 at enmity in a state of hatred. Ironically, Richard next announces that he hates hatred.

64 cousin A term used for a 'cousin' in the modern sense, for any relative or for a close associate. Buckingham and Richard are distant relatives; they share a common ancestor in Edward III (see Appendix 2, p. 232 below).

65 lodged harboured, established.

66 of Dorset This extra 'of' is puzzling if Dorset is included in 'Of you and you'. Perhaps Richard actually says 'of you and you' to Rivers, in keeping with his ironic address to Rivers by each of his other titles in 68 (see 68 n.).

67 all without desert entirely without my having deserved it.

68 Lord Woodville and Lord Scales were both titles for Lord Rivers. Richard thus addresses Rivers at least three times in this one speech. Given the apparent confusion about Rivers/Woodville in the stage directions, many editors have supposed this F line to be a mistake (see Variorum, p. 154). On the other hand, sarcastically acknowledging all of Rivers's titles is completely consistent with Richard's manner toward Elizabeth's relatives throughout the play.

71 jot small particle. From the Latin *iota* (*OED* Jot).

72 More than the soul of a newborn baby is.

75 compounded resolved.

77 to your grace to yourself; into your good graces.

79 flouted outraged.

Who knows not that the gentle duke is dead?   80
          They all start
You do him injury to scorn his corpse.
KING EDWARD Who knows not he is dead?
Who knows he is?
ELIZABETH All-seeing heaven, what a world is this?
BUCKINGHAM Look I so pale, Lord Dorset, as the rest?   85
DORSET Ay, my good lord, and no man in the presence
But his red colour hath forsook his cheeks.
KING EDWARD Is Clarence dead? The order was reversed.
RICHARD But he (poor man) by your first order died,
And that a wingèd Mercury did bear;   90
Some tardy cripple bare the countermand,
That came too lag to see him burièd.
God grant that some, less noble and less loyal,
Nearer in bloody thoughts and not in blood,
Deserve not worse than wretched Clarence did,   95
And yet go current from suspicion.

Enter [STANLEY] EARL OF DERBY

STANLEY A boon, my sovereign, for my service done.
KING EDWARD I prithee, peace, my soul is full of sorrow.
STANLEY I will not rise unless your highness hear me.
KING EDWARD Then say at once what is it thou requests.   100
STANLEY The forfeit, sovereign, of my servant's life,

---

80 gentle] F; noble Qq   80 SD] F; *not in* Qq   82–3] F; *as one line* Qq   82 SH] F; *Ryu.* Q; *Riu.* Q2; *Ri.* Q3–6   84 All-seeing]
F; All seeing Qq   86 man] F; one Qq   86 the] F; this Qq   89 man] F; soule Qq   90 wingèd] F, Q2–6; wingled Q   91
bare] F; bore Qq   94 and] F; but Qq   96 SD STANLEY] *Theobald (Enter Lord Stanly.);* *Enter Earle of Derby.* F; *Enter*
Darby. Qq *(subst.)*   98 prithee] F; pray thee Qq   99 hear me] F; grant Qq *(subst.)*   100 say] F; speake Qq   100 requests]
F; demaundst Qq   101 SH] F *(Der.),* Q, Q2 *(Dar.),* Q4–6 *(Dar.);* *not in* Q3

---

86 the presence the presence of the king.

90 that the 'first order' (89). The regular
iambic metre stresses the word.

90 wingèd Mercury Mercury, messenger to
the Roman gods and patron of thieves, wore
wings on his hat and sandals. It was proverbial
that 'Ill news hath wings' (Tilley 148).

91 Some tardy cripple Both messengers
must be Richard himself. This ironic line may
have suggested the often-used stage business of
Richard's fumbling for the right warrant to give
the two Murderers at 1.3.344.

91 bare did bear, 'did' being understood from
90.

92 lag late.

93–6 God grant that those less noble and

less loyal than Clarence, more bloody in their
thoughts, though not as royal in blood, do not
deserve even worse than Clarence did and yet
walk around unsuspected. Richard clearly aims
at Elizabeth, asserting that these 'less loyal' persons exist, even as he pretends to pray that they
have done nothing to deserve Clarence's fate.

96 go current be generally accepted as genuine (*OED* Current *a* 8).

96 from removed from.

97 boon request for a favour (*OED* Boon *sb*[1]
2b). Stanley alludes to the ancient relationship
between the lord and his subordinates, in which
the lord was expected to grant favours for ser-
vices rendered.

101 The return of my servant's forfeited life.

Who slew today a riotous gentleman
Lately attendant on the Duke of Norfolk.
KING EDWARD Have I a tongue to doom my brother's death,
And shall that tongue give pardon to a slave?   105
My brother killed no man; his fault was thought,
And yet his punishment was bitter death.
Who sued to me for him? Who (in my wrath)
Kneeled at my feet and bid me be advised?
Who spoke of brotherhood? Who spoke of love?   110
Who told me how the poor soul did forsake
The mighty Warwick and did fight for me?
Who told me, in the field at Tewkesbury,
When Oxford had me down, he rescued me
And said 'Dear brother, live, and be a king'?   115
Who told me, when we both lay in the field,
Frozen almost to death, how he did lap me
Even in his garments and did give himself
(All thin and naked) to the numb cold night?
All this from my remembrance brutish wrath   120
Sinfully plucked, and not a man of you
Had so much grace to put it in my mind.
But when your carters or your waiting vassals
Have done a drunken slaughter and defaced
The precious image of our dear redeemer,   125
You straight are on your knees for pardon, pardon,
And I, unjustly too, must grant it you.
But for my brother not a man would speak,
Nor I, ungracious, speak unto myself

---

105 that tongue] F; the same Qq 106 killed] F; slew Qq (*subst.*) 107 bitter] F; cruell Qq 108 wrath] F; rage Qq 109 at] Qq; and F 109 bid] F; bad Qq (*subst.*) 110 Who spoke . . . Who spoke] F; Who spake . . . who Qq 113 at] F; by Qq 115 'Dear . . . king'] *Hanmer (italics); no quotation marks in* F, Qq 116 in] F, Q, Q3–6; ie Q2 118 garments] F; owne garments Q, Q2–5; owne armes Q6 118 did give] F; gave Qq 121 plucked] F, Q2–6 (*subst.*); puckt Q 128 man] F, Q, Q2, Q6; mast Q3–5

104 **doom** decree (*OED* Doom *v* 5).
105 **slave** servant.
106 **killed no man** This is not precisely true, although Clarence's killings were committed during war, and in support of Edward, as Clarence himself has said (1.4.200–1).
106 **thought** Edward believes that Clarence plotted against him but did not act.
114 **he rescued me** Shakespeare does not explicitly represent this scene, although he does show Clarence fighting for Edward (*3H6* 5.4.82 SD).

117 **lap** wrap.
123 **carters** heavy labourers.
123 **vassals** table servants. Edward exaggerates the lowliness of Stanley's 'servant', who may himself be a gentleman, to emphasise his own neglect of a blood relative.
124–5 **defaced . . . redeemer** killed a person, since humans were made in the image of God.

For him, poor soul. The proudest of you all   130
Have been beholding to him in his life,
Yet none of you would once beg for his life.
O God, I fear thy justice will take hold
On me and you, and mine and yours, for this.
Come, Hastings, help me to my closet.   135
Ah, poor Clarence!

                     Exeunt some with K[ing] and Queen

RICHARD   This is the fruits of rashness. Marked you not
How that the guilty kindred of the queen
Looked pale when they did hear of Clarence' death?
Oh, they did urge it still unto the king.   140
God will revenge it. Come, lords, will you go
To comfort Edward with our company?
BUCKINGHAM   We wait upon your grace.

                                          Exeunt

2.2 *Enter the old* DUCHESS OF YORK *with the two children*
[BOY *and* GIRL] *of Clarence*

BOY   Good grandam, tell us, is our father dead?
DUCHESS   No, boy.
GIRL   Why do you weep so oft, and beat your breast,
     And cry, 'O Clarence, my unhappy son'?

---

131 beholding] F, Q, Q2–3; beholden Q4–6   132 beg] F; pleade Qq (*subst.*)   134 yours] F, Q, Q2–5; your Q6   135–6] F; *as one line* Qq   136 Ah] F; oh Qq   136 SD] F (*Exeunt some with K. & Queen.*); *Exit.* Qq   137 fruits] F; fruit Qq (*subst.*)   137 rashness] F, Q, Q2 (*subst.*); rawnes Q3–6 (*subst.*)   141 Come, lords, will you go] F; But come lets in Qq   143] F; *not in* Qq   Act 2, Scene 2   2.2] F (*Scena Secunda.*); *not in* Qq   0 SD] F; *Enter Dutches of Yorke, with Clarence Children.* Qq (*subst.*)   1 SH] Qq; *Edw.* F   1 Good grandam, tell us] F; Tell me good Granam Qq   3 SH] F (*Daugh.*); *Boy* Qq   3 you] Qq; *not in* F   3 weep so oft] F; wring your hands Qq   4 'O . . . son'] *Hanmer* (*italics*); *no quotation marks in* F, Qq

131 beholding beholden, indebted.
134 On me, on all of you, on my family and on yours.
135 closet private room.
139 Looked pale This observation is typical of Richard's half-truths. As the dialogue between Buckingham and Dorset at 85–7 shows, everyone in the scene looks pale at the news of Clarence's death.
140 urge it advocate Clarence's death.
140 still constantly.

Act 2, Scene 2
   This first part of this scene, one of the play's three female triads, has no counterpart in the chronicles (see pp. 9–12 above). Holinshed says that once Edward IV was dead, Richard set about to destroy the queen's kindred, who surrounded the young Prince of Wales. With this purpose 'the duke of Glocester soone set on fire them that were of themselues easie to kindle, &, in speciallie twaine, Edward [actually Henry] duke of Buckingham, and William lord Hastings, then chamberleine' (Holinshed, III, 366). According to Holinshed, the queen herself was persuaded that the prince should not travel with a large force.

   0 SD *children . . . of Clarence* Clarence's two children were Margaret and Edward Plantagenet, who would have been about twelve and ten years old, respectively, at the time of these events.

BOY Why do you look on us, and shake your head,   5
        And call us orphans, wretches, castaways,
        If that our noble father were alive?
DUCHESS My pretty cousins, you mistake me both.
        I do lament the sickness of the king,
        As loath to lose him, not your father's death.   10
        It were lost sorrow to wail one that's lost.
BOY Then you conclude, my grandam, he is dead.
        The king mine uncle is to blame for it.
        God will revenge it, whom I will importune
        With earnest prayers all to that effect.   15
GIRL And so will I.
DUCHESS Peace, children, peace. The king doth love you well.
        Incapable and shallow innocents,
        You cannot guess who caused your father's death.
BOY Grandam, we can, for my good uncle Gloucester   20
        Told me the king, provoked to it by the queen,
        Devised impeachments to imprison him.
        And when my uncle told me so, he wept,
        And pitied me, and kindly kissed my cheek;
        Bade me rely on him as on my father,   25
        And he would love me dearly as a child.
DUCHESS Ah, that deceit should steal such gentle shape
        And with a virtuous visor hide deep vice.
        He is my son, ay, and therein my shame,

---

5 SH] F; *Gerl.* Qq (*subst.*)   6 orphans, wretches] F; wretches, Orphanes Qq   7 were] F; be Qq   8 both] F; much Qq   10 not] F, Q, Q2–5; now Q6   10 death] F, Q, Q2–5; dead Q6   11 sorrow] F; labour Qq (*subst.*)   11 wail] F; weepe for Qq   12 you conclude, my grandam] F; Granam you conclude that Qq   13 mine] F; my Qq   13 it] F; this Qq   15 earnest] F; daily Qq (*subst.*)   16] F; *not in* Qq   16 SH] F (*Daugh.*)   21 provoked to it] F; prouoked Qq   23 my uncle] F; he Qq   24 pitied me] F; hugd me in his arme Qq   25 Bade] F; And bad Qq   25 as on] F; Q2–6; as in Q   26 a] F; his Qq   27 Ah] F; Oh Qq   27 shape] F; shapes Qq   28 visor] F; visard Qq (*subst.*)   28 deep vice] F; foule guile Qq   29 ay] F; yea Q, Q2–3, Q5–6; *not in* Q4

8 cousins relatives.
14 importune beg.
18 Helpless and unknowing children. The word 'innocents' recalls the theatrical roots of all Richard's child victims in the story of the massacre of the innocents, familiar to Shakespeare from medieval drama as well as from the Bible (Matt. 2.16). Richard's character derives in part from the stereotype of wicked King Herod as well as from the Vice figure in the morality plays. (See pp. 7–8 above.)
22 impeachments charges, accusations.
24 kindly This word has connotations of both kinship and benevolence (see *OED* Kindly *a* 2b; *OED* Kindly *adv* 2).

25 rely . . . father Clarence had proved notably unreliable to his relatives, which perhaps was Richard's real point.
27 gentle shape Richard's 'shape' is 'gentle' in the sense that he is well-born, and also in the sense that he pretends to be amiable toward Clarence's children. The phrase ironically recalls Richard's 'deformed' physical shape, as well.
28 visor outward appearance or disguise (*OED* Visor *sb* 3a). Originally, the part of a helmet that covers the face.
28 vice A reminder that Richard is not only vicious, but also related to the Vice of traditional English drama (see pp. 7–8 above).

Yet from my dugs he drew not this deceit. 30
BOY Think you my uncle did dissemble, grandam?
DUCHESS Ay, boy.
BOY I cannot think it. Hark, what noise is this?

Enter the QUEEN [ELIZABETH] *with her hair about her ears,*
RIVERS *and* DORSET *after her*

ELIZABETH Ah, who shall hinder me to wail and weep,
    To chide my fortune and torment myself? 35
    I'll join with black despair against my soul,
    And to myself become an enemy.
DUCHESS What means this scene of rude impatience?
ELIZABETH To make an act of tragic violence.
    Edward, my lord, thy son, our king, is dead. 40
    Why grow the branches when the root is gone?
    Why wither not the leaves that want their sap?
    If you will live, lament; if die, be brief,
    That our swift-wingèd souls may catch the king's,
    Or, like obedient subjects, follow him 45
    To his new kingdom of ne'er-changing night.
DUCHESS Ah, so much interest have I in thy sorrow
    As I had title in thy noble husband.
    I have bewept a worthy husband's death
    And lived with looking on his images, 50
    But now two mirrors of his princely semblance

---

33 SD] F; *Enter the Quee.* Q; *Enter the Queene.* Q2–6 (*subst.*)　34 Ah, who] F; Oh who Q, Q2, Q4; Wh who Q3; Whoy Q5 (*Edinburgh University, Folger 1, Huntington copies*); Who Q5 (*other copies*), Q6　36 soul] F, Q, Q2–4; selfe Q5–6　40 thy] F; your Qq　41 when . . . gone] F; now . . . witherd Qq (*subst.*)　42 that want their sap] F; the sap being gone Qq　44 swift-wingèd] F; swiftwinged Q; swift winged Q2–6　46 ne'er-changing night] F; perpetuall rest Qq　47 I] Qq; *not in* F 50 with] F; by Qq

30 **dugs** breasts.
33 SD *about her ears* hanging down. Loose hair was a conventional sign of distress in women. Riverside, which adopts the SD from Q *Hamlet*, has the mad Ophelia entering *distracted, with her hair down, playing on a lute* (4.5.20).
37 **to myself . . . enemy** I'll kill myself. Compare Anne's idea (1.2.86–8) that despair leads to suicide, making the self its own mortal enemy.
38 **rude** uncivilised.
38 **impatience** lack of the capacity to endure. Compare 1.1.116, where Richard urges Clarence to 'have patience' with his circumstances while in prison.
39 **act** action (that is, suicide), but also a the-

atrical act, responding to the Duchess's suggestion at 38 that Elizabeth is making a 'scene'.
42 **want** lack.
43 **brief** quick.
46 **ne'er-changing night** Elizabeth's lament does not picture King Edward in the Christian heaven, but in the more classical 'kingdom of perpetual night' that also appears in Clarence's dream (1.4.45–63).
48 **title** claim, in this case as a mother.
50 **his images** his sons. Whatever theories of resemblance Richard may hold or invent, the Duchess evidently thinks all her sons look like their father.
51 **semblance** appearance, form.

Are cracked in pieces by malignant death,
And I for comfort have but one false glass,
That grieves me when I see my shame in him.
Thou art a widow, yet thou art a mother   55
And hast the comfort of thy children left.
But death hath snatched my husband from mine arms
And plucked two crutches from my feeble hands,
Clarence and Edward. Oh, what cause have I,
Thine being but a moiety of my moan,   60
To overgo thy woes and drown thy cries.
BOY Ah, aunt, you wept not for our father's death.
    How can we aid you with our kindred tears?
GIRL Our fatherless distress was left unmoaned.
    Your widow-dolour likewise be unwept.   65
ELIZABETH Give me no help in lamentation.
    I am not barren to bring forth complaints.
    All springs reduce their currents to mine eyes,
    That I, being governed by the watery moon,
    May send forth plenteous tears to drown the world.   70
    Ah, for my husband, for my dear lord Edward.
CHILDREN Ah, for our father, for our dear lord Clarence.
DUCHESS Alas for both, both mine Edward and Clarence.
ELIZABETH What stay had I but Edward? And he's gone.
CHILDREN What stay had we but Clarence? And he's gone.   75
DUCHESS What stays had I but they? And they are gone.
ELIZABETH Was never widow had so dear a loss.
CHILDREN Were never orphans had so dear a loss.

---

54 That] F; Which Qq 56 left] F; left thee Qq 57 husband] F; children 58 hands] F; limmes Qq 59 Clarence and
Edward] F; Edward and Clarence Qq 60 Thine] F; Then Qq 60 moan] F; griefe Q, Q2–5; selfe Q6 61 woes] F; plaints
Q, Q3–6; plants Q2 61 thy cries] F, Q, Q2–4; the cries Q5–6 62 Ah] F; Good Qq 63 kindred] F; kindreds Qq 65
widow-dolour] F; widdowes doulours Qq (*subst.*) 67 complaints] F; laments Qq 69 moon] F; moane Qq 71 Ah] F; Oh
Qq 71 dear] F; eire Q; eyre Q2; heire Q3–6 72 SH] F (*Chil.*); *Ambo* Qq (*subst.*) 72 Ah] F; Oh Qq 74 he's] F; he is Q,
Q2–5; is he Q6 75 SH] F (*Chil.*); *Ambo.* Q, Q2–5; *Ambo.* Q6 75 he's] F; he is Q, Q2–5; is he Q6 76 stays] F, Q, Q2–5; stay
Q6 77 never] F, Q, Q2–3, Q5–6; euer Q4 78 SH] F (*Chil.*); *Ambo.* Q, Q2, Q6; *Am.* Q3–5 78 Were never] F; Was neuer
Q; Was euer Q2–6 78 so dear a] F; a dearer Qq

---

53 **false glass** Richard.
54 **my shame in him** Richard is a 'false glass'
(53) because he embodies his mother's shame –
she is ashamed of him – rather than because he
reflects any shameful quality of hers. Compare
30: 'from my dugs he drew not this deceit'.
60 **a moiety of my moan** half as much grief
as mine.
61 **overgo** surpass, outdo.

63 **kindred tears** tears that come from being
in the same family; similar tears.
65 **widow-dolour** widow's sadness.
68 May the water of all the springs in the
world be concentrated in my eyes.
69 **being governed . . . moon** being, like the
ocean tides, controlled by the moon.
74 **stay** support.
77 **dear** costly.

DUCHESS Was never mother had so dear a loss.
        Alas, I am the mother of these griefs; 80
        Their woes are parcelled, mine is general.
        She for an Edward weeps, and so do I;
        I for a Clarence weep, so doth not she.
        These babes for Clarence weep, and so do I;
        I for an Edward weep, so do not they. 85
        Alas, you three, on me, threefold distressed,
        Pour all your tears; I am your sorrow's nurse,
        And I will pamper it with lamentation.
DORSET Comfort, dear mother. God is much displeased
        That you take with unthankfulness his doing. 90
        In common worldly things 'tis called ungrateful
        With dull unwillingness to repay a debt
        Which with a bounteous hand was kindly lent;
        Much more to be thus opposite with heaven,
        For it requires the royal debt it lent you. 95
RIVERS Madam, bethink you like a careful mother
        Of the young prince your son. Send straight for him.
        Let him be crowned. In him your comfort lives.
        Drown desperate sorrow in dead Edward's grave
        And plant your joys in living Edward's throne. 100

Enter RICHARD, BUCKINGHAM, [STANLEY EARL OF]
      DERBY, HASTINGS, *and* RATCLIFFE

RICHARD Sister, have comfort. All of us have cause
        To wail the dimming of our shining star,
        But none can help our harms by wailing them.
        Madam, my mother, I do cry you mercy;
        I did not see your grace. Humbly on my knee 105

---

79 never] F, Q; euer Q2–6 79 so dear a] F; a dearer Qq 80 griefs] F; mones Qq (*subst.*) 81 is] F; are Qq 82 an Edward] F; Edward Qq 83 weep] Qq; weepes F 84–5] Qq; *as one line* F 84 and so do I] Qq; *not in* F 85 I for an Edward weep] Q, Q2–3, Q5–6; I for a Edward Q4; *not in* F 85 so do not] F, Q; and so do Q2–6 (*subst.*) 87 Pour] F (Power), Q (Poure), Q3–6 (Powre); Proue Q2 88 lamentation] F; laminations Qq 89–100] F; *not in* Qq. Qq (*subst.*) *after 88* 101 Sister] F; Madame Qq 103 help our] F; cure their Qq

---

81 **parcelled** partial.
81 **general** inclusive, complete.
84–5 In F, the first half of 84 forms a single line with the second half of 85. The other two half-lines are missing. A plausible explanation for this gap is 'eye-skip', in which the compositor, glancing first at his copy and then at his type, accidentally finished the first line with the ending of the second.
87 **nurse** wet nurse, feeder.
88 **pamper** nurture.

92 **dull** listless.
94 **opposite with** contrary toward.
95 **For** Because.
95 **royal debt** the king.
100 **plant** establish; with a play on 'Plantagenet', the royal family name.
104 **cry you mercy** beg your pardon.
105 **on my knee** Perhaps another implied stage direction. It was common for children to kneel before their parents, as Richard may do here.

I crave your blessing.

DUCHESS God bless thee and put meekness in thy breast,
        Love, charity, obedience, and true duty.

RICHARD Amen. [*Aside*] And make me die a good old man,
        That is the butt-end of a mother's blessing;   110
        I marvel that her grace did leave it out.

BUCKINGHAM You cloudy princes and heart-sorrowing peers
        That bear this heavy mutual load of moan,
        Now cheer each other in each other's love.
        Though we have spent our harvest of this king,   115
        We are to reap the harvest of his son.
        The broken rancour of your high-swoll'n hates,
        But lately splintered, knit, and joined together,
        Must gently be preserved, cherished, and kept.
        Me seemeth good that with some little train   120
        Forthwith from Ludlow the young prince be fet
        Hither to London, to be crowned our king.

RIVERS Why with some little train,
        My lord of Buckingham?

BUCKINGHAM Marry, my lord, lest by a multitude   125
        The new-healed wound of malice should break out,
        Which would be so much the more dangerous
        By how much the estate is green and yet ungoverned.

---

106 your] F, Q, Q2–5; you Q6   107 breast] F; minde Qq (*subst.*)   109 SD] *Hanmer; not in* F, Qq   109 And] F, Q, Q2–5; not in Q6   110 That is] F; Thats Qq   110 butt-end] F; butt end Qq   110 a] F, Q; my Q2–6   111 that] F; why Qq   113 heavy mutual] F; mutuall heavy Qq (*subst.*)   115 of] F, Q; for Q2–6   116 son] F, Q, Q2–5 (sonne); soone Q6   117 high-swoll'n hates] F; high swolne hearts Qq   118 splintered] F, Qq; splinted Q2–6   119 gently] F, Q; greatly Q2–6   121 fet] F; fetcht Qq   123–41 F; *not in* Qq

112 cloudy darkened by grief and anger; gloomy, depressed (see *OED* Cloudy 6).

112 princes . . . peers Buckingham draws a subtle class distinction, splitting the group between 'princes' and mere lords.

113 moan grief.

116 harvest of his son The image of harvesting the young prince is ominous, especially since both Richard and the First Murderer have used similar metaphors in contexts of killing (see 1.2.251, 1.4.231).

117 broken rancour interrupted hostility.

118 splintered This word suggests both splintering in the modern sense of smashing – an echo of 'broken rancour' – and also mending with a splint. The overall image is one of breaking and resetting a bone so it will knit properly.

120 Me seemeth good It seems good to me.

120 some little train a small retinue. The modern railroad 'train' apparently inspired Richard Eyre and Ian McKellen, whose Royal

National Theatre production (1989) was set in the 1930s, to transport the young prince via steam locomotive. Loncraine and McKellen's film version retains the visual pun, along with an echo in 2.4, where little York plays with a toy train.

121 Ludlow Ludlow Castle, a hundred and fifty miles north-west of London, near the Welsh border.

121 fet fetched (see *OED* Fet).

123–4 Rivers's two short lines suggest that his polite 'My lord of Buckingham' is an afterthought, perhaps elicited by a raised eyebrow from Buckingham at being addressed so briefly (124). Some intimidation at this point would help explain Rivers's capitulation at 136 ff.

128 Because the prince's administration is new ('green', unripe) and not yet in control of the state. 'Green' also implies the immaturity of the prince himself.

Where every horse bears his commanding rein
And may direct his course as please himself,   130
As well the fear of harm, as harm apparent,
In my opinion, ought to be prevented.
RICHARD I hope the king made peace with all of us,
And the compact is firm and true in me.
RIVERS And so in me, and so, I think, in all.   135
Yet since it is but green, it should be put
To no apparent likelihood of breach,
Which haply by much company might be urged.
Therefore I say with noble Buckingham
That it is meet so few should fetch the prince.   140
HASTINGS And so say I.
RICHARD Then be it so, and go we to determine
Who they shall be that straight shall post to Ludlow.
Madam, and you my sister, will you go
To give your censures in this business?   145

Exeunt [all but] Buckingham and Richard

BUCKINGHAM My lord, whoever journeys to the prince,
For God's sake let not us two stay at home,
For by the way I'll sort occasion,
As index to the story we late talked of,
To part the queen's proud kindred from the prince.   150

---

143 Ludlow] Qq; London F   144 sister] F; mother Qq   145 this] F; this waighty Qq (*subst.*)   145] F; To . . . busines, /
Ans. With all our hearts. Qq   145 SD] Malone; *Exeunt. Manet Buckingham, and Richard.* F; *Exeunt man. Glo. Buck.* Q,
Q2; *Exeunt manet Glo. Buck.* Q3–6   146 whoever] F, Q, Q2–3, Q5–6; who Q4   147 God's] Qq (Gods); God F   147 stay
at home] F; stay behind Q; be behind Q2–6 (*subst.*)   149 late] F, Q; lately Q2–6   149 of] F, Q, Q2; off Q3–6   150 prince]
F; King Qq

129–30 Where every horse (or horseman) chooses his own direction (rather than all following a strong commander). Buckingham implies an analogy to the state of affairs in England at the moment.

131 Even the fear of trouble, and certainly the appearance of trouble.

137 breach break, rupture. Rivers seems easily swayed by Buckingham's far-fetched argument that a crowd accompanying the prince would somehow encourage suspicion or attacks.

138 haply perhaps.
138 urged incited.
140 meet appropriate.
143 straight immediately.
143 post ride quickly.
143 Ludlow F's 'London' probably results from compositorial carelessness. Wilson speculates that the error 'may be due to "L" written for "Ludlow" in the manuscript' (p. 195).

144 Madam . . . sister In Q, Richard defers to the queen as 'Madam', addressing her before his mother, as protocol requires. In F, however, the order is reversed, allowing Richard to make even this apparently polite request into a subtle insult to Elizabeth. His calling her 'sister', both here and at 101, may also be tinged with sarcasm. Compare his earlier remark that he would do anything to free Clarence from prison, even if he had to call Edward's wife 'sister' (1.1.109).

145 censures opinions.
148 by the way on the way (to Ludlow).
148 sort find.
149 index preface.
149 the story we late talked of the matter we talked about lately.

RICHARD My other self, my counsel's consistory,
       My oracle, my prophet, my dear cousin,
       I, as a child, will go by thy direction.
       Toward Ludlow then, for we'll not stay behind.

                                        Exeunt

2.3 *Enter one* [FIRST] CITIZEN *at one door, and another* [SECOND
CITIZEN] *at the other*

FIRST CITIZEN Good morrow, neighbour. Whither away so fast?
SECOND CITIZEN I promise you, I scarcely know myself.
       Hear you the news abroad?
FIRST CITIZEN Yes, that the king is dead.
SECOND CITIZEN Ill news, by'r Lady; seldom comes the better.   5
       I fear, I fear, 'twill prove a giddy world.

               Enter another [THIRD] CITIZEN

THIRD CITIZEN Neighbours, God speed.
FIRST CITIZEN Give you good morrow, sir.
THIRD CITIZEN Doth the news hold of good King Edward's death?
SECOND CITIZEN Ay, sir, it is too true, God help the while.   10

153 as] F; like Qq   154 Toward] F; Towards Qq   154 Ludlow] Qq; London F   154 we'll] F; we will Qq   154 SD] F; *Exit.*
Q3–6; *not in* Q, Q2   Act 2, Scene 3   2.3] F (*Scena Tertia.*); *not in* Qq   0 SD] F; *Enter two Citizens.* Qq (*subst.*)   0 SD
FIRST] *This edn; not in* F, Qq   0 SD SECOND] *This edn; not in* F, Qq   1 SH] F, Qq (*1. Cit.*) (*subst.*)   1 Good morrow,
neighbour] F; Neighbour well met Qq   2 SH] F, Qq (*2. Cit.*) (*subst.*)   4 Yes] F; I Qq   5 SH] F; *1* Q, Q2–5; *1.* Q6   5 Ill] F;
Bad Qq   6 giddy] F; troublous Q; troublesome Q2–6   6 SD THIRD] *This edn; not in* F, Qq   7 SH] F, Qq (*3.*) (*subst.*)   7
Neighbours, God speed] F; Good morrow neighbours Qq   8] F; *not in* Qq   9 the] F; this Qq   9 King] F, Q, Q2, Q4, Q6;
Kings Q3, Q5   10–11] F; *as one line* Qq   10 SH] F (*2.*); *1* Q, Q2–5; *1.* Q6   10] F (*subst.*); It doth. Qq

151 my counsel's consistory the meeting
place of my advisers, that is, the source of all
good advice.
153 as a child An ironic warning considering Richard's childhood behaviour as described
by his mother: 'frightful, desperate, wild, and
furious' (4.4.170).

Act 2, Scene 3
  This scene reflects portions of the chronicles
that refer to the discontent of the people: 'began
there here and there abouts, some maner of mut-
tering among the people, as though all should not
long be well, though they neither wist what they
feared, nor wherefore: were it, that before such
great things, mens hearts of a secret instinct of
nature misgiue them; as the sea without wind
swelleth of himselfe sometime before a tempest'
(Holinshed, III, 379).
  0 SD *one door . . . other* Shakespeare's
stage probably had two upstage doors which

could stand for houses or other locations not
seen.
  2 promise assure.
  5 SH Here the quartos get out of step with the
Folio in assigning speech headings, a difference
that persists throughout the scene.
  5 by'r Lady by Our Lady (by the Virgin
Mary).
  5 seldom comes the better seldom comes
good news. The phrase was proverbial (see Tilley
B332, citing this line as an example). It carries the
general sense that any news is likely to be bad
news.
  6 giddy inconstant.
  7 God speed God speed you. Usually a
farewell rather than a greeting.
  8 Give you God give you.
  10 God help the while An exclamation of
grief (see *OED* While *sb* 6d).

THIRD CITIZEN Then, masters, look to see a troublous world.
FIRST CITIZEN No, no, by God's good grace his son shall reign.
THIRD CITIZEN Woe to that land that's governed by a child.
SECOND CITIZEN In him there is a hope of government,
 Which in his nonage, council under him,   15
 And in his full and ripened years, himself
 No doubt shall then, and till then, govern well.
FIRST CITIZEN So stood the state when Henry the Sixth
 Was crowned in Paris but at nine months old.
THIRD CITIZEN Stood the state so? No, no, good friends, God wot, 20
 For then this land was famously enriched
 With politic grave counsel. Then the king
 Had virtuous uncles to protect his grace.
FIRST CITIZEN Why, so hath this, both by his father and mother.
THIRD CITIZEN Better it were they all came by his father,   25
 Or by his father there were none at all.
 For emulation who shall now be nearest
 Will touch us all too near, if God prevent not.
 Oh, full of danger is the Duke of Gloucester,
 And the queen's sons and brothers haught and proud. 30
 And were they to be ruled, and not to rule,
 This sickly land might solace as before.
FIRST CITIZEN Come, come, we fear the worst; all will be well.
THIRD CITIZEN When clouds are seen, wise men put on their cloaks;
 When great leaves fall, then winter is at hand;   35
 When the sun sets, who doth not look for night?

---

12 good grace] F, Q; grace Q2–6   15 Which] F; That Qq   18 Henry] F; Harry Qq   19 in] F; at Qq   19 nine months] F, Q3–6 (*subst.*); ix. moneths Q; xi. moneths Q2   20 No, no, good friends, God wot] F; no good my friend not so Qq   24 SH] F; 2 Q, Q2–5; 2. Q6   24 Why, so] F; So Qq   24 his] Q; his] F; the Qq   25 his] F; the Qq   26 his] F; the Qq   27 who shall now] F; now, who shall Qq   28 Will] F, Q; Which Q2–6   30 sons and brothers] F; kindred Qq   30 haught] F; hauty Qq (*subst.*)   31 to rule] F, Q, Q2–5; rule Q6   33 SH] F; 2 Q, Q2–5; 2. Q6   33 will be] F; shalbe Q, Q2; shall Q3–6   34 are seen] F; appeare Qq   35 then] F; the Qq

11 **masters** sirs, gentlemen.
11 **troublous** troubled.
13 Tilley lists this as proverbial, tracing it to Eccles. 10.16: 'Woe to thee, O land, when thy king is a child.' In More, Buckingham uses a similar phrase in his speech to the citizens at the Guildhall (p. 74).
15 **nonage** minority.
15 **council** The king's council of ministers, normally under his control, but in the case of a child, governing in his place. The Second Citizen's sentence is complex, but the thought is clear: the council will no doubt govern well while the king is a child, and the king will no doubt

govern well when he grows up.
20 **wot** knows.
22 **politic** prudent, wise.
23 **uncles** For Shakespeare's portrayals of these uncles, see *1H6* and *2H6*.
27 **emulation** competition.
27 **who . . . nearest** who shall be closest to the king.
32 **solace** console itself, be cheerful.
33 **all will be well** Compare this remark with Queen Elizabeth's pessimism in 1.3 and also with Shakespeare's general distrust of the phrase 'all's well' (see 1.3.40–1n.). The Third Citizen is more cautious (38–9).

Untimely storms makes men expect a dearth.
All may be well, but if God sort it so,
'Tis more than we deserve or I expect.
SECOND CITIZEN Truly, the hearts of men are full of fear. 40
You cannot reason almost with a man
That looks not heavily and full of dread.
THIRD CITIZEN Before the days of change, still is it so.
By a divine instinct, men's minds mistrust
Ensuing danger, as by proof, we see 45
The water swell before a boisterous storm.
But leave it all to God. Whither away?
SECOND CITIZEN Marry, we were sent for to the justices.
THIRD CITIZEN And so was I. I'll bear you company.

Exeunt

2.4 *Enter [the]* ARCHBISHOP [OF YORK], [*the*] *young* [DUKE OF]
YORK, *the* QUEEN [ELIZABETH], *and the* DUCHESS [OF YORK]

ARCHBISHOP Last night, I heard, they lay at Stony Stratford,
And at Northampton they do rest tonight.

37 makes] F; make Qq 38 may] F, Q, Q2–5; men Q6 40 SH] F; *1* Q, Q2–5; *1.* Q6 40 hearts] F; soules Qq 40 fear] F;
bread Q, Q2; dread Q3–6 41 You] F; Yee Q; Ye Q2–6 41 reason almost] F; almost reason Qq (almast Q6) 42 dread]
F; feare Qq 43 days] F; times Qq 45 Ensuing] Qq, F *catchword*; Pursuing F 45 danger] F; dangers Qq 45 see] F; see.
Q, Q2; see, Q3–6 46 water] F; waters Qq 48 Marry, we were] F; we are Qq 48 justices] F; Iustice Qq **Act 2, Scene
4** 2.4] F (*Scena Quarta*); *not in* Qq 0 SD] F; *Enter Cardinall, Dutches of Yorke, Quee. young Yorke.* Qq (*subst.*) 1
SH] F (*Arch.*); *Car.* Qq (*throughout*) 1 heard] F, Q, Q2; heare Q3–6 1 Stony Stratford] F; Northampton Qq 2 And at
Northampton they do rest] F; At Stonistratford will they be Qq

37 **dearth** shortage of food.
41 **You** can hardly talk with a man.
42 **heavily** sad, mournful.
43 **still** always.
44 **mistrust** suspect.
45 **Ensuing** Oncoming.
45 **by proof** by way of evidence.
48 **to the justices** The play offers no details
about the legal matter the three citizens are
involved in, but it may be seen as related to the
generally unsettled condition of the times.

Act 2, Scene 4
Thomas More and the chroniclers describe in
some detail the scene of the queen rushing out
of the palace of Westminster into the sanctuary
of the abbey and the archbishop's rushing after
her. 'The quéene hir selfe sate alone alow on
the rushes all desolate and dismaid, whome the
archbishop comforted in best manner he could'
(Holinshed, III, 368).
0 SD ARCHBISHOP The 'Cardinall' of the

quartos is the Archbishop of Canterbury,
Thomas Cardinal Bourchier. But the Archbishop
of York was chancellor of England and thus
keeper of the great seal, which he says he will
give to Elizabeth at the end of this scene. Holinshed and More both confuse the two archbish-
ops, making York responsible for removing Elizabeth's younger son from sanctuary in 3.1.
1 **Stony Stratford** A village in Bucking-
hamshire.
2 **Northampton** A town in Northampton-
shire about fifteen miles farther from London
than Stony Stratford. Since the Archbishop's
speech seems to imply steady progress toward
London, the order of towns appears reversed
in F. Shakespeare's sources indicate, however,
that the royal party backtracked to Northampton from Stony Stratford after Rivers, Grey and
Vaughan were arrested. Shakespeare evidently
retained the roundabout route without its explanation.

Tomorrow, or next day, they will be here.
DUCHESS I long with all my heart to see the prince.
I hope he is much grown since last I saw him.   5
ELIZABETH But I hear no. They say my son of York
Has almost overta'en him in his growth.
YORK Ay, mother, but I would not have it so.
DUCHESS Why, my good cousin? It is good to grow.
YORK Grandam, one night as we did sit at supper,   10
My uncle Rivers talked how I did grow
More than my brother. 'Ay', quoth my uncle Gloucester,
'Small herbs have grace; great weeds do grow apace.'
And since, methinks, I would not grow so fast,
Because sweet flowers are slow, and weeds make haste.   15
DUCHESS Good faith, good faith, the saying did not hold
In him that did object the same to thee.
He was the wretched'st thing when he was young,
So long a-growing, and so leisurely,
That if his rule were true, he should be gracious.   20
YORK And so no doubt he is, my gracious madam.
DUCHESS I hope he is, but yet let mothers doubt.
YORK Now, by my troth, if I had been remembered,
I could have given my uncle's grace a flout
To touch his growth nearer than he touched mine.   25
DUCHESS How, my young York? I prithee, let me hear it.
YORK Marry, they say my uncle grew so fast

---

7 Has] F; Hath Qq   7 almost F, Q, Q2–5; *not in* Q6   9 good cousin] F; young cousin Qq (*subst.*)   12 'Ay'] *Hanmer* (*italics*); *no quotation marks in* F, Qq   12 uncle] F, Q2–6 (*subst.*); Nnckle Q   12 Gloucester] F, Q, Q2, Q4 (*subst.*); Clo. Q3, Q5; Glo. Q6   13 'Small . . . apace.'] *Hanmer* (*italics*); *no quotation marks in* F, Qq   13 do grow] F; grow Qq   19 a-growing] *Dyce*; a growing F, Qq   20 his rule were true] F; this were a true rule Q, Q2; this were a rule Q3–6   21 SH] F (*Yor.*); *Car.* Qq   21] F; Why Madame, so no doubt he is. Qq   22 he is] F; so too Qq   25] F; That should haue neerer toucht his growth than he did mine. Qq   26] Qq; How . . . Yorke, / I . . . it. F   26 young] F; prety Qq (*subst.*)   26 prithee] F; pray thee Qq   27 say] F, Q; say that Q2–6

---

6 my son of York Richard Duke of York was Elizabeth's younger son by King Edward. Elizabeth's phrase ties the young duke to Richard's pun on 'this son of York' in 1.1.

7 overta'en overtaken.

8–9 The rhyme suggests sympathy between little York and his grandmother.

9 cousin relative; in this case, grandchild.

13 grace virtue.

13 apace quickly.

17 object the same make that argument.

21 SH The quartos give this line to the Archbishop (*Car.*), and it sounds more like the utter-

ance of the cautious prelate than of the irreverent little York. Perhaps the boy is taken aback at his grandmother's evident hostility to her son. The Duchess's next line is uncharacteristically subdued.

23 troth faith, truth.

23 had been remembered had remembered.

24 my uncle's grace his grace, my uncle; the grace my uncle supposedly gained by slow growth.

24 flout insult.

25 touch . . . mine mock his growth more effectively than he mocked mine.

That he could gnaw a crust at two hours old.
'Twas full two years ere I could get a tooth.
Grandam, this would have been a biting jest.   30
DUCHESS I prithee, pretty York, who told thee this?
YORK Grandam, his nurse.
DUCHESS His nurse? Why, she was dead ere thou wast born.
YORK If 'twere not she, I cannot tell who told me.
ELIZABETH A parlous boy; go to, you are too shrewd.   35
DUCHESS Good madam, be not angry with the child.
ELIZABETH Pitchers have ears.

Enter a MESSENGER

ARCHBISHOP Here comes a messenger. What news?
MESSENGER Such news, my lord, as grieves me to report.
ELIZABETH How doth the prince?   40
MESSENGER Well, madam, and in health.
DUCHESS What is thy news?
MESSENGER Lord Rivers and Lord Grey
       Are sent to Pomfret, and with them
       Sir Thomas Vaughan, prisoners.   45
DUCHESS Who hath committed them?
MESSENGER The mighty dukes, Gloucester and Buckingham.
ARCHBISHOP For what offence?

28 old] F, Q, Q2, Q4, Q6 (*subst.*); hold Q3, Q5   30 biting] F, Q; pretie Q2–6 (*subst.*)   31 prithee] F; pray thee Qq   31 this] F; so Qq   33 His nurse?] F, Q; *not in* Q2–6   33 wast] F; wert Qq   35 parlous] F; perilous Qq   36 SH] F (*Dut.*); Car. Qq   37 SD] F; *Enter Dorset.* Qq   38 a messenger] F; your sonne, Lo: M. Dorset. / What newes Lo: Marques? Qq (*subst.*)   39 SH] F (*Mes.*); Dor. Qq (*and throughout*)   39 report] F; vnfolde Qq (*subst.*)   40 doth] F; fares Qq   42 thy] F, Q; the Q2–6   42 news?] F; newes then? Qq   43–5] F; Lo: . . . Pomfret, / With . . . prisoners. Qq (*subst.*)   44 and with] F; With Qq

28 gnaw . . . old The story of Richard's having been born with teeth goes back nearly to his own lifetime, originating in the *Historia Regum Angliae* of John Rous (d. 1491). Young York's difficulty in attributing the story may indicate that Shakespeare saw it as legend rather than fact. The Duchess testifies (18–19) that Richard was slow rather than fast in growing.

35 parlous dangerously mischievous (*OED* Parlous 3). Qq's 'perilous' misses F's implication that little York's cleverness is the source of peril.

35 go to come, come. An expression of disapproval.

35 shrewd sharp-tongued, biting. An appropriate word for little York's joke about his uncle's teeth.

37 Pitchers have ears A proverb in Shakespeare's time (Tilley P363) and today ('little pitchers have big ears'). Elizabeth implies that

York has picked up stories of Richard's 'unnatural' infancy from the adults around him, probably including herself.

37 SD The quartos give the Messenger's part to Dorset.

40–5 Editors often rearrange these lines to bring them closer to iambic pentameter. The raggedness of F, however, may help an actor show the Messenger's distress.

44 Pomfret Pontefract Castle in Yorkshire. Like the Tower of London, it was known as a place of political executions. For Shakespeare's version of the murder of Richard II at Pomfret, see *R2* 5.5.

45 Sir Thomas Vaughan Historically, Vaughan was chamberlain to Edward, Prince of Wales. Richard had him arrested for conspiring with Elizabeth's relatives to control the young prince.

MESSENGER The sum of all I can, I have disclosed.
    Why or for what the nobles were committed   50
    Is all unknown to me, my gracious lord.
ELIZABETH Aye me! I see the ruin of my house.
    The tiger now hath seized the gentle hind;
    Insulting tyranny begins to jut
    Upon the innocent and aweless throne.   55
    Welcome, destruction, blood, and massacre.
    I see, as in a map, the end of all.
DUCHESS Accursèd and unquiet wrangling days,
    How many of you have mine eyes beheld?
    My husband lost his life to get the crown,   60
    And often up and down my sons were tossed
    For me to joy and weep their gain and loss.
    And being seated, and domestic broils
    Clean over-blown, themselves the conquerors
    Make war upon themselves, brother to brother,   65
    Blood to blood, self against self. Oh, preposterous
    And frantic outrage, end thy damnèd spleen,
    Or let me die, to look on earth no more.
ELIZABETH Come, come, my boy, we will to sanctuary.
    Madam, farewell.   70
DUCHESS Stay, I will go with you.
ELIZABETH You have no cause.
ARCHBISHOP My gracious lady, go,
    And thither bear your treasure and your goods.
    For my part, I'll resign unto your grace   75
    The seal I keep, and so betide to me

---

50 or for] F, Q, Q3–6; or Q2 **50** the] F; these Qq **51** lord] F; Lady Qq **52** ruin] F; downfall Qq (*subst.*) **52** my] F; our Qq **54** jut] F; iet Qq **55** aweless] F; lawlesse Qq **56** blood] F; death Qq **65** brother to brother] F; bloud against bloud Qq (*subst.*) **66** Blood to blood] F; *not in* Qq (*see* 65) **68** earth] F; death Qq **70**] F; *not in* Qq **71** Stay, I will go] F; Ile go along Qq

52 house family.
53 hind doe. Elizabeth's word choice suggests her fear for herself and her children.
54 Insulting Abusive (see *OED* Insult *v* 2 and 4).
54 jut encroach (*OED* Jut *v²* b).
55 aweless not awe-inspiring (because it is occupied by a child).
57 map diagram.
63 seated enthroned.
63 broils quarrels.
64 Clean over-blown Completely finished.

67 spleen rage.
69 sanctuary By old English custom, churches and churchyards served as refuges from the law. Elizabeth seeks sanctuary in Westminster Abbey.
76 seal The great seal of England, used by the king and kept by the Archbishop in his civil office as chancellor of England. Since Elizabeth is not the monarch, he has no right to resign the seal to her.
76–7 so . . . yours let my fortunes depend on how well I take care of you and your family.

As well I tender you and all of yours.
Go, I'll conduct you to the sanctuary.

Exeunt

3.1 *The Trumpets sound. Enter young* PRINCE [EDWARD], *the* DUKES OF GLOUCESTER [RICHARD] *and* BUCKINGHAM, LORD CARDINAL [BOURCHIER, CATESBY], *with others*

BUCKINGHAM Welcome, sweet prince, to London, to your chamber.
RICHARD Welcome, dear cousin, my thoughts' sovereign.
  The weary way hath made you melancholy.
PRINCE EDWARD No, uncle, but our crosses on the way
  Have made it tedious, wearisome, and heavy.   5
  I want more uncles here to welcome me.
RICHARD Sweet prince, the untainted virtue of your years
  Hath not yet dived into the world's deceit.
  No more can you distinguish of a man
  Than of his outward show, which God he knows,   10
  Seldom or never jumpeth with the heart.
  Those uncles which you want were dangerous.
  Your grace attended to their sugared words
  But looked not on the poison of their hearts.
  God keep you from them and from such false friends.   15
PRINCE EDWARD God keep me from false friends, but they were none.
RICHARD My lord, the Mayor of London comes to greet you.

Enter LORD MAYOR

MAYOR God bless your grace with health and happy days.

---

78 Go] F; Come Qq   **Act 3, Scene 1** 3.1] F (*Actus Tertius. Scoena Prima.*); *not in* Qq   0 SD DUKES] F, Q, Q2–5; *Duke* Q6   0 SD LORD . . . *others*] F; *Cardinall & c.* Qq   0 SD CATESBY] *Capell; not in* F, Qq   1] Qq; Welcome . . . London, / To . . . Chamber. F   8 Hath] F, Q, Q2–5; Haue Q6   9 No] F; Nor Qq   16] Qq; God . . . Friends, / But . . . none. F   16 from] F, Q, Q2–3, Q5–6; frõ such Q4

Act 3, Scene 1

The chronicles describe the approach of the king to London, where he is met by the mayor and 'fiue hundred horsse of the citizens' (Holinshed, III, 369). This scene precedes the discussion found in Hall and Holinshed during which Buckingham gives a speech about the limits of sanctuary, and Cardinal Bourchier prevails upon the queen to release her younger son.

  1 chamber royal residence (*OED* Chamber *sb* 6). London had long been known as the king's

chamber (Latin, *camera regis*). The prince is now king, although he has not yet been crowned.

  4 crosses troubles. The prince alludes to the arrest of Rivers, Vaughan and Grey.

  6 want lack; desire.

  6 more uncles Among the arrested men, only Rivers was Edward's uncle. Grey was the prince's half-brother.

  10 God he knows God knows.

  11 jumpeth agrees.

PRINCE EDWARD I thank you, good my lord, and thank you all.
　　　　I thought my mother and my brother York　　　　　　20
　　　　Would long ere this have met us on the way.
　　　　Fie, what a slug is Hastings, that he comes not
　　　　To tell us whether they will come or no.

Enter LORD HASTINGS

BUCKINGHAM And in good time, here comes the sweating lord.
PRINCE EDWARD Welcome, my lord. What, will our mother come?　　25
HASTINGS On what occasion God he knows, not I,
　　　　The queen your mother and your brother York
　　　　Have taken sanctuary. The tender prince
　　　　Would fain have come with me to meet your grace,
　　　　But by his mother was perforce withheld.　　　　　30
BUCKINGHAM Fie, what an indirect and peevish course
　　　　Is this of hers. Lord Cardinal, will your grace
　　　　Persuade the queen to send the Duke of York
　　　　Unto his princely brother presently?
　　　　If she deny, Lord Hastings, go with him,　　　　　35
　　　　And from her jealous arms pluck him perforce.
CARDINAL My lord of Buckingham, if my weak oratory
　　　　Can from his mother win the Duke of York,
　　　　Anon expect him here; but if she be obdurate
　　　　To mild entreaties, God forbid　　　　　　40
　　　　We should infringe the holy privilege
　　　　Of blessèd sanctuary. Not for all this land
　　　　Would I be guilty of so great a sin.
BUCKINGHAM You are too senseless obstinate, my lord,
　　　　Too ceremonious and traditional.　　　　　45
　　　　Weigh it but with the grossness of this age:

29 have come] F, Q, Q2, Q4; come Q3, Q5–6　33 to send] F, Q, Q2, Q4, Q6; the send Q3; they send Q5　35 him] F, Q, Q2–4; them Q5–6　38 the] F, Q, Q2, Q4–6; to Q3　40 God] F, Q3–6; God in heauen Q, Q2　43 great] F, Q3–6; deepe Q, Q2　46 grossness] F, Q, Q2–5 (*subst.*); greatnesse Q6

22 **Fie** An exclamation of disgust or reproach.
22 **slug** sluggard, slacker.
22 **Hastings** Hastings had been King Edward's chamberlain, and the prince evidently expects him to continue to serve in that capacity.
29 **fain** gladly.
30 **perforce** by force.
31 **indirect** devious.
31 **peevish** perverse.
34 **presently** immediately.
36 **jealous** grudging; distrustful.

39 **Anon** Soon.
44 **senseless** unreasonably (*OED* Senseless 3b).
45 **ceremonious** precise in observing established procedure.
46 **Weigh it but with** Judge it only according to.
46 **grossness** coarseness, lack of moral refinement (*OED* Grossness 4b). Buckingham implies that the cardinal's scruples are old-fashioned.

You break not sanctuary in seizing him.
The benefit thereof is always granted
To those whose dealings have deserved the place
And those who have the wit to claim the place.   50
This prince hath neither claimed it nor deserved it,
And therefore, in mine opinion, cannot have it.
Then taking him from thence that is not there,
You break no privilege nor charter there.
Oft have I heard of sanctuary men,   55
But sanctuary children ne'er till now.
CARDINAL My lord, you shall o'er-rule my mind for once.
Come on, Lord Hastings, will you go with me?
HASTINGS I go, my lord.
                    [Exeunt] Cardinal and Hastings
PRINCE EDWARD Good lords, make all the speedy haste you may.   60
Say, uncle Gloucester, if our brother come,
Where shall we sojourn till our coronation?
RICHARD Where it think'st best unto your royal self.
If I may counsel you, some day or two
Your highness shall repose you at the Tower,   65
Then where you please and shall be thought most fit
For your best health and recreation.
PRINCE EDWARD I do not like the Tower, of any place.
Did Julius Caesar build that place, my lord?
BUCKINGHAM He did, my gracious lord, begin that place,   70
Which since, succeeding ages have re-edified.
PRINCE EDWARD Is it upon recòrd, or else reported
Successively from age to age, he built it?
BUCKINGHAM Upon recòrd, my gracious lord.
PRINCE EDWARD But say, my lord, it were not registered, 75
Methinks the truth should live from age to age,
As 'twere retailed to all posterity,

---

53 taking] F, Q, Q2–5; take Q6 57 o'er-rule] F; ouerrule Q, Q2–5; ouer-rule Q6 59 SD] F (*Exit*), Q3–6; *not in* Q, Q2
63 think'st] F, Q3–6; seemes Q, Q2

53 taking . . . there taking him from a place that for him is no sanctuary.
54 charter publicly conceded right (*OED* Charter 3).
57 o'er-rule my mind The cardinal appears dazzled by Buckingham's confusing rhetoric.
62 sojourn stay.
69 Julius Caesar The oldest part of the Tower of London is the White Tower, begun by

William the Conqueror. Tradition places a fort built by Julius Caesar on the same site (Brewer 1129).
71 re-edified rebuilt.
72 upon recòrd . . . reported on written record or reported by word of mouth.
75 registered written down.
77 retailed repeated.

Even to the general ending day.

RICHARD [*Aside*] So wise so young, they say, do never live long.

PRINCE EDWARD What say you, uncle?   80

RICHARD I say, without characters fame lives long.

[*Aside*] Thus, like the formal Vice, Iniquity,

I moralise two meanings in one word.

PRINCE EDWARD That Julius Caesar was a famous man.

With what his valour did enrich his wit,   85

His wit set down to make his valour live.

Death makes no conquest of his conqueror,

For now he lives in fame, though not in life.

I'll tell you what, my cousin Buckingham.

BUCKINGHAM What, my gracious lord?   90

PRINCE EDWARD And if I live until I be a man,

I'll win our ancient right in France again

Or die a soldier, as I lived a king.

RICHARD [*Aside*] Short summers lightly have a forward spring.

Enter young YORK, HASTINGS, *and* CARDINAL

BUCKINGHAM Now in good time, here comes the Duke of York.   95

PRINCE EDWARD Richard of York, how fares our noble brother?

YORK Well, my dear lord, so must I call you now.

78 ending] F, Q2–6; all-ending Q   79, 94 SD] *Johnson; not in* F, Qq   82 SD] F2; *not in* F, Qq   82 Thus] F, Q, Q2–5; That Q6   87 his] F, Q2–6; this Q   94 SD *and*] F; *not in* Qq   96 noble] F, Q3–6; louing Q, Q2   97 dear] F, Q3–6; dread Q, Q2

78 general ending day The Christian judgement day, the end of the world.

79 So wise so young Those who are very wise when very young.

81 characters letters; written records. Richard also plays on the sense in which 'character' is synonymous with the collection of qualities that distinguishes an individual (*OED* Character *sb* 11), implying that even when the young princes are dead, their fame will live. As Shakespeare's audience already knew, the princes' posthumous fame would also be the death of Richard's reputation.

82 formal Vice stock villain (from the old morality plays). This character personified human evil and often bore either the name of a particular sin such as Vanity or Fraud, or a general symbolic name such as Iniquity. See pp. 7–8 above.

83 moralise interpret, illustrate. Double meanings and word-play, such as Richard's pun on 'characters', were standard tricks of the Vice.

85–6 With . . . live. Having improved his mind in battle, he used his mind to write down his exploits, thereby securing his fame.

87 Death cannot conquer the one who conquers death.

91 And if If.

91–3 Compare Edward's heroic intentions with the French wars of Shakespeare's hero-king, Henry V. Winning back territory in France was a dream of many English people in Shakespeare's time as well as in Richard's.

94 Early springs usually lead to short summers. Richard's meaning here is substantially the same as what he says at 79. Compare Tilley F775, 'Sharp frosts bite forward springs.'

94 lightly probably (*OED* Lightly 6).

95 Now in good time This phrase from Buckingham usually announces someone whose presence has just been requested. Perhaps he means that the young duke arrives 'in good time' because the atmosphere surrounding Richard and the prince is growing too tense.

97 lord Since the death of the king, Edward has become his brother's lord.

PRINCE EDWARD Ay, brother, to our grief, as it is yours.
          Too late he died that might have kept that title,
          Which by his death hath lost much majesty.   100
RICHARD How fares our cousin, noble lord of York?
YORK I thank you, gentle uncle. O my lord,
          You said that idle weeds are fast in growth;
          The prince my brother hath outgrown me far.
RICHARD He hath, my lord.   105
YORK And therefore is he idle?
RICHARD O my fair cousin, I must not say so.
YORK Then he is more beholding to you than I.
RICHARD He may command me as my sovereign,
          But you have power in me as in a kinsman.   110
YORK I pray you, uncle, give me this dagger.
RICHARD My dagger, little cousin? With all my heart.
PRINCE EDWARD A beggar, brother?
YORK Of my kind uncle, that I know will give,
          And being but a toy, which is no grief to give.   115
RICHARD A greater gift than that I'll give my cousin.
YORK A greater gift? Oh, that's the sword to it.
RICHARD Ay, gentle cousin, were it light enough.
YORK Oh, then I see you will part but with light gifts.
          In weightier things you'll say a beggar nay.   120
RICHARD It is too weighty for your grace to wear.
YORK I weigh it lightly, were it heavier.
RICHARD What, would you have my weapon, little lord?
YORK I would, that I might thank you as you call me.
RICHARD How?   125
YORK Little.
PRINCE EDWARD My lord of York will still be cross in talk.
          Uncle, your grace knows how to bear with him.

112 With all] F, Q3–6; withall Q, Q2 115 grief] F, Q, Q2–5; gift Q6 121 weighty] F, Q2–6; heauy Q 121 your] F, Q,
Q2–5; you Q6 124 as] Q, Q2, Q4–6; as, as F; as as Q3 125–6] F; *as one line* Qq

99 Too late Too recently.
100 Which The title, the kingship.
103 idle worthless.
108 beholding beholden, indebted. The
prince owes Richard a debt because Richard has
refrained from calling him an idle weed, as he
did York.
112 With all my heart Richard agrees to let
the boy have the dagger, but in his heart he wants
to let him have it in the sense of stabbing him
with it.

114 that . . . give that which I know he will
give.
115 And being And that gift being.
115 toy trinket.
117 to it that goes with it.
119 light trivial.
122 I'd consider it trivial even if it weighed
more.
127 still always.
127 cross perverse, annoying.

YORK You mean to bear me, not to bear with me.
   Uncle, my brother mocks both you and me: 130
   Because that I am little, like an ape,
   He thinks that you should bear me on your shoulders.
BUCKINGHAM With what a sharp-provided wit he reasons.
   To mitigate the scorn he gives his uncle,
   He prettily and aptly taunts himself.   135
   So cunning and so young is wonderful.
RICHARD My lord, will't please you pass along?
   Myself and my good cousin Buckingham
   Will to your mother, to entreat of her
   To meet you at the Tower and welcome you.   140
YORK What, will you go unto the Tower, my lord?
PRINCE EDWARD My Lord Protector will have it so.
YORK I shall not sleep in quiet at the Tower.
RICHARD Why, what should you fear?
YORK Marry, my uncle Clarence' angry ghost.   145
   My grandam told me he was murdered there.
PRINCE EDWARD I fear no uncles dead.
RICHARD Nor none that live, I hope.
PRINCE EDWARD And if they live, I hope I need not fear.
   But come, my lord, and with a heavy heart,   150
   Thinking on them, go I unto the Tower.
   A sennet. Exeunt Prince, York, Hastings, [and others, except]
          Richard, Buckingham, and Catesby

---

133 sharp-provided] *Theobald*; sharpe prouided F, Qq 134 gives] F, Q, Q2, Q4; giue Q3, Q5–6 142 will] F, Q2–6; needes will Q 150 and] F; *not in* Qq 151 SD *A sennet.*] F; *not in* Qq 151 SD *and others, except*] *This edn; Exeunt Prince, Yorke, Hastings, and Dorset, Manet Richard, Buckingham, and Catesby.* F; *Exeunt Prin. Yor. Hast. Dors. manet, Rich. Buck.* Qq (*subst.*)

132 bear ... shoulders The idea of Richard's bearing young York on his shoulders 'like an ape' (131) evokes images of ape-bearing from Elizabethan amusements, including tame bears and professional fools carrying apes. Many commentators assume that York means to call attention to Richard's hunch-back (see Variorum, p. 208). In production, this is often a climactic moment, with little York leaping on Richard's back, causing Richard to lose control in a moment of pain and rage (see, for example, the Olivier and McKellen film versions). Such business runs counter to the smoothing-over remarks offered next by Buckingham. A child who leaps on his uncle's back and rides him around the stage like a fury hardly 'prettily and aptly taunts himself' (135).

133 sharp-provided sharply alert.
136 wonderful a cause of wonder.
142 F's headless line, missing the first syllable, gives the prince a chance for ironic emphasis on 'Protector', stressing the first syllable.
149 And if If.
151 on them on his dead relatives.
151 SD *sennet* Series of trumpet notes that signal ceremonial entrances and exits of characters (*OED* Sennet[1]).
151 SD *and others* The 'others' must include the Cardinal, who had re-entered earlier with Hastings, and the Mayor, on stage since his single line at 18. Both F and Qq have an exit for Dorset, although neither specifies an entrance for him.

BUCKINGHAM Think you, my lord, this little prating York
        Was not incensèd by his subtle mother
        To taunt and scorn you thus opprobriously?
RICHARD No doubt, no doubt. Oh, 'tis a perilous boy,   155
        Bold, quick, ingenious, forward, capable.
        He is all the mother's, from the top to toe.
BUCKINGHAM Well, let them rest. Come hither, Catesby.
        Thou art sworn as deeply to effect what we intend
        As closely to conceal what we impart.   160
        Thou know'st our reasons urged upon the way.
        What think'st thou? Is it not an easy matter
        To make William Lord Hastings of our mind
        For the instalment of this noble duke
        In the seat royal of this famous isle?   165
CATESBY He for his father's sake so loves the prince
        That he will not be won to aught against him.
BUCKINGHAM What think'st thou, then, of Stanley? Will not he?
CATESBY He will do all in all as Hastings doth.
BUCKINGHAM Well then, no more but this: 170
        Go, gentle Catesby, and as it were far off,
        Sound thou Lord Hastings
        How he doth stand affected to our purpose,
        And summon him tomorrow to the Tower
        To sit about the coronation.   175
        If thou dost find him tractable to us,
        Encourage him, and tell him all our reasons.

---

155 perilous] F, Q, Q2–6 (*subst.*); perlous Q7–8   168 Will not] F; what will Qq   171 far] F; a farre Qq   172–3] F; Sound . . . affected / Vnto our purpose, if he be willing, Qq (*subst.*)   172 thou] F, Q, Q2; *not in* Q3–6   173 doth stand] F; stands Qq   173 to] F; Vnto Qq   173 our] F, Q, Q2–3, Q5–6; your Q4   174–6] F; *not in* Qq   177 tell] F; shew Qq

152 **prating** chattering.
155 **perilous** Compare this with Elizabeth's 'parlous' at 2.4.35. Some editors follow Q7–8 in tidying up the metre by using 'parlous' here, but a distinction seems deliberately drawn between Elizabeth's word, which suggests that York's tongue will get his family in trouble, and Richard's, which means that York is dangerous to him.
156 **capable** Richard speaks of his child-victims as if they were competent enemies. Contrast this to the protective attitude of the Duchess, who calls her grandchildren 'Incapable and shallow innocents' (2.2.18).

157 **is all the mother's** takes after his mother. In fact, York takes after his uncle Richard in all the qualities listed.
159 **deeply** earnestly.
161 **upon the way** On the journey from Ludlow to London, during which Rivers and the others were arrested.
166 **He . . . sake** Hastings for King Edward's sake.
167 **aught** anything.
171 **as . . . off** distantly, subtly.
172 **Sound** Sound out.
173 **doth stand affected to** feels about.
175 **sit about** attend a meeting about.

If he be leaden, icy, cold, unwilling,
Be thou so too, and so break off the talk,
And give us notice of his inclination.   180
For we tomorrow hold divided councils,
Wherein thyself shalt highly be employed.
RICHARD Commend me to Lord William. Tell him, Catesby,
His ancient knot of dangerous adversaries
Tomorrow are let blood at Pomfret Castle;   185
And bid my lord, for joy of this good news,
Give Mistress Shore one gentle kiss the more.
BUCKINGHAM Good Catesby, go, effect this business soundly.
CATESBY My good lords both, with all the heed I can.
RICHARD Shall we hear from you, Catesby, ere we sleep?   190
CATESBY You shall, my lord.
RICHARD At Crosby House, there shall you find us both.

Exit Catesby

BUCKINGHAM Now, my lord,
What shall we do if we perceive
Lord Hastings will not yield to our complots?   195
RICHARD Chop off his head.
Something we will determine.
And look when I am king, claim thou of me
The earldom of Hereford and all the movables
Whereof the king my brother was possessed.   200
BUCKINGHAM I'll claim that promise at your grace's hand.
RICHARD And look to have it yielded with all kindness.

179 the] F; your Qq   186 lord] F; friend Q, Q2–5; friends Q2 (*one copy, Huntington HEH 69352*), Q6   187 Mistress] F,
Q, Q2; gentle Mistresse Q3–6 (*subst.*)   188 go] F; *not in* Qq   189 can] F; may Qq   192 House] F; place Qq   192 SD] F,
Q3–6; *not in* Q, Q2   193–4] F; *as one line* Qq   195 Lord] F; William Lo: Qq (Lord Q3–6)   196–7] F; Chop off his head
man, somewhat we will do Qq (*subst.*) (chop of Q)   199 Hereford] F, Q, Q2; Herford Q3–5; Hertford Q6   199 all] F; *not
in* Qq   200 was] F; stood Qq   202 all kindness] F; all willingnes Qq; willingnesse Q2–6

181 **divided councils** two different meetings.
184 **knot** group; with the suggestion of a knot
of snakes or other obnoxious animals – given the
context, one might think of leeches. Compare
Grey's exclamation against Richard's faction at
3.3.5: 'A knot you are of damnèd blood-suckers.'
185 **are let blood** will be bled; that is, killed.
Bloodletting was a common surgical procedure.
Richard uses the phrase as an ironic synonym for
execution.
187 **Mistress Shore** According to More
(p. 48), Jane Shore became Hastings's mistress
after the king died. Richard habitually sneers
at the sexual affairs of others (see 1.1.14 ff.).
In terms of the medieval Christian hierarchy of

sins, Richard scorns the less serious vices – sloth,
avarice, gluttony and lust – and pursues the more
dangerous ones – pride, envy and wrath.
195 **complots** conspiracies.
198 **look** expect.
199 **movables** household goods; presumably
those originally belonging to the earldom. Both
the lands and the goods of a lord might revert to
the king's possession if the title were vacated or
disputed.
202 **with all kindness** with all friendliness,
but also 'in the usual way', 'after (one's) kind'. It
is only in the manner of Richard's kind – that is,
treacherously – that he gives Buckingham anything.

Come, let us sup betimes, that afterwards
We may digest our complots in some form.

Exeunt

3.2 *Enter a* MESSENGER *to the door of Hastings*

MESSENGER My lord! My lord!
HASTINGS (*within*) Who knocks?
MESSENGER One from the Lord Stanley.
HASTINGS (*within*) What is't o'clock?
MESSENGER Upon the stroke of four.   5

Enter LORD HASTINGS

HASTINGS Cannot my Lord Stanley sleep these tedious nights?
MESSENGER So it appears by that I have to say.
     First, he commends him to your noble self.
HASTINGS What then?
MESSENGER Then certifies your lordship that this night   10
     He dreamt the boar had razèd off his helm.
     Besides, he says there are two councils kept,
     And that may be determined at the one
     Which may make you and him to rue at th'other.
     Therefore he sends to know your lordship's pleasure,   15
     If you will presently take horse with him

Act 3, Scene 2 3.2] F (*Scena Secunda.*); not in Qq 0 SD *the door of Hastings*] F; *Lo: Hastings.* Qq 1 My lord! My
lord!] F; *What ho My Lord* Qq (*subst.*) 2 SD, 4 SD] *Theobald (the second / Within / implied); not in* F, Qq 2 knocks]
F; *knockes at the dore.* Q; *knockes at the dore?* Q2–5; *knockes at the coore?* Q6 3 One] F; *A messenger* Qq 4 What is't]
F; *Whats* Qq 5 SD] F; *after 3* Qq 6 *my Lord Stanley*] F; *thy Master* Qq (*subst.*) 6 *these tedious*] F, Q; *the tedious* Q2,
Q4, Q6; *the teditous* Q3, Q5 7 *appears*] F; *should seeme* Qq 8 self] F; *Lordship* Qq 9–10] F; *as one line* Qq 9 What]
F; *And* Qq 10] F; *And then he sends you word,* Qq 11 *dreamt*] F; *dreamt to night* Qq 11 *boar*] F, Q6; *beare* Q, Q2–5
(*subst.*) 11 *razèd off*] F; *raste* Q, Q2–4; *caste* Q5; *cast* Q6 12 *kept*] F; *held* Qq 16 *you will presently*] F; *presently you
will* Qq

203 betimes early.
204 digest arrange; with a pun on digesting
supper.
204 in some form in an orderly way.

Act 3, Scene 2
  The scene apparently takes place in front of
Hastings's house. More (pp. 44–6, 49–53) was
the first author to select the sequence of events
Shakespeare portrays here and shape them into
a dramatic narrative.
  1 SD *the door of Hastings* Hastings's house
might have been represented by one of the two
doors thought to be part of the Shakespearean
stage.

2 SD Since Hastings does not enter until 6, he
must speak his first two lines offstage, as if inside
his house.
  8 commends him sends his greetings.
  10 certifies declares to.
  11 boar Richard's heraldic emblem.
  11 razèd knocked, torn.
  11 helm helmet (and by extension, head).
  12 two councils Two separate and simultaneous meetings of the king's advisers. Buckingham
mentions 'divided councils' at 3.1.181.
  16 presently immediately.

And with all speed post with him toward the north,
To shun the danger that his soul divines.
HASTINGS Go, fellow, go, return unto thy lord;
    Bid him not fear the separated council.   20
    His honour and myself are at the one,
    And at the other is my good friend Catesby,
    Where nothing can proceed that toucheth us
    Whereof I shall not have intelligence.
    Tell him his fears are shallow, without instance.   25
    And for his dreams, I wonder he's so simple
    To trust the mockery of unquiet slumbers.
    To fly the boar before the boar pursues
    Were to incense the boar to follow us
    And make pursuit where he did mean no chase.   30
    Go, bid thy master rise and come to me,
    And we will both together to the Tower,
    Where he shall see the boar will use us kindly.
MESSENGER I'll go, my lord, and tell him what you say.   *Exit*

Enter CATESBY

CATESBY Many good morrows to my noble lord.   35
HASTINGS Good morrow, Catesby. You are early stirring.
    What news, what news, in this our tott'ring state?
CATESBY It is a reeling world indeed, my lord,
    And I believe will never stand upright
    Till Richard wear the garland of the realm.   40
HASTINGS How, wear the garland? Dost thou mean the crown?
CATESBY Ay, my good lord.
HASTINGS I'll have this crown of mine cut from my shoulders

---

17 with him toward] F; into Qq   19 Go, fellow] F, Q, Q2; Good fellow Q3–6   20 council] F; counsels Qq (*subst.*)   22 good friend] F; seruant Qq   25 without] F; wanting Qq   25 instance] F, Q; instancie Q2–6 (*subst.*)   26 he's] F; he is Qq   26 so simple] F; so fond Q, Q2–3, Q5–6; fond Q4   28 pursues] F; pursues vs Q, Q2; pursue vs Q3–6   30 no chase] F; Q, Q2–3, Q5–6; to chase Q4   34 I'll go, my lord] F; My gratious Lo; Qq (*subst.*)   34 and] F; Ile Qq   34 SD.1 *Exit*] F, Q3–6; *not in* Q, Q2   35 SD.2 CATESBY] F, Q, Q2 (*subst.*); *Catesby to L. Hastings*; Q3–6 (*subst.*)   39 will] F; it will Q, Q2; twill Q3–6   41] Qq; How . . . Garland / Doest . . . Crowne? F   41 How] F, Q, Q2 (*subst.*); Who Q3–6

17 **post** ride quickly.
18 **divines** predicts, suspects.
21 **His honour** His lordship (Stanley).
24 **intelligence** information.
25 **instance** grounds.
27 **mockery** counterfeit, unreal appearance (*OED* Mockery 2).
32 **will** will go.

33 **kindly** As usual in Shakespeare, this word has a double sense. Hastings means Richard will use them gently, but the word also suggests that he will use them after his kind – that is, as a wild boar would.
43 **crown of mine** my head. Like the self-curses of Buckingham and the others, this oath prefigures Hastings's fate.

Before I'll see the crown so foul misplaced.
But canst thou guess that he doth aim at it?   45
CATESBY Ay, on my life, and hopes to find you forward
Upon his party for the gain thereof.
And thereupon he sends you this good news,
That this same very day your enemies,
The kindred of the queen, must die at Pomfret.   50
HASTINGS Indeed, I am no mourner for that news,
Because they have been still my adversaries.
But that I'll give my voice on Richard's side
To bar my master's heirs in true descent,
God knows I will not do it, to the death.   55
CATESBY God keep your lordship in that gracious mind.
HASTINGS But I shall laugh at this a twelvemonth hence,
That they which brought me in my master's hate,
I live to look upon their tragedy.
Well, Catesby, ere a fortnight make me older,   60
I'll send some packing that yet think not on't.
CATESBY 'Tis a vile thing to die, my gracious lord,
When men are unprepared and look not for it.
HASTINGS Oh, monstrous, monstrous! And so falls it out
With Rivers, Vaughan, Grey; and so 'twill do   65
With some men else that think themselves as safe
As thou and I, who, as thou know'st, are dear
To princely Richard and to Buckingham.
CATESBY The princes both make high account of you.
[*Aside*] For they account his head upon the bridge.   70
HASTINGS I know they do, and I have well deserved it.

Enter LORD STANLEY [EARL OF DERBY]

44 Before I'll] F; Ere I will Qq   46 Ay, on my life] F; Vpon my life my Lo: Qq (*subst.*)   51 that] F, Q, Q2–3, Q5; this Q4,
Q6   52 my adversaries] F; mine enemies Qq   58 which] F; who Qq   60 Well, Catesby] F; I tell thee Catesby. *Cat.* What
my Lord? Qq (*subst.*)   60 older] F; elder Qq   61 on't] F; on it Qq   66 that] F; who Qq   70 SD] F4; *not in* F, Qq

46 forward enthusiastic, eager.
52 still always.
54 master's heirs The children of Edward
IV, whom Hastings had served as chamberlain.
55 to the death though I die for it.
58–9 That I live to see the deaths of those who
caused King Edward to hate me. These lines (57–
9) summarise the manner of Hastings's life and
death, as well as underscoring his obtuseness.
61 send some packing Hastings evidently
has plans to use his power against more of

his enemies, perhaps including the queen's son
Dorset, not among those executed at Pomfret.
69 make high account of value highly.
70 account count on, expect (*OED* Account
v 2d).
70 the bridge Probably London Bridge,
where the severed heads of traitors were stuck up
on poles as gruesome warnings to others. This
is the real 'high account' (69) of Hastings that
Catesby has in mind.

Come on, come on, where is your boar spear, man?
Fear you the boar and go so unprovided?

STANLEY My lord, good morrow. Good morrow, Catesby.
You may jest on, but by the holy rood,   75
I do not like these several councils, I.

HASTINGS My lord, I hold my life as dear as yours,
And never in my days, I do protest,
Was it so precious to me as 'tis now.
Think you, but that I know our state secure,   80
I would be so triumphant as I am?

STANLEY The lords at Pomfret, when they rode from London,
Were jocund and supposed their states were sure,
And they indeed had no cause to mistrust.
But yet you see how soon the day o'ercast.   85
This sudden stab of rancour I misdoubt.
Pray God, I say, I prove a needless coward.
What, shall we toward the Tower? The day is spent.

HASTINGS Come, come, have with you.
Wot you what, my lord?   90
Today the lords you talk of are beheaded.

STANLEY They, for their truth, might better wear their heads
Than some that have accused them wear their hats.
But come, my lord, let's away.

Enter a PURSUIVANT

---

72 Come on, come on] F; What my Lo: Qq (*subst.*) 73 go] F, Q, Q2–5 (*subst.*); goe you Q6 75 but] F, Q, Q2–3, Q5–6; *not in* Q4 77 as yours] F; as you doe yours Qq (*subst.*) 78 days] F; life Qq 79 so] F; more Qq 79 as 'tis] F; then it is Qq 82 at] F, Q, Q2–5; of Q6 83 were sure] F; was sure Qq 84 they] F, Q, Q2; *not in* Q3–6 86 stab] F; scab Qq 87 I say] F, Q, Q2–3, Q5–6; *not in* Q4 88 What] F; But come my Lo: Qq (*subst.*) 88 toward] F; to Qq 88 The day is spent] F; *not in* Qq 89] F; I go: but stay, heare you not the newes, Qq (*subst.*) 90] F; *not in* Qq 91 Today the lords] F; This day those men Qq 91 talk] F, Q3–6; talkt Q, Q2 93 hats] F, Q, Q6; hat Q2–5 94 let's] F; let vs Qq 95 SD] F; *Enter Hastin. a Purssuant.* Qq (*subst.*); *Exit L. Standley, & Cat.* Q3–6 (*subst.*)

---

75 **rood** cross.
76 **several** multiple, separate.
76 **I . . . I** The second 'I' here is used for emphasis, as in *TGV* 5.4.132: 'Sir Valentine, I care not for her, I.'
77 **as yours** as you do yours.
78–9 On stage, Hastings's lust for life at this point is often used as a cue to bring on a silent but significant Mistress Shore.
80 **our state** our positions (Hastings's and Stanley's).
83 **jocund** cheerful.
86 **This . . . misdoubt** This sudden attack (on the queen's kindred) makes me mistrustful.

88 **The day is spent** The hour is late. An evident exaggeration, since the scene begins at four in the morning (5). The phrase is not in the quartos.
89 **have with you** let us go.
90 **Wot** Know.
92 **truth** loyalty (to the new king).
93 **their hats** Possibly their hats of office, their positions. The same idea informs the modern English expression 'to wear two hats' (see *OED* Hat *sb* 3).
95 SD PURSUIVANT Messenger authorised to serve warrants. In Shakespeare's sources, as in the quartos, the pursuivant has the same name

HASTINGS Go on before, I'll talk with this good fellow.   95
                    Exeunt Lord Stanley and Catesby
        How now, sirrah? How goes the world with thee?
PURSUIVANT The better that your lordship please to ask.
HASTINGS I tell thee, man, 'tis better with me now
        Than when thou met'st me last where now we meet.
        Then was I going prisoner to the Tower   100
        By the suggestion of the queen's allies.
        But now I tell thee (keep it to thyself)
        This day those enemies are put to death,
        And I in better state then e'er I was.
PURSUIVANT God hold it to your honour's good content.   105
HASTINGS Gramercy, fellow. There, drink that for me.
                    Throws him his purse
PURSUIVANT I thank your honour.   *Exit Pursuivant*

                    Enter a PRIEST

PRIEST Well met, my lord. I am glad to see your honour.
HASTINGS I thank thee, good Sir John, with all my heart.
        I am in your debt for your last exercise.   110
        Come the next sabbath, and I will content you.
PRIEST I'll wait upon your lordship.

                    Enter BUCKINGHAM

BUCKINGHAM What, talking with a priest, Lord Chamberlain?
        Your friends at Pomfret, they do need the priest.

---

95 on] F; you Qq   95 talk with this good fellow] F; follow presently Qq   95 SD] F, Q3–6 (*after 94*); *not in* Q, Q2   96 How now, sirrah] F; Well met Hastings Qq   97 your lordship please] F; it please your Lo: Q, Q2; it please your good Lordship Q3–6   98 man] F; fellow Qq   99 thou met'st me] F; I met thee Qq   104 e'er] F; euer Qq   106 fellow] F; Hastings Qq   106 There, drink that for me] F; hold spend thou that Qq   106 SD] F; *He giues him his purse.* Qq   107] F; God saue your Lordship. Qq   107 SD.1 *Exit Pursuivant*] F, Q3–6 (*subst.*); *not in* Q, Q2   108] F; *not in* Qq   109] F; What sir Iohn, you are wel met, Qq (*subst.*)   110 in your debt] F; beholding to you Qq   110 exercise] F; daies exercise Qq (*subst.*)   111 you.] F; you. *He whispers in his eare.* Qq   112] F; *not in* Qq   113] F; How now Lo: Chamberlaine, what talking with a priest, Qq (*subst.*)

as Lord Hastings. Ironically, the Lord Chamberlain takes as good omens both the similarity of names and the coincidence of meeting the same official on both his trips to the Tower (see More, p. 51).

96 sirrah Like 'fellow' (95), this salutation indicates that Hastings is socially superior to the Pursuivant.

99 where now we meet In More (p. 51) and Holinshed (III, 382), Hastings meets the pursuivant on Tower wharf. Here, the location seems still to be Hastings's own front door.

105 hold it keep it that way.

106 Gramercy Many thanks.

109 Sir John Priests were given the courtesy title of 'Sir', although they were not knights.

110 exercise sermon or prayer. Hastings vows to make up his lack of offering at 'the next sabbath' (111).

111 content you give you money.

Your honour hath no shriving work in hand.   115
HASTINGS Good faith, and when I met this holy man,
    The men you talk of came into my mind.
    What, go you toward the Tower?
BUCKINGHAM I do, my lord, but long I cannot stay there.
    I shall return before your lordship thence.   120
HASTINGS Nay, like enough, for I stay dinner there.
BUCKINGHAM (*aside*) And supper too, although thou know'st it not.–
    Come, will you go?
HASTINGS I'll wait upon your lordship.

                                 Exeunt

3.3 *Enter* SIR RICHARD RATCLIFFE *with Halberds, carrying the nobles*
[RIVERS, GREY, *and* VAUGHAN] *to death at Pomfret*

RIVERS Sir Richard Ratcliffe, let me tell thee this:
    Today shalt thou behold a subject die
    For truth, for duty, and for loyalty.
GREY God bless the prince from all the pack of you.
    A knot you are of damnèd bloodsuckers.   5
VAUGHAN You live that shall cry woe for this hereafter.
RATCLIFFE Dispatch. The limit of your lives is out.
RIVERS O Pomfret, Pomfret! O thou bloody prison,
    Fatal and ominous to noble peers.
    Within the guilty closure of thy walls   10
    Richard the Second here was hacked to death,

---

117 The] F; Those Qq   118 toward] F; to Qq   118 Tower] F; tower my Lord Qq   119 my lord] F; *not in* Qq   119 cannot
stay there] F; shall not stay Qq   121 Nay] F; Tis Qq   122 SD] *Rowe; not in* F, Qq   122 know'st] F, Q, Q2–5 (*subst.*); knowh
Q6   123] F; Come shall we go along? Qq (*subst.*)   124] F; *not in* Qq   **Act 3, Scene 3**   3.3] F (*Scena Tertia.*); *not in* Qq   0
SD RICHARD RATCLIFFE] F; *Rickard Ratliffe* Q; *Richard Ratliffe* Q2–6 (*Richad* Q6)   0 SD *Halberds, carrying the nobles*]
F; *the Lo*: Qq (*subst.*)   0 SD RIVERS, GREY, *and* VAUGHAN] Qq; *not in* F   0 SD *to death at Pomfret*] F; *prisoners* Qq   1]
F; *Rat.* Come bring foorth the prisoners Qq (*subst.*)   1 Ratcliffe] F; Ratliffe Qq   4 bless] F; keepe Qq (*subst*)   6] F; *not in*
Qq   7] F; *not in* Qq (*compare line 24*)   9 ominous] F, Q, Q6; dominious Q2–3; ominious Q4–5

115 shriving confessing. Buckingham says
ironically that Hastings need not seek absolution,
because he is not near death.
  121 stay wait for.
  121 dinner The midday meal, as contrasted
to supper, the evening meal.
  122 And supper too That is, you will wait
forever for supper.

Act 3, Scene 3
  The nobles were executed at Pomfret (Pontefract) Castle, in Yorkshire.

  0 SD *Halberds* Guards carrying halberds. See
1.2.0. SD n.
  5 knot entwined group, as of snakes or
leeches. Compare Richard's message to Hastings
at 3.1.184–6.
  6 This is the only line Vaughan speaks as a
living person. (He has two lines as a ghost).
  7 Dispatch Hurry up.

And, for more slander to thy dismal seat,
We give to thee our guiltless blood to drink.
GREY Now Margaret's curse is fall'n upon our heads,
      When she exclaimed on Hastings, you, and I   15
      For standing by when Richard stabbed her son.
RIVERS Then cursed she Richard,
      Then cursed she Buckingham,
      Then cursed she Hastings. O remember God,
      To hear her prayer for them, as now for us.   20
      And for my sister and her princely sons,
      Be satisfied, dear God, with our true blood,
      Which, as thou know'st, unjustly must be spilt.
RATCLIFFE Make haste. The hour of death is expiate.
RIVERS Come, Grey, come, Vaughan, let us here embrace.   25
      Farewell, until we meet again in heaven.

                                                          Exeunt

3.4 *Enter* BUCKINGHAM, [STANLEY EARL OF] DERBY, HASTINGS,
BISHOP OF ELY, NORFOLK, RATCLIFFE, LOVELL, *with others, at*
a table

HASTINGS Now, noble peers, the cause why we are met
      Is to determine of the coronation.
      In God's name, speak. When is the royal day?

---

12 seat] F; soule Qq   13 to thee] F; thee vp Qq   13 blood] F; blouds Qq (*subst.*)   15] F; *not in* Qq   17–18] F; *as one*
line Qq   17 Richard] F; Hastings Qq   19 Hastings] F; Richard Qq   20 prayer] F; praiers Qq (*subst.*)   21 sons] F; sonne
Qq   22 blood] F; blouds Qq (*subst.*)   24] F; Come come dispatch, the limit of your liues [linea Q; lines Q2] is out Qq   24
expiate] F; now expir'd F2   25 here] F; all Qq   26] F; And take our leaue [leaues Q6] vntill we meete in heauen Qq   **Act 3,**
Scene 4 3.4] F (*Scoena Quarta.*); *not in* Qq   **0 SD**] F; *Enter the Lords to Councell.* Qq (*subst.*)   **0 SD** STANLEY] *Theobald;*
not in F, Qq   **1** Now, noble peers] F; My Lords at once Qq   **3** speak] F; say Qq   **3** the] F; this Qq

---

12 for . . . seat to increase the scandal linked
to your (Pomfret Castle's) unhappy site.

15 exclaimed on cried out against.

15 Hastings, you, and I Margaret exclaims
against Hastings, Rivers and Dorset at 1.3.208–9,
not mentioning Grey.

21–3 Compare Rivers's prayer with Clarence's
at 1.4.71–2: 'Yet execute thy wrath in me alone.
/ Oh, spare my guiltless wife and my poor children.' In both cases, the prayers of dying men
serve to call attention to the innocence and vul-
nerability of women and children.

24 expiate fully arrived (*OED* Expiate
ppl a, citing this line as the only example).
F2's emendation suggests that the usage was
uncommon.

Act 3, Scene 4
      According to the chronicles, the meeting was
held in the Tower of London.

      0 SD RATCLIFFE Some in the audience may
notice that Ratcliffe was in the north of England
in the previous scene, presiding over the executions at Pomfret. It is still the same day, yet Ratcliffe is now in London, an impossible journey
(approximately 160 miles) in an age of horseback
travel on rough roads. Perhaps Shakespeare's
relatively unrealistic stage made the locations
seem more symbolic than literal. The quick shift
becomes plausible in a modern-dress production
such as Michael Bogdanov's 1990 video, in which
Ratcliffe seems to have caught a mid-morning jet.

      2 determine of decide about.

BUCKINGHAM Is all things ready for the royal time?
STANLEY It is, and wants but nomination.   5
ELY Tomorrow, then, I judge a happy day.
BUCKINGHAM Who knows the Lord Protector's mind herein?
    Who is most inward with the noble duke?
ELY Your grace, we think, should soonest know his mind.
BUCKINGHAM We know each other's faces. For our hearts,   10
    He knows no more of mine than I of yours,
    Or I of his, my lord, than you of mine.
    Lord Hastings, you and he are near in love.
HASTINGS I thank his grace, I know he loves me well.
    But for his purpose in the coronation,   15
    I have not sounded him, nor he delivered
    His gracious pleasure any way therein.
    But you, my honourable lords, may name the time,
    And in the duke's behalf I'll give my voice,
    Which I presume he'll take in gentle part.   20

        Enter [RICHARD DUKE OF] GLOUCESTER

ELY In happy time, here comes the duke himself.
RICHARD My noble lords and cousins all, good morrow.
    I have been long a sleeper, but I trust
    My absence doth neglect no great design
    Which by my presence might have been concluded.   25
BUCKINGHAM Had you not come upon your cue, my lord,

4 Is] F; Are Qq   4 ready] F; fitting Qq   4 the] F; that Qq   5 wants] F, Q, Q2; let Q3, Q5–6; lack Q4   6 SH] F; *Ryu.* Q; *Riu.* Q2; *Bish.* Q3–6   6 judge] F; guesse Qq (*subst.*)   6 day] F; time Qq   9 Your grace, we think] F; Why you my Lo: me thinks you Qq (*subst.*)   10] F; Who I my Lo? We . . . faces: Qq (*subst.*)   11] F; But for our harts, he knowes no more of mine Qq (*subst.*)   12] F; Then I of yours: nor I no more of his, then you of mine: Qq   17 gracious] F; Graces Qq (*subst.*)   18 honourable] F; noble Q, Q2; *not in* Q3–6   18 lords] F; Lo: Q, Q2; L. Q3–6   20 he'll] F; he will Qq   20 gentle] F, Q, Q2–5; good Q6   21 In happy time] F; Now in good time Qq   23 a sleeper] F, Q, Q2–5; a sleepe Q6   23 but] F, Q; but now Q2–6   23 trust] F; hope Qq   24 design] F; designes Qq   26 you not] F; not you Qq   26 cue] F (Q), Qq (kew)

4 Is . . . things Shakespeare often worries less about noun–verb agreement than modern grammarians do (see Abbott 412), but 'things' is probably used here as a singular collective noun, making 'Is' the proper verb form.

5 wants but nomination lacks only the naming of the day.

8 inward intimate. Buckingham lays bait for the overconfident Hastings, who is soon trapped (14).

16 delivered This word, emphasised by its position at the end of a verse line, recalls to the audience the ominous twist Richard habitually gives to his 'deliveries' (see especially 1.1.115 and n.).

19 voice approval.

20 in gentle part with gracious acceptance.

22 cousins friends, close associates.

23 I . . . sleeper Since Richard has called this early-morning meeting himself, his lateness must also be part of his plan. McKellen, who associates Richard with Hitler, notes that Hitler liked to put others at a disadvantage by holding meetings in the middle of the night (p. 176).

24 neglect cause to be neglected (*OED* Neglect *v* 5, citing this passage).

26 upon your cue Buckingham several times makes metadramatic remarks about events in *Richard III*. Compare 2.1.45–6 and 3.1.24, where Buckingham seems almost to summon characters

William Lord Hastings had pronounced your part,
I mean your voice for crowning of the king.
RICHARD Than my Lord Hastings no man might be bolder.
His lordship knows me well and loves me well. –   30
My lord of Ely, when I was last in Holborn,
I saw good strawberries in your garden there.
I do beseech you, send for some of them.
ELY Marry, and will, my lord, with all my heart.   *Exit Bishop*
RICHARD Cousin of Buckingham, a word with you.   35
Catesby hath sounded Hastings in our business,
And finds the testy gentleman so hot
That he will lose his head ere give consent
His master's child, as worshipfully he terms it,
Shall lose the royalty of England's throne.   40
BUCKINGHAM Withdraw yourself a while; I'll go with you.
                                Exeunt [Richard and Buckingham]
STANLEY We have not yet set down this day of triumph.
Tomorrow, in my judgement, is too sudden,
For I myself am not so well provided
As else I would be, were the day prolonged.   45

Enter the BISHOP OF ELY

ELY Where is my lord the Duke of Gloucester?

---

27 had] F; had now Qq   27 your] F, Q, Q2–5; you Q6   30 well.] F; well. / *Hast.* I thanke your Grace. Qq   31 Ely,] F; Elie, *Bish.* My Lo: / *Glo.* When Q, Q2; Elie. / *Bish.* My Lord. / *Glo.* When Q3–6   33 do] F, Q, Q2, Q5–6; now Q4   34] F; I go my Lord. Qq (*subst.*)   34 SD] F; *not in* Qq   35 of] F; *not in* Qq   37 testy] F, Q, Q2–3, Q5–6; resty Q4   38 That] F; As Qq   38 ere] F, Q3–4, Q6; eare Q, Q2 (*British Library copies, Huntington copy 69352*); are Q5   39 child] F; sonne Qq   39 worshipfully] F; worshipfull Qq   41 yourself a while] F; you hence my Lo: Qq (*subst.*)   41 go with] F; follow Qq   41 SD *Exeunt*] F; *Ex. Gl.* Qq (*subst.*)   41 SD *Richard and Buckingham*] Pope (*Glo. And Buck.*); *not in* F   43 my judgement] F; mine opinion Qq   43 sudden] F; sodaine Q; soone Q2–6   46–7] F; *as one line* Qq   46 the Duke of Gloucester] F; protector Qq (*subst.*)

---

from the wings to meet their cues, and his later promise to 'counterfeit the deep tragedian' for Richard's cause (3.5.5).

31 Holborn The location of the bishop's house and gardens in London. Historically, the Bishop of Ely at this time was John Morton, later the patron of Sir Thomas More and a probable source of some details in More's account (see More, p. 47).

32 strawberries Richard's sudden request for strawberries shows him deliberately exhibiting a sunny mood as he tightens his net around Hastings. The strawberries themselves have seemed to many commentators richly symbolic. See, for example, Lawrence. J. Ross, 'The meaning of strawberries in Shakespeare', *Studies in*

the Renaissance 7 (1960), 225–40. Whatever they symbolise, the strawberries also suggest that Richard has a good appetite, which for him seems to be associated with murder. Compare 75–6 and 4.3.31–2, where Richard wants to hear the details of the young princes' death after supper. In some performances of the 1989 Royal National Theatre production, McKellen tasted the blood from Hastings's severed head.

35–41 This private exchange between Richard and Buckingham is not heard by the others in the scene.

44 provided furnished (with proper clothing, etc., for the coronation).

45 prolonged postponed.

I have sent for these strawberries.

HASTINGS His grace looks cheerfully and smooth this morning.
There's some conceit or other likes him well
When that he bids good morrow with such spirit.   50
I think there's never a man in Christendom
Can lesser hide his love or hate, than he,
For by his face straight shall you know his heart.

STANLEY What of his heart perceive you in his face
By any livelihood he showed today?   55

HASTINGS Marry, that with no man here he is offended,
For were he, he had shown it in his looks.

Enter RICHARD *and* BUCKINGHAM

RICHARD I pray you all, tell me what they deserve
That do conspire my death with devilish plots
Of damnèd witchcraft and that have prevailed   60
Upon my body with their hellish charms.

HASTINGS The tender love I bear your grace, my lord,
Makes me most forward in this princely presence
To doom th'offenders, whosoe'er they be.
I say, my lord, they have deservèd death.   65

RICHARD Then be your eyes the witness of their evil.
Look how I am bewitched. Behold, mine arm
Is like a blasted sapling, withered up.
And this is Edward's wife, that monstrous witch,
Consorted with that harlot, strumpet Shore,   70
That by their witchcraft thus have markèd me.

---

48 this morning] F; to day Qq   50 that he bids] F; he doth bid Qq   50 such] F; such a Qq   51 there's] F; there is Qq   52 Can] F; That can Qq   55 livelihood] F; likelihood Qq   57 were he, he had] F; if he were, he would have Qq   57 looks] F, Q; face Q2–6   57 looks.] F; lookes. / Dar. I pray God he be not, I say. Qq   57 SD] F; *Enter Glocester.* Qq (*subst.*)   58 tell me what] F; what doe Qq (*subst.*)   63 princely] F; noble Qq   64 th'offenders] F; the offenders Qq   64 whosoe'er] F; whatsoeuer Qq   66 their evil] F; this ill Qq   67 Look] F; See Qq   69 And this is] F; This is that Qq   71 witchcraft] F, Q; witchcrafts Q2–6

---

48 smooth smoothly, pleasantly.

49 conceit concept, idea.

49 likes pleases.

51 Christendom Christian countries, the domain of Christianity.

55 livelihood liveliness.

60–1 prevailed/Upon controlled.

67 As Richard makes clear in his opening soliloquy (1.1.16–23), and as all the courtiers know, his arm has always been misshapen. In *3H6*, Richard says explicitly that nature deter-

mined while he was still in his mother's womb 'To shrink mine arm up like a wither'd shrub' (3.2.156).

68 blasted blighted, ruined.

69 witch Richard's accusation shows more ferocity than his earlier slur against Margaret (1.3.162), perhaps because it derives from his personal concerns. He associates deformity with birth (1.1.20) and birth with the power of women (1.1.75), which he connects to witchcraft.

70 Consorted Associated.

HASTINGS If they have done this deed, my noble lord –
RICHARD If? Thou protector of this damnèd strumpet,
　　　　Talk'st thou to me of ifs? Thou art a traitor.
　　　　Off with his head! Now by Saint Paul I swear,　　　　　　75
　　　　I will not dine until I see the same.
　　　　Lovell and Ratcliffe, look that it be done.
　　　　The rest that love me, rise and follow me.
　　　　　　Exeunt [all but] Lovell and Ratcliffe, with the Lord Hastings
HASTINGS Woe, woe for England, not a whit for me,
　　　　For I, too fond, might have prevented this.　　　　　　　80
　　　　Stanley did dream the boar did rouse our helms,
　　　　And I did scorn it and disdain to fly.
　　　　Three times today my footcloth horse did stumble,
　　　　And started when he looked upon the Tower,
　　　　As loath to bear me to the slaughterhouse.　　　　　　　85
　　　　Oh, now I need the priest that spake to me.
　　　　I now repent I told the pursuivant,
　　　　As too triumphing, how mine enemies
　　　　Today at Pomfret bloodily were butchered,
　　　　And I myself secure in grace and favour.　　　　　　　　90
　　　　O Margaret, Margaret, now thy heavy curse
　　　　Is lighted on poor Hastings' wretched head.
RATCLIFFE Come, come, dispatch. The duke would be at dinner.
　　　　Make a short shrift; he longs to see your head.
HASTINGS O momentary grace of mortal men,　　　　　　　　95
　　　　Which we more hunt for than the grace of God,
　　　　Who builds his hope in air of your good looks

---

72 deed, my noble] F; thing my gratious Qq (*subst.*)　74 Talk'st thou to] F; Telst thou Qq　75 I swear] F; *not in* Qq
76] F; I will not dine to day I sweare, Qq　77] F; vntill I see the same, some see it done, Qq　78 rise] F; come Qq　78
SD *all but*] Cam.; all, except / Dyce; Manet F; manet Cat. with Ha. Qq (*subst.*)　81 rouse our helms] F (rowse); race his
helme Qq　82] F; but I disdaind it, and did scorne to flie, Qq (*subst.*) (disdaind, and Q4)　84 started] F; startled Qq　86
need] F; want Qq　88 too] F; twere Qq　88 how] F; at Qq　89 Today] F; how they Qq　92 lighted] F; Q, Q2–5; lightened
Q6　93 SH] F (*Ra.*); Cat. Qq　93 Come, come, dispatch] F; Dispatch my Lo: Qq (*subst.*)　95 grace of mortal] F; state of
worldly Qq　96 than] F, Q, Q2; then for Q3–6　96 God] F; heauen Qq　97 hope] F; hopes Qq　97 good] F; faire Qq　97
looks] F, Q, Q2–3, Q5–6; looke Q4

80 **fond** foolish.
81 **rouse** move violently (*OED* Rouse v¹ II).
As reported by his messenger (and repeated here
in Qq), Stanley dreamed the boar had 'razèd off'
his helm (see 3.2.11).
83 **footcloth horse** richly decorated horse. A
footcloth was a drape laid over the back of the
horse, hanging to the feet. Hastings now sees the
stumbling and starting of his horse on the way to
the Tower as evil omens he should have heeded.

88 **triumphing** boastful.
93 **dispatch** hurry up.
94 **short shrift** brief confession. Ratcliffe's
words recall Buckingham's ironic remark that
Hastings has 'no shriving work in hand'
(3.2.115).
95 **grace** Good fortune in worldly matters, as
opposed to the grace of God (96).
97 **in air** on the insubstantial (airy) foundation.

Lives like a drunken sailor on a mast,
Ready with every nod to tumble down
Into the fatal bowels of the deep.   100
LOVELL   Come, come, dispatch; 'tis bootless to exclaim.
HASTINGS   O bloody Richard, miserable England,
I prophesy the fearful'st time to thee
That ever wretched age hath looked upon.
Come, lead me to the block; bear him my head.   105
They smile at me who shortly shall be dead.

Exeunt

3.5   *Enter* RICHARD *and* BUCKINGHAM *in rotten armour,*
marvellous ill-favoured

RICHARD   Come, cousin, canst thou quake and change thy colour,
Murder thy breath in middle of a word,
And then again begin, and stop again,
As if thou were distraught and mad with terror?
BUCKINGHAM   Tut, I can counterfeit the deep tragedian,   5
Speak and look back, and pry on every side,
Tremble and start at wagging of a straw.
Intending deep suspicion, ghastly looks
Are at my service, like enforcèd smiles.

---

98 a drunken sailor] F, Q, Q2–3, Q5–6; drunken Saylers Q4   100 the fatal] F, Q, Q2–5; fatall Q6   101–4] F; *not in* Qq   106 who] F; that Qq   **Act 3, Scene 5**   3.5] *Capell; not in* F, Qq   0 SD *in rotten armour, marvellous ill-favoured*] F; *in armonr* Q; *in armor* Q2–4; *in armour* Q5–6   1] Q; Come . . . Cousin, / Canst . . . colour, F   3 again begin] F; beginne againe Qq (*subst.*)   4 were] F; wert Qq   5] F; Tut feare not me. / I can counterfait the deepe Tragedian: Qq (*subst.*)   7] F; *not in* Qq   8 deep] F, Q, Q2–3, Q5–6; deere Q4

101 **bootless** useless.
101 **exclaim** cry out.

Act 3, Scene 5
Shakespeare's sources say that immediately after dinner, Richard sent for the mayor and 'manie substantial men out of the citie' in order to give them an explanation for Hastings's death (Holinshed, III, 383).
0 SD *rotten* rusty.
0 SD *marvellous ill-favoured* astonishingly ugly. More says that Richard and Buckingham wore rusty armour to make the citizens think the two lords had been the victims of a surprise attack, forcing them to reach for old, worn-out gear (p. 52).

2 **Murder** Kill; stop.
5 **deep tragedian** profound tragic actor. The two dukes describe (6–11) this kind of 'ham' actor's standard devices. Several commentators have observed that Buckingham shows himself to be such an actor – as here before the Mayor (see Variorum, p. 242). Richard, by contrast, is an adaptable and naturalistic performer. Compare, for example, Buckingham's supercilious rhetoric (33–9) to Richard's subsequent speech (41–6).
6 **Speak and look back** Look over my shoulder while speaking.
6 **pry** peer.
8 **Intending** Pretending.
9 **enforcèd** forced.

And both are ready in their offices   10
At any time to grace my stratagems.
But what, is Catesby gone?
RICHARD He is, and see, he brings the Mayor along.

Enter the MAYOR *and* CATESBY

BUCKINGHAM Lord Mayor –
RICHARD Look to the drawbridge there!   15
BUCKINGHAM Hark, a drum!
RICHARD Catesby, o'erlook the walls!
BUCKINGHAM Lord Mayor, the reason we have sent –
RICHARD Look back, defend thee, here are enemies!
BUCKINGHAM God and our innocency defend and guard us!   20

Enter LOVELL *and* RATCLIFFE *with Hastings's head*

RICHARD Be patient; they are friends, Ratcliffe and Lovell.
LOVELL Here is the head of that ignoble traitor,
     The dangerous and unsuspected Hastings.
RICHARD So dear I loved the man that I must weep.
     I took him for the plainest harmless creature   25
     That breathed upon the earth a Christian,
     Made him my book, wherein my soul recorded
     The history of all her secret thoughts.
     So smooth he daubed his vice with show of virtue
     That his apparent open guilt omitted,   30
     I mean his conversation with Shore's wife,
     He lived from all attainder of suspects.
BUCKINGHAM Well, well, he was the covert'st sheltered traitor

---

11 At any time] F; *not in* Qq   12] F; *not in* Qq   13] F; Here comes the Maior. Qq   13 SD] F; *Enter Maior.* Qq (*after 11*)   14 Lord Mayor] F; Let me alone to entertaine him. Lo: Maior Qq (*subst.*)   16] F; The reason we haue sent for you. Qq   18] F; Harke, I heare a drumme. Qq   20 innocency] F (Innocencie), Q2–6; innocence Q   20 and guard] F; *not in* Qq   20 SD] F (Hastings); *Enter Catesby with Hast. head.* Qq (*subst.*)   21] F; O, O, be quiet, it is Catesby. Qq (G, O, . . . Catesby Q)   25 creature] F; man Qq   26 the] F, Q4; this Q, Q2–3, Q5–6   26 Christian,] F; christian, / Looke ye my Lo: Maior. Qq (*subst.*)   27 Made] F, Q, Q2–4; I made Q5–6   32 lived] F; laid Qq   32 suspects] F; suspect Qq

10 **offices** proper functions (see *OED* Office *sb* 3b).
17 **o'erlook** look over. The scene probably takes place outside, on the battlements of the Tower. If not, Catesby needs an exit here to go outside in response to Richard's order.
20 **innocency** innocence.
27 **book** diary; confidant.
29 **daubed** plastered, whitewashed.

30 **his . . . omitted** aside from his publicly evident guilt.
31 **conversation** sexual affair.
32 **from** free from.
32 **attainder** stain. *OED* (Attainder 2b) cites this line as the earliest instance.
32 **suspects** suspicion.
33 **covert'st** most covert.
33 **sheltered** hidden.

That ever lived.
Would you imagine, or almost believe, 35
Were't not that by great preservation
We live to tell it, that the subtle traitor
This day had plotted, in the Council House,
To murder me and my good lord of Gloucester?
MAYOR Had he done so? 40
RICHARD What? Think you we are Turks or infidels?
Or that we would, against the form of law,
Proceed thus rashly in the villain's death,
But that the extreme peril of the case,
The peace of England, and our persons' safety, 45
Enforced us to this execution?
MAYOR Now fair befall you, he deserved his death,
And your good graces both have well proceeded
To warn false traitors from the like attempts.
BUCKINGHAM I never looked for better at his hands 50
After he once fell in with Mistress Shore.
Yet had we not determined he should die
Until your lordship came to see his end,
Which now the loving haste of these our friends,
Something against our meanings, have prevented; 55
Because, my lord, I would have had you heard
The traitor speak and timorously confess
The manner and the purpose of his treasons,
That you might well have signified the same
Unto the citizens, who haply may 60

34 lived.] F; liu'd, would you haue imagined. Qq   35] F; Or almost beleeue, wert not by great preseruation Qq (*subst.*)   36 Were't] F, Q, Q2–5 (wert); were Q6   37 it, that the] F; it you? Qq   38 This day had] F; Had this day Qq   40] F; What, had he so? Qq   41 you] F, Q, Q2; ye Q3–6   42 form] F, Q, Q2; course Q3–6   43 in] F; to Qq   44 extreme] F, Q, Q2, Q5–6; very extreame Q4   46 this] F, Q, Q2–3, Q5–6; that Q4   48 your good graces] F; you my good Lords Qq (*subst.*)   50 SH] F; *not in* Qq   52 Yet] F; *Dut.* Yet Q, Q2; *Clo.* Yet Q3, Q5; *Glo.* Yet Q4, Q6 (*subst.*)   52 we not] F; not we Qq   53 end] F; death Qq   54 loving] F; longing Qq   55 Something] F; Somewhat Qq   55 meanings] F; meaning Qq   56 I] F; we Qq   58 treasons] F; treason Qq

36 **great preservation** preservation by providence or fortune.
41 **Turks or infidels** That is, non-Christians, who, Richard implies, do not respect due process of law. The Elizabethan Book of Common Prayer, used in churches, includes a prayer for the salvation of 'all Jews, Turks, infidels, and heretics' (p. 144). Turks, Tartars and Jews are associated with blasphemy by the witches in *Mac.* (4.1.16–19) and by the Duke in *MV* (4.1.32–4).

47 **fair befall you** good luck to you, bless you.
48 **your good graces** The Mayor means 'your graces', that is, you two dukes.
52 **had we not** we had not.
55 **Something against our meanings** Somewhat against our intentions.
56 **would have had you heard** would you had heard (?).
57 **timorously** fearfully.
60 **haply** perhaps.

Misconster us in him and wail his death.

MAYOR But, my good lord, your graces' words shall serve
      As well as I had seen and heard him speak.
      And do not doubt, right noble princes both,
      But I'll acquaint our duteous citizens   65
      With all your just proceedings in this case.

RICHARD And to that end we wished your lordship here,
      T'avoid the censures of the carping world.

BUCKINGHAM Which, since you come too late of our intent,
      Yet witness what you hear we did intend.   70
      And so, my good Lord Mayor, we bid farewell.

                                              Exit Mayor

RICHARD Go after, after, cousin Buckingham.
      The Mayor towards Guildhall hies him in all post.
      There, at your meetest vantage of the time,
      Infer the bastardy of Edward's children.   75
      Tell them how Edward put to death a citizen
      Only for saying he would make his son
      Heir to the crown, meaning indeed his house,
      Which, by the sign thereof, was termèd so.
      Moreover, urge his hateful luxury   80
      And bestial appetite in change of lust,
      Which stretched unto their servants, daughters, wives,
      Even where his raging eye or savage heart,
      Without control, lusted to make a prey.

---

62 But, my] F, Q, Q2; My Q3–6 62 words] F; word Qq 63 and] F; or Qq 64 do not doubt] F; doubt you not Qq 65 our] F; your Qq 66 case] F; cause Q, Q2–5; ease Q6 67 wished] F, Q, Q2–5 (*subst.*); wish Q6 68 T'avoid] F; To auoyde Qq (*subst.*) 68 censures] F; carping censures Qq (*subst.*) 68 carping world] F; world Q, Q2, Q4–6; word Q3 69 Which] F; But Qq 69 come] F, Q, Q2; came Q3–6 69 intent] F; intents Qq 70 you hear] F; *not in* Qq 70 intend.] F; intend, and so my Lord adue. Qq 71] F; *not in* Qq 71 SD] F; *after 72* Qq 72 Go after] F; After Qq 74 meetest vantage] F; meetst aduantage Q, Q2–5; meetest aduantage Q6 82 unto] F; to Qq 83 raging] F; lustfull Qq 84 lusted] F; listed Qq 84 a] F; his Qq

61 **Misconster us in him** Misconstrue our actions toward him.
  63 **As well as** As well as if.
  70 **witness** testify to.
  73 **Guildhall** London's 'city hall' or primary government building.
  73 **hies him** hurries himself.
  73 **post** haste.
  74 **meetest . . . time** best opportunity.
  75 **Infer** Allege (*OED* Infer *v* 2).
  76–9 This story, from More's account (pp. 70–1), may have come to Shakespeare through Hall, since Holinshed does not give it in detail.

78 **house** The man's house, also his place of business, was called 'The Crown'. More says King Edward deliberately misunderstood the merchant's harmless remark and had him beheaded for suggesting that his son would inherit the throne of England (p. 70, n.15).
  79 **by the sign thereof** by the sign hanging in front of the shop.
  80 **urge** assert; allege.
  80 **luxury** lustfulness.
  81 **change of lust** change of sexual partners.

Nay, for a need, thus far come near my person: 85
Tell them, when that my mother went with child
Of that insatiate Edward, noble York,
My princely father, then had wars in France,
And by true computation of the time
Found that the issue was not his begot,   90
Which well appearèd in his lineaments,
Being nothing like the noble duke, my father.
Yet touch this sparingly, as 'twere far off,
Because, my lord, you know my mother lives.

BUCKINGHAM Doubt not, my lord, I'll play the orator   95
As if the golden fee for which I plead
Were for myself. And so, my lord, adieu.

RICHARD If you thrive well, bring them to Baynard's Castle,
Where you shall find me well accompanied
With reverend fathers and well-learnèd bishops.   100

BUCKINGHAM I go, and towards three or four o'clock
Look for the news that the Guildhall affords.

Exit Buckingham

RICHARD Go, Lovell, with all speed to Doctor Shaw.
Go thou to Friar Penker. Bid them both
Meet me within this hour at Baynard's Castle.   105

Exit [Lovell]

Now will I go to take some privy order
To draw the brats of Clarence out of sight,

---

85 come] F, Q, Q2–3, Q5–6; comes Q4   87 insatiate] F; vnsatiate Qq   89 true] F; iust Qq   93 Yet] F; But Qq   93 'twere far] F; it were farre Q, Q2–3, Q5–6; it were a farre Q4   94 my lord, you know] F; you know, my Lord Qq   94 my mother] F, Q, Q2–4; my brother Q5; me brother Q6   95 Doubt] F; Feare Q, Q2, Q4–6; Faree Q3   97 And . . . adieu] F; *not in* Qq   101] F; About three or foure a clocke look to heare Qq (*subst.*)   102] F; What news Guildhall affordeth, and so my Lord farewell. Qq (*subst.*)   103–5] F; *not in* Qq   104 Penker] *Capell*; Peuker F   105 SD] F (*Exit*); *not in* Qq   105 SD Lovell] *Theobald* (*Exeunt Lov. and Cates. severally*); *not in* F, Qq   106 go] F; in Qq

85 **for a need** if necessary.
86–7 **went with child/Of** was pregnant with.
90 **issue** child.
91 **his lineaments** Edward's features.
96 **golden fee** the crown. Buckingham also expects a fee from Richard, however: the earldom promised at 3.1.198–200.
98 **Baynard's Castle** Residence of the Duchess of York in London.
103 **Doctor Shaw** Historically, Shaw (or Shaa) was the Mayor's brother and a former royal chaplain who preached in favour of Richard.

104 **Go thou** This may be addressed to Lovell, but more likely either to Catesby or Ratcliffe, both still on stage (unless Catesby exits at 17). If Lovell does not undertake both errands, Ratcliffe or Catesby will probably exit after 105 along with Lovell.
104 **Friar Penker** Another religious figure who supported Richard's accession.
106 **take some privy order** give some secret instruction.

And to give order that no manner person
Have any time recourse unto the princes.

Exeunt

3.6 *Enter a* SCRIVENER

SCRIVENER Here is the indictment of the good Lord Hastings,
Which in a set hand fairly is engrossed
That it may be today read o'er in Paul's.
And mark how well the sequel hangs together:
Eleven hours I have spent to write it over,   5
For yesternight by Catesby was it sent me;
The precedent was full as long a-doing.
And yet within these five hours Hastings lived,
Untainted, unexamined, free, at liberty.
Here's a good world the while.   10
Who is so gross that cannot see this palpable device?
Yet who so bold but says he sees it not?

---

108 order] F; notice Qq   **108** manner] F, Q3–4 (*subst.*); manner of Q, Q2, Q5–6   **109** Have any time] F; At any tyme haue Qq (*subst.*)   **109** SD] F; *Exit.* Qq   **Act 3, Scene 6   3.6**] *Capell*; not in F, Qq   **0** SD] F; *Enter a Scriuener with a paper in his hand.* Qq   **1** Here] F; *This* Qq   **3** today] F; this day Qq   **3** o'er] F; ouer Qq   **5** have spent] F; spent Qq   **6** sent] F; brought Qq   **8** Hastings lived] F; liued Lord Hastings Qq (*subst.*)   **10–11**] F; Heeres . . . grosse / That . . . deuice? Qq   **11** Who is] F; Why whoes Qq (who's Q3–6)   **11** cannot see] F; sees not Qq   **12** who] F, Q3–6; whoes Q, Q2   **12** bold] F; blinde Qq (*subst.*)

---

108 no manner person no manner of person; no person whatsoever.

109 any time at any time.

109 recourse access.

Act 3, Scene 6
Shakespeare dramatises More's editorial commentary as passed down through Hall and Holinshed. Holinshed says that upon hearing the indictment read, 'one that was schoolemaister of Powles of chance standing by, and comparing the shortnesse of the time with the length of the matter, said vnto them that stood about him; "Here is a gaie goodlie cast [trick], foule cast awaie for hast." And a merchant answered him, that it was written by prophesie' (III, 383).

0 SD The quartos' additional phrase, *with a paper in his hand*, makes explicit the stage direction already encoded in the Scrivener's opening line, 'Here is the indictment . . .'

1–14 The Scrivener's monologue is a quasi-sonnet. The passage lacks the rhyme-scheme of a Shakespearean sonnet, but it has fourteen lines and ends in a couplet, giving it enough sonnet

features to mark the Scrivener, at least for readers of the play, as a bookish, thoughtful person.

1 indictment written statement of charges.

2 set hand formal handwriting.

2 engrossed written in large characters appropriate to legal documents (*OED* Engross 1).

3 read o'er in Paul's read publicly in St Paul's Cathedral.

4 the sequel the following.

7 precedent preceding document, rough draft.

9 Untainted Unstained with accusation (*OED* Untainted, citing this line as the only example).

9 unexamined not interrogated.

10–11 F's lineation may be a mistake, but coming as it does in the middle of a sonnet-like passage, the disturbed metre may be a formal allusion to palpable devices and to those who cannot see them.

11 gross stupid, slow.

11 palpable device unmistakable trick.

   Bad is the world, and all will come to naught

   When such ill dealing must be seen in thought.   *Exit*

3.7 *Enter* RICHARD *and* BUCKINGHAM *at several doors*

RICHARD How now, how now, what say the citizens?

BUCKINGHAM Now, by the holy mother of our Lord,

   The citizens are mum, say not a word.

RICHARD Touched you the bastardy of Edward's children?

BUCKINGHAM I did, with his contràct with Lady Lucy   5

   And his contràct by deputy in France;

   Th'insatiate greediness of his desire

   And his enforcement of the city wives;

   His tyranny for trifles; his own bastardy,

   As being got, your father then in France,   10

   And his resemblance being not like the duke.

   Withal, I did infer your lineaments,

   Being the right idea of your father

   Both in your form and nobleness of mind;

   Laid open all your victories in Scotland,   15

   Your discipline in war, wisdom in peace,

---

13 naught] Q, Q2; nought F, Q3–6 14 ill] F; bad Qq 14 dealing] F, Q, Q2–3, Q5–6; dealings Q4 Act 3, Scene 7 3.7]
Pope; not in F, Qq 0 SD] F; *Enter Glocester at one doore, Buckingham at another.* Qq (*subst.*) 1 How now, how now] F;
How now my Lord Qq (*subst.*) 3 say] F; and speake Qq 5–6 his . . . France,] F; *not in* Qq 7 Th'insatiate] F (vnsatiate);
the insatiate Qq (*subst.*) 7 desire] F; desires Qq 8] F; *not in* Qq 11] F; *not in* Qq 14 your] F, Q, Q2; one Q3–6 15
open] F, Q, Q2–5; vpon Q6 15 victories] F, Q, Q2–3, Q5–6; victorie Q4

---

13 naught evil. F's 'nought' has the Scrivener suggesting the end of the world rather than its badness.

14 seen in thought only thought about, not spoken.

Act 3, Scene 7
This scene is usually set in a courtyard, with Richard appearing 'aloft' on a balcony with the two bishops (see 93 SD). More explains that Richard stood in a gallery above the crowd at Baynard's Castle as though he suspected the citizens of ill will toward him (p. 77).

 0 SD *several* separate.

 4 Touched you Did you touch on, mention.

 5 Lady Lucy Lady Elizabeth Lucy, to whom More says Edward was betrothed at the time he wooed Elizabeth Grey. Shakespeare alludes to Edward's child by Lady Lucy during the courtship scene between Edward and Elizabeth Grey (*3H6* 3.2).

6 his contràct by deputy See *3H6* 3.3 for Shakespeare's version of Edward's proxy marriage contract with the French king's sister, Bona. Richard and Buckingham argue Edward's pledges to Lady Lucy and to the lady Bona invalidate his subsequent marriage to Elizabeth.

 8 enforcement sexual compulsion, rape.

 9 tyranny for trifles oppression of subjects for trivial reasons.

 10 got conceived.

 12 Withal Besides, in addition.

 12 infer argue, assert.

 12 lineaments features.

 13 right idea accurate image.

 15 Laid open Plainly described.

 15 victories in Scotland Richard III headed a successful expedition against the Scots in 1482.

 16 discipline in war skill in military affairs (*OED* Discipline *sb* 3b).

Your bounty, virtue, fair humility;
Indeed, left nothing fitting for your purpose
Untouched or slightly handled in discourse.
And when my oratory drew toward end, 20
I bid them that did love their country's good
Cry 'God save Richard, England's royal king!'

RICHARD And did they so?

BUCKINGHAM No, so God help me, they spake not a word,
But like dumb statuès or breathing stones 25
Stared each on other and looked deadly pale.
Which when I saw, I reprehended them,
And asked the Mayor what meant this wilful silence.
His answer was, the people were not used
To be spoke to but by the Recorder. 30
Then he was urged to tell my tale again:
'Thus saith the duke, thus hath the duke inferred',
But nothing spoke in warrant from himself.
When he had done, some followers of mine own
At lower end of the hall hurled up their caps, 35
And some ten voices cried 'God save King Richard!'
And thus I took the vantage of those few:
'Thanks, gentle citizens and friends', quoth I,
'This general applause and cheerful shout
Argues your wisdom and your love to Richard.' 40
And even here broke off and came away.

RICHARD What tongueless blocks were they! Would they not speak?
Will not the Mayor, then, and his brethren, come?

BUCKINGHAM The Mayor is here at hand; intend some fear.

---

18 your] F; the Qq 20 my] F, Q3–6; mine Q, Q2 20 drew] F; grew Qq 20 toward] F; to an Q, Q2, Q4 (*subst.*); to Q3, Q5–6 21 bid] F, Q, Q2–4; bad Q5–6 21 did love] F, Q, Q2; loues Q3–6 22 'God . . . king!'] *Malone (italics); no quotation marks in* F, Qq 23 And] F; A and Qq 24 they spake not a word] F; *not in* Qq 25 breathing] F, Q, Q2; breathlesse Q3–6 26 Stared] F; Gazde Qq 28 meant] F, Q, Q2–5; meanes Q6 29 used] F; wont Qq 32 'Thus . . . inferred'] *Johnson (italics); no quotation marks in* F, Qq 33 spoke] F; spake Q, Q2–4, Q6; speake Q5 35 At] F; At the Qq 36 'God . . . Richard!'] *Capell (italics); no quotation marks in* F, Qq 37] F; *not in* Qq 38 'Thanks . . . friends'] *Johnson (italics); no quotation marks in* F, Qq 38 gentle] F; louing Qq 39–40 'This . . . Richard.'] *Johnson (italics); no quotation marks in* F, Qq 39 cheerful] F; louing Qq 40 wisdom] F, Q3–6; wisdoms Q, Q2 40 love] F, Q, Q2; loues Q3–6 41 even here] F; so Qq 42] Qq; What . . . they, / Would . . . speake? F 42 speak?] F; speake? / Buc. No by my troth my Lo; Qq (*subst.*) 44 SH] F (*Buck.*), Q3–6 (*Buc.*); Glo. Q, Q2 44 at hand] F, Q, Q2; *not in* Q3–6 44 intend] F; and intend Qq

---

17 **bounty** generosity. Good leaders were supposed to be generous to their followers in return for loyalty.

19 **handled** dealt with.

19 **discourse** Stressed on the second syllable.

30 **Recorder** Chief legal officer of the City of London.

31 **he** the Recorder.

32 **inferred** alleged, asserted.

33 **in warrant from himself** as an assertion of his own.

37 **the vantage** advantage.

43 **his brethren** his brothers, his fellow citizens.

44 **intend** pretend.

Be not you spoke with but by mighty suit.   45
And look you get a prayer book in your hand
And stand between two churchmen, good my lord,
For on that ground I'll make a holy descant.
And be not easily won to our requests;
Play the maid's part: still answer nay and take it.   50

RICHARD I go; and if you plead as well for them
    As I can say nay to thee for myself,
    No doubt we bring it to a happy issue.

BUCKINGHAM Go, go, up to the leads. The Lord Mayor knocks.

                                        Exit [Richard]

             Enter the MAYOR *and Citizens*

Welcome, my lord. I dance attendance here.   55
I think the duke will not be spoke withal.

                  Enter CATESBY

BUCKINGHAM Now, Catesby, what says your lord to my request?
CATESBY He doth entreat your grace, my noble lord,
    To visit him tomorrow or next day.
    He is within, with two right reverend fathers,   60
    Divinely bent to meditation,
    And in no worldly suits would he be moved
    To draw him from his holy exercise.

---

45 you spoke with] F; spoken withall Qq   45 by] F; with Qq   47 between] F; betwixt Qq   48 make] F; build Qq   49 And be] F; Be Qq   49 easily] F, Q; easie Q2–6   49 requests] F; request Qq   50 still answer nay and] F; say no, but Qq   51 I go; and] F; Feare not me, Qq   51 you] F; thou canst Qq   53 we] F; weele Qq   54] F; You shal see what I can do, get you vp to the leads. Qq (*subst.*)   54 SD. 1 *Exit Richard*] Theobald (*Ex. Glo.*); *Exit*. Qq; *not in* F   54 SD. 2 *Enter . . . Citizens*] F; *not in* Qq   55 Welcome, my lord] F; Now my L. Maior Qq (*subst.*)   56 spoke] F, Q, Q2; spoken Q3–6   57] F; Here coms his seruant: how now *Catesby* what sais he. Qq (*subst.*)   58] F; My Lord, he doth intreat your grace Qq (*subst.*)   60 right reverend] F, Q, Q2; reuerent Q3–6   62 suits] F; suite Qq (*subst.*)

45 **mighty suit** strenuous pleading.

48 **on . . . descant** to that tune I'll make a holy accompaniment. In medieval religious music, the 'ground' was the foundation chant or melody above which the 'descant' or counterpoint was sung (see *OED* Ground *sb* 6c). The 'ground' in Buckingham's metaphor is the sight of Richard, prayer book in hand, standing between two clergymen.

50 **maid's** girl's.

50 **still** always.

50 **and take it** It was (and is) a common saying that women say 'no' to sexual invitations when they really mean 'yes'.

52 As I can answer 'nay' when you plead for them. This ironic remark foreshadows Richard's denial of Buckingham's request (4.2.84–101).

53 **issue** conclusion.

54 **leads** Lead coverings on the roof (*OED* Lead *sb* 7). Most productions have Richard re-enter on an upper balcony rather than on a roof.

54 SD.2 *Citizens* Some productions take this direction as an opportunity to stage a Fascist rally with a mob of citizens. In others, the citizens are few and often subdued, as Buckingham described them in the Guildhall (24–40).

55 **dance attendance** await attention, as a client upon a patron.

56 **spoke withal** spoken with.

BUCKINGHAM Return, good Catesby, to the gracious duke.
    Tell him myself, the Mayor, and aldermen   65
    In deep designs, in matter of great moment,
    No less importing than our general good,
    Are come to have some conference with his grace.
CATESBY I'll signify so much unto him straight.   *Exit*
BUCKINGHAM Ah ha, my lord, this prince is not an Edward.   70
    He is not lulling on a lewd love-bed
    But on his knees at meditation,
    Not dallying with a brace of courtesans
    But meditating with two deep divines,
    Not sleeping to engross his idle body   75
    But praying to enrich his watchful soul.
    Happy were England, would this virtuous prince
    Take on his grace the sovereignty thereof,
    But sure I fear we shall not win him to it.
MAYOR Marry, God defend his grace should say us nay.   80
BUCKINGHAM I fear he will. Here Catesby comes again.

      Enter CATESBY

    Now, Catesby, what says his grace?
CATESBY He wonders to what end you have assembled
    Such troops of citizens to come to him,
    His grace not being warned thereof before.   85
    He fears, my lord, you mean no good to him.
BUCKINGHAM Sorry I am my noble cousin should
    Suspect me that I mean no good to him.
    By heaven, we come to him in perfect love,
    And so once more return and tell his grace.   90
          Exit [*Catesby*]

---

64 the gracious duke] F; thy Lord againe Qq (*subst.*) **65** aldermen] F; Cittizens Qq (*subst.*) **66** in matter] F; and matters Qq **67** than] F, Q, Q2–5; them then Q6 **69**] F; Ile tell him what you say my Lord. Qq (*subst.*) **71** love-bed] F; day bed Qq **77** virtuous] F; gracious Qq **78** his grace] F; himselfe Qq **78** thereof] F; thereon Qq **79** not] F; neuer Qq **80** defend] F; forbid Qq **81** Here Catesby comes again] F; how now Catesby Qq **82**] F; What saies your Lord? Qq (*subst.*) **83** He] F; My Lo. he Qq (*subst.*) **84** come to] F; speake with Qq **86** He fears, my lord] F; My Lord, he feares Qq **89** we . . . love] F; I come in perfect loue to him Qq **90** SD *Catesby*] Qq; *not in* F

---

 65 aldermen municipal legislators, city councillors.
 66 deep designs profound matters.
 67 No less importing Concerning nothing less.

 71 lulling lolling, resting at ease.
 73 brace pair.
 74 deep divines deeply learned clergymen.
 75 engross make gross or fat.
 80 defend forbid.

When holy and devout religious men
Are at their beads, 'tis much to draw them thence,
So sweet is zealous contemplation.

Enter RICHARD *aloft, between two Bishops*

MAYOR See where his grace stands, 'tween two clergymen.
BUCKINGHAM Two props of virtue for a Christian prince,   95
      To stay him from the fall of vanity.
      And see, a book of prayer in his hand,
      True ornaments to know a holy man –
      Famous Plantagenet, most gracious prince,
      Lend favourable ear to our requests,   100
      And pardon us the interruption
      Of thy devotion and right Christian zeal.
RICHARD My lord, there needs no such apology.
      I do beseech your grace to pardon me,
      Who, earnest in the service of my God,   105
      Deferred the visitation of my friends.
      But leaving this, what is your grace's pleasure?
BUCKINGHAM Even that, I hope, which pleaseth God above
      And all good men of this ungoverned isle.
RICHARD I do suspect I have done some offence   110
      That seems disgracious in the city's eye,
      And that you come to reprehend my ignorance.
BUCKINGHAM You have, my lord. Would it might please your grace
      On our entreaties to amend your fault.

---

92 much] F; hard Qq   92 thence] F, Q, Q2–4; hence Q5–6   93 SD *aloft, between two Bishops*] F; *with two bishops a loste* Q; *with two Bishops aloft* Q2; *and two Bishops aloft* Q3–6   94 his grace] F; he Qq   94 'tween] F; between Qq   97–8] F; *not in* Qq   100 ear] F; eares Qq   100 our requests] F; our request Q; my request Q2–6   104 I do beseech your grace to] F; I rather do beseech you Qq   106 Deferred] F; Neglect Qq   111 seems] F, Q, Q2–4; seeme Q5–6   111 eye] F; eies Qq (*subst.*)   113] Qq; You . . . Lord: / Would . . . Grace, F   113 might] F; *not in* Qq   114 On] F; At Qq   114 your] F; that Qq

92 **beads** rosary beads; prayers.
92 **'tis much** it takes much.
93 **contemplation** Latinate words like this one, which a modern English speaker would normally pronounce with four syllables, but which needs five syllables for the metre, are a challenge for the contemporary verse-speaking actor. A common solution uses four syllables plus extra emphasis.
93 SD *aloft* above. Shakespeare's theatre probably contained both a main stage and an upper playing space. Although F and Qq fail to specify an entry for Catesby aloft, his exit from the main stage at 90 must be followed by his reappearance above before he speaks to Richard at 202. Many directors elect to have Catesby re-enter with Richard and the bishops at 93.
93 SD *two Bishops* These two clergymen are probably Shaw and Penker, whom Richard sent for at 3.5.103–4. Historically, neither was a bishop.
96 **stay** keep.
98 **ornaments** i.e. the bishops and the prayer book.
102 **right** true, genuine (*OED* Right *a* 17).
109 **ungoverned** without a proper ruler.
111 **disgracious** displeasing.

RICHARD Else wherefore breathe I in a Christian land?   115
BUCKINGHAM Know, then, it is your fault that you resign
       The supreme seat, the throne majestical,
       The sceptred office of your ancestors,
       Your state of fortune and your due of birth,
       The lineal glory of your royal house,   120
       To the corruption of a blemished stock;
       While in the mildness of your sleepy thoughts,
       Which here we waken to our country's good,
       The noble isle doth want her proper limbs;
       Her face defaced with scars of infamy,   125
       Her royal stock graft with ignoble plants,
       And almost shouldered in the swallowing gulf
       Of dark forgetfulness and deep oblivion.
       Which to recure, we heartily solicit
       Your gracious self to take on you the charge   130
       And kingly government of this your land,
       Not as protector, steward, substitute,
       Or lowly factor for another's gain,
       But as successively from blood to blood,
       Your right of birth, your empery, your own.   135
       For this, consorted with the citizens,
       Your very worshipful and loving friends,

---

116 Know then] F; Then Know Qq   119] F; *not in* Qq   122 While] F; Whilest Q; Whilest Q2–6   122 your] F, Q, Q3–6;
you Q2   123 our] F, Q, Q2–4; your Q5–6   124 The] F; This Qq   124 her] Q, Q2; his Q3–6, F   125 Her] Qq; His F   125
scars] F, Q, Q5–6; stars Q2–4   126] F; *not in* Qq   126 Her] *Pope*; His F; this Q3–6   128 dark] F; blind
Qq   128 deep] F; darke Qq   129 recure] F, Q, Q2–5; recouer Q6   130 charge] F; soueraingtie therof Qq (*subst.*)   131] F;
not in Qq   133 Or] F, Q, Q2; Nor Q3–6   137 very] F, Q, Q2 (*subst.*); *not in* Q3–6   137 loving] F, Q, Q2; very louing Q3–6

115 What else is the purpose of my Christian life (if not to amend my faults)?

119 your state of fortune position you deserve by fortune.

121 the corruption of a blemished stock the degradation sure to follow from the rule of a bastard prince.

122 While While you are.

124 her Since countries are usually feminine, 'his' probably crept into the quartos by mistake and was not corrected when this line was set in the Folio. A second masculine pronoun (125) and a third that occurs only in F (126) may have been changed from those in the manuscript by someone in the printing house who wanted to maintain consistency with the first 'his'.

124 proper limbs own true parts; with a suggestion of the 'plant'/'Plantagenet' pun.

126 graft grafted.

126 ignoble plants the supposed bastards, ignoble because illegitimate, and 'plants' partly for the pun on 'Plantagenet'. Compare 215, 'we will plant some other in the throne'.

127 shouldered sunk up to the shoulders.

127 gulf depth. Buckingham drops his plant metaphor for one in which a dark hole or body of water swallows the royal line.

129 recure remedy, restore to a normal state (*OED* Recure *v* 2b).

133 factor agent.

134 successively consecutively, by inheritance. Buckingham's next phrase, 'from blood to blood', makes his meaning clear.

135 empery empire.

136 consorted with in association with.

137 worshipful respectful.

> And by their vehement instigation,
> In this just cause come I to move your grace.

RICHARD I cannot tell if to depart in silence   140
> Or bitterly to speak in your reproof
> Best fitteth my degree or your condition.
> If not to answer, you might haply think
> Tongue-tied ambition, not replying, yielded
> To bear the golden yoke of sovereignty,   145
> Which fondly you would here impose on me.
> If to reprove you for this suit of yours,
> So seasoned with your faithful love to me,
> Then on the other side I checked my friends.
> Therefore, to speak, and to avoid the first,   150
> And then, in speaking, not to incur the last,
> Definitively thus I answer you:
> Your love deserves my thanks, but my desert
> Unmeritable shuns your high request.
> First, if all obstacles were cut away,   155
> And that my path were even to the crown
> As the ripe revenue and due of birth,
> Yet so much is my poverty of spirit,
> So mighty and so many my defects,
> That I would rather hide me from my greatness,   160
> Being a bark to brook no mighty sea,
> Than in my greatness covet to be hid
> And in the vapour of my glory smothered.

---

139 cause] F; suite Q; sute Q2–6 **140** cannot tell] F; know not whether Qq (*subst.*) **143–52**] F; *not in* Qq **157** the ripe] F; my ripe Q; my right Q2–6 **157** of] F; by Qq **160** That I would] F; As I had Qq

---

142 my degree or your condition my rank or yours. Richard draws an implicit distinction between his high 'degree' as a duke and the lower 'condition' of the citizens. Later, to flatter them, he calls them all 'cousins' (245).

143 haply perhaps.

146 fondly foolishly.

148 seasoned rendered palatable or acceptable.

149 I checked I would have criticised, rebuked.

153–4 my desert/Unmeritable my undeserving, my unworthiness.

155 cut away Richard answers Buckingham's plant metaphor with a subtle reminder of his earlier murderous pruning of Clarence from the family tree.

156 even level, smooth.

157 ripe ready to be passed down.

157 revenue return, proceeds.

160 my greatness the kingship. With this phrase, Richard claims the throne even as he rejects it.

161–3 Richard's figurative language responds to Buckingham's 'swallowing gulf' image (127).

161 bark boat.

161 brook tolerate.

162 hid covered.

163 in . . . smothered be overwhelmed by my own greatness. 'Vapour' suggests the foam of a swallowing sea.

But, God be thanked, there is no need of me,
And much I need to help you, were there need.   165
The royal tree hath left us royal fruit,
Which, mellowed by the stealing hours of time,
Will well become the seat of majesty
And make (no doubt) us happy by his reign.
On him I lay that you would lay on me,   170
The right and fortune of his happy stars,
Which God defend that I should wring from him.
BUCKINGHAM My lord, this argues conscience in your grace,
But the respects thereof are nice and trivial,
All circumstances well considerèd.   175
You say that Edward is your brother's son.
So say we too, but not by Edward's wife,
For first was he contràct to Lady Lucy,
Your mother lives a witness to his vow,
And afterward by substitute betrothed   180
To Bona, sister to the King of France.
These both put off, a poor petitioner,
A care-crazed mother to a many sons,
A beauty-waning and distressèd widow,
Even in the afternoon of her best days,   185
Made prize and purchase of his wanton eye,
Seduced the pitch and height of his degree
To base declension and loathed bigamy.

---

164 there is] F; there's Qq (*subst.*)   164 of] F, Q, Q2; for Q3–6   165 were there need] F; if need were Qq   169 (no doubt)] F; no doubt Qq   170 that] F; what Qq   178 was he] F; he was Qq   178 contràct] F, Q, Q2–5; contracted Q6   179 his] F; that Qq   180 afterward] F, Q, Q2–5; afterwards Q6   182 off] F; by Qq   183 to a many] F; of a many Q; of many Q2–6   183 sons] F; children Qq   186 wanton] F; lustfull Qq   187 Seduced] F, Q, Q2–5 (*subst.*); Seduce Q6   187 his degree] F; al his thoughts Qq (*subst.*)

---

165 much I need to help you I am severely lacking in the ability to help you.

166–7 Compare Richard's metaphor here to Margaret's image of Richard's reign as rotten fruit dropping into the mouth of death (4.4.1–2).

167 stealing stealthy.

169 no doubt F's parentheses underscore the effect Richard seeks with this interjection, which is to cast doubt by saying there is no doubt.

170 that that which.

172 defend forbid.

174 respects thereof points of your argument.

174 nice overly precise.

178 contràct contracted. See 5n. For the verb

form, see 1.4.177n. and Abbott 342.

180 substitute proxy.

182 poor petitioner Elizabeth Grey, who had petitioned the king for the return of her dead husband's lands (see *3H6* 3.2).

186 purchase plunder, that which is taken with violence (*OED* Purchase *sb* 1).

187 pitch . . . degree his high rank. 'Pitch' is a term from falconry meaning the high point in a bird's flight (*OED* Pitch *sb*² 18a).

188 declension decline.

188 bigamy Buckingham argues that Edward's pre-contracts to other women caused him to commit bigamy when he married Elizabeth Grey.

By her, in his unlawful bed, he got
This Edward, whom our manners call the prince.   190
More bitterly could I expostulate,
Save that for reverence to some alive,
I give a sparing limit to my tongue.
Then, good my lord, take to your royal self
This proffered benefit of dignity,   195
If not to bless us and the land withal,
Yet to draw forth your noble ancestry
From the corruption of abusing times
Unto a lineal true-derivèd course.

MAYOR Do, good my lord, your citizens entreat you.   200
BUCKINGHAM Refuse not, mighty lord, this proffered love.
CATESBY Oh, make them joyful. Grant their lawful suit.
RICHARD Alas, why would you heap this care on me?
      I am unfit for state and majesty.
      I do beseech you, take it not amiss;   205
      I cannot nor I will not yield to you.
BUCKINGHAM If you refuse it, as in love and zeal
      Loath to depose the child, your brother's son,
      As well we know your tenderness of heart
      And gentle, kind, effeminate remorse,   210
      Which we have noted in you to your kindred
      And equally indeed to all estates,
      Yet know, whe'er you accept our suit or no,
      Your brother's son shall never reign our king,
      But we will plant some other in the throne   215
      To the disgrace and downfall of your house.

---

189 his] F, Q, Q2–5; this Q6   190 call] F; terme Qq   191 could I] F, Q, Q2–5; could Q6   197 forth your noble ancestry] F; out your royall stocke Qq   198 times] F; time Qq   199 true-derivèd] *Theobald*; true deriued F, Qq; true, derived *Pope*   201] F; *not in* Qq   203 this] F; these Q; those Q2–6   203 care] F; cares Qq   204 majesty] F; dignitie Qq   211 kindred] F; kin Qq   213 know, whe'er] F (where); whether Qq   213 accept] F, Q, Q2–5; except Q6

190 **whom . . . prince** whom we call the prince only for the sake of courtesy.
191 **expostulate** argue.
192 **some alive** i.e. the Duchess of York. Buckingham obeys Richard's orders to allude to Edward's supposed illegitimate birth, but to keep the topic 'as 'twere far off, / Because, my lord, you know my mother lives' (3.5.93–4).
196 **withal** with.
197 **draw forth** extract.

210 **gentle, kind, effeminate remorse** refined, familial, nurturing pity. Compare the Murderer's association of compassion or pity with women at 1.4.252. The scene following this one, 4.1, shows the genuine display of such emotion by the women in Richard's family.
212 **estates** ranks.
213 **whe'er** whether.
215 **plant** Compare word-play on the royal family name, 'Plantagenet', at 126 and at 2.2.100.

And in this resolution here we leave you.
Come, citizens. We will entreat no more.

Exeunt

CATESBY Call him again, sweet prince; accept their suit.
If you deny them, all the land will rue it.   220
RICHARD Will you enforce me to a world of cares?
Call them again. I am not made of stones,
But penetrable to your kind entreaties,
Albeit against my conscience and my soul.

Enter BUCKINGHAM *and the rest*

Cousin of Buckingham, and sage, grave men,   225
Since you will buckle fortune on my back,
To bear her burden, whe'er I will or no,
I must have patience to endure the load.
But if black scandal or foul-faced reproach
Attend the sequel of your imposition,   230
Your mere enforcement shall acquittance me
From all the impure blots and stains thereof;
For God doth know, and you may partly see,
How far I am from the desire of this.
MAYOR God bless your grace; we see it and will say it.   235
RICHARD In saying so, you shall but say the truth.
BUCKINGHAM Then I salute you with this royal title:
Long live King Richard, England's worthy king.

---

218 We will] F; zounds ile Qq   218 more.] F; more. / *Glo.* O do not sweare my Lord of Buckingham. Qq   218 SD] F; *not in* Qq   219 him] F; them Qq   219 sweet prince] F; my lord, and Qq   220] F; *Ano.* Doe, good my lord, least all the land do rew it. Qq   221 Will] F; Would Qq   221 cares] F; care Qq   222 Call] F; Well, call Qq   223 entreaties] F; intreates Qq (*subst.*)   224 SD] F; *not in* Qq   225 sage] F; you sage Qq   226 you] F, Q, Q2, Q4–6; your Q3   227 her] F, Q, Q2; Q3–6   227 whe'er] F (where); whether Qq   229 foul-faced] F; soule-fac't Q, Q2; so foule fac't Q3–5; so foulefac't Q6   233 doth know] F; he knowes Qq   234 of this] F; thereof Qq   237 this royal] F; this kingly Q, Q2–3, Q5–6; the kingly Q4   238 King Richard] F, Q3–6; Richard Q, Q2   238 worthy] F; royall Qq

218 **We will entreat no more** To many editors, the absence from F of the quarto's oath, 'zounds' ('by Christ's wounds'), and Richard's hypocritical admonition, 'O do not sweare my Lord of Buckingham', appears to constitute strong evidence that the F text was purged in obedience to the Statute to Restrain Abuses (1606), a law intended to reduce profanity on stage. Buckingham's oath and Richard's reply, however, may have been added to Qq rather than purged during the composition of F. The quarto versions of *Richard III* contain several strong oaths that do not appear in F, but this fact alone cannot prove that the F text was expurgated.

218 SD *Exeunt* Buckingham, the Mayor and all the citizens probably do not have time to leave the stage before they are called back. At 222, Richard seems to be talking to them again, although the group has not completely re-entered until 224.
221 **enforce me to** force me into.
226 **on my back** Richard calls attention to his hunched back.
230 Follow the duty you impose.
231 **Your . . . me** The simple fact that you forced this on me shall absolve me.

ALL Amen.

BUCKINGHAM Tomorrow may it please you to be crowned?   240
RICHARD Even when you please, for you will have it so.
BUCKINGHAM Tomorrow, then, we will attend your grace,
    And so most joyfully we take our leave.
RICHARD [*to the bishops*] Come, let us to our holy work again.–
    Farewell, my cousins, farewell, gentle friends.   245

                                       Exeunt

4.1 *Enter the Queen* [ELIZABETH], *the* DUCHESS OF YORK, *and*
MARQUESS DORSET [*at one door;*] ANNE DUCHESS OF GLOUCESTER
[*and Clarence's daughter, at another door*]

DUCHESS Who meets us here? My niece Plantagenet
    Led in the hand of her kind aunt of Gloucester?
    Now, for my life, she's wand'ring to the Tower,
    On pure heart's love to greet the tender prince.
    Daughter, well met.
ANNE   God give your graces both   5
    A happy and a joyful time of day.
ELIZABETH As much to you, good sister. Whither away?
ANNE No farther than the Tower, and, as I guess,
    Upon the like devotion as yourselves,

239 SH] F; *M yor.* Q; *Mai.* Q2–4; *May.* Q5–6   **240** may] F; will Qq   **241** please, for] F; will, since Qq   **243** F; *not in* Qq   **244** SD] *Johnson (To the Clergymen.); not in* F, Qq   **244** work] F; task Qq   **245** my] F; good Qq   **245** cousins] F; cousin Qq (*subst.*)   **Act 4, Scene 1   4.1**] F (*Actus Quartus. Scena Prima.*); *not in* Qq   **0** SD] Qq (*Enter Quee. mother, Duchesse of Yorke, Marques Dorset, at one doore, Duchesse of Glocest. at another doore.*); *Enter the Queene, Anne Duchesse of Gloucester, the Duchesse of Yorke, and Marquesse Dorset.* F   **0** SD *and Clarence's daughter*] *Theobald (leading Clarence's young Daughter); not in* F, Qq   **1**] Qq; *Who . . . heere? / My . . . Plantagenet.* F   **2–4**] F; *not in* Qq   **5** Daughter] F; *Qu. Sister* Qq   **5–6** ANNE *God . . . day*] F; *not in* Qq   **5–6** both / A *happie* / And F   **7** As . . . sister] F; *not in* Qq   **7** away] F; awaie so fast Qq (*subst.*)   **8** SH] F; *Duch.* Qq (*subst.*)

245 cousins Richard includes the citizens in this sweeping term of intimacy. Compare his calling the lords at the council meeting 'cousins all' (3.4.22).

Act 4, Scene 1
This scene, the second of the female triads, has no analogue in Hall or Holinshed. It is part of a pattern Shakespeare derived from the motif of the three Marys in the English cycle plays (see pp. 9–12 above).

0 SD As often, the quarto stage directions make explicit what F implies through dialogue (1: 'Who meets us here?'). In this case, however, F may mislead by listing Anne's entrance between rather than after those of Elizabeth and the Duchess.

0 SD Clarence's daughter The girl has no lines in this scene. Her absence from the quartos suggests that the part may have been eliminated in at least some performances. Dramatically, the presence of Clarence's child enhances the strong sense of family feeling among the women – for example, the Duchess calls Anne 'Daughter' (5), and Elizabeth calls her 'sister' (7) – and contrasts their attitude to Richard's.

1 niece relative; in this case, granddaughter.
3 for my life I stake my life on it.
9 like devotion same devout purpose.

To gratulate the gentle princes there.   10
ELIZABETH Kind sister, thanks. We'll enter all together.

Enter the Lieutenant [BRAKENBURY]

And in good time, here the Lieutenant comes.
Master Lieutenant, pray you, by your leave,
How doth the prince and my young son of York?
BRAKENBURY Right well, dear madam. By your patience,   15
I may not suffer you to visit them.
The king hath strictly charged the contrary.
ELIZABETH The king? Who's that?
BRAKENBURY I mean the Lord Protector.
ELIZABETH The Lord protect him from that kingly title.   20
Hath he set bounds between their love and me?
I am their mother. Who shall bar me from them?
DUCHESS I am their father's mother. I will see them.
ANNE Their aunt I am in law, in love their mother.
Then bring me to their sights; I'll bear thy blame   25
And take thy office from thee, on my peril.
BRAKENBURY No, madam, no; I may not leave it so.
I am bound by oath, and therefore pardon me.

Exit Lieutenant

Enter STANLEY [EARL OF DERBY]

STANLEY Let me but meet you ladies one hour hence,
And I'll salute your grace of York as mother   30
And reverend looker-on of two fair queens.
[*To Anne*] Come, madam, you must straight to Westminster,
There to be crownèd Richard's royal queen.

---

10 gentle] F; tender Qq   12 SD BRAKENBURY] *Capell; the Lieutenant* F; *Lieutenant* Q, Q2; *the Lieutenant of the Tower* Q3–6   14] F; How fares the Prince? Qq (feares Q6)   15, 19, 27 SH] *Capell; Lieu.* F, Qq   15] F; Wel Madam, and in health, but by your leaue, Qq (*subst.*)   16 them] F; him Qq   18 Who's] F; whie, whose Qq (*subst.*)   19 I mean] F; I crie you mercie, I meane Qq (*subst.*)   21 between] F; betwixt Qq   22 shall bar] F; should keepe Qq   23 SH] F (*Duch. Yorke.*), Q (*Du. yor.*); *not in* Q2–6   23 their father's mother] F; their Fathers, Mother Q; their Father, Mother Q2–3, Q5–6 (*subst.*); theirs father mother Q4   23 I] F, Q; and Q2–6   25 bring me to their sights] F; feare not thou Qq   27] F; I doe beseech your graces all to pardon me: Qq (*subst.*)   28 and therefore pardon me] F; I may not doe it Qq (*subst.*)   28 SD. 1] F (*Exit Lieutenant.*); *not in* Qq   29 you] F, Q, Q2–5; your Q6   29 one] F; an Q, Q2–4; at an Q5–6   31 reverend] F; reuerente Qq (*subst.*)   32 SD] *Capell; not in* F, Qq   32 straight] F; go with me Qq

10 **gratulate** greet.
16 **suffer** permit.
21 **bounds** boundaries, walls.
26 **office** duty, responsibility.
31 **looker-on** observer.

31 **two fair queens** Elizabeth, wife of the Duchess's son King Edward, and Anne, wife of Richard, who is about to be crowned.
32 **straight** go immediately.

ELIZABETH Ah, cut my lace asunder,
       That my pent heart may have some scope to beat,   35
       Or else I swoon with this dead-killing news.
ANNE Despiteful tidings. Oh, unpleasing news.
DORSET Be of good cheer, mother; how fares your grace?
ELIZABETH O Dorset, speak not to me; get thee gone.
       Death and destruction dogs thee at thy heels.   40
       Thy mother's name is ominous to children.
       If thou wilt outstrip death, go, cross the seas
       And live with Richmond, from the reach of hell.
       Go hie thee, hie thee from this slaughterhouse,
       Lest thou increase the number of the dead   45
       And make me die the thrall of Margaret's curse,
       Nor mother, wife, nor England's counted queen.
STANLEY Full of wise care is this your counsel, madam –
       [*To Dorset*] Take all the swift advantage of the hours.
       You shall have letters from me to my son   50
       In your behalf, to meet you on the way.
       Be not ta'en tardy by unwise delay.
DUCHESS O ill-dispersing wind of misery.
       O my accursèd womb, the bed of death.
       A cockatrice hast thou hatched to the world,   55
       Whose unavoided eye is murderous.

34–6] F; O . . . heart, / May . . . sound, / With . . . newes. Qq   **34** Ah] F; O Qq   **34** asunder] F; in sunder Qq   **36** else I] F, Q, Q3, Q5–6; else Q2, *Huntington copy of* Q3, Q4   **36** swoon] F; sound Qq   **36** dead-killing] F; dead killing Q, Q2–4; dead liking Q5–6   **37**] F; *not in* Qq   **38** Be of good cheer, mother] F; Madam, haue comfort Qq (*subst.*)   **39** gone] F; hence Qq   **40** dogs] F; dogge Qq   **40** thy] F; the Qq   **41** ominous] F, Q, Q2–4, Q6; ominious Q5   **42** outstrip] F, Q, Q2–5; ouerstrip Q6   **43** reach] F, Q, Q2–5; race Q6   **49** SD] *Johnson (using a dash); not in* F, Qq   **49** hours] F; time Qq   **50** my] F; Q, Q2–5; me Q6   **51**] F; To meet you on the way, and welcome you, Qq   **52** ta'en] F, Q (*subst.*); taken Q2–6   **53** ill-dispersing] *Theobald*; ill dispersing F, Qq (*subst.*)   **55** hatched] F, Q2–6 (*subst.*); hatch Q

34 lace String used to lace up a tight bodice or corset.
   34 asunder apart.
   35 pent confined.
   35 scope room.
   41 ominous a bad omen.
   43 Richmond This is the first mention in the play of Henry Tudor, Earl of Richmond. Queen Elizabeth includes the Countess of Richmond as one of her enemies at 1.3.20–4, but here she sees Richmond's exiled household in Brittany as a haven for her son.
   43 hell Richard's government.
   44 hie thee hurry.
   46 thrall subject, captive (*OED* Thrall *sb*[1] 1). Elizabeth escapes the full force of Margaret's

curse, since although she is no longer a queen or a wife, she is still a mother (see 1.3.207).
   47 Nor Neither.
   47 counted acknowledged.
   50 Stanley probably means that he will give Dorset letters of introduction to his stepson, Richmond. Stanley also has a son of his own, George Stanley, whom Richard threatens in Act 5.
   51 to . . . way The letters in 50 (or perhaps Stanley's son) will be sent to Dorset while he is on his way.
   52 ta'en taken.
   53 ill-dispersing evil-spreading.
   55 cockatrice Mythical serpent, also called a 'basilisk', that could kill with a look.

STANLEY Come, madam, come. I in all haste was sent.

ANNE And I with all unwillingness will go.
>   Oh, would to God that the inclusive verge
>   Of golden metal that must round my brow   60
>   Were red-hot steel, to sear me to the brains.
>   Anointed let me be with deadly venom
>   And die ere men can say 'God save the queen.'

ELIZABETH Go, go, poor soul, I envy not thy glory.
>   To feed my humour, wish thyself no harm.   65

ANNE No? Why? When he that is my husband now
>   Came to me as I followed Henry's corpse,
>   When scarce the blood was well washed from his hands
>   Which issued from my other angel husband
>   And that dear saint which then I weeping followed,   70
>   Oh, when, I say, I looked on Richard's face,
>   This was my wish: 'Be thou', quoth I, 'accursed
>   For making me, so young, so old a widow.
>   And when thou wed'st, let sorrow haunt thy bed;
>   And be thy wife, if any be so mad,   75
>   More miserable by the life of thee
>   Than thou hast made me by my dear lord's death.'
>   Lo, ere I can repeat this curse again,
>   Within so small a time, my woman's heart
>   Grossly grew captive to his honey words   80
>   And proved the subject of mine own soul's curse,

---

57 madam, come] F; Madam, Qq   57 sent] F, Q, Q2; sent for Q3–6   58 SH] F; *Duch.* Qq (*subst.*)   58 with] F; in Qq   59 Oh] F; I Qq   61 brains] F; braine Qq   62 let me be] F, Q, Q2, Q4, Q6; let me Q3, Q5   62 venom] F; poyson Qq (*subst.*)   63 'God . . . queen.'] *Johnson* (*italics*); *no quotation marks in* F, Qq   64 Go, go] F; Alas Qq   64 thy] F, Q, Q3–6; the Q2   66 Why?] F; *not in* Qq   67 as I] F, Q, Q2–5; I Q6   67 corpse] F (Corse); course Qq   70 dear] F; dead Qq   72–7 'Be thou' . . . 'accursed . . . death.'] *Pope* (*subst.*); *no quotation marks in* F, Qq   75 mad] F, Q, Q2 (madde); badde Q3–6   76 More] F; As Qq   76 life] F; death Qq   77 Than] F; As Qq   78 ere] F; eare Q; euen Q2–6   79 Within so small a time] F; Euen in so short a space Qq   80 Grossly] F, Q; Crosslie Q2; Crosly Q3–6   81 subject] F, Q; subiectes Q2, Q4–6 (*subst.*); subsects Q3   81 mine] F; my Qq

---

59 inclusive verge enclosing rim (i.e. the crown).

62 Anointed Blessed. Anointing with holy oil was part of the coronation ceremony, but Anne wishes for poison instead.

65 feed my humour humour me.

68 his Richard's.

69 angel husband Edward, son of Henry VI. At the beginning of the play, Anne is his supposed widow.

70 saint Henry VI. Richard admits in 1.2 that he killed both Edward and Henry.

73 old long.

76 life Compare this recollection with Anne's curse at 1.2.26–8 (uttered not to Richard's face but before his entrance). The subtle differences between the scene as written and the scene as Anne remembers it may indicate her changed perspective. She now knows, for example, that anyone who marries Richard must be 'mad' (75).

80 Grossly Stupidly.

> Which hitherto hath held mine eyes from rest.
> For never yet one hour in his bed
> Did I enjoy the golden dew of sleep,
> But with his timorous dreams was still awaked.   85
> Besides, he hates me for my father Warwick,
> And will, no doubt, shortly be rid of me.

ELIZABETH Poor heart, adieu; I pity thy complaining.

ANNE No more than with my soul I mourn for yours.

DORSET Farewell, thou woeful welcomer of glory.   90

ANNE Adieu, poor soul, that tak'st thy leave of it.

DUCHESS Go thou to Richmond, and good fortune guide thee –
> Go thou to Richard, and good angels tend thee –
> Go thou to sanctuary, and good thoughts possess thee;
> I to my grave, where peace and rest lie with me.   95
> Eighty-odd years of sorrow have I seen,
> And each hour's joy wracked with a week of teen.

ELIZABETH Stay, yet look back with me unto the Tower.
> Pity, you ancient stones, those tender babes
> Whom envy hath immured within your walls,   100
> Rough cradle for such little pretty ones.
> Rude, ragged nurse, old sullen playfellow
> For tender princes, use my babies well.
> So foolish sorrows bids your stones farewell.

Exeunt

---

82 hitherto] F; euer since Qq   82 held] F; kept Qq   82 mine] F, Q6; my Q6; my Q, Q2–5   82 rest] F; sleepe Qq   84 Did I enjoy] F; Haue I enjoyed Qq   85 with his timorous dreames was still awaked] F; haue bene waked by his timerous dreames Qq (*subst.*)   87 no doubt] F, Q; *not in* Q2–6   88 Poor heart, adieu] F; Alas poore soule Qq   88 complaining] F; complaints Qq   89 with] F; from Qq   90 SH] F, Q (*subst.*); *Qu.* Q2–6   91 that] F; thou Qq   93 tend] F; garde Qq (*subst.*)   94 and] F; *not in* Qq   96 Eighty-odd] *Bevington*; Eightie odde F, Q2–4   96 odd] F, Q, Q2–4; olde Q5–6 (*subst.*)   98–104] F; *not in* Qq   104 SD] F; *not in* Qq

82 **hitherto** until now.

85 **timorous** fearful. Anne's mention of Richard's nightmares foreshadows both his abrupt display of insecurity once he ascends the throne (4.2.6–7) and his dream on the eve of Bosworth (5.3.121–79). So far, the audience has not seen a fearful Richard.

85 **still** constantly. See 1.3.220n. Compare this description to Macbeth's report of 'terrible dreams / That shake us nightly' (3.3.18–19).

86 **Warwick** The powerful earl who turned against the house of York during the Wars of the Roses.

88 **complaining** reasons to complain.

90 **welcomer of glory** i.e. because she is about to become queen.

97 **teen** grief.

98–104 The Duchess's couplet at 96–7 sounds very much like the close of the scene, which it is in the quartos. These lines of Elizabeth's may have been added after the quarto play diverged from the material that lies behind F.

98 **Stay** Wait.

100 **immured** penned up.

102 **Rude** Rough.

4.2 *Sound a sennet. Enter* RICHARD, *in pomp;* BUCKINGHAM,
CATESBY, RATCLIFFE, LOVELL [, *a* PAGE, *and others*]

RICHARD Stand all apart. Cousin of Buckingham.
BUCKINGHAM My gracious sovereign.
RICHARD Give me thy hand.
                    Sound
          Thus high, by thy advice and thy assistance,
          Is King Richard seated.   5
          But shall we wear these glories for a day?
          Or shall they last, and we rejoice in them?
BUCKINGHAM Still live they, and forever let them last.
RICHARD Ah, Buckingham, now do I play the touch
          To try if thou be current gold indeed.   10
          Young Edward lives; think now what I would speak.
BUCKINGHAM Say on, my loving lord.
RICHARD Why, Buckingham, I say I would be king.
BUCKINGHAM Why, so you are, my thrice-renownèd lord.
RICHARD Ha, am I king? 'Tis so. But Edward lives.   15
BUCKINGHAM True, noble prince.
RICHARD   O bitter consequence,

Act 4, Scene 2   **4.2**] F (*Scena Secunda.*); *not in* Qq   **0 SD**] F; *The Trumpets sound, Enter Richard crownd, Buckingham, Catesby with other Nobles.* Qq (*subst.*)   **0 SD** *a* PAGE] Capell; *not in* F, Qq   **0 SD** *and others*] Qq (*with other Nobles*); *not in* F   **1 SH**] F (*Rich.*); *King* Qq (*and subst. throughout the rest of the play*)   **2**] F; *not in* Qq   **3 SD**] F; *Here he ascendeth the throne.* Qq (*ascendeth throne.* Q3; *ascendeth his throne.* Q4–6)   **4–5**] F; Thus . . . aduice / And . . . seated: Qq   **6** glories] F; honours Qq   **8** forever] F, Q, Q3–6 (for euer); for for euer Q2   **8** let them] F; may they Qq   **9** Ah] F; O Qq   **9** do I] F, Q, Q2; I do Q3–6 (*subst.*)   **11** speak] F; say Qq   **12** loving lord] F; gracious soueraigne Qq (*subst.*)   **14** lord] F; liege Qq   **16**] Steevens; True Prince. / O . . . consequence! F, Qq (*subst.*)

Act 4, Scene 2

The material for this scene follows Richard's coronation in More and the chronicles. As Peggy Endel has pointed out, the odd sense of privacy here may derive from the fact that in the sources Richard's conversation with the Page takes place while the king is seated on the 'draught' or privy (see 'Profane icon: the throne scene of Shakespeare's *Richard III*', *Comparative Drama* 20 (1986), 115–23). Richard then goes looking for Tyrrel and finds him in bed (More, p. 84).

0 SD *sennet* trumpet fanfare.

0 SD *pomp* splendour, magnificent display. Whether the scene is the coronation ceremony, as the Q stage directions imply, or a more intimate setting, as Richard's confidential conversations with Buckingham, Stanley, the Page and Tyrrel suggest, this is his first appearance as king.

0 SD *others* The number of these 'others' depends on the setting; perhaps there are only one or two if the scene takes place in private.

1 apart aside.

3 Typically, the Q stage direction preceding this line literalises the implications of the F dialogue: 'Thus high . . . / Is King Richard seated' (4–5).

3 SD *Sound* Another fanfare.

9 play the touch enact the part of the touchstone, a stone used to test for true gold.

10 current genuine.

16 consequence reply. The split line implies Richard's unusually quick response. As he reveals at 17, he means that Buckingham's answer is bitter to him because Edward, not Richard, is the 'true noble prince'.

> That Edward still should live, true noble prince.
> Cousin, thou wast not wont to be so dull.
> Shall I be plain? I wish the bastards dead,
> And I would have it suddenly performed.   20
> What say'st thou now? Speak suddenly, be brief.

BUCKINGHAM Your grace may do your pleasure.

RICHARD Tut, tut, thou art all ice; thy kindness freezes.
> Say, have I thy consent that they shall die?

BUCKINGHAM Give me some little breath, some pause, dear lord,   25
> Before I positively speak in this.
> I will resolve you herein presently.   *Exit Buckingham*

CATESBY The king is angry; see, he gnaws his lip.

RICHARD I will converse with iron-witted fools
> And unrespective boys. None are for me   30
> That look into me with considerate eyes.
> High-reaching Buckingham grows circumspect. –
> Boy!

PAGE My lord.

RICHARD Know'st thou not any whom corrupting gold   35
> Will tempt unto a close exploit of death?

PAGE I know a discontented gentleman
> Whose humble means match not his haughty spirit.
> Gold were as good as twenty orators
> And will, no doubt, tempt him to anything.   40

RICHARD What is his name?

---

18 wast] F; wert Qq   21 say'st thou now] F; saist thou, Q, Q2–6 (*subst.*)   23 freezes] F; freezeth Qq (*subst.*)   25 little breath, some pause] F; breath, some little pause Qq   25 dear] F; my Qq   26 in this] F; herein Qq   27 you herein presently] F; your grace immediatlie Qq (*subst.*)   27 SD] F, Q (*Exit.*); *not in* Q2–6   28 gnaws his] F; bites the Qq   32 High-reaching] F; Boy high reaching Q, Q2–5; *Boy*, high reaching Q6   33] F; *not in* Qq   34 SH] F; *Boy.* Qq *and throughout*   34 My lord] F, Q, Q2; Lord Q3–6   36 Will] F; Would Qq   37 I] F; My lord, I Qq   38 spirit] F; mind Qq (*subst.*)

18 **wont** accustomed.

20, 21 **suddenly** immediately.

23 **kindness** amiability; similarity to Richard.

27 **herein** in this matter.

27 **presently** shortly. Q has 'immediatlie'. Although 'presently' often means 'immediately' in Shakespeare, Buckingham's request for 'some pause' at 25 shows that this is not the word's meaning here.

28 Catesby may speak this line to any or all of the other bystanders. Many directors solve the problem of the separate conversations taking place in this scene by having Richard seated apart, sometimes talking to himself, as at 29–32,

43–6 and perhaps 61–6. If these passages are private musings, however, they are not soliloquies in the manner of 1.1.1 ff., where Richard actively shares his thoughts with the audience.

29 **converse** keep company (*OED* Converse *v* 2).

29 **iron-witted** stupid.

30 **unrespective** inattentive, heedless.

31 **considerate** thoughtful.

32 **circumspect** careful, wary.

36 **close** covert.

41, 69 The split lines again suggest speed of response. Neither the Page (41) nor Tyrrel (69) hesitates.

PAGE   His name, my lord, is Tyrrel.
RICHARD I partly know the man. Go call him hither, boy.

                                                            Exit [Page]

       The deep-revolving, witty Buckingham
       No more shall be the neighbour to my counsels.
       Hath he so long held out with me, untired,   45
       And stops he now for breath? Well, be it so.

              Enter STANLEY [EARL OF DERBY]

       How now, Lord Stanley, what's the news?
STANLEY Know, my loving lord, the Marquess Dorset,
       As I hear, is fled to Richmond
       In the parts where he abides.   50
RICHARD Come hither, Catesby. Rumour it abroad
       That Anne my wife is very grievous sick.
       I will take order for her keeping close.
       Inquire me out some mean poor gentleman,
       Whom I will marry straight to Clarence' daughter.   55
       The boy is foolish, and I fear not him.
       Look how thou dream'st! I say again, give out
       That Anne my queen is sick and like to die.
       About it, for it stands me much upon
       To stop all hopes whose growth may damage me.   60
       I must be married to my brother's daughter,

41] *Steevens*; *What . . . Name? / His . . . Tirrell.* F, Qq (*subst.*)   42 I partly know the man.] F; *not in* Qq   42 hither, boy.]
Capell; hither, / Boy. F; hither presentile, Qq (*subst.*)   42 SD] *Pope* (*Exit Boy.*); *Exit.* F; *not in* Qq   43 deep-revolving]
Pope; deepe reuoluing F, Qq   44 counsels] F; counsell Qq   46 Well, be it so.] F; *not in* Qq   47 Lord Stanley, what's the
news] F; what neewes vvith you Qq (*subst.*)   48] F; My Lord, I heare the Marques Dorset Qq (*subst.*)   49–50] F; Is fled
to Richmond, in those partes beyond the seas where he abides. Qq (*subst.*)   51] F; King. Catesby. Cat. My Lord. / King.
Rumor it abroad Qq (*subst.*)   51 Come hither] F; *not in* Qq   52 very grievous sick] F; sicke and like to die Qq   54 poor]
F; borne Qq   58 queen] F; wife Qq

---

41 partly slightly.
43 deep-revolving deeply considering, thoughtful (*OED* Revolve *v* 4b).
43 witty clever.
53 take order give orders.
53 keeping close remaining in seclusion.
54 mean low-ranking.
56 boy Clarence's son.
57 Look how thou dream'st A stage direction for Catesby, who is momentarily taken aback by Richard's murderous intentions toward Anne. Catesby has no separate exit in F or Qq, and perhaps he does not leave here, but slips into the background to contemplate his task further, quitting the stage with Buckingham and the rest at 105. Richard may speak 61–6 to Catesby or to himself.

59 stands me much upon is very important to me.
60 growth The word recalls the plant metaphors and the implied pun on 'Plantagenet' at 3.7.124, 126, 155 and 215.
61 my brother's daughter Elizabeth of York, daughter of Queen Elizabeth and King Edward and older sister of the little princes. Elizabeth of York married Henry Tudor, Earl of Richmond, and became the grandmother of Elizabeth I. Richard's idea that only marriage to Edward's daughter can secure his throne would have made a kind of retrospective sense to Shakespeare's audience, who knew that the relative security of the Tudor period had begun with her.

Or else my kingdom stands on brittle glass.
Murder her brothers, and then marry her:
Uncertain way of gain. But I am in
So far in blood that sin will pluck on sin.   65
Tear-falling pity dwells not in this eye.

Enter TYRREL

Is thy name Tyrrel?
TYRREL James Tyrrel, and your most obedient subject.
RICHARD Art thou indeed?
TYRREL   Prove me, my gracious lord.
RICHARD Dar'st thou resolve to kill a friend of mine?   70
TYRREL Please you.
       But I had rather kill two enemies.
RICHARD Why then thou hast it: two deep enemies,
       Foes to my rest and my sweet sleep's disturbers
       Are they that I would have thee deal upon.   75
       Tyrrel, I mean those bastards in the Tower.
TYRREL Let me have open means to come to them,
       And soon I'll rid you from the fear of them.
RICHARD Thou sing'st sweet music. Hark, come hither, Tyrrel.
       Go by this token. Rise, and lend thine ear.   *Whispers*   80
       There is no more but so; say it is done,
       And I will love thee and prefer thee for it.
TYRREL I will dispatch it straight.   *Exit*

Enter BUCKINGHAM

BUCKINGHAM My lord, I have considered in my mind
           The late request that you did sound me in.   85

65 will pluck] F, Q; plucke Q2–5; plucks Q6   66 Tear-falling] F; Teare falling Q, Q2–5; Teares falling Q6   69] *Steevens; as two lines* F, Qq   69 lord] F; soueraigne Qq   71] F; I my Lord, Qq   72 enemies] F, Q; deepe enemies Q2–6   73 then] F; there Qq   74 disturbers] F; disturbs Qq   79] Qq; Thou . . . Musique. / Hearke . . . *Tyrrel,* F   79 Hark] F; *not in* Qq   80 this] F; that Qq   80 SD] F; *he wispers in his eare.* Qq (*subst.*)   81 There is] F; Tis Qq   81 it is] F, Q3–5; is it Q, Q2, Q6   82 for it] F; too Qq   83] F; Tis done my gracious lord. / *King* Shal we heare from thee *Tirrel* ere we sleep? / *Tir.* Ye shall my lord, Qq (*subst.*) (Yea my good Lord. Q6)   83 SD] F; *not in* Qq   85 request] F; demand Qq (*subst.*)

64–5 Compare *Mac.*: 'I am in blood / Stepped in so far that, should I wade no more, / Returning were as tedious as go o'er' (3.4.135–7). See Dent F565.1 and S379.
65 **pluck on** encourage.
69 **Prove** Try; test.
71 **Please you** If it please you.
74 **sleep's disturbers** A foreshadowing of Richard's nightmare in Act 5.
75 **deal upon** act against.

77 **open means to come to them** easy access to them.
80 **Go by** Gain access with. Here Richard probably gives Tyrrel some personal symbol of royal protection, perhaps a ring. After this line he whispers some further instructions not heard by the audience.
82 **prefer** favour, promote.
85 **sound me in** ask me about.

RICHARD Well, let that rest. Dorset is fled to Richmond.

BUCKINGHAM I hear the news, my lord.

RICHARD Stanley, he is your wife's son. Well, look unto it.

BUCKINGHAM My lord, I claim the gift, my due by promise,
    For which your honour and your faith is pawned: 90
    Th'earldom of Hereford and the movables
    Which you have promisèd I shall possess.

RICHARD Stanley, look to your wife. If she convey
    Letters to Richmond, you shall answer it.

BUCKINGHAM What says your highness to my just request?   95

RICHARD I do remember me, Henry the Sixth
    Did prophesy that Richmond should be king,
    When Richmond was a little peevish boy.
    A king, perhaps.

BUCKINGHAM May it please you to resolve me in my suit?   100

RICHARD Thou troublest me; I am not in the vein.   *Exit*

BUCKINGHAM And is it thus? Repays he my deep service
    With such contempt? Made I him king for this?
    Oh, let me think on Hastings and be gone
    To Brecknock, while my fearful head is on.   105

                          Exeunt

4.3 *Enter* TYRREL

TYRREL The tyrannous and bloody act is done,
    The most arch deed of piteous massacre
    That ever yet this land was guilty of.

---

86 rest] F; passe Qq   87 the] F; that Qq   88 son] F, Q4–6; sonnes Q, Q2–3   88 unto] F; to Qq (*subst.*)   89 the] F; your Qq   91 Th'earldom] F; The Earledome Qq   91 Hereford] Q, Q2–3; Herfort Q4; Herford Q5–6; Hertford F   92 Which] F; The which Qq   92 you have] F; you Q, Q3–6; your Q2   92 shall] F; should Qq   95 request] F; demand Qq (*subst.*)   96 I do remember me] F; As I remember Qq   99] F; *twenty additional lines follow 99 in* Qq (*see Appendix 1, pp. 230–1 below*)   99] F, Q4; A king perhaps, perhaps. Q, Q2–3, Q5–6   100 May . . . suit] F; Whie then resolue me whether you wil or no Qq (*subst.*)   101 Thou] F; Tut, tut, thou Qq   102 And is it thus] F; Is it euen so Qq   102 Repays] F; rewardst Q; rewards Q2–6   102 deep] F; true Qq   103 contempt] F; deepe contempt Qq   105 SD] *This edn*; Exit F, Qq   Act 4, Scene 3 4.3] *Pope; not in* F, Qq   0 SD] F; *Enter Sir Francis Tirrell.* Qq   1 act] F; deed Qq   2 deed] F; act Qq

90 pawned pledged.

94 answer it answer for it.

98 peevish fretful. Margaret uses the same word to describe Richard's young brother Rutland, for whose death she was responsible (see 1.3.192).

99 For the 'clock' passage that occurs here in the quartos, see Appendix 1, pp. 220–1 below.

101 vein mood.

101 SD The other courtiers may leave here with Richard rather than at 105 with Buckingham. F and Q do not specify.

105 Brecknock Brecon, Buckingham's family home in Wales.

Act 4, Scene 3
Shakespeare's sources describe the smothering of the princes by Dighton and Forrest, but in more general terms than in Tyrrel's monologue (1–23). Tyrrel's remorseful tone seems to be Shakespeare's invention.

2 arch chief, prime.

Dighton and Forrest, who I did suborn
To do this piece of ruthful butchery,   5
Albeit they were fleshed villains, bloody dogs,
Melted with tenderness and mild compassion,
Wept like to children in their deaths' sad story.
'Oh, thus', quoth Dighton, 'lay the gentle babes.'
'Thus, thus', quoth Forrest, 'girdling one another   10
Within their alabaster innocent arms.
Their lips were four red roses on a stalk,
And in their summer beauty kissed each other.
A book of prayers on their pillow lay,
Which once', quoth Forrest, 'almost changed my mind.   15
But oh, the devil', there the villain stopped.
When Dighton thus told on: 'we smotherèd
The most replenishèd sweet work of nature
That from the prime creation e'er she framed.'
Hence both are gone; with conscience and remorse   20
They could not speak, and so I left them both
To bear this tidings to the bloody king.

Enter RICHARD

And here he comes. All health, my sovereign lord.
RICHARD Kind Tyrrel, am I happy in thy news?
TYRREL If to have done the thing you gave in charge   25
Beget your happiness, be happy then,

---

4 who] F; whom Qq   5 piece of ruthful] F; ruthles peece of Q, Q2 (*subst.*); ruthfull peece of Q3–6   6 Albeit] F; Although Qq   7 Melted] F; Melting Qq   7 mild] F; kind Q, Q2–5; not in Q6   8 to] F; two Qq   8 deaths'] F, Q, Q2–3, Q5–6 (deaths); death Q4   8 story] F; stories Qq   9, 10–15, 16, 17–19] *Quotation marks as Warburton; not in* F, Qq   9 Oh] F; Lo Qq (*subst.*)   9 the] F; those Q, Q2–5; these Q6   9 gentle] F; tender Qq   10 one] F, Q3–6; on Q, Q2   11 alabaster innocent] F; innocent alablaster Qq   12 lips were] F, Q; lips Q2; lips like Q3–6   13 And] F; Which Q, Q2–5; When Q6   15 once] Qq; one F   17 When] F; Whilst Qq (*subst.*)   19 e'er she] F; euer he Qq   20] F, Q, Q2; *not in* Q3–6   20 Hence] F; Thus Q, Q2   22 bear] F; bring Qq   22 this] F, Q, Q2–5; these Q6   23 SD] F; *Enter Ki. Richard.* Qq (*subst.*)   23 comes] F, Q, Q2–5; come Q6   23 health] F; haile Qq   23 lord] F; leige Qq (*subst.*)   24 am] F, Q, Q2–5; and Q6   25 gave] F, Q3–6; giue Q, Q2

---

4 suborn hire, bribe.
5 ruthful pitiful; filled with pity. The coincidence of 'ruthfull' in Q3–6 and in F has led most editors to assume that F repeats a mistake introduced in Q3 and that the more common 'ruthles' of Q and Q2 must be correct.
6 fleshed experienced.
8 in their deaths' sad story in telling the sad story of the princes' deaths.
9 thus This word, repeated by Forrest, implies some kind of pantomime or demonstration.
11 alabaster smooth and pale as alabaster, a variety of limestone.

18 replenishèd perfect (*OED* Replenished, citing this line as the earliest instance).
19 prime first.
19 she nature.
20 gone Since Tyrrel says he left the murderers rather than their leaving him (21), 'gone' probably means 'far gone in remorse' rather than 'departed'.
24 Kind Tyrrel Richard identifies the murderer as his own 'kind'.
25 gave in charge ordered.

        For it is done.

RICHARD   But did'st thou see them dead?

TYRREL I did, my lord.

RICHARD   And buried, gentle Tyrrel?

TYRREL The chaplain of the Tower hath buried them,

        But where, to say the truth, I do not know.   30

RICHARD Come to me, Tyrrel, soon and after supper,

        When thou shalt tell the process of their death.

        Meantime, but think how I may do thee good,

        And be inheritor of thy desire.

        Farewell till then.

TYRREL   I humbly take my leave.   *[Exit]* 35

RICHARD The son of Clarence have I pent up close,

        His daughter meanly have I matched in marriage,

        The sons of Edward sleep in Abraham's bosom,

        And Anne my wife hath bid this world good night.

        Now, for I know the Breton Richmond aims   40

        At young Elizabeth, my brother's daughter,

        And by that knot looks proudly on the crown,

        To her go I, a jolly thriving wooer.

               Enter RATCLIFFE

RATCLIFFE My lord.

27] *Steevens;* For . . . done. / But . . . dead. F; For . . . Lord. / But . . . dead? Qq 27 done] F; done my Lord Qq 28] *Steevens;* I . . . Lord. / And . . . *Tirrel.* F, Qq (*subst.*) 30 where, to say the truth] F; how or in what place Qq 31 SH] F; *Tir.* Q, Q2; *King.* Q3–6 31 and] F; at Qq 32 When] F; And Qq 35] *Steevens;* Farewell . . . then. / I . . . leaue. F 35 then] F; soone Qq 35 TYRREL . . . leave] F; *not in* Qq 35 SD] Qq (*after 34*); *not in* F 39 this] F; the Qq 40 Breton] *Capell;* Britaine F; Brittaine Qq 41 At] F, Q, Q2–5; And Q6 42 on] F; ore Qq 43 go I] F; I go Qq 44 SD RATCLIFFE] F; Catesby Qq 44 SH] F; *Cat.* Qq

27–8 The split lines here indicate Richard's eager questioning of Tyrrel. Similarly, Tyrrel later shows his impatience to be gone by quickly finishing a line begun by Richard (35).

30 According to A. J. Pollard, *Richard III and the Princes in the Tower,* 1991, two children's skeletons were found during the demolition of a staircase in the White Tower in 1674, two hundred years after the events shown in this play.

31 soon and after supper soon, but not until I have eaten. The quartos have 'soon at after supper', meaning during dessert. In F, however, Richard wants to forgo dessert to hear about the murder.

32 process story.

34 be inheritor of thy desire get what you wish.

36–7 Historically, Clarence's son was held captive by Richard and afterward executed by Richmond (Henry VII). Clarence's daughter Margaret married Sir Richard Pole and was executed by Henry VIII, son of Henry VII and father of Elizabeth I.

36 pent up close imprisoned.

37 meanly lowly (that is, matched to a low-ranking husband).

38 Abraham's bosom A biblical phrase (see Luke 16.22) for heaven. Abraham is the patriarch of Hebrew scripture.

40 for because.

40 Breton from Brittany. Richmond was not a Breton, but had taken refuge in Brittany.

42 by that knot through that marriage.

42 on toward.

RICHARD Good or bad news, that thou com'st in so bluntly?   45
RATCLIFFE Bad news, my lord. Morton is fled to Richmond,
            And Buckingham, backed with the hardy Welshmen,
            Is in the field, and still his power increaseth.
RICHARD Ely with Richmond troubles me more near
            Than Buckingham and his rash-levied strength.   50
            Come. I have learned that fearful commenting
            Is leaden servitor to dull delay.
            Delay leads impotent and snail-paced beggary.
            Then fiery expedition be my wing,
            Jove's Mercury, and herald for a king!   55
            Go muster men. My counsel is my shield.
            We must be brief when traitors brave the field.

                                                               Exeunt

4.4 *Enter old* QUEEN MARGARET

MARGARET So now prosperity begins to mellow
            And drop into the rotten mouth of death.
            Here in these confines slyly have I lurked
            To watch the waning of mine enemies.
            A dire induction am I witness to,   5

45 Good or bad news] F; Good newes or bad Qq 45 com'st] F, Q; comest Q2–6 (*subst.*) 46 SH] F; *Cates.* Qq 46 Morton]
F; Ely Qq 50 rash-levied] *Pope*; rash leuied F, Qq 50 strength] F; armie Qq (*subst.*) 51 learned] F; heard Qq 53 leads]
Qq (*subst.*); leds F 54 wing] F, Q, Q2; wings Q3–6 55 Jove's] F, Q, Q2 (Ioues); Ioue, Q3, Q5–6 (*subst.*); Loue, Q4 56
Go] F; Come Qq   **Act 4, Scene 4 4.4**] *Pope*; *Scena Tertia.* F; *not in* Qq 0 SD] F; *Enter Queene Margaret sola.* Qq 4
enemies] F; aduersaries Qq

45 bluntly abruptly, without ceremony.
46 Morton John Morton, Bishop of Ely. This
is the same Ely whom Richard sends out for
strawberries in 3.4.
48 in the field beginning a military campaign.
48 still continually.
48 power army.
50 rash-levied quickly assembled.
51 fearful commenting nervous talk.
52 leaden servitor slow servant.
53 leads precedes.
53 beggary destitution, wretchedness.
54 expedition haste.
55 Haste is Jove's messenger and therefore a
fit herald for a king.
56 My . . . shield My armour is my adviser –
that is, I have no time to talk.
57 brave the field confront us on the battlefield.

Act 4, Scene 4
The scene of the wailing queens has roots in

classical and English religious drama as well as
in the chronicles (see pp. 9–11 above). In the
sources, Richard plots to keep Richmond from
marrying Elizabeth of York and sends letters to
Queen Elizabeth seeking help. Finally, Elizabeth
begins 'somewhat to relent' (Holinshed, III, 429).
In the last part of this scene, Shakespeare condenses material concerning Buckingham's rebellion and the Earl of Richmond's attempts to land
an army in England.
    1 mellow mature. Margaret's image evokes
autumnal fruit just starting to decay. She echoes
and extends Richard's opening metaphor, as
England's 'summer' of peace (1.1.2) gives way
again to war.
    3 confines boundaries (of England).
    5 induction introduction, prologue. Mar-
garet again echoes Richard's opening soliloquy,
where he boasts about his plots and 'inductions
dangerous' (1.1.32).

And will to France, hoping the consequence
Will prove as bitter, black, and tragical.
Withdraw thee, wretched Margaret. Who comes here?

Enter DUCHESS [OF YORK] *and* QUEEN [ELIZABETH]

ELIZABETH Ah, my poor princes! Ah, my tender babes!
My unblowed flowers, new-appearing sweets!   10
If yet your gentle souls fly in the air
And be not fixed in doom perpetual,
Hover about me with your airy wings
And hear your mother's lamentation.
MARGARET [*Aside*] Hover about her; say that right for right   15
Hath dimmed your infant morn to agèd night.
DUCHESS So many miseries have crazed my voice
That my woe-wearied tongue is still and mute.
Edward Plantagenet, why art thou dead?
MARGARET [*Aside*] Plantagenet doth quit Plantagenet;   20
Edward for Edward pays a dying debt.
ELIZABETH Wilt thou, O God, fly from such gentle lambs
And throw them in the entrails of the wolf?
When didst thou sleep when such a deed was done?
MARGARET [*Aside*] When holy Harry died, and my sweet son.   25

---

8 SD] F; *Enter the Qu. and the Dutchesse of Yorke.* Qq (*subst.*)   9 poor] F; *young* Qq (*subst.*)   10 unblowed] F; *unblowne* Qq   10 flowers] F, Q, Q2–5; *flower* Q6   10 new-appearing] *Pope*; *new appearing* F, Qq   13 about] F, Q, Q2–5; *aboue* Q6   15, 20, 25 SD] *Collier; not in* F, Qq   17–19] F; *after 34* Qq   18 still and mute] F; *mute and dumbe* Qq (*subst.*)   20–1] F; *not in* Qq   25 Harry] F, Q, Q2; *Mary* Q3–6

6 will will go. Margaret, a French princess before she married Henry VI, actually left England in 1476.
6 consequence that which follows; conclusion.
8 Withdraw thee Step aside. This implicit stage direction in F suggests that Margaret's speeches at 15–16, 20–1 and 25 are spoken as asides.
10 unblowed unopened, still in the bud.
10 sweets flowers.
12 doom perpetual eternal destiny. 'Doom' means judgement, not necessarily damnation. Elizabeth hopes her sons' souls are still hovering in the air near the earth.
15 right for right right for the sake of right.
16 your infant morn the bright hope of the children.
16 agèd night death.
17–19 The placing of these lines in Qq delays the Duchess's first speech until 26.

17 crazed cracked.
19 Edward Plantagenet Most of the Edwards referred to in the play are Plantagenets, including Margaret's son (Edward, Prince of Wales), the Duchess's son (Edward IV), and Elizabeth's son (Edward V). Most likely the Duchess means her son, the dead king.
20 quit requite; get even for.
21 Edward for Edward Probably, the death of Edward IV, the Duchess's son, pays for the death of Edward, prince of Wales, Margaret's son.
22 gentle lambs Elizabeth returns to the subject of her own dead sons.
23 entrails belly.
25 holy Harry Margaret's husband, Henry VI. Anne has already implied that Henry was a saint (1.2.8).

DUCHESS Dead life, blind sight, poor mortal living ghost;
　　　　Woe's scene, world's shame, grave's due by life usurped;
　　　　Brief abstract and recòrd of tedious days,
　　　　Rest thy unrest on England's lawful earth,
　　　　Unlawfully made drunk with innocent blood.　　　　　　　　　30

ELIZABETH Ah, that thou wouldst as soon afford a grave
　　　　As thou canst yield a melancholy seat.
　　　　Then would I hide my bones, not rest them here.
　　　　Ah, who hath any cause to mourn but we?

MARGARET If ancient sorrow be most reverend,　　　　　　　　　35
　　　　Give mine the benefit of seniory,
　　　　And let my griefs frown on the upper hand,
　　　　If sorrow can admit society.
　　　　I had an Edward, till a Richard killed him;
　　　　I had a husband, till a Richard killed him.　　　　　　　　40
　　　　Thou hadst an Edward, till a Richard killed him;
　　　　Thou hadst a Richard, till a Richard killed him.

DUCHESS I had a Richard too, and thou didst kill him;
　　　　I had a Rutland too, thou holp'st to kill him.

---

26 Dead life, blind sight] F; Blind sight, dead life Qq   28] F; *not in* Qq   29 thy] F, Q, Q2–4; they Q5; their Q6   30 Unlawfully] F, Q, Q2–5; Vnlawfull Q6   30 innocent] F; innocents Qq   31 Ah] F; O Qq   31 as soon] F; aswel Q; as well Q2–6   35 reverend] *Reed*; reuerent F, Qq   36 seniory] Qq (signorie); signeurie F   37 griefs] F; woes Qq   38] F; If . . . societie, / Tell ouer your woes againe by vewing mine, Qq (*subst.*)   40 husband] F; Richard Qq   44 thou holp'st] F (hop'st); hopst Q, Q2; and thou holpst Q3–6

26 **mortal living ghost** living dead person. The Duchess apparently speaks to herself, although she may also mean to describe Elizabeth as a walking ghost.
27 **grave's due by life usurped** a person who should be in the grave but lives on past her time. This is the Duchess's way of saying she wishes she were dead.
28 **abstract** summary.
29 **Rest thy unrest** Although restless, rest. Many editors add a direction here for the Duchess to sit down.
30 **made drunk** That is, the earth has been made drunk.
32 **thou** the earth. Perhaps Elizabeth also sits down. Sitting on the ground was a traditional sign of grief.
35 **reverend** worthy of deference. Margaret joins the other women here, perhaps also sitting down with them.
36 **seniory** seniority.
37 **let . . . hand** let my sorrows take precedence.

38 The line that follows this in the quartos, 'Tell ouer your woes againe by vewing mine', may have been omitted accidentally by the F compositor, but it is not essential to the meaning of Margaret's sentence.
39 **Edward** Margaret's son, killed by Richard and his brothers at Tewkesbury (see *3H6* 5.3).
40 **husband** Henry VI, killed by Richard in the Tower (*3H6* 5.6).
41 **Edward** Elizabeth's son, the older prince, killed in this play by Richard's order (see 4.3).
42 **Richard** Elizabeth's younger son, killed with his brother in the Tower.
43 **Richard** The Duchess's husband, Richard, Duke of York, killed by Margaret and Clifford (*3H6* 1.4).
44 **Rutland** The Duchess's son, represented by Shakespeare as a child, and killed by Clifford in *3H6* 1.3.
44 **holp'st** helped.

MARGARET Thou hadst a Clarence, too,   45
　　　And Richard killed him.
　　　From forth the kennel of thy womb hath crept
　　　A hell-hound that doth hunt us all to death:
　　　That dog, that had his teeth before his eyes
　　　To worry lambs and lap their gentle blood,   50
　　　That foul defacer of God's handiwork
　　　That reigns in gallèd eyes of weeping souls,
　　　That excellent grand tyrant of the earth
　　　Thy womb let loose to chase us to our graves.
　　　O upright, just, and true-disposing God,   55
　　　How do I thank thee, that this carnal cur
　　　Preys on the issue of his mother's body
　　　And makes her pew-fellow with others' moan.
DUCHESS O Harry's wife, triumph not in my woes.
　　　God witness with me, I have wept for thine.   60
MARGARET Bear with me. I am hungry for revenge,
　　　And now I cloy me with beholding it.
　　　Thy Edward he is dead that killed my Edward;
　　　The other Edward dead to quit my Edward;
　　　Young York he is but boot, because both they   65

45–6] F; *as one line* Qq　46 And] F, Q; till Q2–6 (*subst.*)　50 blood] F; bloods Qq　52–3] F; *not in* Qq　55 true-disposing]
F; true disposing Qq　59 wife] F, Q2–6; wifes Q　60 thine] F, Q,; thee Q2–6　63 killed] F; stabd Qq　64 The] F; Thy
Qq　64 quit] F, Q2–5; quitte Q; quite Q6

45–6 This is one of many instances in which
the Folio arrangement of a pentameter as two
short lines seems calculated for dramatic effect.
The break after 'too' creates a strong rhetorical
pause as Margaret lets her point sink in.

45 Clarence Richard's brother, killed on
Richard's orders in this play (1.4).

47–50 Margaret creates a revolting picture of
Richard as a dog born of a woman. Milton probably borrowed this image for his portrait of Sin
in book II of *Paradise Lost*. See R. W. F. Martin,
'Milton's hell-hounds', *NQ* 36 (1989), 31–2.

49 had his teeth before his eyes Margaret
refers to the legend that Richard had teeth at
birth. Since he is a 'dog', she also pictures him
born blind, as puppies are.

50 worry bite in the throat; said of dogs or
wolves (*OED* Worry *v* 3a).

51, 53 Many editors have exchanged these two
lines, supposing them to be wrongly ordered in
F because 'tyrant' must be the subject of 'reigns'.
The F ordering, however, reveals a sequence of

word associations: 'defacer' suggests the 'eyes',
where the defacer rains and reigns. 'Reigns' then
suggests 'tyrant of the earth', and 'earth' leads to
the 'graves' in 54.

51 God's handiwork Human beings.

52 gallèd irritated (with weeping).

53 excellent unequalled, incomparable.

56 carnal carnivorous.

58 pew-fellow associate. The metaphor
implies that all the mourners attend the church
of grief and occupy the same bench or pew.

62 cloy me gorge myself.

63 Edward IV, who killed Edward, Prince of
Wales, is dead.

64 other Edward The Duchess's grandson,
the young prince of this play. Margaret says that
both Edwards died because Margaret's son was
killed, yet only the young prince's death really
begins to pay the price ('to quit my Edward').

65 boot That which is given in addition to
make up a deficiency of value (*OED* Boot *sb*[1] 2).

65 both they the two Edwards.

Matched not the high perfection of my loss.
Thy Clarence he is dead that stabbed my Edward,
And the beholders of this frantic play,
Th'adulterate Hastings, Rivers, Vaughan, Grey,
Untimely smothered in their dusky graves.   70
Richard yet lives, hell's black intelligencer,
Only reserved their factor to buy souls
And send them thither. But at hand, at hand
Ensues his piteous and unpitied end.
Earth gapes, hell burns, fiends roar, saints pray,   75
To have him suddenly conveyed from hence.
Cancel his bond of life, dear God, I pray,
That I may live and say the dog is dead.

ELIZABETH Oh, thou didst prophesy the time would come
That I should wish for thee to help me curse   80
That bottled spider, that foul bunch-backed toad.

MARGARET I called thee then vain flourish of my fortune;
I called thee then poor shadow, painted queen,
The presentation of but what I was,
The flattering index of a direful pageant,   85
One heaved a-high to be hurled down below,
A mother only mocked with two fair babes,
A dream of what thou wast, a garish flag
To be the aim of every dangerous shot,
A sign of dignity, a breath, a bubble,   90
A queen in jest, only to fill the scene.

---

66 Matched] F; Match Qq   67 stabbed] F; kild Qq   68 frantic] F; tragicke Qq   73 at hand, at hand] F, Q2–6; at hand at
handes Q   75 hell] F, Q, Q2–5; hels Q6   76 from hence] F; away Qq   78 and] F; to Qq   81 bunch-backed] F, Q; hunch-
backt Q2–6   87 fair] F; sweete Qq (*subst.*)   88–90] F; A dreame of which thou wert a breath, a bubble, / A signe of
dignitie, a garish flagge, / To be the aime of euerie dangerous shot, Qq (*subst.*)

---

68 frantic play frenzied scene, the death of
Margaret's Edward.
69 adulterate Margaret refers to Hastings's
adultery with Jane Shore.
70 smothered buried.
71 intelligencer spy.
72 their factor the agent of the devils in hell.
Margaret says that the only reason Richard is
allowed to live is to send others to hell before
him. He is a 'scourge of God', permitted for a
while to punish evil with evil (see pp. 6–7 above).
74 piteous dreadful.
81 bottled bottle-shaped. See 1.3.242 and
n. Elizabeth repeats the words of Margaret's
prophecy.

81 bunch-backed hunch-backed.
82 vain . . . fortune worthless decoration of
a life that properly belongs to me. As Margaret
points out, she had used exactly the same phrase
earlier (1.3.241).
83 painted queen picture of a queen.
84 presentation copy, reproduction.
85 index preface.
85 pageant spectacle, drama.
90 sign empty symbol.
91 fill the scene round out the company of
actors. Margaret continues her metaphor from
85 of Elizabeth's reign as a stage play.

Where is thy husband now? Where be thy brothers?
Where be thy two sons? Wherein dost thou joy?
Who sues and kneels and says 'God save the queen'?
Where be the bending peers that flattered thee?   95
Where be the thronging troops that followed thee?
Decline all this, and see what now thou art:
For happy wife, a most distressèd widow;
For joyful mother, one that wails the name;
For one being sued to, one that humbly sues;   100
For queen, a very caitiff crowned with care;
For she that scorned at me, now scorned of me;
For she being feared of all, now fearing one;
For she commanding all, obeyed of none.
Thus hath the course of justice whirled about   105
And left thee but a very prey to time,
Having no more but thought of what thou wast
To torture thee the more, being what thou art.
Thou didst usurp my place, and dost thou not
Usurp the just proportion of my sorrow?   110
Now thy proud neck bears half my burdened yoke,
From which even here I slip my wearied head
And leave the burden of it all on thee.
Farewell, York's wife, and queen of sad mischance.
These English woes shall make me smile in France.   115
ELIZABETH O thou well skilled in curses, stay awhile,
And teach me how to curse mine enemies.
MARGARET Forbear to sleep the night, and fast the day;
Compare dead happiness with living woe;
Think that thy babes were sweeter than they were   120
And he that slew them fouler than he is.
Bett'ring thy loss makes the bad causer worse;
Revolving this will teach thee how to curse.

---

93 be] F, Q3–6; are Q, Q2   93 two sons] F; children Qq   94 and kneels, and says] F; to thee, and cries Qq   94 'God. . . . queen'] *Malone (–God . . . queen); no quotation marks in* F, Qq   100–2, 104] F; *order in* Qq: *101, 100, 104, 102*   102 she] F; one Qq   103] F; *not in* Qq   104 she] F; one Qq   105 whirled] F; whe'eld Q; wheel'd Q2–6 (*subst.*)   107 wast] F; wert Q, Q2; art Q3–6   112 wearied] F, Q6; wearie Q, Q2–5 (*subst.*)   112 head] F; necke Qq   115 woes] F, Q, Q2–3, Q5–6; wars Q4   115 shall] F; will Qq   118 night . . . day] F, Q3–6; nights . . . daies Q, Q2   120 thy babes] F, Q, Q2–3, Q5–6; babes Q4   120 sweeter] F; fairer Qq   122 causer] F, Q, Q2–3, Q5–6; causes Q4

    95 **bending** bowing.
    97 **Decline** Recite in order, as one would recite a grammar lesson.
     100 **sued to** appealed to; petitioned.
     101 **caitiff** wretch.

    107 Having only the memory of what you were.
     122 **Bett'ring** Exaggerating.
     123 **Revolving** Thinking about, brooding on.

ELIZABETH My words are dull. Oh, quicken them with thine.
MARGARET Thy woes will make them sharp, and pierce like mine.   125

Exit Margaret

DUCHESS Why should calamity be full of words?
ELIZABETH Windy attorneys to their clients' woes,
    Airy succeeders of intestine joys,
    Poor breathing orators of miseries,
    Let them have scope. Though what they will impart   130
    Help nothing else, yet do they ease the heart.
DUCHESS If so, then be not tongue-tied. Go with me,
    And in the breath of bitter words let's smother
    My damnèd son that thy two sweet sons smothered.
    The trumpet sounds. Be copious in exclaims.   135

Enter RICHARD *and his train*

RICHARD Who intercepts me in my expedition?
DUCHESS Oh, she that might have intercepted thee,
    By strangling thee in her accursèd womb,
    From all the slaughters, wretch, that thou hast done.
ELIZABETH Hid'st thou that forehead with a golden crown   140
    Where should be branded, if that right were right,
    The slaughter of the prince that owed that crown
    And the dire death of my poor sons and brothers?
    Tell me, thou villain slave, where are my children?
DUCHESS Thou toad, thou toad, where is thy brother Clarence,   145
    And little Ned Plantagenet, his son?

125] Qq; Thy . . . sharpe, / And . . . mine. F   127 their clients'] F (their Clients); your Client Q, Q2–3, Q5–6 (*subst.*); your clients Q4   128 intestine] F; intestate Qq   130 will] F; do Qq   131 nothing else] F; not at al Qq (*subst.*)   134 that] F; which Qq   134 sweet] F, Q, Q2; *not in* Q3–6   135 The trumpet sounds] F; I heare his drum Qq   135 SD *and his trains*] F; *marching with Drummes and Trumpets* Qq (*subst.*)   136 me in] F; *not in* Qq   137 Oh] F; A Qq   141 Where] Qq; Where't F   141 should] F, Q, Q2–3, Q5–6; would Q4   141 branded] F; grauen Qq   143 poor] F; two Qq   145] Qq; Thou . . . Toade, / Where . . . *Clarence?* F   146 Plantagenet] F, Q, Q2, Q6; Plantaget Q3–5

124 **quicken** enliven, animate.
126 The Duchess's remark may be a criticism of Margaret's long speech, but more likely it is a genuine question: will it do us any good to talk? After hearing Elizabeth's opinion, the Duchess resolves to use words against Richard (132–5).
128 **intestine** internal; domestic as opposed to public. Many editors prefer 'intestate' from the quartos, continuing the legal metaphor of 'Windy attorneys'. On the other hand, 'intestine' sustains a ruder metaphor of words as farts, windy outward successors to now-defunct internal pleasures.
135 **exclaims** exclamations.

135 SD **train** retinue. This group should include trumpeters and drummers to play at 151, and possibly Catesby. He must enter before Richard speaks to him at 448, but he may instead come on with Ratcliffe at 437.
136 **expedition** When last seen, Richard had proclaimed 'fiery expedition' as the king's herald and was preparing to march against his enemies (4.3.54–7). The women here cross his path.
142 **owed** owned.
146 **Ned Plantagenet** Clarence's son is yet another Edward Plantagenet victimised by Richard in this play.

ELIZABETH Where is the gentle Rivers, Vaughan, Grey?
DUCHESS Where is kind Hastings?
RICHARD A flourish, trumpets! Strike alarum, drums!
   Let not the heavens hear these telltale women   150
   Rail on the Lord's anointed. Strike, I say!
       Flourish. Alarums
   Either be patient and entreat me fair,
   Or with the clamorous report of war
   Thus will I drown your exclamations.
DUCHESS Art thou my son?   155
RICHARD Ay, I thank God, my father, and yourself.
DUCHESS Then patiently hear my impatience.
RICHARD Madam, I have a touch of your condition,
   That cannot brook the accent of reproof.
DUCHESS Oh, let me speak.
RICHARD   Do then, but I'll not hear. 160
DUCHESS I will be mild and gentle in my words.
RICHARD And brief, good mother, for I am in haste.
DUCHESS Art thou so hasty? I have stayed for thee,
   God knows, in torment and in agony.
RICHARD And came I not at last to comfort you? 165
DUCHESS No, by the holy rood, thou know'st it well,
   Thou cam'st on earth to make the earth my hell.
   A grievous burden was thy birth to me.
   Tetchy and wayward was thy infancy;
   Thy schooldays frightful, desperate, wild, and furious; 170
   Thy prime of manhood, daring, bold, and venturous;
   Thy age confirmed, proud, subtle, sly, and bloody:

---

147 the gentle] F; kind Hastings Qq   148] F; *not in* Qq   151 SD] F; *The trumpets* Q; *The trumpets sound* Q2; *The trumpets sounds* Q3–6   153 clamorous] F, Q, Q2–3, Q5–6; clamour Q4   159 That] F; Which Qq   160] *Steevens*; O . . . speake. /. Do . . . heare. F; *not in* Qq   161 words] F; speach Qq (*subst.*)   164 torment and in agony] F; anguish, paine and agonie Qq   171] F, Q, Q2; *not in* Q3–6   172 sly, and bloody] F; bloudie, trecherous Qq

149 flourish fanfare.
149 alarum the call to arms. Richard has now returned to the state of war that he longed for in Act I, when he regretted the Yorkists' 'stern alarums changed to merry meetings' (1.1.7).
151 Rail on the Lord's anointed Abuse God's blessed king.
152 entreat me fair treat me politely.
153 report noise, especially of guns or explosive (*OED* Report *sb* 7a).
158 condition nature, personality.

159 brook endure.
159 accent sound.
163 stayed waited. The Duchess speaks of her pains at Richard's birth.
166 rood cross.
167 The accusation recalls Anne's charge that Richard has made 'the happy earth thy hell' (1.2.51).
169 Tetchy Fretful.
172 age confirmed full maturity. Historically, Richard died aged thirty-three.

More mild, but yet more harmful, kind in hatred.
What comfortable hour canst thou name
That ever graced me with thy company?   175
RICHARD Faith, none but Humphrey Hower, that called your grace
To breakfast once, forth of my company.
If I be so disgracious in your eye,
Let me march on and not offend you, madam.
Strike up the drum!
DUCHESS   I prithee, hear me speak.   180
RICHARD You speak too bitterly.
DUCHESS   Hear me a word,
For I shall never speak to thee again.
RICHARD So.
DUCHESS Either thou wilt die by God's just ordinance
Ere from this war thou turn a conqueror,   185
Or I with grief and extreme age shall perish
And nevermore behold thy face again.
Therefore take with thee my most grievous curse,
Which in the day of battle tire thee more
Than all the còmplete armour that thou wear'st.   190
My prayers on the adverse party fight,
And there the little souls of Edward's children
Whisper the spirits of thine enemies
And promise them success and victory.
Bloody thou art, bloody will be thy end;   195
Shame serves thy life and doth thy death attend.   *Exit*

173] F; *not in* Qq   175 with] F; in Qq   176] Qq; Faith . . . *Hower*, / That . . . Grace F   176 Hower] F; houre Qq   177 my company] F, Q, Q2–3, Q5–6; companie Q4   178 If I] F, Q; If it Q2–3, Q5–6; If Q4   178 disgracious] F, Q, Q2; gratious Q3–6   178 eye] F; sight Qq   179 you, madam] F; your grace Qq   180] *Steevens*; Strike . . . Drumme. / I . . . speake. F; *not in* Qq   180 I . . . speak] F; O heare me speake for I shal neuer see thee more Qq (*subst.*)   181] *Steevens*; You . . . bitterly. / Heare . . . word: F; Come, come, you art too bitter. Qq (are Q2–6)   182–3] *not in* Qq (*see 180*)   187 nevermore behold] F; neuer looke vpon Qq   188 grievous] F; heauy Qq (*subst.*)   193 spirits] F, Q, Q2–3, Q5–6; spirit Q4   195 art] F, Q, Q2–5; art, and Q6

173 kind in hatred apparently kind though actually hateful. The word also suggests that it is in Richard's nature or 'kind' to be despicable.
176 Humphrey Hower This joke or pun has remained obscure through centuries of editorial commentary. Malone and others suggest that Richard alludes to the expression 'dining with Duke Humphrey', or going hungry. It is also possible that he refers to a person, now unknown, called Humphrey Hower. Gary Taylor proposes 'Humfrey Hewer' (also pronounced 'Hour') as the name of a servant; see 'Humfrey Hower', *SQ* 33 (1982), 95–7.

177 forth of away from.
185 turn return.
189 tire i.e. I hope will tire. The Duchess puns on 'attire', wishing that in battle Richard will be attired in his mother's heavy curse as well as in his armour.
190 còmplete full; head-to-toe.
191 adverse party the side opposite to Richard's.
192 there on Richmond's side.
193 Whisper Whisper to.

ELIZABETH Though far more cause, yet much less spirit to curse
  Abides in me. I say amen to her.
RICHARD Stay, madam. I must talk a word with you.
ELIZABETH I have no more sons of the royal blood   200
  For thee to slaughter. For my daughters, Richard,
  They shall be praying nuns, not weeping queens,
  And therefore level not to hit their lives.
RICHARD You have a daughter called Elizabeth,
  Virtuous and fair, royal and gracious.   205
ELIZABETH And must she die for this? Oh, let her live,
  And I'll corrupt her manners, stain her beauty,
  Slander myself as false to Edward's bed,
  Throw over her the veil of infamy.
  So she may live unscarred of bleeding slaughter, 210
  I will confess she was not Edward's daughter.
RICHARD Wrong not her birth; she is a royal princess.
ELIZABETH To save her life, I'll say she is not so.
RICHARD Her life is safest only in her birth.
ELIZABETH And only in that safety died her brothers. 215
RICHARD Lo, at their birth good stars were opposite.
ELIZABETH No, to their lives ill friends were contrary.
RICHARD All unavoided is the doom of destiny.
ELIZABETH True, when avoided grace makes destiny.
  My babes were destined to a fairer death,   220
  If grace had blest thee with a fairer life.
RICHARD You speak as if that I had slain my cousins.
ELIZABETH Cousins indeed, and by their uncle cozened
  Of comfort, kingdom, kindred, freedom, life.
  Whose hand soever lanch'd their tender hearts, 225

198 her] F; all Qq   199 talk] F; speake Qq   201 slaughter. For] F; murther for Q; murther, for Q2–6   210 of] F; from
Qq   212 a royal princess] F; of roiall bloud Qq (*subst.*)   214 safest only] F; onlie safest Qq (*subst.*)   216 birth] F; births
Qq   217 ill] F; bad Qq   222–35] F; *not in* Qq

201 For my As for my.
203 level aim.
209 infamy disgrace.
210 So Provided that.
210–11 The couplet may imply that Elizabeth thinks the argument is over. She has confessed herself exhausted with grief (197–8).
214 safest only in her birth made secure by her high birth alone.
216 opposite hostile.
218 unavoided unavoidable.
219 avoided grace the absence of God's grace. Elizabeth does not imply that Richard has

rejected or avoided God's grace, which, according to Protestant theology, could not be avoided if God wished to bestow it. Rather, Richard's life holds a void where others have grace.
223 cozened cheated. Elizabeth puns on 'cousins'.
225 Whose hand soever Whoever it was whose hand.
225 lanch'd pierced (*OED* Launch *v* 1a). Elizabeth speaks as if the young princes had been stabbed, although both Tyrrel and the Duchess describe them as having been smothered (4.3.17, 4.4.134).

Thy head all indirectly gave direction.
No doubt the murderous knife was dull and blunt
Till it was whetted on thy stone-hard heart
To revel in the entrails of my lambs.
But that still use of grief makes wild grief tame,   230
My tongue should to thy ears not name my boys
Till that my nails were anchored in thine eyes,
And I in such a desperate bay of death,
Like a poor bark of sails and tackling reft,
Rush all to pieces on thy rocky bosom.   235

RICHARD Madam, so thrive I in my enterprise
And dangerous success of bloody wars
As I intend more good to you and yours
Than ever you and yours by me were harmed.

ELIZABETH What good is covered with the face of heaven   240
To be discovered, that can do me good?

RICHARD Th'advancement of your children, gentle lady.

ELIZABETH Up to some scaffold, there to lose their heads.

RICHARD Unto the dignity and height of fortune,
The high imperial type of this earth's glory.   245

ELIZABETH Flatter my sorrow with report of it.
Tell me what state, what dignity, what honour,
Canst thou demise to any child of mine?

RICHARD Even all I have, ay, and myself and all,
Will I withal endow a child of thine,   250
So in the Lethe of thy angry soul
Thou drown the sad remembrance of those wrongs
Which thou supposest I have done to thee.

236–7] F; Madam, so thriue *I* in my dangerous attempt of hostile armes Qq (*subst.*) 238 I intend] F, Q, Q2–5; Intend Q6 239 and] F, Q6; or Q, Q2–5 239 by me were harmed] F; were by me wrongd Qq (*subst.*) 242 Th'advancement] F; The aduancement Qq 242 gentle] F; mightie Qq 244 Unto] F; No to Qq 244 fortune] F; honor Qq 245 high] F, Q; height Q2–6 246 sorrow] F; sorrowes Qq 249 ay] F (I); yea Qq

230 **But that** Only because.
230 **still** constant.
233 **in such a desperate bay** desperately at bay, as a hunted animal bayed by hounds. As the following two lines show, 'bay' also suggests a harbour or cove in which a 'poor bark' runs aground.
234 **bark** boat.
234 **reft** bereft.
236 **so thrive I** may I only thrive. Richard here curses himself by linking his success in war to his supposed good intentions toward Elizabeth.

238 **As** Only as far as.
240–1 **covered . . . heaven** as yet unrevealed by heaven.
245 **type** symbol.
248 **demise** convey or transmit (*OED* Demise *v* 2 cites this line as the earliest example in the general sense, although more strictly legal uses begin much earlier).
250 **withal** with.
251 **So** Provided that.
251 **Lethe** The river of forgetfulness in the classical underworld.

ELIZABETH Be brief, lest that the process of thy kindness
            Last longer telling than thy kindness date.   255
RICHARD Then know that from my soul I love thy daughter.
ELIZABETH My daughter's mother thinks it with her soul.
RICHARD What do you think?
ELIZABETH That thou dost love my daughter from thy soul.
            So from thy soul's love didst thou love her brothers,   260
            And from my heart's love I do thank thee for it.
RICHARD Be not so hasty to confound my meaning.
            I mean that with my soul I love thy daughter
            And do intend to make her Queen of England.
ELIZABETH Well then, who dost thou mean shall be her king?   265
RICHARD Even he that makes her queen. Who else should be?
ELIZABETH What, thou?
RICHARD Even so. How think you of it?
ELIZABETH How canst thou woo her?
RICHARD That I would learn of you,   270
            As one being best acquainted with her humour.
ELIZABETH And wilt thou learn of me?
RICHARD Madam, with all my heart.
ELIZABETH Send to her by the man that slew her brothers
            A pair of bleeding hearts; thereon engrave   275
            Edward and York; then haply will she weep.
            Therefore present to her, as sometime Margaret
            Did to thy father, steeped in Rutland's blood,
            A handkerchief, which, say to her, did drain
            The purple sap from her sweet brother's body,   280
            And bid her wipe her weeping eyes withal.

---

255 date] F; doe Qq (*subst.*)   **256**] Qq; Then know, / That . . . Daughter. F   **260** soul's love] F, Q, Q2–5; soule Q6   **260** thou love] F, Q, Q6; thou Q2–5   **264** do intend] F; meane Qq   **265** Well] F; Saie Qq (*subst.*)   **266**] Qq; Euen . . . Queene: / Who . . . bee? F   **266** Who else should be] F; who should be else Q; who should else Q2–4, Q6; how should else Q5   **268**] F; I euen I, what thinke you of it Maddame? Qq (*subst.*)   **270** I would] F, Q3–6; would I Q, Q2   **271** being] F; that are Q, Q2, that were Q3–6   **276** haply will she] F; happelie she wil Qq   **277** sometime] F, Q3–6; sometimes Q, Q2   **278–80**] F; Did to thy father, a handkercher steept in Rutlands bloud, Qq   **280** The . . . body] F; *not in* Qq   **281** wipe] F; drie Qq (*subst.*)   **281** withal] F; therewith Qq

---

254 process narrative.
255 date endure.
259 from apart from. Elizabeth means that Richard's love is only an appearance, distinct from the real feelings of his soul. She makes the same play on 'from' again in the next two lines. Each time the pentameter stresses the word, as it does for Richard's contrary 'with' in 263.
    262 confound distort, misunderstand.
    271 humour disposition, character.

274 by on behalf of; through the agency of. Elizabeth may also be suggesting that Richard use the actual murderer of the princes as a messenger to their sister.
277–81 See *3H6* 1.4.79–83. Richard has shown that he remembers and resents this crime (1.3.173–6).
    277 sometime once.
    281 withal with it.

> If this inducement move her not to love,
> Send her a letter of thy noble deeds.
> Tell her thou mad'st away her uncle Clarence,
> Her uncle Rivers, ay, and for her sake   285
> Mad'st quick conveyance with her good aunt Anne.
>
> RICHARD You mock me, madam, this is not the way
>   To win your daughter.
>
> ELIZABETH There is no other way,
>   Unless thou couldst put on some other shape   290
>   And not be Richard that hath done all this.
>
> RICHARD Say that I did all this for love of her.
>
> ELIZABETH Nay, then indeed she cannot choose but hate thee,
>   Having bought love with such a bloody spoil.
>
> RICHARD Look what is done, cannot be now amended.   295
>   Men shall deal unadvisedly sometimes,
>   Which after-hours gives leisure to repent.
>   If I did take the kingdom from your sons,
>   To make amends I'll give it to your daughter.
>   If I have killed the issue of your womb,   300
>   To quicken your increase I will beget
>   Mine issue of your blood upon your daughter.
>   A grandam's name is little less in love
>   Than is the doting title of a mother;
>   They are as children but one step below,   305
>   Even of your metal, of your very blood,
>   Of all one pain, save for a night of groans
>   Endured of her for whom you bid like sorrow.
>   Your children were vexation to your youth,
>   But mine shall be a comfort to your age.   310
>   The loss you have is but a son being king,
>   And by that loss your daughter is made queen.

---

282 move] F; force Qq   283 letter] F; storie Qq (*subst.*)   283 deeds] F; acts Qq   285 ay] F (I); yea Qq   287 You] F; Come, come, you Q, Q2; Come, come ye Q3–6   287 me, madam] F; me Qq   287 is] Qq; *not in* F   292–346] F; *not in* Qq

284 mad'st away did away with.
286 Mad'st quick conveyance Quickly disposed of.
294 spoil An object or article of pillage; prey (*OED* Spoil *sb* 4).
295 Look what Whatever.
296 Everyone makes mistakes.
301 quicken your increase put new life in your family (*OED* Increase *sb* 2b).

304 doting tender, loving.
305 They Grandchildren.
306 metal substance.
307 Of all one pain Children and grandchildren cause the same amount of pain.
308 Suffered by her (the younger Elizabeth) for whom you endured similar pain.
308 bid endured (see *OED* Bide *v* 9).

I cannot make you what amends I would;
Therefore accept such kindness as I can.
Dorset, your son, that with a fearful soul   315
Leads discontented steps in foreign soil,
This fair alliance quickly shall call home
To high promotions and great dignity.
The king that calls your beauteous daughter wife
Familiarly shall call thy Dorset brother.   320
Again shall you be mother to a king,
And all the ruins of distressful times
Repaired with double riches of content.
What? We have many goodly days to see.
The liquid drops of tears that you have shed   325
Shall come again, transformed to orient pearl,
Advantaging their love with interest
Of ten times double gain of happiness.
Go then, my mother, to thy daughter go.
Make bold her bashful years with your experience;   330
Prepare her ears to hear a wooer's tale;
Put in her tender heart th'aspiring flame
Of golden sovereignty; acquaint the princess
With the sweet silent hours of marriage joys.
And when this arm of mine hath chastisèd   335
The petty rebel, dull-brained Buckingham,
Bound with triumphant garlands will I come
And lead thy daughter to a conqueror's bed;
To whom I will retail my conquest won,
And she shall be sole victoress, Caesar's Caesar.   340
ELIZABETH What were I best to say? Her father's brother
Would be her lord? Or shall I say her uncle?
Or he that slew her brothers and her uncles?

328 Of ten times] *Theobald*; Often-times F

320 **Familiarly** In the manner of family.
320 **brother** Richard begins to ease himself
into the younger generation, no longer Elizabeth's brother, but her son's. At 329 and 417,
he insists on calling Elizabeth his 'mother'.
321 Elizabeth has been briefly mother to a
king. Her son Edward, although uncrowned,
nevertheless became king at his father's death.
326 **orient** lustrous, shining. The adjective
probably originated in describing pearls from the
east ('orient'). See *OED* Orient *a* 2.

327 **Advantaging** Increasing.
327 **their love** the love that caused the tears
(325).
337 **triumphant garlands** Wreaths such as
Roman military heroes wore in triumphal pro-
cessions.
339 **retail** recount.
341–3 Elizabeth recalls Richard's true relationship to her daughter.

Under what title shall I woo for thee

That God, the law, my honour, and her love   345

Can make seem pleasing to her tender years?

RICHARD Infer fair England's peace by this alliance.

ELIZABETH Which she shall purchase with still-lasting war.

RICHARD Tell her the king, that may command, entreats.

ELIZABETH That at her hands which the king's King forbids.   350

RICHARD Say she shall be a high and mighty queen.

ELIZABETH To vail the title, as her mother doth.

RICHARD Say I will love her everlastingly.

ELIZABETH But how long shall that title ever last?

RICHARD Sweetly in force unto her fair life's end.   355

ELIZABETH But how long fairly shall her sweet life last?

RICHARD As long as heaven and nature lengthens it.

ELIZABETH As long as hell and Richard likes of it.

RICHARD Say I, her sovereign, am her subject low.

ELIZABETH But she, your subject, loathes such sovereignty,   360

RICHARD Be eloquent in my behalf to her.

ELIZABETH An honest tale speeds best being plainly told.

RICHARD Then plainly to her tell my loving tale.

ELIZABETH Plain and not honest is too harsh a style.

RICHARD Your reasons are too shallow and too quick.   365

ELIZABETH Oh, no, my reasons are too deep and dead,

Too deep and dead, poor infants, in their graves.

RICHARD Harp not on that string, madam. That is past.

ELIZABETH Harp on it still shall I till heartstrings break.

RICHARD Now, by my George, my Garter, and my crown –   370

347 this] F, Q, Q2–3, Q5; tuis Q4; his Q6   349 Tell her] F; Saie that Qq (*subst.*)   349 that] F; which Qq   350 forbids] F, Q; forbid Q2–6   352 vail] F; waile Qq   354 ever] F, Q, Q2–4, Q6 (euer); *not in* Q5   356 her sweet life] F, Q, Q2; that title Q3–6   357 As] F; So Qq   358 As] F; So Qq   359 low] F; loue Qq   363 plainly to her tell] F; in plaine termes tell her Qq (*subst.*)   365 Your] F; Madame your Qq   367 graves] F; graue Qq   368] Q; *after 369* F; *not in* Q2–6   368 on] F; one Q   369 SH] F, Q (*Qu.*); King. Q2; *not in* Q3–6

347 **Infer** Allege.

348 **still-lasting** everlasting (in her personal life).

350 **the king's King** God, who forbids marriage between uncle and niece (see Lev. 18).

352 **vail** yield (*OED* Vail *v²* 4a).

360 **loathes** Elizabeth plays on the sound of Richard's phrase, 'subject low' (359).

365 **quick** hastily invented. In her reply (366), Elizabeth plays on 'quick' meaning 'alive'.

368 This line, dropped from the later quartos, was probably re-inserted in the wrong spot during the composition of the Folio.

369 **heartstrings** Elizabeth turns Richard's musical cliché into an anatomical image of the heart and its tendons as an instrument of grief that she will play until it breaks.

370 **George** Emblem of St George, England's patron saint. This emblem was part of the Garter insignia, although not until after Richard's time.

370 **Garter** Badge signifying Richard's membership of the Order of the Garter, England's highest order of knighthood. In *Shakespeare's Garter Plays: 'Edward III' to 'Merry Wives of Windsor'* (1994), Giorgio Melchiori argues that Shakespeare associates the Garter with issues of

ELIZABETH Profaned, dishonoured, and the third usurped.

RICHARD I swear –

ELIZABETH   By nothing, for this is no oath.
          Thy George, profaned, hath lost his lordly honour;
          Thy Garter, blemished, pawned his knightly virtue;
          Thy crown, usurped, disgraced his kingly glory: 375
          If something thou wouldst swear to be believed,
          Swear then by something that thou hast not wronged.

RICHARD Then by myself.

ELIZABETH   Thyself is self-misused.

RICHARD Now, by the world –

ELIZABETH   'Tis full of thy foul wrongs.

RICHARD My father's death.

ELIZABETH   Thy life hath it dishonoured.   380

RICHARD Why then, by heaven.

ELIZABETH   Heaven's wrong is most of all.
          If thou didst fear to break an oath with Him,
          The unity the king my husband made
          Thou hadst not broken, nor my brothers died.
          If thou hadst feared to break an oath by Him,   385
          Th'imperial metal circling now thy head
          Had graced the tender temples of my child,
          And both the princes had been breathing here,
          Which now, two tender bedfellows for dust,
          Thy broken faith hath made the prey for worms.   390
          What canst thou swear by now?

372] *Steevens*; I sweare. / *Qu.* By . . . Oath: F; I sweare by nothing. / *Qu.* By nothing, . . . oath. Qq   373 Thy] F; The
Qq   373 lordly] F; holy Qq   374 Thy] F; The Qq   375 Thy] F; The Qq   375 glory] F; dignitie Qq   376 wouldst] F; wilt
Qq   378–81] *Steevens*: Then . . . Selfe. / Thy . . . selfe-misvs'd. / Now . . . World. / 'Tis . . . wrongs. / My . . .
death. / Thy . . . dishonor'd. / Why . . . Heauen. / Heauens . . . all: F; Now . . . world. / Tis . . . wrongs. / My . . .
death. / Thy . . . dishonord. / Then . . . selfe. / Thy . . . misusest. / Whie, then by God. / Gods . . . all, Qq   378
is self-misused] F; thy selfe misusest Qq (*subst.*)   380 life] F, Q, Q2; selfe Q3–6   380 it] F; that Qq   381 heaven] F; God
Qq   381 Heaven's] F; God's Q   382 didst fear] F; hadst feard Qq (*subst.*)   382 with] F; by Qq   383 my] F; my Q, Q2–5, Q6
(*most copies*); thy (*BL C.34.k.50, BL C.12.g.14, Folger copies*)   383 husband] F; brother Qq   384 Thou hadst not] F; Had
not bene Qq (*subst.*)   384 brothers died] F; brother slaine Qq   386 head] F; brow Qq   389 bedfellows] F; plaie-fellowes
Qq (*subst.*)   390 the] F; a Qq   390 worms] F, Q, Q2–5; worme Q6   391] F; *not in* Qq

---

honour, power and sexuality throughout his
work, although he mentions it explicitly only
three times, in *1H6, R3* and *Wiv.* As Melchiori
points out, all three references are associated with
characters who lack true honour (p. 113). The
Order's ambiguous motto, *Honi soit qui mal y
pense* – Evil (or shame) to him who thinks evil –
applies more directly to dishonourable knights
than it does to the truly chivalrous.

373, 374, 375 **his** its.

378–81 This sequence of split lines forms a
climax to the long passage of stichomythia –
exchange of single lines – that precedes it (347–
71).

382, 385 **Him** God.

383 The reconciliation between rival court
factions that Edward IV tried to make in 2.1.

384 **brothers** Rivers is Elizabeth's only
brother in the play (see 1.3.37n.).

RICHARD The time to come.

ELIZABETH That thou hast wrongèd in the time o'erpast,
   For I myself have many tears to wash
   Hereafter time, for time past wrongèd by thee.   395
   The children live whose fathers thou hast slaughtered,
   Ungoverned youth, to wail it with their age;
   The parents live whose children thou hast butchered,
   Old barren plants, to wail it with their age.
   Swear not by time to come, for that thou hast   400
   Misused ere used, by times ill-used repassed.

RICHARD As I intend to prosper and repent,
   So thrive I in my dangerous affairs
   Of hostile arms. Myself myself confound!
   Heaven and fortune bar me happy hours!   405
   Day, yield me not thy light, nor night, thy rest!
   Be opposite, all planets of good luck
   To my proceeding if, with dear heart's love,
   Immaculate devotion, holy thoughts,
   I tender not thy beauteous, princely daughter!   410
   In her consists my happiness and thine.
   Without her follows to myself and thee,
   Herself, the land, and many a Christian soul,
   Death, desolation, ruin, and decay.
   It cannot be avoided but by this.   415
   It will not be avoided but by this.
   Therefore, dear mother, I must call you so,
   Be the attorney of my love to her.

---

392 The] F; By the Qq   393 in the time] F; in time Qq   395 past wronged by thee] F; by the past wrongd Q, Q2–4 (*subst.*); by the past wrongd Q5–6 (*subst.*)   396 fathers] F; parents Qq   397 with their] F, Q5; in their Q, Q2–4; with her Q6   399 barren] F; withered Qq   401 ere] F, Q6; eare Q, Q2–3, Q5; nere Q4   401 times ill-used] F; time misused Qq   401 repassed] F (repast); orepast Qq   403 affairs] F; attempt Qq   405] F; *not in* Qq   408 proceeding] F; proceedings Qq   408 dear] F; pure Qq   409 Immaculate] F, Q; Immaculatd Q2; Immaculated Q3–6   410 tender] F, Q, Q2, Q4; render Q3, Q5–6   412 myself and thee] F; this land and me Qq   413 Herself, the land] F; To thee her selfe Qq (*subst.*)   414 Death, desolation] F; Sad desolation Qq   416 by this] F, Q2–6; this Q   417 dear] F; good Qq

395 Hereafter time In the future.

397 Ungoverned Lacking a father's control.

397 with their age 'in their age' (Q, Q2–4) implies that the young will mourn when they get old. In the Folio, this line and its parallel, 399, suggest that both young and old mourn 'with their age', at whatever age they have attained.

401 Ruined (the future) before it arrived by abuse of past time. The quartos' 'orepast' is a more common word than 'repassed', which usually means 'to pass again' (*OED* Repass) but here means 'finished, completed'.

402–3 Richard again ties his success in war to the sincerity of his repentance (compare 236).

404 Myself . . . confound May I destroy myself (if I don't love your daughter). The 'if' does not come until 408.

407 opposite hostile.

409 Immaculate devotion Worship.

410 tender hold dear.

412–16 Following his pledge with a threat, Richard outlines the complete ruin of England as the consequence of Elizabeth's refusal.

Plead what I will be, not what I have been,
Not my deserts, but what I will deserve.   420
Urge the necessity and state of times,
And be not peevish found in great designs.
ELIZABETH Shall I be tempted of the devil thus?
RICHARD Ay, if the devil tempt you to do good.
ELIZABETH Shall I forget myself to be myself?   425
RICHARD Ay, if your self's remembrance wrong yourself.
ELIZABETH Yet thou didst kill my children.
RICHARD But in your daughter's womb I bury them,
    Where in that nest of spicery they will breed
    Selves of themselves, to your recomforture.   430
ELIZABETH Shall I go win my daughter to thy will?
RICHARD And be a happy mother by the deed.
ELIZABETH I go. Write to me very shortly,
    And you shall understand from me her mind.
RICHARD Bear her my true love's kiss, and so farewell.   435

Exit Q[ueen Elizabeth]

Relenting fool and shallow, changing woman.
How now, what news?

Enter RATCLIFFE [*and* CATESBY]

RATCLIFFE Most mighty sovereign, on the western coast
    Rideth a puissant navy. To our shores

---

420 my] F; by Qq   422 found] F; fond Qq   424 you] F; thee Qq   427 Yet] F; But Qq   428 I bury] F, Q3; I buried Q, Q2;
Ile burie Q4–6   429 they will] F; they shall Q, Q2; there shall Q3–6   434] F; *not in* Qq   435 and so farewell] F; farewell Qq
(*subst.*)   435 SD] Qq; *after 434* F   437] F; *not in* Qq   437 SD] F; *after 436* Qq   438 Most mighty] F; My gracious Qq   439
our shores] F; the shore Qq

421 necessity and state of times pressing
political situation.
421–2 The couplet again implies that the
speaker thinks he has clinched his argument
(compare 210–11).
422 be . . . designs do not be discovered fret-
fully complaining when great deeds are being
planned.
424 if . . . good Both Richard and Elizabeth
doubtless know that the devil cannot tempt to
good, but Richard senses victory and slights theology to score a rhetorical hit.
425 Shall I forget the wrongs you did to me in
order to be again myself as mother to a monarch?
428–30 Steevens observed that 'nest of spicery'
(429) recalls the fable of the phoenix, a mythical bird that was reborn from the nest of spices
on which it had burned to death in its previous
life. Here the nest – the princess's womb – is
transformed into a compost pit in which Richard

proposes to bury the dead boys to stimulate
fertility in their sister. This spectacularly inap-
propriate metaphor shows Richard's language at
its most strained, emphasising his disgust with
women and breeding at just the wrong moment
in his duel with Elizabeth.
430 recomforture consolation (*OED* Recomforture, citing only this line).
436 Richard assumes that he has won, but the
next time the audience hears of Elizabeth (4.5.7–
8) she has promised her daughter to Richmond.
In many productions, Elizabeth clearly holds out
against Richard, only speaking evasively at the
end as an excuse to leave him. Colley Cibber
gave her an aside saying she would 'seemingly
comply, and thus / By sending *Richmond* Word
of his Intent / Shall gain some time to let my
Child escape him' (Cibber, p. 43).
439 puissant powerful.

> Throng many doubtful, hollow-hearted friends,   440
> Unarmed and unresolved to beat them back.
> 'Tis thought that Richmond is their admiral;
> And there they hull, expecting but the aid
> Of Buckingham to welcome them ashore.

RICHARD Some light-foot friend post to the Duke of Norfolk: 445
> Ratcliffe, thyself, or Catesby; where is he?

CATESBY Here, my good lord.

RICHARD Catesby, fly to the duke.

CATESBY I will, my lord, with all convenient haste.

RICHARD Ratcliffe, come hither. Post to Salisbury.   450
> When thou com'st thither – Dull, unmindful villain,
> Why stay'st thou here, and go'st not to the duke?

CATESBY First, mighty liege, tell me your highness' pleasure,
> What from your grace I shall deliver to him.

RICHARD Oh, true, good Catesby. Bid him levy straight   455
> The greatest strength and power that he can make
> And meet me suddenly at Salisbury.

CATESBY I go.   *Exit*

RATCLIFFE What, may it please you, shall I do at Salisbury?

RICHARD Why, what wouldst thou do there before I go?   460

RATCLIFFE Your highness told me I should post before.

RICHARD My mind is changed.

> *Enter* LORD STANLEY [EARL OF DERBY]

> Stanley, what news with you?

STANLEY None good, my liege, to please you with the hearing,
> Nor none so bad but well may be reported.   465

RICHARD Hoyday, a riddle! Neither good nor bad.

443 they] F, Q, Q3–6; thy Q2   447 good lord] F; Lord Qq   448 Catesby, fly] F; Flie Qq   448 duke.] F; Duke, post thou to
Salisburie Qq (*subst.*)   449–50] F; *not in* Qq   450 Ratcliffe] F; *Rowe*; *Catesby* F   451 com'st thither] F; comst there Q; comest
there Q2–6   451 villain] F, Q, Q2–5; villanie Q6   452 stay'st] F; standst Q, Q2–3, Q5–6; stands Q4   452 here] F; still Qq
(*subst.*)   453 liege] F; Soueraigne Qq   453 tell me your highness' pleasure] F (Highnesse); let me know your minde Qq
(*subst.*)   454 to him] F; them Q, Q2; him Q3–6   456 that he] F; be Qq   457 suddenly] F; presentlie Qq (*subst.*)   458] F;
not in Qq   458 SD] F; *not in* Qq   459 may it please you, shall I] F; is it [it is Q5; is Q6] your highnes pleasure, I shall Qq
(*subst.*)   460 wouldst] F, Q, Q2–3, Q5–6; woulds Q4   462 changed.] F; changd sir, my minde is changd. Qq   462 SD] F;
after 463 Qq   463 Stanley] F; How now Qq   464 liege] F; Lord Qq   465 well may] F; it may well Qq   465 reported] F;
told Qq

442 **their admiral** Admiral of the navy mentioned at 439.
443 **hull** float, wait.
443 **expecting but** only waiting for.
445 **post** ride quickly.
450 **Ratcliffe** Perhaps the absence of an exit
for Catesby after 449 confused the F compositor

and caused him to substitute 'Catesby' for the
'Ratcliffe' written in his copy.
451 **Dull, unmindful villain** As 453 indicates, Richard speaks to Catesby.
455 **levy** gather armed forces or soldiers.
456 **make** assemble.
466 **Hoyday** An expression of surprise.

What need'st thou run so many miles about,
When thou mayst tell thy tale the nearest way?
Once more, what news?
STANLEY   Richmond is on the seas.
RICHARD There let him sink, and be the seas on him!   470
White-livered runagate, what doth he there?
STANLEY I know not, mighty sovereign, but by guess.
RICHARD Well, as you guess.
STANLEY Stirred up by Dorset, Buckingham, and Morton,
He makes for England, here to claim the crown.   475
RICHARD Is the chair empty? Is the sword unswayed?
Is the king dead? The empire unpossessed?
What heir of York is there alive but we?
And who is England's king but great York's heir?
Then tell me, what makes he upon the seas?   480
STANLEY Unless for that, my liege, I cannot guess.
RICHARD Unless for that he comes to be your liege,
You cannot guess wherefore the Welshman comes.
Thou wilt revolt and fly to him, I fear.
STANLEY No, my good lord; therefore mistrust me not.   485
RICHARD Where is thy power then, to beat him back?
Where be thy tenants and thy followers?
Are they not now upon the western shore,
Safe-cònducting the rebels from their ships?
STANLEY No, my good lord, my friends are in the north.   490
RICHARD Cold friends to me. What do they in the north
When they should serve their sovereign in the west?
STANLEY They have not been commanded, mighty king.
Pleaseth your majesty to give me leave,
I'll muster up my friends and meet your grace   495
Where and what time your majesty shall please.
RICHARD Ay, thou wouldst be gone, to join with Richmond.

---

467 What need'st] F; Why doest Qq (*subst.*)   467 miles] F; mile Qq   468 the nearest] F; a neerer Qq (*subst.*)   469] *Steevens*; Once . . . newes? / *Stan.* Richmond . . . Seas. F, Qq (*subst.*)   473] F; Well sir, as you guesse, as you guesse. Qq (*subst.*)   474 Morton] F; Elie Qq (*subst.*)   475 here] F; there Qq   480 makes] F; doeth Qq (*subst.*)   480 seas] F; sea Qq   485 my good lord] F; mightie liege Qq   487 be] F; are Qq   491 me] F; Richard Qq   493 king] F; soueraigne Qq   494 Pleaseth] F; Please it Qq   497 Ay] F (I); I, I Qq

469 The split line shows Stanley's haste to comply.
471 **White-livered   runagate**   Cowardly renegade.
476 **chair** throne.
476 **sword** sword of office.

480 **makes he** is he doing.
483 **Welshman** Richmond was the grandson of the Welshman Owen Tudor and Katherine of Valois, widow of Henry V.
486 **power** military force.
494 **Pleaseth** If it pleases.

But I'll not trust thee.

STANLEY Most mighty sovereign,
You have no cause to hold my friendship doubtful.   500
I never was nor never will be false.

RICHARD Go then and muster men, but leave behind
Your son George Stanley. Look your heart be firm,
Or else his head's assurance is but frail.

STANLEY So deal with him as I prove true to you   *Exit Stanley*   505

Enter a MESSENGER

MESSENGER My gracious sovereign, now in Devonshire,
As I by friends am well advertisèd,
Sir Edward Courtney and the haughty prelate,
Bishop of Exeter, his elder brother,
With many more confederates, are in arms.   510

Enter another MESSENGER

SECOND MESSENGER In Kent, my liege, the Guilfords are in arms,
And every hour more competitors
Flock to the rebels, and their power grows strong.

Enter another MESSENGER

THIRD MESSENGER My lord, the army of great Buckingham –
RICHARD Out on ye, owls, nothing but songs of death!   515
He striketh him
There, take thou that, till thou bring better news.
THIRD MESSENGER The news I have to tell your majesty
Is that by sudden floods and fall of waters
Buckingham's army is dispersed and scattered,

498] F; I will not trust you Sir. Qq (*subst.*)   502 Go then and] F; Well, go Qq   502 leave] F; heare you, leaue Qq   503 heart] F; faith Qq   505 So deal] F, Q, Q2–3, Q5–6; Deale Q4   505 SD. 1] F; *Exit. Dar.* Q3–5 (*subst.*); *Exit.* Q6; *not in* Q, Q2   508 Edward] F; William Qq   509 elder brother] F; brother there Qq   511 SH] *Capell; Mess.* F, Qq   511 In Kent, my liege] F; My Liege, in Kent Qq (*subst.*)   513 the rebels, and their power grows strong] F; their aide, and still their power increaseth Qq (*subst.*)   514, 517, 526, 527 SH] *Capell; Mess.* F, Qq   514 My lord] F, Q, Q2, Q5–6; Lord Q4   514 great] F; the Duke of Qq   515 ye] F, Q6; you Q, Q2–5   515 SD] F; *after 514* Qq   516] F; Take that vntill thou [you Q6] bring me better newes. Qq   517] F; Your grace mistakes, the newes I bring is good, Qq (*subst.*)   518] F; My newes is that by sudden floud, and fall of water, Qq (*subst.*)   519 Buckingham's] F; The Duke of Buckinghams Qq

504 assurance safety.
506–47 Shakespeare condenses two years of military history into these lines. Successive messengers bring news of events that actually took place between October 1483, when Richmond first attempted to land in England, and August

1485, just before the battle of Bosworth Field.
507 advertisèd advised, told.
515 owls Birds whose mournful cries were supposed to predict death.
518 fall of waters storms, rain.

And he himself wandered away alone,   520
No man knows whither.
RICHARD I cry thee mercy.
There is my purse to cure that blow of thine.
Hath any well-advisèd friend proclaimed
Reward to him that brings the traitor in?   525
THIRD MESSENGER Such proclamation hath been made, my lord.

Enter another MESSENGER

FOURTH MESSENGER Sir Thomas Lovell and Lord Marquess Dorset,
'Tis said, my liege, in Yorkshire are in arms.
But this good comfort bring I to your highness:
The Breton navy is dispersed by tempest.   530
Richmond, in Dorsetshire, sent out a boat
Unto the shore, to ask those on the banks
If they were his assistants, yea or no,
Who answered him they came from Buckingham
Upon his party. He, mistrusting them,   535
Hoised sail and made his course again for Bretagne.
RICHARD March on, march on, since we are up in arms,
If not to fight with foreign enemies,
Yet to beat down these rebels here at home.

Enter CATESBY

CATESBY My liege, the Duke of Buckingham is taken.   540
That is the best news. That the Earl of Richmond
Is with a mighty power landed at Milford
Is colder news, but yet they must be told.
RICHARD Away towards Salisbury! While we reason here
A royal battle might be won and lost.   545

---

520 wandered away alone] F; fled, no man knowes whether Qq (whither Q2–6)   521 No . . . whither] F; *as part of 520* Qq   522] F; O I crie you mercie, I did mistake, Qq (*subst.*)   523] F; Ratcliffe reward him, for the blow I gaue him, Qq   524 proclaimed] F; giuen out Qq   525 Reward to] F; Rewardes for Qq (*subst.*)   525 the traitor in] F; in Buckingham Qq   526 lord] F; liege Qq   528 in Yorkshire are] F; are vp Qq   529 But] F; Yet Qq   529 highness] F; grace Qq   530 Breton] *Theobald* (*Bretagne*); Brittaine F, Qq   530 dispersed by tempest] F; disperst, Richmond in Dorshire Qq (*Dorsetshire* Q6)   531–2] F; Sent out a boate to aske them on the shore, Qq   532 Unto the shore] F; *not in* Qq   536 his course again] F; away Qq   536 Bretagne] *Theobald*; Brittaine F, Qq   541 That is] F; Thats Qq   543 news, but yet] F; tidings, yet Q, Q2–5 (*subst.*); newes, yet Q6

522 **Pardon me.**
524 **well-advisèd** judicious, wise.
527 **Sir Thomas Lovell** Not the same Lovell who serves Richard in 3.4 and 3.5.
536 **Hoised** Hoisted.

544 **reason** talk, debate.
545 **royal battle** battle in which royalty (the throne) is in dispute; a 'battle royal' or general engagement (see *OED* Battle *sb* 3).

Someone take order Buckingham be brought
To Salisbury. The rest march on with me.

Flourish. Exeunt

4.5   *Enter* [STANLEY EARL OF] DERBY, *and* SIR CHRISTOPHER
[URSWICK, *a priest*]

STANLEY   Sir Christopher, tell Richmond this from me,
    That in the sty of the most deadly boar
    My son George Stanley is franked up in hold.
    If I revolt, off goes young George's head;
    The fear of that holds off my present aid.   5
    So get thee gone; commend me to thy lord.
    Withal say that the queen hath heartily consented
    He should espouse Elizabeth her daughter.
    But tell me, where is princely Richmond now?
CHRISTOPHER   At Pembroke, or at Ha'rfordwest, in Wales.   10
STANLEY   What men of name resort to him?
CHRISTOPHER   Sir Walter Herbert, a renownèd soldier,
    Sir Gilbert Talbot, Sir William Stanley,
    Oxford, redoubted Pembroke, Sir James Blunt,
    And Rice ap Thomas, with a valiant crew,   15
    And many other of great name and worth;
    And towards London do they bend their power,
    If by the way they be not fought withal.

---

547 SD *Flourish*] F; *not in* Qq   547 SD *Exeunt*] F, Q; *not in* Q2–6   Act 4, Scene 5   4.5] Capell; *Scena Quarta.* F; *not in* Qq   0 SD *and*] F; *not in* Qq   0 SD URSWICK] Theobald; *not in* F, Qq   2 of the] F; of this Qq   2 deadly] F; bloudie Qq   5 holds off] F; with holdes Qq (*subst.*)   6] F; *not in* Qq   7–8] F; *after* 19 Qq   7 Withal say that] F; Tell him Qq   8 should] F; shall Qq   10 Ha'rfordwest] Capell; Hertford West F; Harford-west Q; Herford-west Q2, Q5; Hertford-west Q3–4, Q6 (*subst.*)   14 redoubted] F; Q2–3, Q5–6; doubted Q4   15 And] F; *not in* Qq   15 ap] F, Q6; vp Q, Q2–5   16 And] F; With Qq   16 other] F; moe Qq   16 great name] F; noble fame Qq   17 do they] F; they do Qq   17 power] F; course Qq

546 take order give order that.

Act 4, Scene 5
Shakespeare dramatises the chronicles' narrative assertion of Stanley's secret loyalty to Richmond. In Holinshed, it is the Countess of Richmond who sends Sir Christopher Urswick with messages to her son.

0 SD URSWICK Christopher Urswick was chaplain to the Countess of Richmond, who was Stanley's wife and Richmond's mother.

3 franked up in hold shut up, as a pig being fattened for slaughter, Richard uses the same expression for Clarence's imprisonment at 1.3.314.

7 Withal In addition.
10 Pembroke A town in Wales, near Richmond's landing-place at Milford Haven.
10 Ha'rfordwest Haverfordwest, another town in the west of Wales.
11 of name of title or rank.
14 Oxford Earl of Oxford.
14 redoubted awe-inspiring; feared.
14 Pembroke Earl of Pembroke.
17 bend their power turn their army.
18 by the way along the way. Richmond's forces met Richard's near Market Bosworth, in Leicestershire.
18 withal with.

STANLEY Well, hie thee to thy lord; I kiss his hand.
My letter will resolve him of my mind.   20
Farewell.

Exeunt

5.1 *Enter* [SHERIFF *and*] BUCKINGHAM *with Halberds, led to execution*

BUCKINGHAM Will not King Richard let me speak with him?
SHERIFF No, my good lord. Therefore be patient.
BUCKINGHAM Hastings and Edward's children, Grey and Rivers,
Holy King Henry, and thy fair son Edward,
Vaughan, and all that have miscarrièd   5
By underhand corrupted foul injustice,
If that your moody, discontented souls
Do through the clouds behold this present hour,
Even for revenge mock my destruction.
This is All Souls' Day, fellow, is it not?   10
SHERIFF It is.
BUCKINGHAM Why, then, All Souls' Day is my body's doomsday.
This is the day which, in King Edward's time,
I wished might fall on me when I was found
False to his children and his wife's allies.   15
This is the day wherein I wished to fall
By the false faith of him whom most I trusted.
This, this All Souls' Day to my fearful soul
Is the determined respite of my wrongs.

19 Well, hie thee to] F; Retourne vnto Qq   19 thy] F; Q; my Q2–6   19 I kiss his hand] F; commend me to him Qq   20
My letter] F; These letters Qq   Act 5, Scene 1   5.1] F (*Actus Quintus. Scene Prima.*); *not in* Qq   0 SD SHERIFF *and*]
Rowe; not in F, Qq   0 SD *with Halberds, led*] F; *not in* Qq   2, 11 SH] F (*Sher.*); *Rat.* Qq   2 good] F; *not in* Qq   3 Grey
and Rivers] F; Riuers, Gray Qq   10 fellow] F; fellowes Qq   11] F; It is my Lord. Qq   13 which] F; that Qq   15 and] F;
or Qq   17 whom most I trusted] F; I trusted most Qq

19 hie hurry.
20 resolve tell.

Act 5, Scene 1
  Historically, Buckingham was executed on
2 November 1483, almost two years before the
battle of Bosworth (22 August 1485). In the play,
Buckingham's death in November fits the pattern
of seasonal imagery begun by Richard in 1.1 and
renewed by Margaret in 4.4. Metaphorically, it is
the late autumn of Richard's reign, even though
the end actually came in summer.
  0 SD *Halberds* Guards carrying halberds or
pole-axes. The sheriff would not be so armed.

4 thy King Henry's.
5 miscarrièd died.
7 moody angry.
10 All Souls' Day 2 November, a day of
prayer for the souls in purgatory (see *The Oxford
Dictionary of Saints*, 1984, p. 12).
  13–17 See 2.1.32–40.
  19 determined respite of my wrongs predestined day to which the punishment of my
wrongs has been postponed (see *OED* Respite *sb*
5). Buckingham acknowledges the ironic congru-
ence of determinism and his own will, as he once
expressed it 'in jest' (2.1.32–40).

That high All-Seer which I dallied with   20
Hath turned my feignèd prayer on my head
And given in earnest what I begged in jest.
Thus doth he force the swords of wicked men
To turn their own points in their masters' bosoms.
Thus Margaret's curse falls heavy on my neck: 25
'When he', quoth she, 'shall split thy heart with sorrow,
Remember Margaret was a prophetess.'
Come, lead me, officers, to the block of shame;
Wrong hath but wrong, and blames the due of blame.

Exeunt Buckingham with officers

5.2 *Enter* RICHMOND, OXFORD, BLUNT, HERBERT, *and others,*
with drum and colours

RICHMOND Fellows in arms, and my most loving friends,
Bruised underneath the yoke of tyranny,
Thus far into the bowels of the land
Have we marched on without impediment;
And here receive we from our father Stanley   5
Lines of fair comfort and encouragement.
The wretched, bloody, and usurping boar,
That spoiled your summer fields and fruitful vines,
Swills your warm blood like wash, and makes his trough
In your embowelled bosoms, this foul swine   10
Is now even in the centre of this isle,

---

20 That] F, Q, Q3–6; What Q2   20 which] F; that Qq   23 swords] F, Q, Q2 (*subst.*); sword Q3–6 (*subst.*)   24 own] F; Q,
Q2; *not in* Q3–6   24 in] F; on Qq   24 bosoms] F; bosome Qq   25 Thus] F; Now Qq   25 falls heavy on] F; is fallen vpon
Qq   25 neck] F; head Qq   26–7 'When he' . . . 'shall . . . prophetess'] *Capell (italics); no quotation marks in* F, Qq   26
quoth] F, Q2–6; quorh Q   28 lead me, officers] F; sirs, conuey me Qq   29 SD] F; *not in* Qq   Act 5, Scene 2   5.2] F
(*Scena Secunda.*); *not in* Qq   0 SD] F; *Enter Richmond with drums and trumpets.* Qq   1 Fellows] F, Q, Q2–4, Q6; Fellowe
Q5   8 fields] F, Q, Q2; field Q3–6   11 Is] F; Lies Qq   11 centre] Qq; Centry F

20 **dallied** pretended, trifled.
26 **he** Richard.

Act 5, Scene 2
Richmond, according to the chronicles,
camped at Tamworth, which he names at 13.
   0 SD *drum and colours* drummers and flag-
bearers.
   3 **bowels** interior.
   5 **our father** Richmond's stepfather. He uses
the royal plural.

6 **Lines** Writings, letters.
7 **boar** Richard.
8 Richmond implies that Richard, the enemy
of summer and sun (see 1.1), has created a barren
land.
8 **spoiled** despoiled, ravaged.
9 **Swills** Guzzles, gulps.
9 **wash** hogwash, slops.
10 **embowelled** disembowelled, gutted.

Near to the town of Leicester, as we learn.
From Tamworth thither is but one day's march.
In God's name, cheerly on, courageous friends,
To reap the harvest of perpetual peace   15
By this one bloody trial of sharp war.
OXFORD Every man's conscience is a thousand men
To fight against this guilty homicide.
HERBERT I doubt not but his friends will turn to us.
BLUNT He hath no friends but what are friends for fear,   20
Which in his dearest need will fly from him.
RICHMOND All for our vantage. Then in God's name march!
True hope is swift and flies with swallow's wings;
Kings it makes gods, and meaner creatures kings.

Exeunt

5.3 *Enter* RICHARD *in arms, with* NORFOLK, RATCLIFFE, *the* EARL
OF SURREY [*with others*]

RICHARD Here pitch our tent, even here in Bosworth field.
My lord of Surrey, why look you so sad?

14 cheerly] F, Q; cheere Q2; cheare Q3–6   17 SH] F; *1 Lo.* Qq   17 men] F; swordes Qq (*subst.*)   18 this guilty] F; that
bloudie Qq (*subst.*)   19 SH] F; *2 Lo.* Qq   19 turn] F; flie Qq   20 SH] F; *3 Lo.* Qq   20 what] F; who Qq   21 dearest] F;
greatest Qq   21 fly] F; shrinke Qq   24 makes] F, Q6; make Q, Q2–5   24 SD] F (*Exeunt Omnes.*), Q (*Exit.*); *not in* Q2–6   **Act
5, Scene 3** 5.3] *Pope; not in* F, Qq   0 SD *in arms*] F; *not in* Qq   0 SD *the* EARL OF SURREY] F; *Catesbie* Qq   0 SD *with
others*] Qq; *not in* F   1 tent] F; tentes Qq (*subst.*)   2 My lord of Surrey] F; Whie, how now Catesbie Qq   2 look you] F;
lookst thou Q; lookest thou Q2–6   2 sad] F; Q2–6; bad Q

14 cheerly cheerfully.
15 reap . . . peace Richmond's rather conventional metaphor gains force by contrast with
earlier links between harvest and death (see
1.2.251, 1.4.231 and 2.2.116). See also Margaret's
imagery of ripening and rotting at 1.3.217 and
4.4.1–2.
17 It was proverbial that 'conscience is a thousand witnesses' (Tilley C601). Richard, by contrast, calls conscience a 'coward' and the word of
cowards (5.3.182, 311).
20–1 Compare *Mac.*: 'And none serve with
him but constrainèd things/Whose hearts are
absent too' (5.4.13–14).
21 dearest greatest.
24 meaner of lower status.

Act 5, Scene 3
The chronicles describe a rumour that Richard
had 'a dreadfull and terrible dreame: for it
séemed to him being asleepe, that he did see
diuerse images like terrible diuels, which pulled
and haled him, not suffering him to take anie

quiet or rest' (Holinshed, III, 438). After the
dream, says Holinshed, Richard did not show
'the alacritie and mirth of mind and countenance
as he was accustomed to doo before he came
toward the battell' (III, 438). The paired ora-
tions (238–71 and 316–43) also appear in Holinshed, although Shakespeare has reversed their
order. This scene is usually staged with two tents
pitched on opposite sides of the stage. Albert
Weiner argues that the scene requires only a single tent. See 'Two tents in *Richard III*?', *SQ* 13
(1962), 258–60.
0 SD RATCLIFFE Ratcliffe participates silently
in this part of the scene (1–18), just as Catesby
does after his second entrance at 271. The
unspecified 'others' of the quartos are included
here to indicate Richard's role as head of an army
in the process of establishing camp. Most directors provide Richard and Richmond with several
silent aides and guards during the early parts of
the scene.
1 Bosworth Historically, the battle of
Bosworth was fought on 22 August 1485.

SURREY My heart is ten times lighter than my looks.
RICHARD My lord of Norfolk.
NORFOLK   Here, most gracious liege.
RICHARD Norfolk, we must have knocks, ha, must we not?   5
NORFOLK We must both give and take, my loving lord.
RICHARD Up with my tent. Here will I lie tonight,
    But where tomorrow? Well, all's one for that.
    Who hath descried the number of the traitors?
NORFOLK Six or seven thousand is their utmost power.   10
RICHARD Why, our battalia trebles that account.
    Besides, the king's name is a tower of strength,
    Which they upon the adverse faction want.
    Up with the tent. Come, noble gentlemen,
    Let us survey the vantage of the ground.   15
    Call for some men of sound direction.
    Let's lack no discipline, make no delay,
    For lords, tomorrow is a busy day.

                                        Exeunt

    Enter RICHMOND, SIR WILLIAM BRANDON, OXFORD,
     and DORSET, [HERBERT, BLUNT, *and others*]

RICHMOND The weary sun hath made a golden set,
    And by the bright tract of his fiery car,   20
    Gives token of a goodly day tomorrow.

---

3 SH] F; *Cat*, Q; *Cat.* Q2–6   4] *Steevens*; My . . . Norfolke. / *Nor.* Heere . . . Liege. F; Norffolke, come hether. Qq (*subst.*)   5] Qq; Norfolke . . . knockes: / Ha . . . not? F   6 loving] F; gracious Qq   7 tent] F; tent there Qq   8 all's] F; all is Qq   9 traitors] F; foe Qq   10 utmost] F, Q; greatest Q (*Huntington copy*), Q2–6   10 power] F; number Qq   11 battalia] F; battalion Q, Q4, Q6 (*subst.*); battailon Q2–3, Q5   13 faction] F; partie Qq   14 the tent. Come, noble] F; my tent there, valiant Qq   15 ground] F; field Qq   17 lack] F; want Qq   18 SD.2 SIR WILLIAM BRANDON, OXFORD, *and* DORSET] F; *with the Lordes* Qq (*subst.*)   18 SD.3 HERBERT, BLUNT] *Capell; not in* F, Qq   18 SD.3 *and others*] Q, Q2 (&c.); *not in* Q3–6, F   19 sun] F, Q2–6; sonne Q   19 set] F; sete Q; seate Q2–5; seat Q6   20 tract] F; tracke Qq   21 token] F; signall Qq

8 **all's one for that** that doesn't matter.
9 **descried** ascertained.
11 **battalia** force, army. 'Battle' often carries this same meaning, as at 91, 141, 294 and 301.
12 Compare *R2*: 'Is not the king's name twenty thousand names? / Arm, arm, my name!' (3.2.85–6).
13 **want** lack.
14 **Up . . . tent** An implicit stage direction suggesting that the first tent goes up at this point.
15 **vantage of the ground** military advantages offered by the terrain.
16 **direction** military judgement.
19 SD.3 DORSET Dorset says nothing in this scene, and no one speaks to him. Nevertheless,

after all the talk of Dorset's fleeing to Richmond (4.1.42–3, 4.2.48–50, 4.2.86), it seems appropriate for the audience to see him at Richmond's side.
20 **tract** track, trace.
20 **car** chariot; an allusion to the sun as the chariot of the sun god. Evoking the play's thematic metaphors of sun and shadow, Richmond confirms himself as Richard's opposite, noting the omen of the setting sun under circumstances in which Richard does not.
21 Signals good weather for tomorrow's battle. It is still proverbial that a 'red sky at night' predicts a fair day. See Tilley E191, S515.

Sir William Brandon, you shall bear my standard.
Give me some ink and paper in my tent.
I'll draw the form and model of our battle,
Limit each leader to his several charge,   25
And part in just proportion our small power.
My lord of Oxford, you, Sir William Brandon,
And you, Sir Walter Herbert, stay with me.
The Earl of Pembroke keeps his regiment.
Good Captain Blunt, bear my goodnight to him   30
And by the second hour in the morning
Desire the earl to see me in my tent.
Yet one thing more, good captain, do for me:
Where is Lord Stanley quartered, do you know?
BLUNT Unless I have mista'en his colours much,   35
Which well I am assured I have not done,
His regiment lies half a mile at least
South from the mighty power of the king.
RICHMOND If without peril it be possible,
Sweet Blunt, make some good means to speak with him   40
And give him from me this most needful note.
BLUNT Upon my life, my lord, I'll undertake it.
And so, God give you quiet rest tonight.
RICHMOND Good night, good Captain Blunt.
Come, gentlemen,   45
Let us consult upon tomorrow's business.
Into my tent; the dew is raw and cold.

They withdraw into the tent

Enter RICHARD, RATCLIFFE, NORFOLK, *and* CATESBY

---

22 Sir] F; Where is Sir Qq 22 you] F; he Qq   23–6] F; *after 44* Qq 26 power] F; strength Qq   27–8] F; *not in* Qq 28 you] F2; your F 29 keeps] F; keepe Qq (*subst.*) 33 captain, do for me] F; Blunt before thou goest Qq 34 do you] F; doest thou Qq 37 lies] F, Q, Q2; liet Q3–5; lieth Q4, Q6 40] F; Good captaine Blunt beare my good night to him, Qq 41 note] F; scrowle Qq 43] F; *not in* Qq 44] F; Farewell good Blunt. Qq 45] F; *not in* Qq 46 Let] F; Come, let Qq 47 my] F; our Qq 47 dew] F; aire Qq 47 SD.1 *They withdraw into the tent*] F; *not in* Qq 47 SD.2 CATESBY] F; Q3–6 (*subst.*); Catesbie, & *c.* Q, Q2

---

22 **standard** flag.
23 Richmond probably addresses this to an aide, although perhaps Sir William Brandon waits on him as Ratcliffe waits on Richard.
24 **draw the form and model** draft the plan.
25 **Limit** Assign.
25 **several charge** particular command.
26 **part . . . power** proportionately divide our small army.
29 **keeps** remains with.

38 **power** forces.
47 SD.1 *into the tent* Like Richard's, Richmond's tent can be set up on stage while the actors talk before it. Richmond has only asked Oxford, Brandon and Herbert to stay in the tent with him, and Blunt, at least, must leave the stage, since he must carry a message to Stanley. The departures of Blunt, Dorset and others may have been managed by having them all step into the tent and thence off stage.

RICHARD What is't o'clock?

CATESBY It's supper time, my lord; it's nine o'clock.

RICHARD I will not sup tonight.   50
        Give me some ink and paper.
        What, is my beaver easier than it was,
        And all my armour laid into my tent?

CATESBY It is, my liege, and all things are in readiness.

RICHARD Good Norfolk, hie thee to thy charge.   55
        Use careful watch; choose trusty sentinels.

NORFOLK I go, my lord.

RICHARD Stir with the lark tomorrow, gentle Norfolk.

NORFOLK I warrant you, my lord.   *Exit*

RICHARD Ratcliffe.   60

RATCLIFFE My lord.

RICHARD Send out a pursuivant at arms
        To Stanley's regiment. Bid him bring his power
        Before sunrising, lest his son George fall
        Into the blind cave of eternal night.   65
        Fill me a bowl of wine. Give me a watch.
        Saddle white Surrey for the field tomorrow.
        Look that my staves be sound and not too heavy. Ratcliffe!

RATCLIFFE My lord.

RICHARD Saw'st the melancholy Lord Northumberland?   70

RATCLIFFE Thomas the Earl of Surrey and himself,
        Much about cockshut time, from troop to troop

---

48 is't] F; is Qq   49] F; It is sixe of clocke [of the clocke Q3–6], full supper time. Qq   50–1] F; *as one line* Qq   56 sentinels] F; centinell Qq   59 SD] F; *not in* Qq   60 Ratcliffe] F; Catesby Qq   68 heavy. Ratcliffe] F; heauy Ratliffe Q, Q2–5; heauy *Ratcliffe* Q6   70 Saw'st] F; Saw'st thou Qq (*subst.*)   72 about] F, Q, Q2–5; like Q6

---

49 nine o'clock The quartos' 'sixe of the clocke' has seemed to many a more normal time for supper (see Variorum, p. 382). Since Richard's army is bedding down on an English summer night after sunset, it must be later than six. Perhaps under such circumstances, 'nine o'clock' was supper time.

52 beaver visor of a helmet.

52 easier working more smoothly.

55 hie hurry.

59 warrant guarantee.

60 Ratcliffe The quartos have 'Catesby', which many editors follow, supplying an exit for Catesby after 65. There is no reason for anyone to leave the stage to send out a pursuivant, however, and given the string of demands Richard issues in 66–8, the Folio seems wise to keep both Ratcliffe and Catesby on hand. Richard may also

be served by other attendants.

62 pursuivant at arms military messenger.

63 power troops.

64 Richard contrasts the rising sun with the falling son. The metre stresses 'ris[e]' and 'fall'.

66 watch Perhaps a watch candle (night light), or perhaps a guard.

68 staves wooden lance shafts.

70 melancholy Richard perceives his nobles as 'sad' (2) and 'melancholy', perhaps reflecting his own lack of cheer (75–6). Historically, this Lord Northumberland was the son of the one Buckingham describes weeping for the death of Rutland (1.3.185).

72 cockshut twilight; possibly because chickens were shut up for the night at that hour (*OED* Cockshut).

Went through the army, cheering up the soldiers.
RICHARD So, I am satisfied. Give me a bowl of wine.
     I have not that alacrity of spirit   75
     Nor cheer of mind that I was wont to have.
     Set it down. Is ink and paper ready?
RATCLIFFE It is, my lord.
RICHARD Bid my guard watch. Leave me.
     Ratcliffe, about the mid of night come to my tent   80
     And help to arm me. Leave me, I say.
                              Exeunt Ratcliffe [and Catesby]

Enter [STANLEY EARL OF] DERBY *to* RICHMOND *in his tent*

STANLEY Fortune and victory sit on thy helm.
RICHMOND All comfort that the dark night can afford
     Be to thy person, noble father-in-law.
     Tell me, how fares our noble mother?   85
STANLEY I by attorney bless thee from thy mother,
     Who prays continually for Richmond's good.
     So much for that. The silent hours steal on,
     And flaky darkness breaks within the east.
     In brief, for so the season bids us be,   90
     Prepare thy battle early in the morning,
     And put thy fortune to th'arbitrement
     Of bloody strokes and mortal-staring war.
     I, as I may (that which I would I cannot),
     With best advantage will deceive the time   95
     And aid thee in this doubtful shock of arms.

---

80 Ratcliffe] F; Q3, Q5–6; Ratliffe Q, Q2,Q4   80 mid] F; Q, Q2–5; midst Q6   81 SD.1 *and Catesby*] Malone; *Exit Ratclif.* F,
Q6 (*subst.*); *Exit. Ratliffe*, Q, Q2–5   82 sit] F, Q2–6; set Q   85 noble] F, Q3–6; loving Q, Q2   93 mortal-staring] *Steevens*;
mortall staring F, Qq (*subst.*)

75 **alacrity** liveliness.
76 **wont** accustomed.
81 SD.1 Since Richard twice insists that he be
left alone, both Ratcliffe and Catesby should exit,
with Richard remaining on stage, perhaps hidden from view in his tent, or perhaps still visible
during the conversation between Richmond and
Stanley and Richmond's prayer (82–120).
82 **helm** helmet.
84 **father-in-law** Here, stepfather.
86 **by attorney** as substitute.
89 **flaky darkness** darkness flecked with light.
Rather than seeing the breaking of dawn or day,
Stanley sees the darkness breaking into flakes as
light invades it.

90 **season** time.
91 **battle** army.
92 **arbitrement** arbitration, judgement.
93 **mortal-staring** Both (1) causing death by
its stare, and (2) staring into the face of death.
94 **that which I would** what I would like to
do for you.
95 **deceive the time** disguise what I do
(from Richard). In the event, Stanley offers no
deception at all, but simply refuses to fight on
Richard's side (344–5).
96 **shock** clash.

But on thy side I may not be too forward,
Lest being seen, thy brother, tender George,
Be executed in his father's sight.
Farewell. The leisure and the fearful time   100
Cuts off the ceremonious vows of love
And ample interchange of sweet discourse
Which so long sundered friends should dwell upon.
God give us leisure for these rites of love.
Once more adieu. Be valiant, and speed well.   105
RICHMOND   Good lords, conduct him to his regiment.
I'll strive with troubled noise to take a nap,
Lest leaden slumber peise me down tomorrow,
When I should mount with wings of victory.
Once more, good night, kind lords and gentlemen.   110

Exeunt [*all but Richmond*]

O thou whose captain I account myself,
Look on my forces with a gracious eye.
Put in their hands thy bruising irons of wrath,
That they may crush down with a heavy fall
Th'usurping helmets of our adversaries.   115
Make us thy ministers of chastisement,
That we may praise thee in thy victory.
To thee I do commend my watchful soul
Ere I let fall the windows of mine eyes.
Sleeping, and waking, oh, defend me still. *Sleeps*   120

---

98 brother, tender] F, Q, Q2–5; tender brother Q6   99 his father's sight] F, Q, Q2–3, Q5–6; thy fathers fight Q4   103 sundered] F, Q5–6 (*subst.*); sundried Q, Q2; sundired Q3–4   104 rites] F; rights Qq   106 lords] F, Q, Q2–3, Q5–6; Lord Q4   107 noise] F; thoughts Qq   110 SD] *This edn; Exeunt. Manet Richmond.* F; *Exeunt.* Qq (*subst.*)   115 Th'usurping] F; the vsurping Qq   115 helmets] F, Q, Q2–4; helmet Q5–6   117 thy] F, Q3–5; the Q, Q2, Q6   120 SD.1] F; *not in* Qq

98 tender young. Elsewhere in the play, 'tender' applies to children, especially the boy-princes. Using the word here lets Shakespeare borrow some of the pathos surrounding those victims for George Stanley, historically an adult in 1485. In their film McKellen and Loncraine go a step further, making young George a very small boy with thick glasses, the most helpless of all Richard's victims.

100 leisure pressure; small amount of free time.

105 speed succeed, prosper.

107 strive contend. It is not clear what noise Richmond is striving against. Many editors have substituted Q's 'troubled thoughts', but

Richmond, as the ghosts of Hastings and Anne both testify, has an 'untroubled' and a 'quiet' soul (152, 167). Perhaps he refers to the noise of battle preparations, as in *H5*: 'and from the tents / The armourers, accomplishing the knights, / With busy hammers closing rivets up, / Give dreadful note of preparation' (4.11–14).

108 peise weigh.

111 thou God.

113–14 Compare Ps. 2.9: 'Thou shalt krush them with a scepter of yron.' The Psalter of the Elizabethan prayer book reads 'Thou shalt bruise them with a rod of iron.'

119 windows covers, lids.

120 still always.

Enter the GHOST OF PRINCE EDWARD, *son to Henry the Sixth*

GHOST [OF PRINCE EDWARD] *(To Richard)* Let me sit heavy on thy
    soul tomorrow.
    Think how thou stab'st me in my prime of youth
    At Tewkesbury. Despair therefore, and die.
    (To Richmond) Be cheerful, Richmond, for the wrongèd souls
    Of butchered princes fight in thy behalf.   125
    King Henry's issue, Richmond, comforts thee.

Enter the GHOST OF HENRY THE SIXTH

GHOST [OF HENRY] [*To Richard*] When I was mortal, my anointed
    body
    By thee was punchèd full of holes.
    Think on the Tower and me. Despair, and die.
    Harry the Sixth bids thee despair and die.   130
    (To Richmond) Virtuous and holy, be thou conqueror.
    Harry, that prophesied thou shouldst be king,
    Doth comfort thee in sleep. Live and flourish.

Enter the GHOST OF CLARENCE

GHOST [OF CLARENCE] [*To Richard*] Let me sit heavy in thy soul
    tomorrow,
    I, that was washed to death with fulsome wine,   135
    Poor Clarence, by thy guile betrayed to death.

120 SD.2 PRINCE] F, Q3–6; *young Prince* Q, Q2 (*subst.*)   120 SD.2 *Henry*] F, Q2–6; *Harry* Q   120 SD.2 *Sixth*] F, Q3–6; *sixt,
to Ri.* Q, Q2   121 SH] *This edn*; *Gh.* F; *Ghost* Qq (*subst.*)   124 SD] Qq; *Ghost to Richm.* F   124] Qq; *Be . . . Richmond, /
For . . . Soules* F   127 SH] *This edn*; *Ghost* F; *Ghost to Ri.* Qq (*subst.*)   128 holes] F, Q2–6; *deadlie holes* Q   133 sleep] F;
thy sleep Qq   134 SH] *This edn*; *Ghost.* F, Qq (*subst.*)   134, 142, 149, 154 SD] *Rowe*; *not in* F, Qq   134 sit] F, Q2–6; *set*
Q   134 in] F, Q, Q2–4; *on* Q5–6

120 SD.2 GHOST The ghosts appear in the
order in which Richard killed them. In Q and Q2,
the young princes enter before Hastings, a mistake evidently recognised by the Q3 compositor,
who exchanged the two entrances. Neither the
Folio nor the quartos provide exits for any of the
ghosts. Following Rowe, eighteenth-century editors had the ghosts 'vanish' after 180, but in the
twentieth century, most have followed Wilson,
who thought it ridiculous to have the ghosts 'lin-
ing up on the stage' (p. 248), and inserted an exit
for each ghost before the next entered. As recent
productions have shown, however, a line-up of
ghosts can effectively underscore the magnitude
of Richard's crimes, and decisions about their
departure may be left to individual directors.
   123 Despair . . . die Each of the ghosts –
eleven in all – orders Richard to commit the

ultimate sin of despair. Marlowe's Dr Faustus pronounces the same curse on himself –
'Damned art thou, Faustus, damned! Despair
and die' (5.1.54). See pp. 12–13 above.
   127 SD Both F and Q lack some stage directions for the ghosts' alternating speeches to
Richard and to Richmond. The dialogue in each
case makes clear the addressee.
   127 anointed consecrated in the coronation
ceremony; blessed by God.
   128 Editors often add 'deadly' from the quartos, but the form of F's shortened line imitates
its subject by creating a hole in the metre, and
may be deliberate.
   129 the Tower Where Richard murdered
Henry VI (see *3H6* 5.6).
   135 fulsome nauseating (*OED* Fulsome 3b,
citing 1601 as the earliest instance).

Tomorrow in the battle think on me,
And fall thy edgeless sword, despair, and die.
(*To Richmond*) Thou offspring of the house of Lancaster,
The wrongèd heirs of York do pray for thee.   140
Good angels guard thy battle. Live and flourish.

Enter the GHOSTS OF RIVERS, GREY, *and* VAUGHAN

[GHOST OF] RIV[ERS]   [*To Richard*] Let me sit heavy in thy soul
    tomorrow.
    Rivers that died at Pomfret. Despair, and die.
[GHOST OF] GREY   Think upon Grey, and let thy soul despair.
[GHOST OF] VAUGHAN   Think upon Vaughan, and with guilty fear   145
    Let fall thy lance. Despair, and die.
ALL [THREE GHOSTS]   (*To Richmond*) Awake, and think our wrongs
    in Richard's bosom
    Will conquer him. Awake, and win the day.

Enter the GHOST OF LORD HASTINGS

GHOST [OF HASTINGS]   [*To Richard*] Bloody and guilty, guiltily awake
    And in a bloody battle end thy days.   150
    Think on Lord Hastings. Despair, and die.
    (*Hast[ings] to Richmond*) Quiet untroubled soul, awake, awake.
    Arm, fight, and conquer, for fair England's sake.

Enter the GHOSTS OF THE TWO YOUNG PRINCES

GHOSTS [OF PRINCES]   [*To Richard*] Dream on thy cousins smothered
    in the Tower.
    Let us be laid within thy bosom, Richard,   155
    And weigh thee down to ruin, shame, and death.
    Thy nephews' soul bids thee despair and die.

141 SD GHOSTS] F, Q, Q2,Q6; Ghoast Q3–5; (*subst.*)   141 SD *and* VAUGHAN] F; *Vaughan* Qq   142 SH] *Dyce; Riu* F, Q3–6; *King* Q, Q2   142 in] F, Q, Q2–4; on Q5–6   144 SH] *Dyce; Grey.* F, Qq (*subst.*)   145 SH] *Dyce; Vaugh.* F, Qq (*subst.*)   147 SH] *This edn; All* F, Qq (*subst.*)   147] Qq: Awake, / And . . . Bosome, F   148 Will] F, Q2–6; Wel Q   148 SD LORD HASTINGS] F, Q3–6 (*subst.*); *Hastings* Q, Q2   149–53] F; Q3–6; *after 161* Q, Q2   149 SH] *This edn; Gho.* F, Qq (*subst.*)   152 SD] F (*Hast. to Rich.*), Qq (*subst.*)   152 Qq; Quiet . . . soule, / Awake, awake: F   153 SD THE TWO] F, Q, Q2–5; two Q6   154–61] F, Q3–6; *after 148* Q, Q2   154 SH] *This edn; Ghosts.* F; *Ghost* Q, Q2, Q6; *Gho.* Q3–5   154] Qq; Dreame . . . Cousins / Smothered . . . Tower: F   155 laid] F, Q2–6; lead Q   157 soul bids] F; soules bid Qq

138, 166 fall let fall, drop.
138, 166 edgeless blunt.
139 offspring . . . Lancaster Richmond was
a descendant of the house of Lancaster through
his mother, Margaret Beaufort. This support
from the 'heirs of York' (140) foreshadows Richmond's union with Princess Elizabeth and the

symbolic merging of the houses of Lancaster and
York.
141 battle army.
154 cousins relatives.
157 soul bids The quartos have 'soules bid'.
The Folio's grammatical error may indicate that
the child-ghosts were to speak in unison.

(*To Richmond*) Sleep, Richmond, sleep in peace, and wake in
     joy.
Good angels guard thee from the boar's annoy.
Live, and beget a happy race of kings.   160
Edward's unhappy sons do bid thee flourish.

Enter the GHOST OF ANNE, *his wife*

GHOST [OF ANNE] (*To Richard*) Richard, thy wife, that wretched
     Anne, thy wife,
That never slept a quiet hour with thee,
Now fills thy sleep with perturbations.
Tomorrow in the battle think on me,   165
And fall thy edgeless sword. Despair, and die.
(*To Richmond*) Thou quiet soul, sleep thou a quiet sleep.
Dream of success and happy victory.
Thy adversary's wife doth pray for thee.

Enter the GHOST OF BUCKINGHAM

GHOST [OF BUCKINGHAM] (*To Richard*) The first was I that helped
     thee to the crown.   170
The last was I that felt thy tyranny.
Oh, in the battle think on Buckingham,
And die in terror of thy guiltiness.
Dream on, dream on, of bloody deeds and death.
Fainting, despair; despairing, yield thy breath.   175
(*To Richmond*) I died for hope ere I could lend thee aid.
But cheer thy heart and be thou not dismayed.
God and good angels fight on Richmond's side,
And Richard fall in height of all his pride.
     Richard starts out of his dream

158 SD] Qq; *Ghost to Richm.* F   158] Qq; Sleep Richmond, / Sleepe . . . Ioy, F   161 SD   ANNE] F; *Lady Anne* Q, Q2;
Queene Anne Q3–6   162 SH] *This edn; Ghost* F; *not in* Qq   162 SD] F; *not in* Qq   162] Qq; *Richard,* . . . Wife, / That . . .
Wife, F   164 perturbations] F, Q2–6; preturbations Q   167 SD] Qq; *Ghost to Richm.* F   167] Qq; Thou . . . soule, /
Sleepe . . . sleepe: F   170 SH] *This edn; Ghost* F; *not in* Qq   170 SD] F; *not in* Qq   170] Qq; The . . . I / That . . . Crowne:
F   176 SD] Qq; *Ghost to Richm.* F   176] Qq; I . . . hope / Ere . . . Ayde; F   179 fall] F; fals Qq   179 SD *starts*] F; *starteth
vp* Q, Q2; *starteth* Q3–6   179 SD *his*] F; *a* Qq

159 **boar's annoy** Richard's assault.
160 **race of kings** The young princes, who
would have begun a Yorkist 'race of kings',
confer dynastic legitimacy on Richmond, whose
descendants were to include Henry VIII and
Elizabeth I. In a similar compliment to James I,
Shakespeare has the witches reveal to Macbeth
'a show of eight Kings' (4.1.111 SD), including
James, who claim descent from Banquo.

174–9 This sequence of three couplets implies
closure for the dream and triumph for Richmond.
175 **Fainting** Growing faint of heart, losing
confidence.
176 **for hope** Either for hoping to help Richmond or for lack of hope that he could help.
179 **Richard fall** may Richard fall.

RICHARD Give me another horse! Bind up my wounds!   180
    Have mercy, Jesu! Soft, I did but dream.
    O coward conscience, how dost thou afflict me?
    The lights burn blue. It is not dead midnight.
    Cold, fearful drops stand on my trembling flesh.
    What? Do I fear myself? There's none else by.   185
    Richard loves Richard, that is, I am I.
    Is there a murderer here? No. Yes, I am.
    Then fly. What, from myself? Great reason why:
    Lest I revenge. What, myself upon myself?
    Alack, I love myself. Wherefore? For any good   190
    That I myself have done unto myself?
    Oh, no. Alas, I rather hate myself
    For hateful deeds committed by myself.
    I am a villain. Yet I lie, I am not.
    Fool, of thyself speak well. Fool, do not flatter.   195
    My conscience hath a thousand several tongues,
    And every tongue brings in a several tale,
    And every tale condemns me for a villain.
    Perjury in the highest degree,
    Murder, stern murder, in the direst degree,   200
    All several sins, all used in each degree,
    Throng all to th'bar, crying all 'Guilty, guilty!'
    I shall despair. There is no creature loves me,
    And if I die no soul shall pity me.

---

183 not] F, Q2–6; now Q   184 stand] F, Q, Q2–4, Q6; stands Q5   186 am] F, Q2–6; and Q   191 I] F, Q, Q2–5; *not in* Q6   199 Perjury] F, Q3–6; Periurie, periurie Q, Q2   202 all to th'] F; to the Q, Q2; all to the Q3–6   204 shall] F, Q3–6; will Q, Q2

181 Richard stops himself as soon as he half-consciously begins to pray for mercy.

183 burn blue Blue-burning candles were thought to signal the presence of ghosts or devils. Here, they may also signal that the ghosts are still on stage.

183 not dead midnight not exactly midnight. Perhaps Richard remarks on the hour because ghosts were supposed to come at midnight, or perhaps this midnight is not 'dead' because it is populated by ghosts. Many editions accept the quartos' 'now'.

185 none else by This remark is ironic if the ghosts remain visible to the audience.

188–95 Pope demoted these lines, along with 205–6, to footnote status, evidently thinking them less fine than the rest of Richard's solil-

oquy. From another point of view, these same speeches elevate *Richard III* to the level of tragedy (see pp. 12–16 above).

190 Wherefore Why.

196, 197 several separate.

201 used . . . degree committed at every step or stage of intensity, as third-degree murder, second-degree murder, etc. See *OED* Degree *sb* 5d.

202 bar court.

203 I shall despair The emphasis is on 'shall', as Richard realises that the despair first urged on him by Anne (1.2.86–7), and lately by all the ghosts, is a real possibility.

203 There . . . me Like Edmund, Richard thinks suddenly of love at the end of a life of villainy (see *Lear* 5.3.240–2).

Nay, wherefore should they, since that I myself   205
Find in myself no pity to myself?
Methought the souls of all that I had murdered
Came to my tent, and every one did threat
Tomorrow's vengeance on the head of Richard.

Enter RATCLIFFE

RATCLIFFE My lord.   210
RICHARD Who's there?
RATCLIFFE Ratcliffe, my lord, 'tis I. The early village cock
    Hath twice done salutation to the morn.
    Your friends are up and buckle on their armour.
RICHARD O Ratcliffe, I fear, I fear.   215
RATCLIFFE Nay, good my lord, be not afraid of shadows.
RICHARD By the apostle Paul, shadows tonight
    Have struck more terror to the soul of Richard
    Than can the substance of ten thousand soldiers
    Armèd in proof and led by shallow Richmond.   220
    'Tis not yet near day. Come, go with me.
    Under our tents I'll play the eavesdropper,
    To hear if any mean to shrink from me.
Exeunt Richard and Ratcliffe

Enter the LORDS *to Richmond sitting in his tent*

LORDS Good morrow, Richmond.
RICHMOND Cry mercy, lords and watchful gentlemen,   225
    That you have ta'en a tardy sluggard here.
LORD How have you slept, my lord?

---

205 Nay] F; And Qq   207 had murdered] F, Q (*subst.*); murtherd Q2–6 (*subst.*)   208 Came] F, Q, Q2; Came all Q3–6   211
Who's there] F; Zoundes, who is there Q, Q2–3, Q5–6 (*subst.*); Zounds, who is heare Q4   214 armour.] F; armor. / *King.*
O Ratcliffe, I have dreamd a fearefull dreame, / What thinkst thou, will our friendes proue all true? / *Rat.* No doubt
(dopt Q4) my Lord. Qq (*subst.*)   222 eavesdropper] F4; Ease-dropper F; ease dropper Q; ewse dropper Q2; ewse-dropper
Q3; eawse-dropper Q4; ewese-dropper Q5–6   223 hear] F, Q3–6; see Q, Q2   223 mean] F, Q, Q2–3, Q5–6; means Q4   223
SD.1 *Richard and Ratcliffe*] F (*Ratliffe*); *not in* Qq   223 SD.2 *sitting in his tent*] F; *not in* Qq   224 SH] Qq (*subst.*); *Richm.*
F   226 a tardy] F, Q, Q2–3, Q5–6; tardie Q4   227 SH] *Hammond* (*1 Lord.*); *Lords.* F, Q3–6; *Lo.* Q; *Lor.* Q2

214 The additional lines in the quartos may
have been dropped from F by accident as the
compositor's eye skipped from one speech beginning with 'O Ratcliffe' to a second one starting
the same way.
  216 **shadows** obscure premonitions (*OED*
Shadow *sb* 6c). The word could also mean
both delusions (*OED* Shadow *sb* 6a) and ghosts
(*OED* Shadow *sb* 7). Richard declares his affinity
with shadows and his hatred of the sun at the

beginning of the play (e.g. 1.1.24–7), and here
these preferences return to haunt him.
  219 **ten thousand** Richard inflates the size of
Richmond's forces, which his agents have said
number seven thousand at most (10).
  220 **proof** armour.
  220 **shallow** inconsequential, insignificant.
  225 **Cry mercy** I beg your pardon.
  226 **ta'en** taken.

RICHMOND   The sweetest sleep and fairest-boding dreams
            That ever entered in a drowsy head
            Have I since your departure had, my lords.   230
            Methought their souls whose bodies Richard murdered
            Came to my tent and cried on victory.
            I promise you, my heart is very jocund
            In the remembrance of so fair a dream.
            How far into the morning is it, lords?   235
LORD   Upon the stroke of four.
RICHMOND   Why, then 'tis time to arm and give direction.
                    His oration to his soldiers
            More than I have said, loving countrymen,
            The leisure and enforcement of the time
            Forbids to dwell upon. Yet remember this: 240
            God and our good cause fight upon our side.
            The prayers of holy saints and wrongèd souls,
            Like high-reared bulwarks, stand before our faces.
            Richard except, those whom we fight against
            Had rather have us win than him they follow.   245
            For what is he they follow? Truly, gentlemen,
            A bloody tyrant, and a homicide;
            One raised in blood, and one in blood established;
            One that made means to come by what he hath,
            And slaughtered those that were the means to help him;   250
            A base, foul stone made precious by the foil
            Of England's chair, where he is falsely set;
            One that hath ever been God's enemy.

228] Qq; The . . . sleepe, / And . . . Dreames, F   228 fairest-boding] *Theobald*; fairest boding F, Qq (*subst.*)   233 heart] F; soule Qq   236 SH] *Hammond* (*I Lord.*); *Lor.* F, Q3–6; *Lo.* Q, Q2   243 high-reared] *Pope*; high rear'd F, Q, Q2–3, Q5–6 (*subst.*); high read Q4   250 slaughtered] F, Q, Q2–3, Q5–6 (*subst.*); slandered Q4   251 foil] Q, Q2; soyle F, Q3–6 (*subst.*)

232 cried on invoked, appealed to (*OED* Cry *v* 17).

233 jocund joyful.

238 SD This unusual SD labels Richmond's speech rather than specifying any action. Most likely it was taken from Holinshed's chronicle, which prints 'The oration of King Henrie the seauenth to his armie' as a heading before Richmond's speech. Richard's speech, with a corresponding heading, precedes Richmond's in Holinshed. Q follows Holinshed more closely than F in this regard, since it distinguishes both speeches with headings. Some scholars have seen the presence of such 'literary' stage directions as evidence that the text containing them derives from Shakespeare's own manuscript (see Textual Analysis, p. 227 below).

239 leisure lack of leisure.

243 bulwarks fortifications.

248 raised raised in status, promoted.

249 made means seized opportunities.

251 foil precious metal backing, as in jewellery. The metaphor pictures Richard as a worthless stone in a precious setting, the throne of England.

252 chair throne.

Then if you fight against God's enemy,
God will in justice ward you as his soldiers;   255
If you do swear to put a tyrant down,
You sleep in peace, the tyrant being slain;
If you do fight against your country's foes,
Your country's fat shall pay your pains the hire;
If you do fight in safeguard of your wives,   260
Your wives shall welcome home the conquerors;
If you do free your children from the sword,
Your children's children quits it in your age.
Then in the name of God and all these rights,
Advance your standards, draw your willing swords.   265
For me, the ransom of my bold attempt
Shall be this cold corpse on the earth's cold face.
But if I thrive, the gain of my attempt
The least of you shall share his part thereof.
Sound drums and trumpets boldly and cheerfully.   270
God and Saint George, Richmond and victory!

Enter RICHARD, RATCLIFFE, *and* CATESBY

RICHARD What said Northumberland as touching Richmond?
RATCLIFFE That he was never trainèd up in arms.
RICHARD He said the truth. And what said Surrey then?
RATCLIFFE He smiled and said 'The better for our purpose'.   275
RICHARD He was in the right, and so indeed it is.
    Tell the clock there.
                    Clock strikes
    Give me a calendar. Who saw the sun today?
RATCLIFFE Not I, my lord.

---

256 do swear] F, Q3–5; doe sweate Q, Q2; sweare Q6   271 SD *and* CATESBY] F; & *c* Qq   273 trainèd] F, Q, Q2–5 (trained);
train'd Q6   277 SD *Clock strikes*] F; *The clocke striketh.* Qq

255 ward protect.
256 swear The quartos' 'sweat' forms a clearer contrast with the 'sleep' of the next line, but 'swear' is not obviously a mistake.
 259 fat wealth.
 259 hire compensation.
 263 quits will requite; will repay.
 263 in your age when you are old.
266–7 High-ranking military leaders were often taken as hostages rather than killed in battle. Like Shakespeare's Henry V, Richmond

promises to die rather than let himself be held for ransom (see *H5* 3.6.154).
 271 Richmond and his followers may leave the stage after this speech, or they may stay, completing their preparations while the audience listens to Richard. The early texts provide no directions here.
 277 Tell Count the strokes of.
 278 SD The clock begins to strike before Richard's line and finishes after it.
 278 calendar almanac.

RICHARD Then he disdains to shine, for by the book   280
    He should have braved the east an hour ago.
    A black day will it be to somebody. Ratcliffe!
RATCLIFFE My lord.
RICHARD The sun will not be seen today;
    The sky doth frown and lour upon our army.   285
    I would these dewy tears were from the ground.
    Not shine today? Why, what is that to me
    More than to Richmond? For the self-same heaven
    That frowns on me looks sadly upon him.

Enter NORFOLK

NORFOLK Arm, arm, my lord! The foe vaunts in the field!   290
RICHARD Come, bustle, bustle. Caparison my horse.
    Call up Lord Stanley; bid him bring his power.
    I will lead forth my soldiers to the plain,
    And thus my battle shall be orderèd:
    My foreward shall be drawn in length,   295
    Consisting equally of horse and foot;
    Our archers shall be placèd in the midst.
    John Duke of Norfolk, Thomas Earl of Surrey,
    Shall have the leading of the foot and horse.
    They thus directed, we will follow   300
    In the main battle, whose puissance on either side
    Shall be well-wingèd with our chiefest horse.
    This, and Saint George to boot! What think'st thou, Norfolk?
NORFOLK A good direction, warlike sovereign.

---

284 not] F, Q2–6; nor Q   289 looks] F, Q, Q2–5; looke Q6   295 drawn] F, Q2–6; drawn out all Q   299 the foot] F, Q3–6; this foote Q, Q2   301 main] F, Q2–6; matne Q   302 well-wingèd] F; well winged Qq   303] Qq; This . . . boote. / What . . . Norfolke. F   303 boot] F, Q3–6; bootes Q, Q2   303 Norfolk] F, Q; Nor. Q2–5; not. Q6   304 sovereign] F; soueraigne, *he sheweth him a paper.* Qq

280 **he disdains to shine** Richard, of course, disdained the sun before the sun disdained him.
   280 **book** almanac.
   281 **braved** adorned, made splendid (*OED* Brave *v* 5 cites this line, though not as the earliest instance).
   285 **lour** scowl. Like almost all the other major characters, Richard gets what he wished for; in his opening soliloquy he declared himself nostalgic for 'all the clouds that loured upon our house' (1.1.3).
   286 **from** gone from.
   290 **vaunts** swaggers, blusters.
   291 **bustle** hurry, be active. This is what

Richard does best. Compare his wish at 1.1.153 that his brothers would die 'And leave the world for me to bustle in!'
   291 **Caparison** Equip.
   294 **battle** troops.
   295 **foreward** vanguard or front-line forces.
   295 **drawn** extended.
   296 **horse and foot** horse soldiers (cavalry) and foot soldiers.
   301 **puissance** power.
   302 **wingèd** flanked.
   302 **chiefest horse** best cavalry.
   303 **This . . . boot** This plan, and the help of St George besides.

This found I on my tent this morning:　　　　　　305
'Jockey of Norfolk, be not so bold,
For Dickon thy master is bought and sold.'
RICHARD A thing devisèd by the enemy.
Go, gentlemen, every man to his charge.
Let not our babbling dreams affright our souls,　　310
For conscience is a word that cowards use,
Devised at first to keep the strong in awe.
Our strong arms be our conscience, swords our law!
March on! Join bravely! Let us to't pell mell,
If not to heaven, then hand in hand to hell.　　　315
　　　　　　[*His oration to his army*]
What shall I say more than I have inferred?
Remember whom you are to cope withal:
A sort of vagabonds, rascals, and runaways,
A scum of Bretons and base lackey peasants,
Whom their o'ercloyèd country vomits forth　　320
To desperate adventures and assured destruction.
You sleeping safe, they bring you to unrest;
You having lands, and blest with beauteous wives,
They would restrain the one, distain the other.
And who doth lead them but a paltry fellow,　　325
Long kept in Bretagne at our mother's cost?
A milksop, one that never in his life

306–7 'Jockey . . . sold.'] F, Qq (*indicated by indentation and italics; no quotation marks*)　306 so] F, Q, Q2–5; to Q6　309 to] F; unto Qq　311 For conscience] F; Conscience Qq　311 a word] F, Q3–6; but a word Q, Q2　312 at] F, Q, Q2–4; as Q5–6　314 to't] F (too't); to it Q, Q2; too it Q3–6　315 SD] Qq; *not in* F　319 Bretons] *Capell*; Brittains F, Qq (*subst.*)　322 you to] F, Q2–6; to you Q　326 Bretagne] *Theobald*; Britaine F, Qq (*subst.*)

306–7 Many editors have found it impossible to believe that Norfolk would read such a message to his king, and they have inserted a direction for Richard to read it instead.

306 Jockey A contemptuous nickname for John or 'Jock' of Norfolk, just as 'Dickon' (307) is for Richard.

307 bought and sold finished.

314 Join Engage in battle.

314 pell mell at close quarters, hand-to-hand (*OED* Pell Mell 2) – not an order to abandon the battle plan, but an exhortation to fight to the death.

316 SD This direction was apparently dropped from the Folio by mistake.

316 inferred alleged.

317 cope withal cope with, confront.

318 A sort An assortment.

319 lackey menial.

320 o'ercloyèd overstuffed.

324 restrain withhold, take.

324 distain stain, rape.

325 paltry insignificant, contemptible.

326 Bretagne Brittany.

326 our mother's Probably, at the expense of England, our mother country. Neither England nor Richard's own mother paid Richmond's keep; Richard speaks instead of the psychological and political costs to his government of Richmond's threatening presence in exile. Boswell-Stone points out that 'mother's' follows a misprint in the 1587 edition of Holinshed, showing that Shakespeare used that edition. Hammond emends to 'brother's', as in the first edition of Holinshed, but 'mother's' evidently made sense to Shakespeare.

Felt so much cold as over shoes in snow.
Let's whip these stragglers o'er the seas again;
Lash hence these overweening rags of France,   330
These famished beggars, weary of their lives,
Who, but for dreaming on this fond exploit,
For want of means, poor rats, had hanged themselves.
If we be conquered, let men conquer us,
And not these bastard Bretons, whom our fathers   335
Have in their own land beaten, bobbed, and thumped,
And on recòrd left them the heirs of shame.
Shall these enjoy our lands, lie with our wives?
Ravish our daughters?
                              (*Drum afar off*)
                              Hark, I hear their drum!
Fight, gentlemen of England! Fight boldly, yeomen!   340
Draw, archers, draw your arrows to the head!
Spur your proud horses hard and ride in blood;
Amaze the welkin with your broken staves!

                    Enter a MESSENGER

What says Lord Stanley? Will he bring his power?
MESSENGER My lord, he doth deny to come.   345
RICHARD Off with his son George's head!
NORFOLK My lord, the enemy is past the marsh;
          After the battle let George Stanley die.
RICHARD A thousand hearts are great within my bosom.
          Advance our standards! Set upon our foes!   350
          Our ancient word of courage, fair Saint George,
          Inspire us with the spleen of fiery dragons!

---

335 Bretons] *Capell*; Britaines F, Qq (*subst.*) 337 on] F, Q3–6; in Q, Q2 339] Qq; Rauish . . . daughters? / Hearke . . . Drumme, F 339 SD] F; *not in* Qq 340 Fight, gentlemen] Q, Q2; Right Gentlemen F, Q3–6 340 boldly] F, Q2–6; bold Q 343 SD] F; *not in* Qq

330 rags ragged relics.
332 fond foolish.
336 bobbed battered (see *OED* Bob v² 1).
337 on recòrd in the historical record. Richard alludes to the conquests of Henry V in France. To Richard, Richmond's forces are 'Bretons', and therefore French, and he tries to use anti-French feeling to rally his troops.
340 yeomen small landholders. A yeoman ranked below a gentleman.
343 welkin sky.
352 spleen anger. The spleen was supposed to be the organ of anger as the heart was the organ of love.
352 fiery dragons St George, of course, was known not for resembling a dragon, but for killing one.

Upon them! Victory sits on our helms!

                              [Exeunt]

5.4 *Alarum. Excursions. Enter* CATESBY

CATESBY Rescue, my lord of Norfolk, rescue, rescue!
        The king enacts more wonders than a man,
        Daring an opposite to every danger.
        His horse is slain, and all on foot he fights,
        Seeking for Richmond in the throat of death.   5
        Rescue, fair lord, or else the day is lost.

            Alarums. Enter RICHARD

RICHARD A horse, a horse, my kingdom for a horse!
CATESBY Withdraw, my lord; I'll help you to a horse.
RICHARD Slave, I have set my life upon a cast,
        And I will stand the hazard of the die.   10
        I think there be six Richmonds in the field;
        Five have I slain today instead of him.
        A horse, a horse, my kingdom for a horse!

                           [Exeunt]

---

353 helms] Q, Q2, Q4; helpes F, Q3, Q5–6   353 SD] Q, Q2; *not in* F, Q3–6   **Act 5, Scene 4**   **5.4**] *Capell; not in* F, Qq   1]
Qq; Rescue . . . Norfolke, / Rescue, Rescue: F   6 SD *Alarums.*] F; *not in* Qq   10 die] F, Q, Q2–3, Q5–6 (*subst.*); day Q4   13
SD] *Theobald; not in* F, Qq

353 helms F's 'helpes' makes some sense –
victory awaits only our help – but it seems likely
that the line is meant to echo Stanley's earlier
wish for Richmond, 'Fortune and victory sit on
thy helm' (82), as much of Richard's oration to
his troops echoes and travesties Richmond's.

Act 5, Scene 4
This scene may derive more directly from
a similar small scene in *The True Tragedie of
Richard III* (scene 19) than from the chronicles.
Holinshed mentions that Richard refuses to save
his life by running because he knows the ill will
the common people bear him (III, 445).

0 SD *Excursions* Movements on and off stage
of actors representing military combatants.

1 Norfolk Capell and many subsequent editors have provided an entrance for Norfolk. He
need not be seen, however, for Catesby to address
him.

3 Daring an opposite to Facing off against.

7 As Antony Sher has remarked, this is 'probably the second most famous line in the whole of
Shakespeare ("To be or not to be" is probably
in first place)' (p. 200). In *The True Tragedie of
Richard the Third*, Richard says 'A horse, a horse,
a fresh horse', perhaps an echo of Shakespeare,
perhaps a precursor.

9 Slave Richard calls Catesby 'slave' for suggesting that he should withdraw from the battle,
even for the purpose of finding another horse.

9 cast throw of the dice.

10 stand the hazard accept the fortune.
Richard uses a metaphor characteristic of one
who regards his will as identical to fate.

10 die One of a pair of dice.

11 six Richmonds This may mean that Richmond, like Henry IV in *1H4*, has other men
dressed like himself on the battlefield, or it may
only mean that in the heat of battle Richard has
mistaken five others for Richmond.

5.5 *Alarum. Enter* RICHARD *and* RICHMOND. *They fight. Richard is
slain. Retreat and flourish. Enter* RICHMOND, [STANLEY EARL OF]
DERBY *bearing the crown, with diverse other lords*

RICHMOND   God and your arms be praised, victorious friends!
     The day is ours; the bloody dog is dead.
STANLEY   Courageous Richmond, well hast thou acquit thee.
     Lo, here these long usurpèd royalties
     From the dead temples of this bloody wretch   5
     Have I plucked off to grace thy brows withal.
     Wear it and make much of it.
RICHMOND   Great God of heaven, say amen to all.
     But tell me, is young George Stanley living?
STANLEY   He is, my lord, and safe in Leicester town,   10
     Whither, if you please, we may withdraw us.
RICHMOND   What men of name are slain on either side?
STANLEY   John Duke of Norfolk, Walter Lord Ferris,
     Sir Robert Brakenbury, and Sir William Brandon.
RICHMOND   Inter their bodies as become their births.   15
     Proclaim a pardon to the soldiers fled
     That in submission will return to us,
     And then, as we have ta'en the sacrament,
     We will unite the white rose and the red.
     Smile heaven upon this fair conjunction,   20
     That long have frowned upon their enmity.

Act 5, Scene 5   **5.5**] *Dyce; not in* F, Qq   o SD.1 *Alarum*] Qq; Alatum F   o SD.2 *Retreat and flourish*] F; *then retrait being
sounded* Qq (*subst.*)   o SD.3 *diverse other lords*] F; *other Lords, &* c. Q, Q2; *other Lords* Q3–6   1] Qq; God . . . Armes /
Be . . . Friends; F   3–4 Courageous . . . Lo,] Qq; Couragious Richmond, / Well . . . thee: Loe, F   4 these] F; this Qq   4
royalties] F, Q2–6 (*subst.*); roialtie Q   7] F, Q3–6; Weare it, enjoy it, and make much of it Q, Q2   11 if you please] F;
if it please you Qq   11 may] F; may now Qq   13–14] F; *Iohn . . . Ferris, sir / Robert . . .* Q; *. . . Ferris, sir Robert /
Brookenbury . . .* Q2–6 (*subst.*)   13 SH] (*Der.*); *not in* Qq   13 Walter] F, Q6; Water Q, Q2–5   13 Ferris] F, Qq; Ferrers
Capell   14 Brakenbury] F4; Brokenbury F, Qq (*subst.*)   17 to us] F, Q, Q2–5; vs Q6   21 have] F, Q, Q2–5, hath Q6

Act 5, Scene 5
  In Holinshed, Richmond speaks to his victorious soldiers from 'the top of a little mounteine' (III, 445).
  o SD.2 Retreat and flourish A trumpet call for retreat, followed by a fanfare for the entrance of Richmond.
  2 the bloody dog is dead Richmond unknowingly echoes Margaret, who wished to 'live and say the dog is dead' (4.4.78). Some recent directors have taken this echo, together with 'What traitor hears me and says not amen?' (22), as evidence that Richmond begins to be vengeful and tyrannical as soon as he ascends the throne.
  4 royalties the crown with its decorations.

6 withal with.
12 name rank of gentleman or above.
18 as we have ta'en the sacrament as I have promised with an oath sworn on the sacrament. Richmond uses the royal plural.
19 I will unite the houses of York (white rose) and Lancaster (red rose) by marrying Elizabeth of York.
20 Smile heaven May heaven smile. Richmond banishes the frowning heavens that Richard had ignored (5.3.287–9).
20 conjunction union.
21 That . . . have Heaven, which is taken as a plural.
21 enmity hatred.

What traitor hears me and says not amen?
England hath long been mad, and scarred herself;
The brother blindly shed the brother's blood;
The father rashly slaughtered his own son;   25
The son, compelled, been butcher to the sire;
All this divided York and Lancaster,
Divided in their dire division.
Oh, now let Richmond and Elizabeth,
The true succeeders of each royal house,   30
By God's fair ordinance conjoin together.
And let thy heirs, God, if thy will be so,
Enrich the time to come with smooth-faced peace,
With smiling plenty and fair prosperous days.
Abate the edge of traitors, gracious Lord,   35
That would reduce these bloody days again
And make poor England weep in streams of blood.
Let them not live to taste this land's increase
That would with treason wound this fair land's peace.
Now civil wounds are stopped; peace lives again.   40
That she may long live here, God say amen.

Exeunt

FINIS.

32 thy heirs] F, Q3–6; their heires Q, Q2   32 thy will] F, Q, Q2–4; they will Q5–6   41 SD] F; *not in* Qq

25–6 Shakespeare shows the symbolic slaughter of father by son and son by father in *3H6*, 2.5.
27–8 The events just recounted further divided York and Lancaster, already divided by their terrible quarrel.
30 succeeders heirs. Richmond could claim Lancastrian ancestry through his mother. Elizabeth was the Yorkist heir to the throne.

31 ordinance decree.
32 thy heirs the heirs of Richmond and Elizabeth. They are also God's heirs because sanctified by God as true royalty.
35 Abate the edge Blunt the swords.
36 reduce bring back.
38 increase fruitful multiplication of crops.
40 stopped stopped from bleeding.

TEXTUAL ANALYSIS

As the twentieth century comes to an end, so do certain traditions of twentieth-century Shakespearean editing. Scholars are less certain than they once were, for example, about the origins of the printed books that have come down to us as the plays of Shakespeare. Once-secure (though hypothetical) lines of descent from Shakespeare's originating manuscripts or 'foul papers' to fair copies, playhouse prompt-books and actors' reconstructions have been called into question. Revision theorists argue that some of Shakespeare's plays may have existed in several manuscript versions because Shakespeare wrote several drafts.[1] Others, influenced by post-structuralism, Marxism and New Historicism, have attacked the whole enterprise of trying to reconstruct Shakespeare's lost manuscripts, pointing instead to the material evidence of the printed books and the historical circumstances of a collaborative theatrical community.[2]

The effects of such criticism on the editing of Shakespeare may be seen in publications such as the Oxford Complete Shakespeare, which offers two versions of *King Lear*, and in the increasing availability of separate editions of multiple-text plays, as in the current New Cambridge series. Most editors still envision Shakespeare as an individual author with designs and intentions for his plays, but many also see modern editions as presentations of particular texts rather than as ideal reconstructions of the author's original intentions. The purpose of such editions becomes not so much to approximate a lost Shakespearean original as to enhance the contemporary reader's understanding of the circumstances and meanings of early modern printed playtexts.

The printed texts of *Richard III*

The First Folio text of *Richard III* (F), called *The Tragedy of Richard III* (running title, *The Life and Death of Richard the Third*), was published in 1623. It occupies signatures q5 to t2^v in the Histories section of the First Folio, between *3 Henry VI* and *Henry VIII*. Another version, substantially different from F, had already been published in a quarto edition in 1597 (Q) and reprinted five times, in 1598, 1602, 1605, 1612 and 1622 (Q2–6). The later quartos were set from the earlier ones, so that

---

[1] For revision theory, see Honigmann, *Stability*, Ioppolo, Taylor and Warren, and Urkowitz.

[2] See, for example, Stephen Orgel, 'What is a text?', *Research Opportunities in Renaissance Drama* 24 (1981), 3–6; Margreta de Grazia, 'The essential Shakespeare and the material book', *Textual Practice* 2 (1988), 69–86; Paul Werstine, '"Foul papers" and "prompt-books": printer's copy for Shakespeare's *Comedy of Errors*', *Studies in Bibliography* 41 (1988), 234–46; Werstine, 'McKerrow's "Suggestion" and twentieth-century Shakespeare textual criticism', *Renaissance Drama* n. s. 19 (1988), 149–73; Werstine, 'Narratives about printed Shakespeare texts: "foul papers" and "bad" quartos', *SQ* 41 (1990), 65–86.

all derive ultimately from Q.[1] When the First Folio text was set, the printers evidently worked from copies of the early quartos – probably Q3 and Q6 – and also from a manuscript source. Two additional quarto versions were printed after the publication of the Folio, in 1629 (Q7) and 1634 (Q8). These later quartos are essentially reprints of the earlier ones. Their compilers may have consulted the Folio version, but they did so only intermittently.

The origins of Q

The desire of twentieth-century scholars to trace each of Shakespeare's play to a single originating manuscript has influenced the explanations put forward for Q *Richard III*.[2] Since the First Folio version of the play is longer and many of its readings have proved more appealing to editors and critics, it has been argued that the F printers probably had access to a manuscript closely related to Shakespeare's autograph manuscript. Most readers think that, on the whole, the variants in F reveal more careful writing. For example, F shows finer rhetorical control at 1.2.14–16, where Anne laments the death of Henry VI:

> Oh, cursèd be the hand that made these holes,
> Cursed the heart that had the heart to do it,
> Cursed the blood that let this blood from hence.

Q has only two lines:

> Curst be the hand that made these fatall holes,
> Curst be the heart that had the heart to doe it.

F varies its lines with 'cursèd be' and 'Cursed the heart', where Q merely repeats 'Curst be'. The metaphorical progression in F moves from 'hand' to 'heart' to 'blood' and from the outside to the inside of the body, increasing in abstraction as it goes. The last half-line closes the circle by returning to the real blood that Anne and the audience can see. By comparison, Q's progression seems truncated.

At 2.2.27–8, the Duchess laments 'that deceit should steal such gentle shape / And with a virtuous visor hide deep vice'. The quartos' reading, 'with a vertuous visard hide foule guile', loses the pun on 'visor' and 'vice' as well as the allusion to Richard's common ground with the Vice character from the morality plays. In a later

---

[1] Two lines (1.1.101–2) that appear in Q2 and subsequent quartos are missing from all known copies of Q. They probably came from a corrected form of Q of which no examples survive. It was common practice in Elizabethan printing houses to make stop-press corrections during a print run. The uncorrected sheets were not discarded, but bound and sold, so that one copy of a book might contain the page in the uncorrected state while another copy showed the correction. If the printers of Q2 *Richard III* had access to such a corrected copy of Q – now lost – it would explain where they found the two extra lines.

[2] Laurie E. Maguire interestingly connects the desire for a single originating text to the biography of New Bibliographer A. W. Pollard: 'Pollard was born in 1859, the year of publication of *The Origin of Species*, a coincidence of date of which he was very proud. In *Shakespeare Folios and Quartos* Pollard, like Darwin, traces his subject back to one founding original: multiple texts derived from a single authorial version' (p. 52).

scene, Buckingham replies to Ely's remark that Buckingham should know Richard's mind:

> We know each other's faces. For our hearts,
> He knows no more of mine than I of yours,
> Or I of his, my lord, than you of mine.   (3.4.10–12)

The first line of the corresponding speech in Q seems padded, while the last is crammed with three extra feet:

> Who I my Lo? we know each others faces:
> But for our harts, he knowes no more of mine,
> Then I of yours: nor I no more of his, then you of mine:

One can also find examples where the Q reading seems better than F, but most readers agree that, overall, F shows higher literary quality.

Q, although printed earlier, probably derived in some way from the manuscript behind F. In the twentieth century, the most popular idea of how that derivation occurred has been 'memorial reconstruction', the process by which actors were supposed to have reconstructed a play in which they had acted but whose script for some reason was not available to them. Just as our era possesses no Shakespearean manuscripts, however, we also have no example of a playtext known to have been reconstructed from memory in Shakespeare's time. Together with the subjectivity of twentieth-century arguments for memorial reconstruction, the scarcity of evidence for the practice in any era makes the hypothesis vulnerable.[1] An alternative

---

[1] See Patrick, Urkowitz, Irace, Maguire. Urkowitz challenges Patrick's conclusion that Q *Richard III* shows unmistakable signs of reconstruction by actors, pointing out that the process of actors' assembling a playtext from memory has 'never been practically tested or empirically demonstrated' (p. 463). Urkowitz also stresses that the supposedly 'memorial' signs found by Patrick – 'transpositions of words and phrases, substitutions of one word for another, and repetitions of words or phrases found elsewhere' – could represent authorial revisions rather than actors' faulty memories (Urkowitz, p. 463). Irace's computer-assisted study of Q *Hamlet* supports the impression of earlier scholars, beginning with H. D. Gray in 1915, that Q was recollected and reported by an actor who had played Marcellus in a version closer to that of the Folio. As Maguire says, however, Irace's study follows the traditional circular reasoning associated with memorial reconstruction, first assuming that Q is a reported text, then identifying Marcellus as the reporter because his scenes most accurately reflect the 'good' text (F), and concluding that this differential accuracy confirms memorial reconstruction (Maguire, pp. 11–12). Maguire argues that the term 'memorial reconstruction' was carelessly and inconsistently used by its originators, and she offers a careful definition of her own: 'the reproduction of a playtext in whole or in part by someone who had at some stage substantial knowledge of the original playtext as written or performed' (p. 225). She examines forty-one 'suspect texts', including Q *Richard III*, for evidence of memorial reconstruction so defined. Her evidentiary criteria, features such as internal repetitions and extra-metrical additions (fifteen in all), are derived from the speculations of earlier critics about what a memorial reconstruction would look like, but Maguire uses them selectively, after testing the arguments for each one. From the scarcity of such characteristics in Q *R3*, she concludes that it is not a memorial reconstruction (pp. 299–300). Peter Davison, on the other hand, reaffirms the traditional explanation (1) that 'Shakespeare's company, the Chamberlain's Men, lost a combined prompt-book used for its London and touring performances of *Richard III* on one of the visits it made to the provinces in 1596 and 1597 and had no alternative available; (2) that the actors recalled their parts and one or more scribes took them down to produce a memorially reconstructed text; and (3) that this memorially reconstructed text provided the manuscript for the 1597 quarto' (p. 5). Like Patrick and others, Davison avoids presenting a clear definition of what it means for a playtext to be 'memorially reconstructed'.

explanation for the origin of Q, which has been encouraged by scholarly acceptance of revision hypotheses, is that Q comes from one Shakespearean draft of the play, and F from another. Many critics, however, resist the idea that Shakespeare himself wrote the Q version and then painstakingly made the numerous verbal changes needed to produce F. Gary Taylor, for instance, says that the verbal variants of the two texts 'do not cluster or coalesce into patterns which imply any discernible strategy of revision'.[1] E. A. J. Honigmann points out that 'the high *incidence* of substitution in Q, and in particular the frequency with which words are moved a few lines out of position, remains, so far as I know, without parallel' in documented revisions.[2] Yet Grace Ioppolo discerns in some F-only passages – such as Richard's retelling of the death of Rutland (1.2.160–71) – a revision strategy designed to unify the first tetralogy by making *Richard III* recall important events in the *Henry VI* plays.[3] In addition, both Honigmann and John Kerrigan have shown that detailed tinkering with verbal variants occurs frequently in revisions of Renaissance plays, and that it is a strategy more characteristic of playwrights revising their own work than of outside adapters.[4]

On the other hand, few commentators believe that Shakespeare himself wrote the F version and then carefully revised it to produce Q. Performance-oriented critics such as Steven Urkowitz gladly give Shakespeare credit for Q's dramatic acuity, but even Kristian Smidt, who wrote two books arguing that Q is a revision rather than a reconstruction of the F manuscript, finally abstained from accusing Shakespeare of Q's clumsier lines. As Smidt pointed out, however, F, too, has its bad verses.[5] There are even moments, as Smidt says, in which it is F that seems to be guilty of the kinds of extra-metrical padding usually attributed to actors.[6] At 1.4.252, for instance, the First Murderer argues against changing his mind: 'Relent? No. 'Tis cowardly and womanish.' In Q he says, 'Relent, tis cowardly and womanish.' In F, Hastings must say, 'Cannot my Lord Stanley sleep these tedious nights?' (3.2.6). Q has 'Cannot thy Master sleepe these tedious nights?' Shakespeare must be convicted of some weak writing if he composed either version of *Richard III*, and the simplest assumption is that he wrote them both. The Q title page links this script firmly to 'the Lord Chamberlaine his seruants'. Even if Q did not come from an authorial draft, it is probable that Shakespeare at least participated in the preparation of this version for acting by his company, and he should be considered its author. The F readings generally show stronger verse and more nuanced diction, and to many this implies that, if either text reflects a Shakespearean revision of the other, the revision must be F. The conclusions of those who have studied writers' revisions support this assumption; most critics see improvement in writers' second drafts, although there are exceptions.[7] Without evidence external to the two texts, however, nothing can be proved.

---

[1] Wells and Taylor, p. 228.   [2] Honigmann, 'Text', p. 53.   [3] Ioppolo, p. 130.

[4] See Honigmann, *Stability*; John Kerrigan, 'Revision, adaptation and the Fool in *King Lear*', in Taylor and Warren, pp. 195–245.

[5] Smidt, *Memorial*, p. 20.   [6] *Ibid.*, p. 20.

[7] See, for example, David Madden and Richard Powers, *Writers' Revisions: An Annotated Bibliography of Articles and Books About Writers' Revisions and Their Comments on the Creative Process*, 1981.

The order of the two substantive texts

It appears reasonable to conclude that Shakespeare authored both versions of *Richard III*, but since one cannot credibly be designated a revision of the other, this conclusion does not help answer the question of which came first. Perhaps the most persuasive argument for Q as the later version is the Q-only 'clock' passage in 4.2. Most critics think that this incident must have been added in Q rather than eliminated in F because no competent playwright or player would have cut it. Taylor calls it a 'dramatic gem', finding it 'difficult to believe that anyone would have deliberately singled it out as the only passage in the play which should be cut'.[1] Some explanations have been offered for the cut – if it was a cut rather than an addition. Edward H. Pickersgill, for example, observed that the clock dialogue contains irregular lines, and postulated an F corrector who was devoted to rigidly metrical verse.[2] Peter Alexander argued that since the detail of the castle at Rugemont derives from Holinshed, Q must be the earlier version.[3] William J. Griffin thought the passage might have been omitted from F in 1623 to avoid offending the then-powerful Duke of Buckingham, King James's favourite.[4] In spite of many such suggestions, most editors have embraced the theory that the clock passage was added to Q rather than cut from F, and that Q thus reflects a later version of the play.

Whether the clock segment is a 'dramatic gem' is a question of literary and theatrical judgement. The first post-Restoration editor to use it was Alexander Pope, who commented that the lines 'have been left out ever since the first editions, but I like them well enough to replace them'.[5] Since Pope, there has been near-universal agreement that this passage is an asset to the play, though one dissenter, P. A. Daniel, thought the passage was an actor's creation, a typical 'bit of fat' added in performance.[6] It remains possible that Shakespeare or someone else responsible for the transmission of this play through its various written and printed forms disliked the clock passage, and that the scene as it appears in F is actually a revision of the scene in Q. It would not be the only time a reviser or adapter made a change that later readers found unfortunate.

Even the argument that F reflects the influence of the study rather than of the stage, and that therefore the more stage-worthy Q must be later, relies on literary judgement. Neither version contains stage directions adequate for a 'prompt-book' or stage manager's notebook as used in the modern theatre, yet both might be seen as dramatically well-developed and playable for somewhat different reasons.[7] Shakespeare and his audiences may actually have liked what many modern critics regard as the wordy elaboration of F, and this longer, more 'poetic' version of *Richard III* may have had a life of its own on the stage. The F manuscript would then reflect

---

[1] Wells and Taylor, p. 228.

[2] Edward H. Pickersgill, New Shakespere Society, *Transactions* (1875–6), p. 94.   [3] Alexander, p. 161.

[4] Griffin, 'An omission in the Folio text of *Richard III*', *RES* (1937), 329–32.   [5] Pope, p. 398.

[6] P. A. Daniel, introduction to Griggs facsimile, p. ix.

[7] On the anachronistic use of the term 'prompt-book' to describe Renaissance playbooks, see William B. Long, '"A bed / for woodstock": a warning for the unwary', *Medieval and Renaissance Drama in England* 2 (1985), 91–118.

those performances, with Q deriving from a different performance version. The argument from stageworthiness thus appears weak as a means of determining which version came first.

To summarise, questions about the origins of Q and the temporal relationship of Q to F remain unresolved. The hypothesis of memorial reconstruction appears doubtful, and no current theory of revision offers a reliable way to tell from the texts alone which came first. Yet the scholarly debate over these matters has produced some progress for textual criticism. There is less inclination now than in the past to label Q 'corrupt' or to insist that in each and every pair of variants one reading must possess literary superiority. There is somewhat less irritable reaching after certainty in advance of convincing evidence. More and more critics and scholars are urging readers to compare the different versions of *Richard III* and other multiple-text Shakespearean plays for themselves instead of relying entirely on conflated editions. Such procedures bring readers closer to the documentary evidence that does exist and to the experience of Shakespeare's plays as they appeared in print and perhaps on stage in his own era.

The printed copy for F

F and Q are not two completely independent texts of *Richard III*, since F itself derives partly from Qq. Judging by substantive agreements, two sections of F were printed with minimal correction from Q3. J. K. Walton argued in 1955 that Q3 was the only quarto used in the printing of F.[1] But the number of readings in which F and Q6 agree against the other quartos – significantly more than between F and any other single quarto – have persuaded most observers that the Folio printers also used at least one copy of Q6.[2] Another strong piece of evidence for the use of quarto copy in F *Richard III*, this time for Q3 in particular, appears at 3.1.124, where F has little York affirming that he wants his uncle's weapon, 'that I might thanke you *as, as,* you call me' (emphasis added). In Q3, the phrase reads 'that I might thanke you *as as* you call me'. None of the other quarto editions has the double 'as', and the chances of the F compositor's making the same meaningless mistake in the same line as Q3 without having looked at Q3 must be very small. In addition, the commas inserted by the F compositor suggest that he was setting what he saw and perhaps trying to make sense

---

[1] Before Walton, textual scholars generally believed that the manuscript from which F was printed had holes in it, and that the holes had been patched with leaves from a copy of Q3. These hypothetical Q3 patches must have been in the manuscript and not in the copy of Q6 used by the F printers, it was argued, because the Q3 passages in F do not correspond to whole pages either in Q3 or Q6 (Greg, p. 87 n. 2). Walton, however, asserted that the patched-manuscript hypothesis was unnecessary if one assumed that the Folio version relied on Q3 as printed copy, and most scholars accepted this hypothesis for the passages in question, although not for all of F.

[2] In his introduction to the Griggs facsimile of Q, Daniel says that F shares two substantive readings exclusively with Q, none with Q2, one with Q3, one with Q4, one with Q5 and twelve with Q6. This edition collates fourteen F/Q6 agreements, not counting the three conjectural emendations Daniel thought were derived from Q6. Daniel's proportions, however, seem about right.

of it through punctuation. This line is part of one of the sections in F that appears to have been set from Q3 with little correction from the manuscript (3.1.1–167). The other such section occurs between 5.3.50 and the end of the play.

In other places, however, F agrees with the later quartos against Q3, and several times with Q6 against the other quartos. Most of these F/Q6 agreements could have occurred independently in F, either because they appeared in the F manuscript or because the F compositor made the change on his own. At 1.4.12–13, for example, Clarence tells of dreaming of his brother Gloucester:

> Who from my cabin tempted me to walk
> Upon the hatches. There we looked toward England

Q6 agrees with F in reading 'There', while Q and Q2–5 have 'thence'. 'There' might easily derive from the F manuscript, however, and not from Q6. There are at least thirteen other similar agreements, none of which by itself clinches the argument for Q6 as copy. At 1.4.228, for example, Clarence tells the murderers to 'Bid Gloucester think on this, and he will weep.' In Q and Q2–5, he says 'think of this'. In 5.3.251, F and Q6 share the spelling 'soyle' as against 'soile' in Q3–5 (Q and Q2 have 'foil', which is probably what the author intended). This spelling agreement may look like a promising parallel to the modern eye, but F consistently uses the 'oyle' spelling in words such as 'Toyle', 'broyles' and 'spoyle', so this instance may be an example of compositor consistency rather than an indication of Q6 printed copy. Perhaps the strongest case for Q6 as copy for some part of F is based on Catesby's lines at 4.4.541–3:

> That the Earl of Richmond
> Is with a mighty power landed at Milford
> Is colder news, but yet they must be told.

At 543, Q and Q2–5 read 'tidings, yet', while Q6 has 'newes, yet'. If 'newes' came into F from Q6, then the F compositor could have added 'but' to fill the gap in the metre. Alternatively, the F reading could have come from the manuscript, making 'newes' in Q6 a substitution by a compositor who approximated the manuscript reading without having access to the manuscript. A similar instance occurs at 3.5.74, where F has 'There, at your meetest vantage of the time', Q6 has 'meetest aduantage', and Q and Q2–5 'meetst aduantage'. Either the Q6 compositor coincidentally made a correction in his Q5 copy that happened to move toward agreement with the F manuscript, or the F compositor took 'meetest' from Q6 and then fixed the metre by substituting 'vantage'. In each case, either explanation is possible, but the use of Q6 as copy looks more likely.

At present, then, the least elaborate hypothesis that seems to fit all observed features of F holds that some portion was set from a copy of Q3 and some from a copy of Q6, both quartos corrected somehow against a manuscript source. As several students of the question have pointed out, only a complete comparison of all early quarto variants – including so-called 'accidentals' such as spelling, punctuation and capitalisation – holds out much hope for specifying the Folio's use of the quartos in greater detail.[1]

Preparation of Folio copy

The printers of F *Richard III* probably set type from at least three documents – Q3, Q6 and a manuscript. Presumably they used the quartos even though they possessed a manuscript they considered authoritative because the printed books were easier to read. Still, the printers needed some method of correcting their quarto copy when it differed from the manuscript. Perhaps a print-shop collator corrected both a copy of Q3 and a copy of Q6 against the manuscript, thereby enabling two compositors to work on the play at the same time. As Smidt and others have noted, however, such a correcting procedure would have involved a great deal of messy annotation in the margins of the printed quartos, possibly creating as much difficulty for the compositors as setting type from the manuscript alone.[2] Perhaps, as Antony Hammond suggests, a clean scribal transcript was made in the printer's shop using one or both of the quartos corrected against the manuscript.[3] Taylor has proposed a third possibility – that the F compositors used Q3 and Q6 in an alternating pattern, with 'major insertions from the manuscript' interleaved into each section.[4] Although none of these speculations has been accepted by all textual critics, Hammond's hypothesis has the advantage of simplicity and appears to be most plausible based on available evidence. The ongoing work of scholars such as Taylor and Peter Blayney may show which hypotheses about the printing of F *Richard III* conform most closely to ordinary print-shop procedure in Shakespeare's era.[5]

'Corruptions' and omissions in F

Earlier editors of *Richard III* worried about undetectable quarto 'contamination' of the Folio text. Since there could have been places where the printed quarto disagreed with the F manuscript, but the compositors failed to make the correction, scholars who believed in the inferiority of Q saw the agreement of Q and F on a questionable reading as a possible symptom of error – a place where the print-shop corrector had failed to do his job – rather than as a sign of textual health. John Dover Wilson, for example, refers to such uncertainties as the 'deep seated disease of the text before us'.[6] If one does not regard Q as corrupt, however, but only as a different version of the play, the disease becomes less acute. One would still like to know if the F compositors caught all the differences between the quartos and the manuscript.

---

[1] Quarto accidentals would also need to be compared to the known habits of the Folio compositors, who characteristically took liberties with the accidentals of their copy. Taylor has initiated a study of Q3 and Q6 accidentals and their relations to Compositors A and B in his unpublished monograph *'Richard III': The Nature and Preparation of the Folio Text*.

[2] Smidt, *Memorial*, p. 205.   [3] Hammond, p. 42.   [4] Wells and Taylor, p. 229.

[5] See Peter Blayney, *The Texts of King Lear and Their Origins: Vol. 1, Nicholas Okes and the First Quarto*, 1982.

[6] Wilson, p. 155.

Nevertheless, both Q and F reflect choices that Shakespeare may have sanctioned at some point, as author-director or as actor-collaborator, and should not lightly be changed to suit modern tastes. This edition of F follows a policy of restrained emendation, especially where F and Q agree.

The manuscript behind F

Whatever quarto edition a particular F compositor was following while setting a section of *Richard III*, a third source – probably a manuscript provided by Shakespeare's colleagues, Heminge and Condell – supplied the many readings in which F differs substantively from all existing quartos. The evidence for the existence of such a manuscript comes entirely from the F text itself: it is longer than the quarto texts, partly because it contains several extended passages that do not appear in the quartos (1.2.160–71, 1.4.69–72, 3.7.143–52, 4.1.98–104, 4.4.222–35 and 4.4.292–346). In addition, F differs from Q in hundreds and hundreds of substantive readings – a word here, a phrase there – that suggest systematic correction of the quartos from a source the printers considered authoritative. The perceived literary superiority of these F readings lies at the root of modern editors' preference for F as copy text. Since F shows higher literary quality, most editors have argued, F – or rather the lost manuscript behind F – has the better claim to Shakespearean origins.

Some students of *Richard III* have held that the lost F manuscript was Shakespeare's 'foul papers'. Alice Walker, for example, pointed out that F contains 'literary' stage directions such as *She looks scornfully at him* (1.2.175) that read more like an author's imaginings than like a script used in the playhouse.[1] The term 'foul papers', however, which was widely accepted by Shakespeareans at mid century, has come under attack at the end of the century from scholars such as Paul Werstine and Laurie Maguire. As Maguire does for 'memorial reconstruction', Werstine shows that the expression 'foul papers' was never rigorously defined by the critics who popularised its use(s).[2] Unlike 'memorial reconstruction', the term 'foul papers' originated in Shakespeare's own time, but as Werstine points out, surviving seventeenth-century documents do not apply it either to an author's rough draft or to a final draft in the author's hand, but to 'fragmentary or incomplete copies of plays'.[3] In addition, since no Shakespearean manuscript – either rough or final – is known to survive today, there is no direct evidence that Shakespeare's drafts – if that is what 'foul papers' means – actually contained descriptive stage directions or inconsistent speech prefixes or any of the other characteristics that appeared to earlier critics as clear signs of underlying authorial scripts.

Rather than a Shakespearean original, the missing manuscript from which F was set may have been a 'fair copy' or cleaned-up draft of Shakespeare's original, perhaps made for theatrical use, if not precisely for a 'prompt-book' in the modern sense. If such a playhouse manuscript had been cleaned up again, after the passage of the 1606 law against profanity on stage, this self-censorship would account for the

---

[1] Walker, pp. 18–19.   [2] See Werstine, 'Narratives'.   [3] *Ibid.*, p. 72.

relative absence of strong oaths such as 'Zounds' in F as compared to Q. (F does not always have the weaker word, however. At 3.4.95–6, for example, Hastings invokes the 'momentary grace of mortal men, / Which we more hunt for than the grace of God'; the quartos have 'the grace of heauen'.) Another possibility, that F derives from a literary transcript made for a patron to read rather than for a company to act, has been supported by Gary Taylor. He argues that F lacks signs of theatrical provenance, and that 'misreadings' in F (that is, the relatively few words or phrases in F generally judged inferior to their counterparts in Q) imply that the lost transcript was a copy of Shakespeare's original draft made by a scribe who misread his copy at certain key points.[1]

Manuscripts from sixteenth-century playhouses and copies of plays made for private patrons do survive today, although as Werstine points out, they do not necessarily show the features that are supposed to distinguish 'prompt-books' and 'fair copies' from 'foul papers'.[2] For Shakespeare's plays, modern editors still have only the printed texts and no certain knowledge about how those texts made their way into print. Having admitted as much, perhaps it is best to assert only that F *Richard III* was probably influenced by some sort of document that allowed its printers to correct the quarto version in well over a thousand readings. These corrections have seemed to most readers generally superior to the quarto readings they replace, and most have preferred to believe that Shakespeare thought so, too, and that F somehow reflects the playwright's best or final or most considered intentions for this play.[3] Yet in the absence of new evidence, which all scholars hope for, a preference for the First Folio of *Richard III* continues to be a matter of literary judgement.

Conclusion

In recent years, theories of authorship and play production grounded in such disciplines as philosophy, history and cultural studies have made their mark on the editing of Shakespeare. These approaches have brought out the inconsistencies and implausibilities in hypothetical constructs that had seemed well established in editorial theory. Editors have been reminded of how easy it is to slip into speaking of hypothetical entities – Shakespeare's manuscripts or memorial reconstructions – as if we had physical evidence of their existence. Like other scholarly editors, Shakespeareans have also begun to question the goal of reconstructing texts as authors intended them, finding that 'intention' and 'author' are more complicated categories

---

[1] Wells and Taylor, p. 230. The 'misreadings' Taylor refers to are those such as 'play' for 'prey' (1.1.133–4): 'More pity that the eagles should be mewed / Whiles kites and buzzards play at liberty'. Generations of editors have singled out F's word as a mistake, by which they have meant that literary judgement leads them to prefer the reading in Q (see, for example, Wilson, pp. 152–3; Hammond, 1.1.133 n).

[2] Werstine, 'Suggestion'. Both 'memorial reconstruction' and 'foul papers', Werstine writes, 'are hypothetical constructs that have yet to be empirically validated with reference to any extant Shakespeare quarto' ('Narratives', p. 81).

[3] For some editorial theorists, of course, 'best', 'final' and 'most considered' intentions are not necessarily the same things. See especially Hershel Parker, *Flawed Texts and Verbal Icons: Literary Authority in American Fiction*, 1984.

than they once seemed, especially since the texts in question were written for performance.[1] Such scrutiny of tradition promises to lead Shakespeareans toward more rigorous historical scholarship, more inquiry into the circumstances of early modern theatrical production, and more study of the printing process in Shakespeare's time. Historical scholarship, however, cannot answer such questions as the nature of an author's intentions. Editorial theory needs the philosopher as well as the historian, the psychologist as well as the bibliographer. To some, this opening of the editing process to interdisciplinary influence may seem a step backward. We appear to know less about the textual history of Shakespeare's plays than we did fifty years ago. If textual hypotheses cannot stand examination, however, we must admit that they never really represented knowledge, and that the texts we edit today will almost certainly have to be re-edited when more is known.

In the case of *Richard III*, much remains to be resolved. Where did the quarto version come from? How is it related to the (hypothetical) manuscript used by the printers of the First Folio? How does the decision of the Folio printers to use three (or more) different documents in the typesetting process square with the customary work habits of Renaissance printers? The answers to such questions cannot come from the evidence of the texts alone. Like the physical nature of Shakespeare's theatre, which recent archaeological discoveries promise to illuminate, the textual history of Shakespeare's plays can be clarified by new cultural and historical evidence. If editors and readers must therefore wait for some of the answers about the texts of *Richard III*, they may at least look forward to answers more firmly grounded in history and logic than some of those that have recently come under attack.

[1] See, for instance, Jerome J. McGann, *A Critique of Modern Textual Criticism*, 1983.

APPENDIX 1
THE Q-ONLY 'CLOCK' PASSAGE

Following 4.2.99, the quartos have the following passage, which does not appear in F:

> *Buck.* My lord.
> *King* How chance the prophet could not at that time,
> Haue told me I being by, that I should kill him.
> *Buck.* My lord, your promise for the Earledome.
> *King* Richmond, when last I was at Exeter,
> The Maior in curtesie showd me the Castle,
> And called it Ruge-mount, at which name I started,
> Because a Bard of Ireland told me once
> I should not liue long after I saw Richmond.
> *Buck.* My lord.
> *King.* I, whats a clocke?
> *Buck.* I am thus bold to put your grace in mind
> Of what you promised me.
> *King.* Wel, but whats a clocke?
> *Buck.* Vpon the stroke of ten.
> *King.* Well, let it strike.
> *Buck.* Whie let it strike?
> *King.* Because that like a Iacke thou keepst the stroke
> Betwixt thy begging and my meditation,
> I am not in the giuing vaine to day.
> *Buck.* Whie then resolue me whether you wil or no?

The story of Richard's visit to the castle at Exeter appears in Holinshed:

And during his abode here he went about the citie, & viewed the seat of the same, & at length he came to the castell: and when he vnderstood that it was called Rugemont, suddenlie he fell into a dumpe, and (as one astonied) said; Well, I see my daies be not long. He spake this of a prophesie told him, that when he came once to Richmond he should not long liue after: which fell out in the end to be true, not in respect of this castle, but in respect of Henrie earle of Richmond, who the next yeare following met him at Bosworth field where he was slaine.

(III, 421)

The dialogue about the clock accords with Shakespeare's dramatic use of clocks throughout the play. The first occurs when Hastings is awakened by a messenger from Stanley at an ominous early hour:

HASTINGS [*Within*] What is't o'clock?
MESSENGER Upon the stroke of four.   (3.2.4–5)

230

Later, Buckingham is associated with the clock, as he promises Richard to persuade the citizens to support him:

> I go, and towards three or four o'clock
> Look for the news that the Guildhall affords. 　　　　　　　*Exit Buckingham*
> 　　　　　　　　　　　　　　　　　　　　　　　　　(3.5.101–2)

Just before his nightmare on the battlefield, Richard asks the time:

> RICHARD What is't o'clock?
> CATESBY It's supper time, my lord; it's nine o'clock. 　　　　　　(5.3.48–9)

Finally, the clock actually strikes, signalling the sun's absence and Richard's doom:

> Tell the clock there.
> 　　　　　　　　　　　*Clock strikes*
> Give me a calendar. Who saw the sun today? 　　　　　　　(5.3.277–8)

The clock of the 'clock' passage, then, may derive from the verbal texture of the play itself, but if it does, this fact does not reveal who added or subtracted these lines, or when (see Textual Analysis, p. 223 above).

APPENDIX 2
THE PLANTAGENET FAMILY TREE

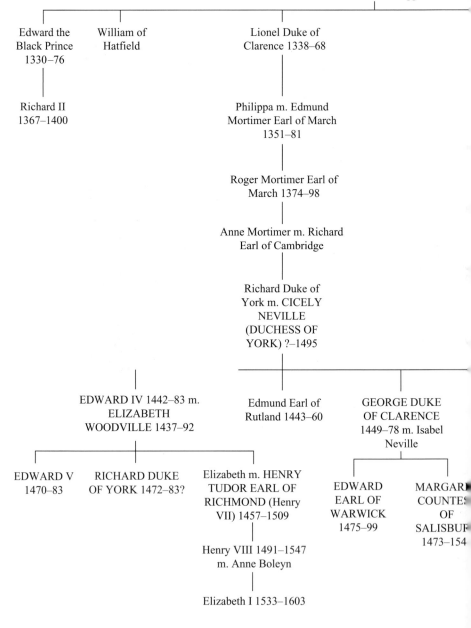

Edward III 1312–77 m. Philippa of Hainau

Edward the
Black Prince
1330–76

William of
Hatfield

Lionel Duke of
Clarence 1338–68

Richard II
1367–1400

Philippa m. Edmund
Mortimer Earl of March
1351–81

Roger Mortimer Earl of
March 1374–98

Anne Mortimer m. Richard
Earl of Cambridge

Richard Duke of
York m. CICELY
NEVILLE
(DUCHESS OF
YORK) ?–1495

EDWARD IV 1442–83 m.
ELIZABETH
WOODVILLE 1437–92

Edmund Earl of
Rutland 1443–60

GEORGE DUKE
OF CLARENCE
1449–78 m. Isabel
Neville

EDWARD V
1470–83

RICHARD DUKE
OF YORK 1472–83?

Elizabeth m. HENRY
TUDOR EARL OF
RICHMOND (Henry
VII) 1457–1509

EDWARD
EARL OF
WARWICK
1475–99

MARGARI
COUNTES
OF
SALISBUF
1473–154

Henry VIII 1491–1547
m. Anne Boleyn

Elizabeth I 1533–1603

Names of characters in the play appear in capitals.
Many persons not significant to *Richard III* are omitted.
See Notes to the List of Characters, pp. 57–60 above.

John of Gaunt Duke of
Lancaster 1340–99

Edmund of
Langley Duke
of York
1341–1402

Thomas of
Woodstock Earl
of Buckingham
and Duke of
Gloucester

William of
Windsor

m. Blanche of
Lancaster

m. Katharine
Swynford

Richard Earl of
Cambridge
?–1415 m.
Anne Mortimer

Anne m.
Edmund Earl of
Stafford ?–1403

ary IV 1367–1413

John Beaufort Earl of
Somerset 1373?–1410

Henry V
1387–1422 m.
therine of France

John Beaufort Duke
of Somerset 1403–44

Richard Duke
of York m.
CICELY
NEVILLE
(DUCHESS
OF YORK)

Humphrey Earl
of Stafford and
Duke of
Buckingham

HENRY VI
1421–71 m.
MARGARET OF
ANJOU 1430–82

Margaret Beaufort
m. Edmund Tudor
Earl of Richmond
?–1456

Humphrey
Stafford ?–1455

EDWARD
PRINCE OF
WALES 1453–71

HENRY TUDOR
EARL OF
RICHMOND (Henry
VII) 1457–1509 m.
Elizabeth of York

HENRY
STAFFORD
DUKE OF
BUCKINGHAM
1454?–83

RICHARD III
1452–85 m.
ANNE NEVILLE
1456–85

READING LIST

This list includes a selection of books and articles which may serve as guides for
further study of the play.

Adelman, Janet. *Suffocating Mothers*, 1992
Baldwin, T. W. *William Shakespere's Small Latine & Lesse Greeke*, 2 vols., 1944
Barber, C. L., and Richard P. Wheeler. *The Whole Journey: Shakespeare's Power of
Development*, 1986
Bate, Jonathan and Eric Rasmussen (eds.). *RSC Shakespeare Complete Works*, 2007
Berkeley, David S. '"Determined" in *Richard III*, I.i.30', *SQ* 14 (1963), 483–4
Boswell-Stone, W. G. *Shakespeare's Holinshed: The Chronicle and the Historical Plays
Compared*, 1896
Braunmuller, A. R. 'Early Shakespearean tragedy and the contemporary context:
cause and emotion in *Titus Andronicus, Richard III*, and *The Rape of Lucrece*',
in D. J. Palmer (ed.), *Shakespearian Tragedy*, Stratford-upon-Avon Studies 20,
1984, pp. 96–128
Brownlow, F. W. *Two Shakespearean Sequences*, 1977
Bullough, Geoffrey (ed.). *Narrative and Dramatic Sources of Shakespeare*, 8 vols.,
1957–75
Campbell, Lily B. *Shakespeare's 'Histories': Mirrors of Elizabethan Policy*, 1947
Churchill, George Bosworth. *Richard the Third up to Shakespeare*, 1900
Cibber, Colley. *The Tragical History of King Richard III, c.* 1700; reprinted 1969
Clemen, Wolfgang. *A Commentary on Shakespeare's 'Richard III'*, 1957; trans. Jean
Bonheim, 1968
Colley, Scott. *Richard's Himself Again: A Stage History of 'Richard III'*, 1992
The Crowland Chronicle Continuations, 1459–1486, ed. Nicholas Pronay and John
Cox, 1986
Day, Gillian. *King Richard III*, 2002
De Grazia, Margreta. 'The essential Shakespeare and the material book', *Textual
Practice* 2 (1988), 69–86
Dessen, Alan C. *Shakespeare and the Late Moral Plays*, 1986
Erne, Lukas. *Shakespeare as Literary Dramatist*, 2003
Gurr, Andrew. *The Shakespearean Stage*, 3rd edn, 1992
Hankey, Julie (ed.). *Richard III* (Plays in Performance), 1981
Hassel, R. Chris, Jr. *Songs of Death: Performance, Interpretation, and the Text of
'Richard III'*, 1987
Hatchuel, Sarah and Nathalie Vienne-Guérin (eds.). *Shakespeare on Screen: 'Richard
III'*, 2005
Hibbard, G. R. *The Making of Shakespeare's Dramatic Poetry*, 1981

Honigmann, E. A. J. *The Stability of Shakespeare's Text*, 1965

Ioppolo, Grace. *Revising Shakespeare*, 1991

Irace, Kathleen O. 'Origins and agents of Q1 Hamlet', in Thomas Clayton (ed.), *The 'Hamlet' First Published (Q1, 1603)*, 1992, pp. 90–122

    Reforming the 'Bad' Quartos: Performance and Provenance of Six Shakespearean First Editions, 1994

Jones, Emrys. *The Origins of Shakespeare*, 1977

Jowett, John (ed.). *The Tragedy of King Richard III*, 2000 (The Oxford Shakespeare)

Kelly, Henry Ansgar. *Divine Providence in the England of Shakespeare's Histories*, 1971

Lenz, Carolyn Ruth, Gayle Greene, and Carol Thomas Neely (eds.). *The Woman's Part: Feminist Criticism of Shakespeare*, 1980

McGann, Jerome J. *A Critique of Modern Textual Criticism*, 1983

McKellen, Ian, and Richard Loncraine. *William Shakespeare's 'Richard III'*, 1996

Maguire, Laurie E. *Shakespearean Suspect Texts: The 'Bad' Quartos and Their Contexts*, 1996

Mancini, Dominic. *The Usurpation of Richard III*, ed. C. A. J. Armstrong, 1969

More, Thomas. *The History of King Richard the Third*, ed. Richard S. Sylvester, 1963

Muir, Kenneth. *The Sources of Shakespeare's Plays*, 1978

Orgel, Stephen. 'What is a text?', *Research Opportunities in Renaissance Drama* 24 (1981), 3–6

Ornstein, Robert. *A Kingdom for a Stage: The Achievement of Shakespeare's History Plays*, 1972

Paris, Bernard J. *Character as a Subversive Force in Shakespeare*, 1991

Patrick, David Lyall. *The Textual History of 'Richard III'*, 1936

Pollard, A. J. *Richard III and the Princes in the Tower*, 1991

Rackin, Phyllis. *Stages of History: Shakespeare's English Chronicles*, 1990

Ribner, Irving. *The English History Play in the Age of Shakespeare*, 1957

Richmond, Hugh M. *King Richard III*, 1989 (Shakespeare in Performance)

Ross, Charles. *Richard III*, 1981

Rossiter, A. P. *English Drama from Early Times to the Elizabethans*, 1950

Royster, J. F. 'Richard III, IV.4 and the three Marys of mediaeval drama', *Modern Language Notes* 25 (1910), 173–4

Saccio, Peter. *Shakespeare's English Kings*, 1977

Sher, Antony. *The Year of the King*, 1987

Smidt, Kristian. *Iniurious Impostors and 'Richard III'*, 1963

    Memorial Transmission and Quarto Copy in 'Richard III': A Reassessment, 1970

Spivack, Bernard. *Shakespeare and the Allegory of Evil*, 1958

Taylor, Gary, and Michael Warren (eds.). *The Division of the Kingdoms*, 1983

Thayer, C. G. *Shakespearean Politics: Government and Misgovernment in the Great Histories*, 1983

Tillyard, E. M. W. *Shakespeare's History Plays*, 1944

Urkowitz, Steven. 'Reconsidering the relationship of quarto and Folio texts of *Richard III*', *ELR* 16 (1986), 442–66

Vickers, Brian. 'Shakespeare's use of rhetoric', in Kenneth Muir and Samuel Schoen-
baum (eds.), *A New Companion to Shakespeare Studies*, 1971
Walker, Alice. *Textual Problems of the First Folio*, 1953
Walton, J. K. *The Copy of the Folio Text of 'Richard III'*, 1955
Weimann, Robert. *Shakespeare and the Popular Tradition in the Theater*, 1978
Wells, Robin Headlam. *Shakespeare, Politics and the State*, 1986
Wells, Stanley, and Gary Taylor. *William Shakespeare: A Textual Companion*, 1987
Werstine, Paul. 'McKerrow's "Suggestion" and twentieth-century Shakespeare tex-
tual criticism', *Renaissance Drama* n.s. 19 (1988), 149–73
'Narratives about printed Shakespeare texts: "foul papers" and "bad" quartos', *SQ*
41 (1990), 65–86
Wright, George T. *Shakespeare's Metrical Art*, 1988